Sasha Pechersky

On October 14, 1943, Aleksandr "Sasha" Pechersky led a mass escape of inmates from Sobibor, a Nazi death camp in Poland. Despite leading the only successful prisoner revolt at a World War II death camp, Pechersky never received the public recognition he deserved in his home country of Russia. This story of a forgotten hero reveals the tremendous difference in memorial cultures between societies in the West and societies in the former Communist world.

Pechersky, along with other Russian and Jewish inmates who had been prisoners of the Nazis, was considered suspect by the Russian government simply because he had been imprisoned. In this volume, Selma Leydesdorff describes the official silence in the Eastern Bloc about Pechersky's role in the Sobibor escape and how an effort was made to recognize his actions. The narrative is based on eyewitness accounts from people in Pechersky's life and a discussion of the mechanism of memory, mixing written sources with varied recollections and assessing the collisions of collective memory held by the East and the West. Specifically, this book critiques the ideological refusal of many societies to acknowledge the suffering of Jews at Sobibor.

Offering fascinating insights into a crucial period of history, emphasizing that Jews were not passive in the face of German violence, and exploring the history of the Jews who fell victim to Stalinism after surviving Nazism, this is valuable reading for students and scholars of the Holocaust and the position of Jews under Communism.

Selma Leydesdorff is a professor emerita of oral history and culture at the University of Amsterdam in the Netherlands. Her publications include *We Lived with Dignity: The Jewish Proletariat of Amsterdam 1900–1940* (1998), *Surviving the Bosnian Genocide: The Women of Srebrenica Speak* (2011), and *The Tapestry of Memory, Testimony and Evidence in Life-Story Narratives* (2013, co-edited with Nanci Adler).

Memory and Narrative
Series editors:
Selma Leydesdorff, Nanci Adler, Albert Lichtblau, Yifat Gutman, Mark Cave and Anna Sheftel

Please send any book proposals for this series to Anna Sheftel (asheftel@gmail. com) for consideration.

The Migration Journey
The Ethiopian Jewish Exodus
Gadi BenEzer

Oral Tradition
A Study in Historical Methodology
Jan Vansina

Family Love in the Diaspora
Migration and the Anglo-Caribbean Experience
Mary Chamberlain

Dwellers of Memory
Youth and Violence in Medellin, Colombia
Pilar Riano-Alcala

Memories of Mass Repression
Narrating Life Stories in the Aftermath of Atrocity
Edited by Nanci Adler, Selma Leydesdorff, Mary Chamberlain and Leyla Neyzi

Witnessing Australian Stories
History, Testimony, and Memory in Contemporary Culture
Kelly Jean Butler

Tapestry of Memory
Evidence and Testimony in Life-Story Narratives
Edited by Nanci Adler and Selma Leydesdorff

Double Exposure
Memory and Photography
Edited by Olga Shevchenko

Negotiating Normality
Everyday Lives in Socialist Institutions
Edited by Daniela Koleva

Sasha Pechersky

Holocaust Hero, Sobibor Resistance Leader, and Hostage of History

Selma Leydesdorff

NEW YORK AND LONDON

First published 2017
by Routledge
711 Third Avenue, New York, NY 10017

and by Routledge
2 Park Square, Milton Park, Abingdon, Oxon OX14 4RN

Routledge is an imprint of the Taylor & Francis Group, an informa business

© 2017 Selma Leydesdorff

The right of Selma Leydesdorff to be identified as author of this work
has been asserted by her in accordance with sections 77 and 78 of the
Copyright, Designs and Patents Act 1988.

All rights reserved. No part of this book may be reprinted or reproduced
or utilised in any form or by any electronic, mechanical, or other means,
now known or hereafter invented, including photocopying and recording,
or in any information storage or retrieval system, without permission in
writing from the publishers.

Trademark notice: Product or corporate names may be trademarks or
registered trademarks, and are used only for identification and explanation
without intent to infringe.

Library of Congress Cataloging-in-Publication Data
Names: Leydesdorff, Selma, author.
Title: Sasha Pechersky : Holocaust hero, Sobibor resistance leader, and
    hostage of history / Selma Leydesdorff.
Description: Abingdon, Oxon ; New York, NY : Routledge, [2017] |
    Series: Memory and narrative | Includes bibliographical references
    and index.
Identifiers: LCCN 2017022361 | ISBN 9781412865258 (hardback :
    alk. paper) | ISBN 9781315114262 (ebook)
Subjects: LCSH: Pecherskiæi, Aleksandr Aronovich, 1909–1990. |
    Sobibâor (Concentration camp) | World War, 1939–1945—Jewish
    resistance—Poland—Sobibâor. | Holocaust survivors—Soviet Union—
    Biography. | Soviet Union—Politics and government—1945–1991. |
    Collective memory—Soviet Union.
Classification: LCC D805.5.S64 L49 2017 | DDC 940.53/18092 [B]—dc23
LC record available at https://lccn.loc.gov/2017022361

ISBN: 978-1-4128-6525-8 (hbk)
ISBN: 978-1-315-11426-2 (ebk)

Typeset in Goudy
by Apex CoVantage, LLC

In memory of my grandparents I never met, both killed in Sobibor.

Stumbling Stones
Photograph courtesy of Eefje Leydesdorff.

Contents

List of Illustrations	x
Acknowledgments	xi
Chronology: Important Dates in the Life of Aleksandr ("Sasha") Aronowitz Pechersky	xiv

Introduction   1

How the Project Started 2
The Unknown Camps in Eastern Poland 6
Political and Academic Silence 8
The Beginning of a Life Story in Moscow (October 2012) 9
Michael Lev and Other Friends of Pechersky in Israel 11
Washington (February 2013): Many Letters 13
Who Was This Man? 14
Minsk (May 2013) 14
I Tried to Hear His Voice, to Understand His Language
and His Sadness 15
And After the Revolt? Rostov-on-Don 16
Reshaping Narratives, Changing Memories 18

1 Jews in a Post-Revolutionary World: Integration and Exclusion   22
Crossing Borders, Looking at the Region 24
The Camps of Operation Reinhard and the History of Pechersky 24
Kremenchuk: Family Background and the Memory of
Persecution 27
A Dangerous Trek Through Chaotic Territory 34
Life in a New Town: Rostov-on-Don 36
War Comes to Rostov-on-Don 42

2 A Trajectory of Misery: The Army and Imprisonment   48
The War, 1941 50
Not a Step Back! Order 270 54

viii   *Contents*

Pechersky's Trajectory: Vyazma, Borisov, Minsk, Stalag 352 55
Changing Times: The Need for Slave Labor, Stalingrad, and the
  Germans Need to Eat 58
The Need for Labor Versus the Wish to Kill All Jews 59
To Be Caught as a Jew 61
To Escape and to Resist 64
The Minsk Ghetto 67
The Prison at Shirokaya Street 69

3   Sobibor Through the Eyes of Survivors   79
The Prisms of the Narrative 80
Eighty Russian Soldiers and a German Miscalculation 84
An Unimaginable Crime 86
The Sobibor Facility: Accounts of a Death Factory 87
Who Speaks? First-person and Other Narratives 89
The Camp: A Place of Violence and Death 91
And Then . . . 93
A Prisoner in Sobibor 94
The Other Side: Experienced Perpetrators 96
Not Only Jews, But Mostly Jewish Victims: Mythologies 98
Psychological Survival and the Russian Soldiers 99
Human Bonding and Hope for a Better World 102
The Tide Turns 105

4   Resist and Tell the World   109
Partisans and Resistance in Poland and Byelorussia 111
The Russians—Experienced Fighters Arrive 115
Not Slaughtered Like Sheep 116
Resistance in Sobibor: To Die With Honor 118
Learning to Fight and to Kill 119
Organizing an Escape 121
Not Mass Escape but Revolt 125
Myth and Reality in Stories about the Revolt 129
Shame and Guilt in Testimonies 134

5   After the Escape: Life With the Partisans and the Red Army   138
Memories of Survival after the Escape 142
Forever Traumatized 147
Further to the East, to the Territory Controlled by the Red
  Army 148
Communist Policies in Byelorussia 152
Partisans Under the Control of Moscow 153

Contents   ix

Life as a Partisan 154
A Culture of Mistrust 155
The Schors Battalion 156
Joining the Red Army 158
Back in Rostov-on-Don after the War 160

6   Return to Rostov: Spreading the Word About Sobibor   164
There Were No Jews, Only Citizens 167
Changing Times and the Rise of Anti-Semitism 167
The Crackdown on Jewish Culture 169
Coping with Stalinist Anti-Semitism in Rostov-on-Don 172
To Reconnect With the Other Survivors 175
The Post-War Trials and the Collective Punishment 179
The Emergence of the Voice of the Survivor and Oral History 181

7   Traumatized and Alone in Front of "Justice"   187
Alone, Isolated, and Bitter 192
The Trial and the Story 194
A Hostage of an Unwanted History 197
*Always Alone: Bitterness, Depression, and Withdrawal from
    the World 198*
Getting Lost in a Hostile World; Unrecognized Trauma 201
To Find the Others and to Remember 201
Depression and No Freedom 205

Conclusion: To Speak and to Be Silenced   210
Competing Victims and Historical Clarity 214
Changing Perspectives 215
Who Was Aleksandr Pechersky? 218

Bibliography   222
Index   232

Illustrations

Figures

0.1	A photograph honoring a young Aleksandr Pechersky in the window of the Bolshaya Bronaya synagogue in Moscow	10
0.2	Aleksandr Pechersky with Simion Rosenfeld in the early 1960s	12
1.1	Aleksandr Pechersky with Michael Lev	31
1.2	Aleksandr Pechersky with his daughter Ella in a snapshot he managed to keep even in Sobibor	31
1.3	Aleksandr Pechersky acting in a theater in Rostov-on-Don in the 1930s	37
6.1	Aleksandr Pechersky teaching at a Russian school in 1962	169
6.2	Aleksandr Pechersky at the Red Square in Moscow in 1980	178
6.3	Aleksandr Pechersky in his sixties	182
7.1	Aleksandr Pechersky with his family in Rostov-on-Don in the 1980s	207
8.1	Aleksandr Pechersky in later life	211
8.2	The Lane of Memory in Sobibor	219

Maps

0.1	German camps in Eastern Europe in 1943	5
1.1	The locations of Kremenchuk in Ukraine and Rostov-on-Don in Russia	28
1.2	Operation Barbarossa in 1941	43

Acknowledgments

A book like this can only be written with the help and advice of many others who make you feel you are on the right track. Sometimes these are small gestures or hints, and sometimes people devote large amounts of their time to giving help. These words of gratitude are chronological and without hierarchy.

The initiative to interview survivors on the occasion of the Demjanjuk trial came from Jetje Manheim and Mirjam Huffener of the Sobibor Foundation. They were soulmates throughout the project. Later I continued to work with the Sobibor Foundation and was supported by Maarten Eddes. These three, together with Jules Schelvis, who established the Sobibor Foundation, were the pillars of my research. Jules also provided me with parts of his archive.

When I decided to expand the interviews into an in-depth study of the life of Aleksandr Pechersky, I needed both financial and practical support. For years the Faculty of Humanities of the University of Amsterdam has enabled me to continue. I wish to thank the former dean Frank van Vree and Astrit Blommestijn en Hotze Mulder, both working at the research office of the faculty, for their practical support. Financial support came through the Dutch embassy in Moscow in collaboration with the Netherlands Institute in St. Petersburg, and also from the Anne Frank Foundation in Amsterdam. I owe thanks also to Mila Chevalier in St. Petersburg, to Hugo Brouwer from the Dutch Embassy in Moscow, and to Jan Erik Dobbelman from the Anne Frank Foundation. Further financial support came from the Wilhelmina E. Jansen Fund and the Memorial Foundation for Jewish Culture in New York. For a generous financial grant that made possible many trips, I am deeply grateful to The Conference on Jewish Material Claims against Germany.

In October 2012 archivist Leonid Terushkin at the Russian Holocaust Center in Moscow gave me access to all the material available in his archive. I owe a debt of gratitude to him and to his colleagues at the Center, which is under the supervision of Ilya Altman. Both at that time and later, Anna Aabakunova never tired of helping me, including with translations. I profited also from Sergei Kulchevich's extensive knowledge of Moscow. On that trip I met Svetlana Bogdanova, who sent me to Lazar Lubarsky in Holon, near Tel Aviv. With him I visited for a second and again for a third time Simion Rosenfeld, who introduced me to Michael Lev, a friend of Aleksandr Pechersky.

In February 2013 I visited the U.S. Holocaust Memorial Museum. An introduction to the library and archives was provided by Jan Lambertz, whose excellent

xii *Acknowledgments*

advice kept turning up in my mailbox. Megan Lewis was a very efficient librarian, and good advice was also provided by Vadim Altskan and Juergen Matthias. I was instructed how to find the testimony given by Pechersky in Kiev in 1962 by Professor Lev Simkin from Moscow. My interpreter at that time and later was Yedida Kanfer. In Washington, D.C., I met Richard Räshke, the author of *Escape from Sobibor*. In the weeks that followed, I received informative e-mails from Vladimir Rafalovitch, a member of the Pechersky family currently living in the United States.

Around this period I renewed contact with Dan Michman, the Director of Research in Yad Vashem, who helped me on several occasions. Through him I became acquainted with Dan Zeits, an incredibly generous historian who was never too tired to read or send material and to help in many other ways. Without his help I would never have understood what happened in Belarus, where I traveled in search of archives. Kuzma Kozak of the History Workshop and his assistant Antonina Chumakova were loyal and pleasant to work with. Antonina and I visited several places where Jews had lived and where they had been killed. Most impressive was the small Jewish historical museum, whose director, Vadim Akopyan, received us.

In Israel my guide for a long time was Lazar Lubarsky, thanks to whom I had the chance to meet several times with survivor Simion Rosenfeld. We both liked the elderly gentleman. Lazar's role was taken over by Polina Lev, the daughter of Michael Lev. At Yad Vashem there were director Arkadi Seltzer and David Silberklang, who provided good advice, and Lital Beer, Shaul Ferrero, and Rita Margolin, who helped me to find my way around in the archives. At that time I had the privilege of meeting Yitzhak Arad and discussing my project with him, as I was also able to do with Yehuda Bauer when he visited the Netherlands.

In New York I had a long talk with Jan T. Gross, whom I had first met when I was affiliated with the CNRS/ NYU programme on Memory and Memorialization directed by Denis Peschansky, who became a dear friend. I had been invited to New York before by Tony Judt, the director of the Remarque Center at NYU, and I realized while writing this book how much I had learned from some of the seminars there. Being in New York also reminds me gratefully of memorable lunches with Marion Kaplan, Linda Gordon, Atina Grossman, Nanette Funk, and Vera Zolberg. They all made me feel at ease in different ways. Polly Zavadivker was generous with her knowledge of the Shirokaya Prison. Dawn Skorczewski and Molly Andrews read early texts and advised.

Visiting the Shoah Visual History Archive was made possible by a kind invitation from Wolf Gruber, the Director of Research. A workshop he organized broadened my perspective. In Los Angeles I was guided by Karen Jungblut, who made arrangements for places to work, and by Christain Cercel and Dan Leshem, who helped me with the interviews in Russian and Hebrew. Andrea Szoni from Budapest, who works for the Shoah Visual History Archive, helped me again and again with interviews. They all have been extremely generous.

Anna Muller invited me to present a paper at the University of Florida in Gainesville, where I also met Dean Alice Freifeld.

Acknowledgments   xiii

Special gratitude is for Mykola Makhortykh in Amsterdam, who helped me immensely; as a Ukrainian historian he sorted out questions I could not answer

I received help by mail from Barbara Epstein, Zvi Gitelman, Amir Weiner, and Dori Laub, all of whom have a prominent place in this book thanks to their outstanding academic work. I thank Andras Kovacs from the Central European University in Budapest, who supported my search for financial support.

My visits to YIVO were fascinating because no one had ever looked at some of the material there. YIVO is a place where one literally feels the rich heritage of the Jewish communities of Eastern Europe. I thank Fruma Mohrer, the chief archivist, and also Lyudmila Sholokhova, Leo Greenbaum, Gunnar Berg, Yeshaya Metal, and Ettie Goldwasser. Near the end of our contact, I also met their new director, Jonathan Brent. Rivka Schiller did some of the translations.

Patrice Bensimon helped me with the Yahad-In Unum Archives, as did Omar Gonzales. Their archives confirmed the truism that the institution that interviews also shapes the interviews. I thank Franziska Bruder from Berlin for her thoughtful comments.

Paul van der Woerd was never too busy to help me with Russian texts. His role was taken over by Polina Lev, who did much more than translate. She guided me through difficult passages of Russian Jewish history and often gave me moral support. It was a pleasure to be in her house in Rechovot. Her friend Elena Petrova from Moscow helped me to solve some of the last problems in my research and translated my discussions with Aleksander Marutyan.

Visiting Pechersky's family in Rostov-on-Don was a very special event. I thank Ella Grinevich and Natasha Laditchenko (sometimes called Natalia in a more formal way) for their extreme generosity. Elena Loginova facilitated the meeting with her excellent English.

The stories of the survivors I interviewed are all unforgettable. I have mentioned Jules Schelvis; there were also Toivi Blatt, Arkady Waiszpapir, Esther Raab, Simcha Bialowitz, Philip Bialowitz, Simion Rosenfield, Aleksey Vaytsen, Selma Wijnberg, and Regina Zielinski. They made me suffer because I loved them and was scared to inflict pain by asking them to remember.

James Morrisson edited first drafts and refining of the texts was done by Gene Moors. Not being a native speaker I am immensely grateful.

Books like this are written because people care for you. My cousin in Israel, Tsiwjah Tauber, and her husband, Chanan, showed me loving hospitality. Nanci Adler of the Center for Holocaust and Genocide studies in Amsterdam traveled with me to Ryazan; she was always keen to be in contact with Russia, and her friend Vilensky.

But most of all there was Siep Stuurman, my husband whom I love so much and by whom I feel loved when I am tired, and during all the work on this book, and most of all when I am ill. He saved me from loneliness during a very arduous period and never stops mixing our intellectual exchanges with the message that whenever it rains, I should look for the rainbow.

Chronology: Important Dates in the Life of Aleksandr ("Sasha") Aronowitz Pechersky

1909	Born in Kremenchuk, Ukraine
1915	The family flees to Rostov-on-Don
1917	Russian Revolution
1931–33	Military service
1933	Marriage with Lyudmila Vasilyevna
1941	Conscripted into Russian army; taken prisoner at the defense of Moscow near Smolensk; deportation to Borisov
1941–42	In various camps around Minsk: Stalag 352, Shiroka Street
Sept. 18, 1943	Arrival in Sobibor
Oct. 14, 1943	Revolt and escape
1943–44	Partisan in Schors Brigade, later soldier in a Red Army; penal battalion
1944	First deposition in Moscow; wounded; second marriage with Olga Kotova
1945	Return to Rostov-on-Don
1948	False accusation of corruption
1953	Death of Stalin
1953–70	Process of slow destalinization
1970–2003	Protest movement of Jews who want to go to Israel; Pechersky wants to stay in Russia
1970–87	Decline of health, depression, isolation, and poverty
1990	Death in Rostov-on-Don

Introduction

It all began in Munich. When I interviewed survivors of the Sobibor death camp at the time of the trial of John Demjanjuk (2009–11), they all praised and loved Aleksandr ("Sasha") Pechersky, the Russian Jew and Red Army lieutenant who led the revolt on October 14, 1943.[1] Pechersky had arrived in Sobibor as the commander of a group of eighty Russian prisoners. The Germans kept them alive because they needed their workforce in order to build a new part of the camp.[2] Pechersky, the uncontested leader, was mentioned in every individual story, since the escape he organized had saved their lives.

The uprising in Sobibor was the most successful instance of the resistance of Jews to their annihilation. Although we know of many examples of resistance by Jews in ghettos, the Sobibor uprising took place in the middle of the war inside a camp created solely for the murder of Jews, far away from the eyes of the world. Sobibor was one of three camps created for the organized industrial killing that the Nazis named Operation Reinhard.[3] All three camps were hidden in the moors and forests of Eastern Poland, not far from Lublin near the border with Belarus.[4] According to the latest research, more than 170,000 people were killed in Sobibor.[5]

The revolt took place in a desperate situation, after meticulous, bold, and imaginative planning by a small group. There is an agreement among survivors that without the leadership of Sasha the revolt would not have succeeded, and they all spoke of him as a respected commander whose authority seems to have come to him in quite a natural way. With his fellow Russian prisoners of war (POWs) he maintained the discipline of the Russian army, but even more important, his position was supported because he inspired trust. For his Russian company, he was an officer they had to obey; the soldiers had learned the hard way to do as they were told. They came from an army where disobedience was severely punished. But most of all his prominent place and the confidence he inspired seem to have come automatically; there was something inspiring about him. He was not born as such a leader, but during the various stages of his life he had become one. He had been an enthusiastic stage director of amateur theater, and he had directed a large orchestra. He clearly loved to organize others. When he entered the camp, people immediately recognized his authority, and they were also aware that he was more mature and older than the soldiers around him. The arrival of a group

2   Introduction

of Russian Jewish men who were not arrested in the ghettos but had been taken prisoner in combat and who had been fighting against the Germans was a major event. The soldiers also brought with them news of the advances of the Red Army, which gave hope.

This book is the record of my attempt to understand Sasha Pechersky and is based on a lengthy search in archives that have opened slowly since the fall of Communism, on eyewitness accounts, and on stories told by those who knew him personally. During the first stage of my inquiry there were bits and scraps of information that I did not understand, but later, within the context of his life story, they became meaningful.

How the Project Started

During the Demjanjuk trial (2009–11), I had the unexpected privilege to interview the so-called *Nebenklager* (co-plaintiffs) who spoke up at the trial in Munich. I had met them because I belonged to a group of volunteers who, together with the Sobibor Foundation, supervised and helped those *Nebenklager* who had decided to travel to be present at the court.

Demjanjuk was accused of being one of the perpetrators at the Sobibor death camp in Eastern Poland, and the co-plaintiffs' role was the result of a particularity in German law that confers rights to the relatives of victims and makes it legally possible for them to be present in the court; they are allowed to testify, not as witnesses but as those whose lives have been irreparably harmed by the accused. As result of legal maneuvers, the *Nebenklager* played an even more prominent role in the Demjanjuk trial and obtained a real chance to speak up in court.

Soon the Sobibor Foundation and I decided to create a website as a unique virtual "place of memory" in order to bring what had happened in Sobibor before a wider audience. We wanted our website to show that, although the war ended in 1945, it did not end for children who had never known their murdered parents; they felt lonely and deserted, even though separation from their loved ones and hiding with those who took care of them had saved their lives. Between them and me, there was a world of difference, since I was born after the war and had never suffered as they had, although they were only a few years older. But there was also common ground and similar involvement, since two of my grandparents were killed in Sobibor. We all had strong emotional reasons to engage with such a project because the Shoah was a major factor in our mental world. Of course, the war was not over for the survivors, as became clear as they began talking and remembering. Indeed, war and peace are not mutually exclusive phenomena in history or memory.

There was also a historiographical issue. The mainstream view still holds that there was little Jewish resistance against the Nazis, and that the Jews let themselves be slaughtered like sheep. From this perspective, the revolt at Sobibor can only figure as a contingent anomaly. Since the 1970s, Israeli historians in particular began to question this myth of passivity, arguing that the old historiography simply ignored the witnesses and that there were indeed sources confirming

Jewish resistance.[6] However, the dominant memorial culture went along with mainstream historiography, while for a long time the personal knowledge of survivors was not validated. Holocaust history and collective memory had remained largely confined to written sources and court testimonials.

A further problem was that several survivors lived in the former Communist Bloc or had lived there for a long time. It soon became clear to me that their narratives were dealing with an altogether different collective memory, one embedded in a system of totalitarian control, censored speech, and a politically imposed "official" collective memory. After 1945 Communist ideologues had created an amorphous category of Russian war victims that did not acknowledge the specificity of Jewish suffering under Nazism.[7] All suffering had been homogenized, and interviewees were imprisoned in the discourse of the "Great Patriotic War," in which "innocent Soviet citizens" had been killed by the fascist invader.

I proposed to the Sobibor Foundation to interview all survivors who were still alive and to post their stories on a website alongside the life stories of the co-plaintiffs in order to create a monument to the suffering in and after Sobibor. We believed it should be possible to find these survivors through the international network of the Foundation and through the contacts of Marek Bem, the former Polish custodian at the site of Sobibor, who at that time was writing a book about the camp that was published in English in 2015.[8] It turned out that the survivors had emigrated to several continents, and it would take me nearly three years (2009–12) to find and interview all of them. To prepare for the interviews, I read and listened to as much audiovisual material I could find, some of it dating back to the late 1940s.

By the time of the Demjanjuk trial, most of the survivors of Sobibor were too old to make the trip to the court in Germany; only Jules Schelvis, Thomas Blatt, and Philip Bialowicz could come. Of course, when I interviewed these elderly people their accounts were most impressive. I am happy to have spoken with them, since most of the actual survivors are dead by now. In court the co-plaintiffs provided the audience with shocking accounts; they spoke to a large and breathless international audience as the children, spouses, brothers, and sisters of victims.

The survivors I interviewed had become public figures. Some of them were no longer able to reflect on a life of suffering, mourning, and enduring hardship. With age, the extreme traumatization had become an obstacle to memory. They had created personal narratives that avoided too much pain, and they were used to telling them. They understood I wanted more, and thus they wanted to create a credible life story. With nearly all of them I succeeded in going back and recovering a more authentic narration. At the same time, no one was able to answer my question about why Pechersky had become such an undisputed leader.

The many accounts represented different stages of dealing with the past. Most of the survivors had been interviewed often and had testified in trials against the brutes who had been their guards. What I read in transcripts of the various interviews and learned from the stories they told in the past was not always clear, because to understand an interview or a testimony one needs to know its

4 Introduction

context. One needs to know why the story is being told, and where and when it is told. For instance, in court words are used for judgments; there is no room for nuances. A courtroom is not the place for understanding the mourning and the pain the survivors wanted to express. The many (audio)visual interviews I had found contained almost no information about the various times and places in which the interviews were conducted. Moreover, the interviews sometimes provided contradictory information. Since I often knew nothing of the context of the interview, nor anything about the interviewer, I remained aghast.

I wondered what kind of (witness) accounts these were. For what purposes and from which historical perspectives were they made? Were the interviewees speaking to journalists or to lawyers, and would their accounts later be used in court proceedings? Were they part of the memorial culture in a particular country, or had the interviewees constructed their own memorial community? What was the historical status of this material? We know that interviews are always framed by the collection that initiates them and by the interaction between interviewer and narrator. Methods of storing and practices of interviewing also vary. As historian Noah Shenker puts it: "Never perfectly enacted, testimonies are contingent upon the specific dialogue fostered among interviewees, interviewers, and the institutions the latter represent."[9]

In addition, how was one to assess the heroic role assigned to Pechersky by people who had barely known him personally, or not at all, but had at most stared at him from a distance or heard about him from others? Over the years, some interviewees' closeness to him seemed to have increased, resulting in an emotional identification that I could only deconstruct as a shifting balance of myth and reality. Most of them said they knew him well.

The interviews with survivors took me all over the world. I traveled from Kiev to Ryazan east of Moscow, to Tel Aviv, Warsaw, Washington, and New York. I conducted my last interview in 2012, when I interviewed an elderly woman named Regina Zielinksi in Adelaide, Australia. We spent a few days together, and I was constantly aware of the fact that we were talking about a world that was gone and about memories that had been sifted and transformed over a lifetime. She loved to talk to me, and like many other narrators she told me again and again that the interviews felt so different from a public testimony or a lecture in a school. I cherished her trust and the way she wanted to "tell it all." Regina was old and frail, like the other survivors. Most of them had been in contact with other escapees for a considerable time; they had attended commemorations and competed with each other with their stories, trying to convey their personal impressions to the outer world, and very often they had disagreed with their fellow survivors. But about Pechersky there appeared to be consensus: he was their savior.

Pechersky was able to act at a moment when the war was turning against the Nazis. Even before the battle of Stalingrad ended in February 1943, it was clear that the Germans could not win the war. Indoctrinated by victorious talk, the German guards thought they were invincible and were arrogant about their strength. This psychological attitude made them not realize how dangerous

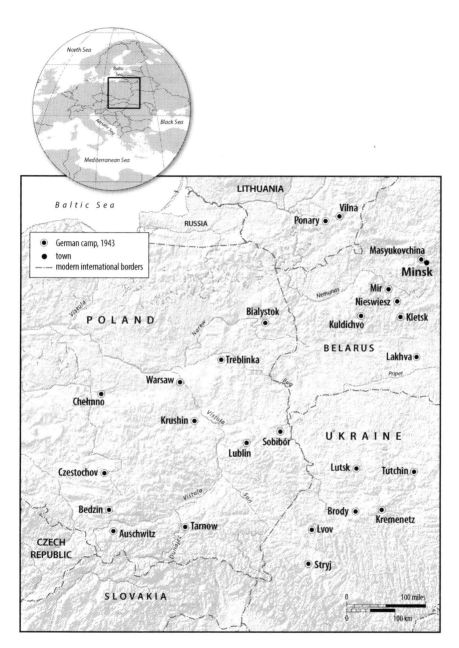

Map 0.1 German camps in Eastern Europe in 1943
Source: Map produced by Isabella Lewis.

6 *Introduction*

a group of well-organized Russian soldiers could be. They thought these half-starved prisoners arriving from Minsk, ragged and dirty like all those who arrived with the trains, had no agency and would be intimidated. They allowed eighty Russian soldiers to remain together as a group and thought they could control them. They were no longer living in reality. As another survivor, Esther Raab, once said: "The Nazis were only scared of being sent to the Russian front and they just wanted to survive in the camp. Therefore they put a tremendous effort into building a labor camp where profit could be made, and for this purpose they selected men they considered strong."[10]

I began to wonder: who was this man, and why did we know so little about him? I wanted to know how he could have become such a leader. What kind of responsible man could become such a daredevil? Where did his ingenuity come from, and how did he get his endurance? Why was he persecuted after the war, as everybody told me? Did he become a special victim of the anti-Semitic policies in the Soviet Union under Stalinism? I wondered how he managed to survive such tremendous horror. Where did he find such strong resilience?

Some information seemed obvious enough: after the escape from Sobibor he joined the partisans, and in the last year of the war he was again a soldier of the Red Army. After the war Pechersky was persecuted in the same way that Stalin dealt with most Soviet soldiers who had been prisoners of war; according to the policy of that time, they were all suspected of collaboration with the Germans, and their having surrendered was considered treason. It was argued that a good Red Army soldier would defend his country to the death and would never be caught alive.

When Pechersky rejoined the Red Army in Belarus at the end of the war in 1944, it was not a moment of liberation but a time of retribution. He expected to be punished, and to avoid the worst, he opted to be sent to a penal battalion of the Red Army that was moving westward into Germany. He did so in order to avoid the Gulag or execution, which was the usual sentence for soldiers who had been imprisoned by the Germans. He was later wounded on the battlefield, and, after a long hospitalization near Moscow, he returned to his native Rostov-on-Don, where he married a nurse named Olga, whom he had taken care of him in the hospital. Never recognized as a hero, Pechersky was falsely accused of corruption and lost his position and social network during the Stalinist anti-cosmopolitan campaign (1948–53). He remained poor and unrecognized in the years afterward and felt that he lived as a pariah. In 1990 he died in poverty, social isolation, and despair.

After the war Pechersky never received the public recognition he deserved. Most public attention was directed to Auschwitz, although during the trial of Adolf Eichmann in 1961 in Jerusalem, Moshe Bahir (formerly called Moshe Shalek) testified about Sobibor and mentioned the man who had been his leader in the insurrection that saved his life.

The Unknown Camps in Eastern Poland

For a long time, the camps in eastern Poland at Treblinka, Sobibor, and Belzec were unknown to the larger public, though more than a million and a half people were killed during Aktion Reinhard, which was the German code name for the camps.[11] Not until the release of the movie *Escape from Sobibor* in 1987 did the Sobibor revolt receive massive public attention. For instance, the Pulitzer-prize-winning historian Saul Friedländer does not seem well informed about the camp, nor about the revolt. Friedländer pays little attention to the killing sites in Eastern Poland. He writes about the "collaboration of Jewish inmates and Soviet POWs" during the revolt, but does not mention that these POWs were Jewish.[12] In his large volume, less than a page is devoted to Sobibor.

In the film *Escape from Sobibor* Pechersky was portrayed as a superhero, hardly recognizable as an ordinary human being, let alone as a Jew. After the film's tremendous success, a lot of stories circulated, particularly on the internet. Some of these fables claimed that Pechersky and his brother were imprisoned and that his brother died (or was killed) while they were in prison together. The latter claim is not true: the circumstances of his brother's death are dubious, but it happened much later, in the Khrushchev era, in the late 1950s. He was probably killed in prison, and stories about a diabetic coma were possibly the result of random use of insulin as a way to force prisoners to confess by inducing delirium.

An aging Pechersky can be seen in several documentaries, speaking almost always about Sobibor and in a sense always telling the same story. He did not like to talk about other episodes of his life. In 1984 Pechersky was interviewed by Sobibor survivor Jules Schelvis and the documentary filmmaker Dunya Breur; both were Dutch. The unedited transcript contains unique information about Pechersky's adolescence, and the story gives us a glimpse into why Pechersky chose not to speak or write about anything other than what happened in Sobibor. When Dunya Breur asked him to recall other events in his life, Pechersky conceded that he could remember his family and said: "Of course I can remember, but whether or not this needs to be told is an open question. I could say some words, not because I am ashamed or feel embarrassed, but is there any point in wearying those who have to listen?"[13] He had built a wall in order not to have to talk about anything else; he wanted to spread the word about the revolt, not about his later travails and disappointments. I became convinced that only by looking beyond the Sobibor insurrection would I be able to understand the wellsprings of his leadership in 1943, as well as the price he had to pay after the "victory" of 1945, when his country punished him instead of giving him his due.

In 2010 a documentary film called *Mathematical Calculation of Freedom* was made in Russia by Aleksander Marutyan with the collaboration of Pechersky's daughter Ella and focused on the fate of her father and his isolation. She talked about her father's life before and after his heroic role at Sobibor.[14] I knew quite early during my research that Pechersky's family was alive, but I did not know how to trace them. Finally, in 2012, I found his daughter's address in Rostov-on-Don, but only after I had gone to Moscow, where activists hoping to win late recognition for Pechersky had turned up several contacts, especially a former neighbor from Rostov-on-Don who now lived near Tel Aviv. The activists gave me the address of Lazar Lubarsky, who had loved Pechersky, tried to console him, and was forced to leave the Soviet Union after years in the Gulag (his trial began in 1973, and he was finally released in 1976).

8 *Introduction*

It turned out that Sasha Pechersky had been a typical Russian man from an average lower-middle-class, partly secularized Jewish family that had tried to assimilate and climb the social ladder with the Communist tide. However, even those Jews who tried hard remained "aliens" in the eyes of most non-Jewish Russians and in the dominant mindset of Communist culture. In his youth, Pechersky profited from the new opportunities available to Jews to acquire knowledge and professional skills in post-revolutionary Soviet society. When the war came in 1941, he was swept along by the storm, like many millions of his countrymen. In German captivity his Jewish identity acquired a novel and sinister significance. Sobibor was meant to be a final destination for all the Jews sent there, but Pechersky managed to escape the Nazi death machinery.

While Hitler was losing, Stalin was winning. Pechersky returned to the Red Army after his escape from Sobibor and after spending nearly a year with the partisans. He suffered the consequences of having been a POW, once more caught up in a massive current of repression that engulfed hundreds of thousands of his countrymen. For the remainder of his life, he was an unrecognized hero, admired and venerated by only a small minority of Russian and West European Jews, while relegated to oblivion by the state for which he had fought and risked his life. What makes his fate all the more tragic is his lifelong pride in having fought to defend his motherland and the hope connected with Communism against the German invaders.

Political and Academic Silence

When I went to meet Lazar Lubarsky at his home near Tel Aviv, he was not the first acquaintance of Pechersky I had met. In the company of historian Nanci Adler, who is more familiar with Russia and with travel in Russia than I could possibly be, I had journeyed to Ryazan, east of Moscow, through slowly melting and re-freezing snow. The Russian trains turned out to be well heated but dirty. One of the last survivors of Sobibor, Aleksey Vaytsen, lived in Ryazan, and I wanted to interview him and ask him about Pechersky. Aleksey had been Pechersky's confidant and had worked with him during the preparations for the revolt. They had escaped together. The first day of interviewing turned out to be difficult, partly due to a brain injury Aleksey had suffered some weeks earlier. But on the second day, after I told him that my grandparents were killed in Sobibor, there was a sudden intimacy that made possible an unforgettable narrative. Eating pie with him and his grandson at their kitchen table made a special moment. For the first time I was physically confronted with a narrative about the fear in Communist times of talking about the fate of the Jews.

Aleksey talked to his grandson in a language distorted by braindamage, who in his turn spoke to Nanci Adler. She translated to me how before the late 1990s he had been not able to talk about his experiences. As he expressed it: "I did not talk to anyone about it, not even to my wife. It was not okay to talk about it. I had no one to talk to. My relatives were all killed. I really felt unable to talk about it." A different behavior would have been dangerous given the constant

KGB surveillance. Moreover, Aleksey remained in the army until the late 1970s, and speaking about Sobibor and the fate of the Jews would have ruined his career.

Mentioning the fate of the Jews meant taking a huge risk at a time when many Jews wanted to emigrate to Israel but were refused permission to do so. Therefore the story of Jewish suffering was "closed," as Aleksey put it. He was not certain what would have happened if he had spoken about such a forbidden subject. I realized how lonely he must have been. From that moment, the story of the imposed silence surrounding Sobibor did not leave me. What had happened to the memory of the massacre of Jews in the former Communist world made me rethink my entire research project. I realized that I would have to tackle fundamental theoretical and methodological problems if I wanted to pursue my research. After the interview with Aleksey in Ryazan, I knew in a deeper way that this widespread, state-controlled silence was probably just one example of what had happened, not only to the handful of Sobibor survivors but to virtually all Shoah survivors in Russia.

I had to deal with multiple interpretations of the past and multiple locations; with German, Polish, and Russian historical memorial culture; and with the politics of several countries that interact. I soon realized that history is framed in national terms and that every nation has its own canonized collective memory and archives. Sobibor was in Poland, but many Russian POWs were killed there after having passed through concentration camps in Belarus and the Soviet Union. Still, their fate was considered part of the Polish history of the Shoah and the German occupation of Poland. National and local histories can speak contradictory languages when one crosses borders, and in this case they seemed to exclude one another. In each country the archives are organized in radically different ways, and so is memory. I was looking for a Russian hero in a Polish camp that, according to official Russian historians, did not belong to Russian history. And, to make things even more complicated, some material had to come from archives in Belarus.

The Beginning of a Life Story in Moscow (October 2012)

I decided to write Pechersky's entire life story and to look for answers to the many questions I now had. If I really wanted to understand him, I needed to find traces of other parts of his life. In Moscow I found the Russian Research and Educational Holocaust Center, whose generous archivist Leonid Terushkin had piles of material. Together with other historians, he had recently published a book about Sobibor.[15]

The archive also held early Russian publications about Sobibor, often written by Jewish intellectuals, along with memoirs and descriptions of other places where Pechersky had been, including Minsk and a camp in the woods near Minsk. His testimony in Moscow in 1944 included a deposition about the crimes committed against him in Sobibor and earlier. The résumé was edited by the NKGB (secret police) and was also preserved in the archive, together with his unpublished memoirs of 1972. But his movements following his escape from Sobibor presented a puzzle.

Several partisan groups in Belarus claimed that Pechersky had been a member. I hoped to find out more with a visit to the partisan archives in Minsk. I also wanted to find his family in his home town of Rostov-on-Don. It was clear to me that most of those who had records about Pechersky were mostly interested in his leadership role in the Sobibor insurrection. At times it felt as if I had been too optimistic when I embarked on my quest, not sufficiently realizing that tracing the life of Pechersky would depend on the assistance and trust of others:

Figure 0.1 A photograph honoring a young Aleksandr Pechersky in the window of the Bolshaya Bronaya synagogue in Moscow

Source: Photograph courtesy of Selma Leydesdorff.

archivists in former Communist countries, surviving relatives and those who had met or known him, and of course people who could decipher his terrible handwriting. I admired those activists and historians who, like his daughter, had tried to break the silence around him after the fall of the Communist regime.

One afternoon I entered the Bolshaya Bronaya synagogue in Moscow and saw to my surprise that Pechersky's portrait occupied a prominent place. He was the centerpiece in an exhibition designed to show the Jewish participation in the heroic struggle against the German invader. I met Svetlana Bogdanova, the custodian in charge of the exhibition, and she advised me to approach Pechersky's friends, who in the meantime had emigrated to Israel. Once I met them, they told a different story, filled with compassion for this man who had become so sad and lonely. They had not been with him in Sobibor, but they had witnessed his slow decline in later years. Again I was lucky.

Michael Lev and Other Friends of Pechersky in Israel

It was Svetlana from the Moscow synagogue who had sent me to Lazar Lubarsky. Lazar was close to another survivor, Simion Rosenfeld, whom I had met in 2010 when I interviewed him for the Sobibor Foundation website. At that time Simion was not able to tell me much except that he wanted to convey his admiration for Pechersky. He read a kind of poem or eulogy to express his feelings and his memory. Here is a part of it:

Our hunted people, the people of the Thora book, paid with mountains of corpses, and with the ashes of Dachau, Auschwitz, Treblinka, and Sobibor.
This is what you get from schizophrenic gibberish.
But the time passed, the end came for the patience of our people, the fires of the Warsaw ghetto flared up in the twinkling of an eye.
The Warsaw Jews stood firm: for twenty days no fascist foot was set in the ghetto.
In the footsteps of the courageous Warsawers rose Sobibor death camp.
With axes, with knives we killed the fascists.
We tore apart the barbed wire with our bare hands.
The fourteenth of October became a funeral repast for eleven fascists.
This day was for many prisoners their last one.
They gave their lives not in vain, Sobibor death camp was extinguished forever.[16]

Simion was in contact with the kibbutz Lohamei HaGeta'ot (the kibbutz of the Ghetto Fighters) in Northern Israel and with a group that sought recognition for Pechersky, some of whom still lived in Moscow, while others had become Israelis. Decades ago one member of this kibbutz, Miriam Novitch, had published the first book (1980) based on eyewitness accounts of Sobibor, in which Pechersky had a prominent place. Born in Byelorussia, Miriam Novitch had traveled before the war to France, where she later joined the resistance against the Germans. In

1946, she emigrated to Palestine and co-founded Lohamei HaGeta'ot. In 1949, she co-founded the Itzhak Katzenelson Holocaust and Jewish Resistance Heritage Museum, Documentation, and Study Center as a part of the kibbutz. Her book of short excerpts marks the early years of Israeli historiography in the 1980s, which sought to explode the myth of Jewish non-resistance.[17]

Along with providing information about Pechersky's later years, Lazar introduced me to Michael Lev, the Yiddish author who in the 1970s and 1980s had helped Pechersky reply to the many letters he received.[18] I spoke with Michael Lev only a few months before he died. He had published a book on Pechersky and Sobibor which is a mixture of history and fiction. Lev had been editorial secretary of *Sovetish Heymland*, the major cultural outlet for Soviet Yiddish culture. Besides this task, Lev had published twelve books in Yiddish before he migrated to Israel in 1996.[19] He had loved Pechersky, whom he described as a cultivated, artistic man who felt rejected, and they had been close. He had helped Pechersky to correspond with former prisoners and to reach out with his story to the world. According to Lev, Pechersky had been de-Judaized in public memory while the authorities used his story of resistance in their propaganda against what they called the struggle against fascism and the West. Lev explained that names in Russian traditionally include a patronymic. Pechersky was born Aleksandr Aronowitch Pechersky, but the authorities left out the Jewish Aronowitch, son of Aaron. Later on, in Poland, his official name was changed to Aleksandr Ivanovich Pechersky. Insofar as he became a public figure, Pechersky was thus Russified and de-Judaized.

Figure 0.2 Aleksandr Pechersky with Simion Rosenfeld in the early 1960s
Source: Photograph courtesy of Selma Leydesdorff.

In talking about the past, Pechersky had to use the idiom of Communist totalitarianism, and even his ego-documents had not escaped the grid of political control and newspeak. Recently the German historian Franziska Bruder has published an admirable account of the trajectory of the various editions of Pechersky's memoir manuscripts and their modifications and adaptations in later editions up until his death in 1990.[20] Pechersky rewrote his memoirs several times. They were also translated into Yiddish and Polish. Each time the memories were adapted to the expected audience and the political climate. Bruder also compared omitted texts with other statements by Pechersky. The 1944 memoir started as a letter written to his mother to tell her what had happened. In the (Russian) edition published in 1945, the word "Jew" does not turn up at all. The book refers only to the "Soviet Citizens" who were killed by the fascists. In retrospect, even when writing to his mother, his victimhood was homogenized into conformity with the standard language of the time. As Bruder mentions: "The word Jew was silenced. Differences in nationality or in language are not mentioned. Nor was the language most of the prisoners spoke: Yiddish. In the Polish and Yiddish editions the word Jew is used much more often."[21] Bruder uses the 1952 Polish edition for most of her quotations. It is indeed the most extensive version. I myself rely mostly on the 1972 Russian revised manuscript, which was never published. Avoiding "dangerous" ground and affirming the official version of contemporary history had become normal for so many, and to be excluded or misrepresented in official histories was part of everyday life under Communism. Silence and adaptation permeated Pechersky's work.

Washington (February 2013): Many Letters

Michael Lev sent his files of Pechersky's correspondence to the U.S. Holocaust Memorial Museum in Washington, D.C. He told me I should go there. So, my next stop was Washington. The search was becoming more and more complicated and expensive.[22] In Washington I got a glimpse of Pechersky's forlorn years after 1945. It turned out there was a huge collection of letters, which often contained detailed descriptions of Pechersky's later life. For decades he had been trying to write about the fate of the inmates of Sobibor. He wanted to tell his story about Jewish resistance, but he was not allowed to testify in Nuremberg in 1948, nor at the Eichmann trial in Jerusalem in 1961. His first public testimony after the war was at a tribunal in Kiev (1962), which was of course stage-managed by the authorities. Once more, Pechersky recounted events in Sobibor without mentioning the word "Jews" a single time. His attempts to maintain contact with the other Russian inmates of the camp were also frustrated. At times he could not even get a permit to travel to Moscow.

In November 1980 he wrote to Michael Lev: "I feel so weak, I don't feel well,"[23] mentioning the onset of the diabetes that would trouble the rest of his life. According to Pechersky, he could fight his illness only by working, which to him meant testifying. These were letters of despair; his only consolation lay in his exchanges with the other Russian survivors of Sobibor and with prominent former inmates of other camps. He described how he was approached by film

14   *Introduction*

crews and journalists. He did not want to collaborate with them because life was already made difficult enough. There was a shortage of food in Rostov, and prices on the market were staggering.[24]

Who Was This Man?

The documents in the archives were vast and rich, especially in Moscow and Washington. Even so, I had to navigate documents with so many contradictions, so many silences. Slowly I began to understand how this complicated person had been attractive to so many inmates in Sobibor but had fallen silent after the war. In several respects he exemplified the changes brought about in Jewish life after the Bolshevik Revolution. He grew up as a young Communist in Rostov-on-Don, where his family found shelter after fleeing their home in Kremenchuk, a smaller town in Ukraine. Compared with Kremenchuk, Rostov-on-Don was a more tolerant city, a major commercial hub with a large, more secularized Jewish community. The "modern" Soviet society expected Jews to assimilate to its secularist culture, which meant minimizing or hiding their Jewishness. Pechersky was clearly a member of this new breed of assimilated Jews.[25] How much he suffered from prejudice before the outbreak of war in 1941 we will never know, but certainly his fate during the war made him more Jewish than he himself probably ever imagined.

As Leonid Terushkin, the archivist at the Center for Holocaust Research in Moscow, wrote: "Until his very death, Pechersky had to rationalize something. This prewar generation of Jews who grew up during the Soviet era was Soviet through and through, accepting the spirit of internationalism that was propagated."[26] His Sovietized self-image makes it understandable why Pechersky found it so hard to cope with the silences and misrepresentations of the post-1945 era.

Minsk (May 2013)

When Germany attacked the Soviet Union in 1941, Pechersky was convinced it was his moral duty to defend the Soviet Union against the invaders. Throughout his life, he remained proud of his contribution to the war effort. He was a leader from the moment he entered Sobibor, surrounded by some friends he had met in Minsk. The deep impression their arrival made in Sobibor is mentioned in many testimonies. He had by then survived one and a half years of imprisonment, including an effort to kill him and several others in a cellar outside of Minsk.

Where was this cellar? I went to Minsk to find out and to collect more information about the partisans who were fighting in 1943–44 in Belarus, among whom Pechersky spent some time after the escape from Sobibor. He had described the cellar in Minsk as a "hell-hole" that only a few prisoners managed to survive. Investigating the topography of the Minsk prison system, I finally identified Stalag 352, of which there are several descriptions, as the place of Pechersky's imprisonment. Much of the material I found in Minsk was unique and provided invaluable knowledge about his trajectory before his deportation to Sobibor. How

Introduction 15

and why did he land there and not (for instance) in an extermination camp in Belarus? Could the German need for labor explain this?[27] The Belarus archives are not easily accessible, even with the assistance of the local archivists. They did not give much of an answer.

I Tried to Hear His Voice, to Understand His Language and His Sadness

When they left the prison in Minsk, the Jews were told they were going to Germany to work. They would travel together with their families. The column of the doomed passed the ghetto of Minsk on its way to an unknown destiny.

When the Russian POWs arrived at Sobibor, the Germans made a huge mistake. They allowed an extremely hostile group to enter the camp, a group of soldiers who were accustomed to military discipline and knew how to handle weapons. As Pechersky put it: "Our arrival at the camp made a great impression on the older prisoners; they knew well that the war was going on, but they had never seen the men who were fighting in it. All these newcomers could handle arms!"[28]

The uprising was not only a fight against the annihilation of the inmates; it was also the product of changing conditions of war, and it was rooted in a tradition of resistance and insurgence in other places, particularly in Byelorussia. It is also important to understand that while the Germans tried to destroy the masses of Jews physically, they were also keen to destroy the spirits of those Jews who were not killed immediately but had to work in order to keep the Germans' murderous industry going. Therefore, those who belonged to the workforce were also tortured psychologically. The Nazis believed that eradicating the prisoners' personalities would prevent any resistance. The revolt provides evidence that the Nazis did not succeed in this objective, and the written and oral memories tell us how a person can retain his/her individuality.

Pechersky organized the revolt in twenty-two days with the help of an already existing Polish underground network and his Russian comrades. In his view, not giving in to the destruction of one's personal identity was a form of resistance. As he wrote:

> By not killing all prisoners and despite terror and punishment, the SS did not kill humanity and the will to struggle and achieve victory.
>
> —Most awful was the atmosphere of psychological oppression, a nearly scientific system of individual pressure and the destruction of the human personality. The SS wanted to corrode all that was human, they wanted to reduce their emotions to the level of an animal, like the instincts of dogs.[29]

Indeed, little research has been done into the mechanism of survival in a world where life and death have become totally arbitrary. It is a theme very much present in the literature of survivors, where names like Primo Levi and Elie Wiesel stand out. This literature demonstrates that despite the constant terror, some

16 *Introduction*

normal gestures and actions of mutual help, friendship, and even love kept the camp inmates afloat. Those who survived were the ones who could resist the moral and physical mechanisms of disintegration. The basis for this resistance was the ability to mobilize the positive values of life against the fear of death.

The Russians had a circle of their own, an identity averse to fascism, a language, jokes, pride, and above all, songs. They stayed together and supported each other. One of them was ordered to sing Russian songs, and Pechersky's friend Tsibulski asked him what they should sing. Pechersky told him to sing an old patriotic song, "Yesli Zavtra Voyna" (If Tomorrow War Comes), which was the only song they all knew. In his 1952 testimony, Perchersky recalled, "It was like lightning in the spring":

> If tomorrow war comes, if the enemy attacks
> If dark forces come up,
> All the Soviet people, like one man
> Shall rise for the free Motherland

The Russians sang in the evenings; it held them together and reinforced their bonds.

And After the Revolt? Rostov-on-Don

After the revolt, where did Pechersky go? To which partisan unit? In Minsk I finally found Pechersky's release papers, showing that he belonged to the Schors partisans. I knew that after the war he tried to resume his former life. In Rostov he found his family after a stay in the hospital where he met Olga. He married her, and she came to live with him and would stay with him until his death. He gave testimony on his ordeal in Moscow in 1944, but the papers were politically correct minutes, and there is hardly anything in them that is authentic. He was never recognized for his role and disillusion permeated the last part of his life. Still, I did not really understand his amazing strength during the insurrection.

In the first years after his return, Pechersky was invited to speak at meetings of veterans and in schools, on the condition that he would speak and act as a "normal" soldier who had defended his country. He was recognized as a war veteran and not as a leader in Sobibor. With the increase of anti-Semitism at the end of the 1940s, he became isolated.[30] Unemployed, he lived in a small house with Olga, where he was sometimes joined by his daughter Ella and her family. The lack of recognition and the fact that he had no chance to tell his story affected his personality. Whoever reads his letters carefully will see a depressed man desperately reaching out to those who can confirm his role. Visits to others were often impossible. Poverty, illness, and official harassment complicated or prevented his traveling to other cities, such as Moscow. These were the times when many Jews wanted to emigrate to Israel but were forbidden to do so. Pechersky, however, identified himself as a Russian and chose to stay. Jewishness once more had become a hot issue in international politics and a danger spot in the Soviet Union. I tried to improve my understanding by visiting the Shoah Visual Archive in Los Angeles. I looked at their videos for hours. Back in Europe, I was helped in continuing my search to understand various patterns.

Introduction   17

It was time to speak with his family in Rostov. I met them in August 2013. Finally I got the story from his daughter, Ella, and his granddaughter Natasha. There were piles of letters from schoolchildren, a huge correspondence that had been going on for decades. In most of his letters Pechersky retold the story of Sobibor. Ella did not think her father was depressed. According to her, he was in poor health physically, but suffered psychologically only in 1987 when he was not allowed to attend the premiere of the movie *Escape from Sobibor*. The uprising in Sobibor was the theme of the movie, which made the heroic narrative of resistance known to a very large audience in the West. One could doubt whether viewers, while admiring the hero Pechersky, learned any more about Sobibor than they did from movies about other concentration camps.

Of all those who remembered Pechersky during my interviews and in the vast literature, no one was able to answer my question: why had Pechersky become such an undisputed leader? At the same time, it took decades before Sobibor emerged from the darkness of oblivion. Nowadays the participation of Jews in the Russian war effort is gaining recognition, but this undeniable fact of history has been slow to rise to the surface.[31] The sad story of the very few survivors has been recorded, but no common narrative has emerged despite impressive efforts to publish as many autobiographies as possible. According to Professor Ilya Altman, the director of the Educational Holocaust Center in Moscow, the Holocaust is finally being spoken and written about in Russia, but the term has been given various meanings by different people and has in some cases been used for the "Russian genocide." According to Altman:

> Our schoolchildren, whose main source of information is the Internet, can only be confused and misled by much that they read there, since dozens of sites describe the Holocaust as a myth. Around the turn of our new century, Russian publishers brought out blockbuster editions of 'compositions' written by Holocaust deniers; the recently closed newspaper *Duel*, the journal *Our Contemporary* and other publications have been trying to persuade us that the subject should not even be raised in Russia today, since it belittles not only the heroic exploits of the Red Army, but people of other ethnicities who died in World War II.[32]

Altman is optimistic, though, since there are major changes in the writing of history, and the fate of Jews during the Holocaust has begun to be acknowledged. Still, outside of Moscow, there are hardly any public events in Russia commemorating it, and "the school history curriculum rightly highlights the wartime heroism of the Red Army, but devotes little attention to such things as life under Nazi occupation."[33]

In the late summer of 2015 a collection of letters archived at YIVO in New York turned up unexpectedly. It was a correspondence between Pechersky and Reuven Ainsztein (1907–81), a well-known publicist who had fled from Poland and settled in England, where he started writing about the resistance of the Jews.[34] Reading Ainsztein's articles I was amazed to find references to data on Pechersky

18 *Introduction*

I had never seen before. It is now clear that Ainsztein found the information in these letters. The letters were written in a pompous Soviet style that will be discussed later in this book.

Reshaping Narratives, Changing Memories

Memories of the revolt have been shaped and continuously re-articulated by the experiences and the political aftermath of Nazism and Communism. Stories also change over time, as did the ways in which people remember Pechersky. He was an unrecognized hero, and all of the survivors regretted this. His life story shows us how Nazism and Communism interacted in an individual life, and how people in a part of Europe that had been occupied by Germans and Russians became disoriented as national borders were modified and one totalitarian regime was replaced by another.

Enormous advances have been made in our historical knowledge about what happened in this region thanks to the opening of archives in the former Communist world and by the rapprochement of historians of the East and the West. Our knowledge about what has been destroyed, the communities and Jewish life, has in a way become a shared endeavor.[35] These changes have also made it possible to speak more freely about memory.

While contemporary history writing often relies largely on memory, we know that memory is contextual and ever-changing. Although memories are remarkably unstable, many histories can be passed on only through individual recollections that provide unique knowledge. In this book I have integrated personal accounts and testimonies into the historical reconstruction as equal in validity to other types of documentation. The documentation includes contemporary accounts and diaries, as well as post-war interviews from various decades after the events; written, oral, audiotaped, and videotaped testimonies; courtroom witness depositions; public interviews; and memoirs. These sources bring into history events that would otherwise remain completely unknown, and they often provide a different perspective on events that are already known.

The Israeli historian Omer Bartov has argued that one must "integrate personal accounts, or testimonies into the historical reconstruction of the Holocaust," which he considers "equal in validity to other forms of documentation." He added that "personal accounts can at times save events from oblivion." In a fascinating study of the Ukrainian town of Buchach, Bartov made visible how a combination of these two methods can provide new insights. He showed for instance that Jews and Christians (or non-Jews) were much more in contact than was believed before now, and he came up with a new pattern of interrelations. In his view, testimonies should be treated on the same level as written documentation.[36] I agree with him, and in the end, the story presented here is correcting earlier interpretations that have become common collective knowledge, as well as providing additional knowledge.

Pechersky died in 1990, when the post-Communist era had not really started. One can only wonder if he would have been officially recognized if the new regime had arrived sooner. It is still difficult and politically unwelcome to talk about the

Introduction   19

fate of Jews in Russia. Pechersky's life and the mystery surrounding him provide a window on a politically imposed silence and its malignant consequences during the bleak decades of Soviet society after Stalin. Pechersky's bitter mood and his dwindling hope for better times resonate with the broader cultural and psychological currents of Russian life. But his situation also makes us aware of the value of retrieving and restoring the stories of individual lives, even if refracted in the cruel mirror of Sobibor. Beyond that, it warns us against reducing a human being to his heroic role in a "spectacular" insurrection.

Since the Communist master narrative unraveled after the fall of Communism, groups in Russia and Israel have managed to draw attention to Pechersky, but the his story remains focused solely on Sobibor and the crimes of the Nazis. Lately the Polish government awarded him a posthumous medal, but in the speeches, only his role as a hero was mentioned. Never was he identified as a Russian Jew. How he was victimized by two totalitarian systems again went unnoticed. In 2016 he was awarded a Medal of Courage by President Vladimir Putin, marking the enormous success of a group around Ilya Vasilyev who had campaigned relentlessly for his recognition.[37] But this recognition came late. Unlike the Sobibor insurrection, the story presented here has no place in the heroic struggle against Nazism. He did not become part of the collective memory of Jewish resistance. With this book I hope to give him his rightful place.

Notes

1 Demjanjuk was a Ukraine-born camp guard at Sobibor who was accused of participating in the murders at the camp. See www.longshadowofsobibor.com.

2 See Michael Lev, *Sobibor* (Jerusalem: Gefen Publishing House, 2007). This beautiful novel is based on Yiddish writer Lev's close acquaintance with Pechersky and his assistance with Pechersky's international correspondence. See also: Jules Schelvis, *Sobibor: A History of a Nazi Death Camp* (Oxford and New York: Berg Publishers, 2010).

3 See Yitzhak Arad, *Belzec, Sobibor, Treblinka: The Operation Reinhard Death Camps* (Bloomington: Indiana University Press, 1987); and also: Jules Schelvis, *Ooggetuigen van Sobibor* (Amsterdam: Ambo/Anthos, 2010); Thomas (Toivi) Blatt, *From the Ashes of Sobibor* (Włodawa, Poland: Muzeum Pojezierza Łęczyńsko-Włodawskiego, 2008); Andrew Zielinski, *Conversations with Regina* (Włodawa, Poland: Muzeum Pojezierza Łęczyńsk-Włodawskiego, 2008); Kalmen Wewryk, *To Sobibor and Back* (Włodawa, Poland: Muzeum Pojezierza Łęczyńsko-Włodawskiego, 2008); Kurt Ticho, *My Legacy, Holocaust, History and the Unfinished Task of Pope John Paul II* (Włodawa, Poland: Muzeum Pojezierza Łęczyńsko-Włodawskiego, 2008).

4 Dieter Pohl, *Nationalsozialistische Judenverfolgung in Ostgalizien, 1941–1944, Organisation und Durchführung eines staatlichen Massenverbrechens* (Munich: Oldenbourg, 1996). *Reihe: Studien zur Zeitgeschichte*, 50.

5 Peter Witte and Stephen Tyas, "A New Document on the Deportation and Murder of Jews during 'Einsatz Reinhardt' 1942," *Holocaust and Genocide Studies* 15:3 (Winter 2001): 468–486.

6 Benjamin Ginsberg, *How the Jews Defeated Hitler: Exploding the Myth of Jewish Passivity in the Face of Nazism* (New York: Rowman & Littlefield Publishers, 2013). I do not agree with this book entirely, but it gives an oversight of the arguments.

7 Tony Judt, *Postwar: A History of Europe Since 1945* (London: Penguin Books, 2005), especially "From the House of the Dead, an Essay on Modern European Memory," 803–831.

20 Introduction

8 Marek Bem, *Sobibor Extermination Camp 1942–1943*, trans. Tomasz Karpiński and Natalia Sarzyńska-Wójtowicz (Amsterdam: Stichting Sobibor, 2015), 10.

9 Noah Shenker, *Reframing Holocaust Testimony* (Bloomington: Indiana University Press, 2015), 7.

10 Ester Raab, www.getuigenverhalen.nl/interview/late-gevolgen-van-sobibor-overlev enden-van-de-opstand-interview-07-esther-raab. This was part of our discussion, not the interview.

11 Belzec: 600,000; Sobibor: 250,000; Treblinka: 900,000; Total: 1,750,000 Jewish victims. From: Wolfgang Benz, ed., *Dimension der Völkermords: Die Zahl der jüdischen Opfer des Nationalsozialismus* (München: Oldenbourg Verlag, 1991), 17. The website of the U.S. Holocaust Memorial Museum mentions 1,700,000. Benz still mentions 250,000 for Sobibor. This number has been revised to 170,000.

12 Saul Friedländer, *Nazi Germany and the Jews 1939–1945, the Years of Extermination* (New York: Harper Colins, 2007), 559.

13 A transcript is held in the archives of NIOD (the Netherlands Institute for War Documentation, Amsterdam). The interview was conducted in Russian and translated into Dutch. I have translated it from Dutch into English.

14 The Russian movie with his daughter is Alexander Marutyan's *Арифметика свободы* (*The Arithmetic of Freedom*).

15 С. С. Виленский, Г. Б. Горбовицкий and Л. А. Терушкин]. [Semen Samuilovich Vilenski; G. B. Gorbovitskii? and Leonid A. Terushkin], Собибор (Sobibor). (Moskva: Vozvrashchenie, 2008).

16 Simion Rosenfeld, 2010, www.getuigenverhalen.nl/interview/late-gevolgen-van-sobi bor-overlevenden-van-de-opstand-interview-02-semion-rozenfeld.

17 Miriam Novitch, *Sobibor, Martyrdom and Revolt* (New York: Holocaust Library, 1980).

18 Mijhail Krutikov, "Introduction to: Michael Lev, 'Sobibor', and Soviet Yiddish Culture," in *Michael Lev, Sobibor* (Jerusalem: Gefen Publishing House, 2007), i-ix.

19 Verbal information by Polina Lev, his daughter.

20 Franziska Bruder, *Hunderte solcher Helden: Der Aufstand jüdischer Gefangener im NS-Vernichtungslager Sobibor* (Münster: Unrast, 2013).

21 Ibid., 61.

22 I am grateful to many institutions for their generosity and mention them in my acknowledgments. The most important has been The Conference on Jewish Material Claims Against Germany.

23 Letter Michael Lev of 10 November 1980. USHMM 68118, Washington, D.C., translated by Yedida Kanfer and me.

24 Letter Michael Lev of 16 March 1982. USHMM 68118, Washington.

25 Zvi Gitelman, *A Century of Ambivalence: The Jews of Russia and the Soviet Union, 1881 to the Present* (Bloomington: Indiana University Press, 1988; reprinted 2001).

26 Leonid Terushkin, *The History of Sobibor and the Fate of the Participants in the Uprising* [materials from Russian archives and museums] (Warsaw: Holocaust Center for Research and Education [CBE], 2013).

27 In my search I was helped by Israeli historian Dan Zeits and by the History Workshop of Minsk, in particular by Kuzma Kozak.

28 Novitch, "Sobibor," 91.

29 Aleksandr Pechersky, Unpublished manuscript 1972, Moscow. Russian Research and Educational Holocaust Center.

30 Arno Lustiger, *Stalin and the Jews: The Tragedy of the Soviet Jews and the Jewish Anti-Fascist Committee* (New York: Enigma Books, 2003).

31 Yitzhak Arad, *In the Shadow of the Red Banner: Soviet Jews in the War Against Nazi Germany* (Jerusalem: Gefen Publishing House, Yad Vashem Publications), 2010.

32 Ilya Altman, "Russia and the Holocaust- Whose Genocide Was It Anyway?," www. opendemocracy.net/od-russia/ilya-altman/russia-and-holocaust-%E2%80%93-whose-genocide-was-it-anyway, accessed 27 January 2014.

33 Ibid.

34 Reuben Ainsztein, *Jewish Resistance in Nazi-occupied Eastern Europe* (London: Paul Elek, 1974); in German as *Jüdischer Widerstand im deutschbesetzten Osteuropa während des Zweiten Weltkriegs* (Bibliothek und Informationssystem der Universität Oldenburg, 1993).

35 Examples include: Zvi Gitelman, *Bitter Legacy: Confronting the Holocaust in the USSR* (Bloomington: Indiana University Press, 1997); Jack Kagan and Dov Cohen, *Surviving the Holocaust with the Russian Jewish Partisans* (Edgware and Portland: Vallentine Mitchell, 1998); Yitzchak Arad, *In the Shadow of the Red Banner* (Jerusalem: Gefen Publishing House, 2010); Ilya Altman, *Zhertvy Nenavisti: Kholokost v SSSR, 1941–1945gg.* (Victims of Hatred: The Holocaust in the USSR, 1941–1945. Moscow: Foundation Kovcheg, 2002); Ray Brandon and Wendy Lower, *The Shoah in the Ukraine: History, Testimony, Memorialization* (Bloomington: Indiana University Press, 2008); and Yehuda Bauer, *The Death of the Shtetl* (New Haven: Yale University Press, 2010).

36 Omer Bartov, "Wartime Lies and Other Testimonies: Jewish-Christian Relations in Buczacz, 1939–1944," *East European Politics and Societies* 25:3 (August 2011): 486–487.

37 Ilya Vasilyev, *Александр Печерский, прорыв в весмертие* (Aleksandr Pechersky: Breakthrough to Immortality. Moscow: Vremya, 2013).

1 Jews in a Post-Revolutionary World
Integration and Exclusion*

The Communist revolution of 1917 dramatically changed the lives of Russian Jews, who up until then had been excluded from public life. Of course there were exceptions, but cultural isolation was the norm. By proclaiming equality for all Russians and declaring Jews to be Soviet citizens equal to all other citizens, the revolution and Communism created possibilities to live a trajectory different from that of previous generations of Jews. However, the newly created identity of Soviet citizen presumed that people would give up their old identities and cultures. Jews became one of the many minorities who, unlike other minorities, were not connected to a particular geography but spread over the whole territory.[1]

Pechersky's early life must be placed in the context of the Jews' difficult position and the chaotic years following the victory of Communism and its politics toward minorities.[2] While Bolshevism proclaimed equality, even the most assimilated Jews would always meet with discrimination and rejection. Jews belonged to a minority that had to give up their cultural background as the price to be paid in order to become full Soviet citizens. As historian Nora Levin wrote: "The Revolution not only destroyed traditional Jewish religious and cultural life but shattered the old economic and social roles and relationships that had formed a precarious but familiar Jewish economy."[3] Within the framework of the further development of Soviet society, they would occupy a particular place: that of the scapegoat. Many Jews had believed in the future of what was called "a Red Communist Dawn"; they had given up their cultural roots but were never rewarded as they had hoped.

Pechersky belonged to those who grew up in a climate of optimism, culture, and creativity, the background of his adolescence. Jewish traditional life was attacked in various stages of the development of the Soviet state, but for Jews there remained the possibility to opt for a new future within certain parameters. One had to follow a Russian education, speak Russian, and become a member of the many organizations Soviet life offered. Communist cultural life was intense, with youth organizations, singing contests, and amateur theater. There was a new standard image of the worker: someone with technical skills ready to join the labor force the new economy was keen to create.

However, the status of Jews was constantly threatened by the anti-Semitism that had always flourished and turned out to be much more persistent than was

Jews in a Post-Revolutionary World   23

expected in the first years after the revolution. While Communism did not exclude Jews on the grounds of any racial theory or racial politics, as was the case with Nazism, prejudice, superstition, and hate could be deployed for political reasons. In a world of bias and suspicion, equality became a slogan, while indeed at the same time one could opt for a modern Communist lifestyle and believe in a better future.

Pechersky's life is also part of the Russian history of World War II and of the millions who joined the army wanting to defend the Motherland, or were forced to do so. In Pechersky's case, it was his own choice, and his role in the revolt was also a matter of choice. But throughout most of his life he was a victim who had to surrender to two totalitarian systems, Nazism and Communism, while life for Jews reached a new low under Stalinist repression. Stalin's death in 1953 marked another phase of Pechersky's life, in which there were moments when it looked like Jews could breathe again. However, the persecution of Jews and the prejudices against them never ended. Like all Jews, Pechersky lived in a context of ambivalence about the choices to be made and decisions imposed by others.

We know little about his life before the war. He married in 1933, became a father, and, as was normal, worked. From 1931 to 1933 he was in the army doing normal military service.[4] I kept wondering what had turned him into a strong man able to survive so many atrocities of Nazism. How could he become so powerless against the Stalinist repression? It seems that part of the answer can be found in his belief in the ideals with which he joined the Red Army to fight Nazism. He frequently said he was proud of having done so, and he never grew tired of telling how aggressive and barbarous fascism was. It was his duty to fight for Communism and defend the Motherland; these were his words. However, we know that in Russia one was expected to talk about history in certain approved terms and to adapt to the official discourse. Since Pechersky died in 1990, he never enjoyed the freedom to speak out openly.

He also never spoke out against Communism, not even in his later years when he was excluded from his surrounding society and gloomily had to accept that he would never be recognized for his heroic role. He was probably scared, and he could not speak or write in any other way. All he could do was to express himself in innocuous general terms, which included the discourse of how he had been fighting invaders who killed innocent citizens. Such terms belonged to life in a totalitarian world where one was not allowed to express opinions about the special fate of Jews under Nazism. It is also possible that he never stopped believing in his old Communist ideals. To persevere in such a belief is not uncommon, even among persecuted Russians who sometimes, despite years in prisons and the Gulag, remained convinced that they were only dealing with a deformation of originally good ideals.[5] They had been fighting for a cause, and it is very human to believe that the cause for which you gave the best part of your life was worth it.

Pechersky is important for understanding the uprising as a historical event, and his trajectory provides a window into a general history of how Jews in that corner of the world faced persecution. His fate is tragic, and I believe that everyone would agree that such a Jewish hero who did not hesitate to take enormous

24   Jews in a Post-Revolutionary World

risks deserved a better fate. He was also a civilized man who had profited from the chances given to Jews after the Russian Revolution to be educated; he was creative and was a professional soldier. An assimilated Jew, he became an officer of the Soviet Army early in the war, which would have been unthinkable in tsarist times, and everyone respected him. Pechersky and his allies, most of them soldiers from Russia, had been strengthened by their desire to defend good against evil; for them it was a choice of Communism against fascism.

Crossing Borders, Looking at the Region

In order to understand his life, I had to overcome the fragmentation of the writing of history into subfields: there are historians of the Shoah, and there are historians of the Soviet Union. Each group has its own publications and networks, but they remain separate academic worlds. This dilemma forced me to take a step beyond national history writing, to cross boundaries and look at the history of the whole region where Pechersky lived and suffered. My research took me to the region called "Bloodlands" by the American historian Timothy Snyder.[6] In these lands the regimes of Stalin and Hitler caused a degree of suffering and bloodshed far greater than any seen in Western Europe during World War II. In this book I also include Rostov-on-Don as part of this area of mass murder. The town is located slightly further to the east and has always been part of Russia, but the population was similarly ravaged. Armies marched through these lands, advancing and retreating in turn, leaving death and devastation in their wake. Since the publication of *Bloodlands*, academic attention to this region has grown. Snyder's research explicitly crossed borders. He chose the name Bloodlands because "the place where all of the victims died, the Bloodlands, extends from central Poland to western Russia, through Ukraine, Belarus and the Baltic States . . . The victims were chiefly Jews, Belarusians, Ukrainians, Poles, Russians, and Balts, the peoples native to these lands."[7] It is a vast transnational landscape where two murderous regimes interacted and killed. Here tens of millions of people perished, including most of the Jews who lived there.[8]

The Polish historian Darius Stola has argued that such an approach overcomes the tendency of national historiographies of the region toward separate, insular perspectives, and that in this vast terrain we are dealing with a "human geography of victims"; he calls this a "spatial turn in explaining mass murder," where space is more the focus than any of its national territories or policies, as was usually the case in the past.[9] This framework of precise attention to local histories helps us to understand better the actors in the drama: the perpetrators, the victims, and the bystanders.

The Camps of Operation Reinhard and the History of Pechersky

From March 1942 onward, Operation Reinhard was a major step in the systematic elimination of the Jews of Europe. Three Reinhard camps—Sobibor, Belzec, and Treblinka—were created in order to murder thousands of people in a systematic manner. What happened there remained an open secret, with people living in the region or involved in the provisions of the camp aware of what was happening there. Although SS soldiers were forbidden to talk about it, they would talk when they were on leave and were sent home.

Many knew about the camps, despite their being officially secret. For instance, in the archive of video testimonies at Yahad-In Unum (Paris) there is an audiovisual file in which a Pole named Jan speaks openly about what happened at Sobibor. He lived in a village nearby and had to transport goods and people to and from the camp. Although he was never allowed to enter the camp and made his deliveries at the entrance, he was well aware of the mass murder there, though he would not describe it that way. He thought the smell of burning people was horrible and very well understood that thousands were being killed there.[10]

The creation of the extermination camps of Operation Reinhard was the result of a conviction that the systematic industrial killing of people and the burning of corpses would be more efficient and "cleaner" than primitive mass executions by shooting, as had been the practice in Ukraine. Also, the extreme violence before and during the mass shootings was supposed to have negative side effects on the morale of the soldiers who had to carry them out. This negative image would disrupt the heroism of an "unconquerable army" whose soldiers' uniforms were in reality spotted with blood and who were doing filthy work, as has been described in the *The Holocaust by Bullets*, an impressive account by Patrick Desbois that describes the mass shootings in Ukraine.[11] The mass graves, with heaps of slowly decomposing bodies, the stench, and the shrieks and wailing of the people who would be killed would haunt the shooting soldiers.

In the U.S. Holocaust Memorial Museum in Washington, D.C., I found among court proceedings after the war the forced confessions of such soldiers who "had to shoot." Their job was made possible with the help of vodka and schnapps, consumed in great quantities in the evenings and during the shooting to rid the perpetrators of images of execution. Pervitin (now known as crystal meth) was also widely used to endure the unpleasant circumstances; it is an amphetamine-like drug that heightens aggression and diminishes human warmth and empathy.

Franz Hess was a German major tried in Minsk in 1946 in *The Trial of the Nazi Invaders Who Committed Acts of Horror in Belarus*.[12] He wrote his own confession, probably because there was no one to translate.[13] Other confessions I found in Russian were shorter, more standardized, and fitted better the proceedings of that moment. Hess described how he drank his first vodka in Minsk: "There was not a day on which a rough quantity of schnapps was not consumed," he complained. Israeli historian Yitzhak Arad mentions in his work on the Holocaust in the Soviet Union how one of the German officers, Von dem Bach-Zelewski, said to Himmler during a visit to Minsk in 1941: "Look at the eyes of the men in this Kommando, how deeply shaken they are! Those men are finished [*fertig*] for the rest of their lives. What kind of followers are we training here? Either neurotics or savages."[14]

Although crematoria blackened the surroundings with ashes mixed with fatty sediment and produced the nauseating stench of burning flesh, they were preferred

26 Jews in a Post-Revolutionary World

to multiplying mass graves, which were covered only with a thin layer of sand and earth where the stench of death and decay remained. The decision to industrialize the killing was a conscious step to speed up the destruction of the Jews, but even more, an effort to erase all proof of what happened and make the process invisible. The Germans were concerned that their crimes would be discovered by the wider world and that this knowledge about them would destroy what was left of their reputation. Therefore, the corpses also needed to be destroyed by burning, especially once the Germans realized they were losing the war. They worried they would be punished, and they were scared. In the war's later stages, tremendous efforts were made to exhume the corpses and erase all traces of the atrocities.

The story of the Treblinka camp is the best known of the three camps, which is certainly the result of Russian journalists entering there with the Soviet army. But our general lack of knowledge about the sites of Operation Reinhard is also grounded in the fact that there were very few survivors, and therefore we lack eyewitness accounts. Only two people survived Belzec. The prisoners fought back in Treblinka in August 1943, which resulted in a higher number of survivors, as was the case with Sobibor a few months later.

A major workforce was needed to profit from the killing of hundreds of thousands of people and to smooth the process. Rucksacks filled with clothes, food, and the personal belongings of victims arriving on many trains from all over Europe had to be sorted in order to send valuable items to Germany, where the production of goods other than those needed for the war had slowed. Of course, the guards did not hesitate to profit from goods that were collected or to engage sometimes very skilled Jewish artisans to provide gifts for their families or themselves. When 15-year-old Stanisław Szmajzner (born in the Polish town of Puławy on March 13, 1927) arrived, the guards discovered he was a goldsmith and demanded that he make something beautiful.[15] The camps also required a lot of routine work and engaged mainly males in forced, hard physical labor. Some men worked as medical staff, jewelry makers, or tailors; women did the sorting, sewing, cleaning, and cooking. Ukrainians who had received special training in a nearby facility called Trawnik assisted the small group of German guards at Sobibor.[16] They, too, needed good food, clean clothes, care, and lodging.

Many survivors of the Nazis' effort to annihilate the Jews have written about their mental resistance and survival in autobiographical accounts, and I have talked with many of them about their strength to do so. But more resilience was needed: after the escape from Sobibor, survival depended upon another kind of strength and on luck and fate. In interviews, I learned about survival in a hostile environment. In most narratives, escape is intertwined with the period after the camp when the former inmates were on the run. These narratives break a wall of silence that has often been self-imposed or has been created by politics, collective and individual self-repression; they often accuse and tell of betrayal, theft, robbery, and hostility in Poland.

However there is another explanation for the silence about the Reinhard camps that needed to be broken: it is very human that we, the audience, do not want to listen to stories about how people could be industrially processed in six hours. The story is too horrendous, too physical, and too painful for our ability to listen and digest. The listener is filled with shame about the evil side of the human race. I, too, feel shame when I think of my grandparents, who, like a third of Dutch Jewry, were killed at Sobibor. I seldom talk about it.

Kremenchuk: Family Background and the Memory of Persecution

Let us now take a closer look at the life story of this elusive hero. Aleksandr Pechersky was born in 1909 in Kremenchuk, a large town in Ukraine on the left bank of the Dniepr. Pechersky does not mention this town much in his memoirs, probably since at a young age he moved with his family to the Russian town of Rostov-on-Don, a little more than 500 kilometers away. It is assumed that the family moved or fled in 1915, but some people, including members of the extended family, believe it was later. The dominant language of Kremenchuk was Russian, not Ukrainian, which was spoken in the surrounding countryside. So there was no language barrier to settling in Rostov-on-Don, which was in Russian and not Ukrainian territory. Most people arriving were looking for safety because, during World War I and the Civil War (during and after the Russian Revolution), Kremenchuk experienced periods of long and intense violence. During the Civil War in 1919 Kremenchuk was reconquered by the Red Army; however, armed hostilities continued until 1921. From a place where Jews could live in peace and relative security, the town had become a dangerous place and the fate of Jews had become harsh and unpredictable. The number of Jewish inhabitants declined dramatically after World War I but grew again until the Nazi occupation. The 1926 census indicates that the Jewish population in Kremenchuk was 28,900, or 46 percent of the overall population of the city.[17]

The origins of the Jewish community of Kremenchuk can be traced back to the end of the eighteenth century, when the Russian Empire became the country with the largest Jewish population in the world.[18] The three partitions of Poland—in 1772, 1793, and 1795—had left many of the Jews of Poland subjects of the Russian monarchy.[19] In 1791, an imperial decree created what became known as the Pale of Settlement (in Russian: *cherta osedlosti*), constricting the territory where Jews could live.[20] Originally, the Pale of Settlement limited the area of settlement to the Mohilevskaya and Polovskaya provinces (territories of what is now Byelorussia) and the Black Sea region (territories of what is now Ukraine).[21] In the following decades, the borders of the Pale of Settlement changed a few times; however, most of the Jewish population settled in these two regions. Kremenchuk, a district capital, was an important urban center on the way from Byelorussia to the Black Sea and soon became an important center of Jewish life in Central Ukraine.

In 1905, Jews made up approximately half the population of the town.[22] The growth of the Jewish community of Kremenchuk in the second half of the nineteenth century can be explained by the active participation of Jews in the industrial development of the region. Jewish workers and Jewish capital were important

28 Jews in a Post-Revolutionary World

Map 1.1 The locations of Kremenchuk in Ukraine and Rostov-on Don in Russia
Source: Map produced by Isabella Lewis.

factors in the growth of modern capitalism. As a result, a number of Jewish institutions were established, including several elementary and specialized schools and two institutes for secondary education. Local Jewish youths participated in the activities of "almost all the revolutionary parties"—both Jewish (such as the Jewish Bund and Poale Zion) and non-Jewish (like the Socialist Revolutionary Party of Russia, Mensheviks and Bolsheviks). Irritation about this involvement in radical politics was one of the reasons for the brutal pogrom in Kremenchuk of October 18–20, 1905, after the suppression of the Revolution in that year, when a wave of social and political unrest spread all over Russia and Ukraine. The real reason was of course the deeply rooted anti-Semitism. The government could only stop the pogrom by declaring martial law. Until then, the Jews of Kremenchuk, like those in many other towns, had given a large "gift" to the chief of police every year, who then guaranteed there would not be any pogroms in the town. However, 1905 saw several attempts to break with this tradition, and in Kremenchuk the arrival of the "gift" was delayed. At many levels, the times were chaotic, and disorder was rampant.

The pogrom of 1905 began with clashes between Jews and police on October 18. Later, when Jewish youngsters gathered to protest against the police, Cossacks opened fire on the Jewish crowd. Several people were killed, and many were wounded. As the result of a rumor that spread the next day accusing Jews of having desecrated the portrait of the Russian Emperor and of arming themselves, crowds attacked Jewish stores. This happened with demonstrative indifference—if not active participation—from the side of the police. In some cases, these attacks were thwarted by Jewish self-defense groups, which were able to defend Kremenchuk's synagogue. The pogrom continued the next day; windows of Jewish apartments were broken and victims were driven into the streets, where they were beaten. Order was restored in Kremenchuk the following day by means of martial law and the arrival of temporary Governor-General Kalitin. The new governor-general tried to organize a symbolic reconciliation between representatives of the Jewish and non-Jewish communities of Kremenchuk, but without any significant results.

Nevertheless, the pogrom of 1905 was relatively "innocent" compared with what followed. It also happened in an epoch of worldwide violence on the borders of Russia. The Russo-Japanese war caused social unrest and a feeling that the Russian nation should defend Russian identity. Such collective psychological turmoil has always influenced the position of Jews. There is a plethora of historical literature on the wave of violence of 1905 and its causes.[23] The literature usually makes a sharp distinction between what happened in 1905 and later violence against Jews, which became extreme in 1918–19. According to several authors, the 1905 pogroms were a side effect of the dire poverty in the countryside and the rise of a Jewish middle class in the towns. These 1905 events were also part of a clash between nationalistic forces and the various political forces that supported or were opposed to the Russian Revolution.

Anti-Semitism in the Russian Empire continued to grow during the period from 1905 to 1917. The chaos of World War I is of particular interest for the history of the Pechersky family. In his book on the history of Russian Jews during the Russian Civil War, Oleg Budnitski argues that the origins of the bloody pogroms of 1918–20 can be traced back to these war years.[24] From the beginning of the war, a few pogroms had occurred in areas where there was a concentration of Russian troops.[25] In general, anti-Jewish attitudes were particularly strong in the front-line areas and usually took the form of a widespread assumption that Jews were enemy spies, a view that circulated among both soldiers and officers. Such an accusation had become a popular explanation for Russian military failures, and this pathological distrust of the Jewish population resulted not only in widespread violence and in the execution of Jews without trial, but also in arbitrary deportations that were often accompanied by pogroms, widespread rape, and even murder.[26] The pogroms were most violent when Russian troops seized territories with a substantial Jewish population.

The rise of anti-Semitism during the war years and the increasing alienation of the Jewish population explains why the Jews as an urbanized and ethnic community produced a considerable number of revolutionary cadres. As a result, the Jews of Kremenchuk were excited about the February Revolution of 1917 and, in particular, the lifting of former limitations on settlement and freedom of movement, and the opening of formerly closed education to Jews by the decrees of the Provisional Government. However, despite the rhetoric of equality, as early as the summer of 1917, anti-Semitic resentment grew with the general chaos in the

30 *Jews in a Post-Revolutionary World*

whole Russian Empire and Ukraine. Political opponents were accused of being Jews or the descendants of Jews, and the failure of an individual politician was explained by identifying him as a Jew.

The situation gradually stabilized after the end of the Russian Civil War in 1921, but the standard of living of Ukrainian Jews worsened in Soviet times as a result of the economic decline that followed the violence. Small businesses had been destroyed, vendors had been killed, and the Jewish community became poor. I assume that, besides the memory of slaughter, death, and fear, there was at that time also a collective memory that some people could escape by resisting or by negotiating for their lives. Otherwise, the Jews of various communities could not have not tried to offer money or to fight. During World War I, the living conditions of Jews deteriorated, partly due to the fact that in that part of Russia/Ukraine, the political situation had become increasingly uncontrollable. It was common knowledge that in that part of the world, fury was often directed toward Jews at such moments of acute political crisis.

There is some information about the Pechersky family at that time in the account of Sobibor written by the Yiddish novelist Michael Lev, who used sources and material that he derived from talking with Pechersky.[27] As I wrote in the introduction, the two men had known each other in Rostov-on-Don, and Lev had even been given charge of some foreign and Russian correspondence when Pechersky's mood and health did not allow him to reply to appeals. Pechersky was not physically able to reply to the many letters that reached him, and it pained him that he was obliged to write in a vocabulary that was not his. He could not tell what he wanted to tell, only a curtailed version of the uprising. Lev told me that a major aim in this last part of his own life was to make the heroism and suffering of Pechersky known to the world. I admired Lev's work for its style and its connection to Russian authors like Tolstoy. Until Lev pointed it out to me, I had not been aware that information he had received from Pechersky was behind the more fictional descriptions in his book on Sobibor, which contained historical elements.

These fictionalized accounts include his description of Pechersky on the train to Sobibor: it is hot and crowded in the freight car, and Pechersky is holding in his arms a small girl named Ettele, who has golden curls, blue eyes, and shiny white teeth. The girl makes him think about Ella, his daughter (in the text her name is Eloshke), whom I had a chance to meet in 2013. "Eloshke was now farther away than the moon," he thought at that moment.[28] In Lev's book, Pechersky knows that Ella is with her mother in Rostov-on-Don (although this part must be fiction, because he could not have known this). Pechersky said after the war that Ella was always in his thoughts. He carried a snapshot of her with him throughout the war.

A major element in Lev's description at that moment is Pechersky's love for the softness his mother emanated. He missed her presence at that terrible moment, and while describing her, Lev suddenly shifts from fiction to historical information. Pechersky's mother would light the candles on Friday evening and bless them. She served gefilte fish, "as was the custom among Ashkenazi Jews."[29]

Jews in a Post-Revolutionary World 31

Figure 1.1 Aleksandr Pechersky with Michael Lev
Source: Photograph courtesy of Natasha (Nathalya) Ladychenko.

Figure 1.2 Aleksandr Pechersky with his daughter Ella in a snapshot he managed to keep even in Sobibor
Source: Photograph courtesy of Natalya Ladychenko.

She spoke more Yiddish than Russian, "which was a rarity in those days" when Yiddish was mainly used between parents so that the children would not understand. According to Lev's description, in daily life most people spoke Russian.[30] Pechersky's father was educated and was considered "all-knowing." Lev continues

32 Jews in a Post-Revolutionary World

with a literary description of the relationship between father and son, and we should realize that when Pechersky read these pages, he was well aware that the book was largely fictional. In his letters in 1965 to Ainzstein, the chronicler of Jewish resistance, Pechersky compared Lev's book on Sobibor in Yiddish[31] with the book by the Russian authors Tomin and Sinelnikov.[32] Pechersky admitted that one cannot trust a literary description and implored Ainzstein not to trust all the "facts." He categorized both writings as documentary novels and judged them in the following way: "Tomin and Sinelnikov wrote a documentary novel, which is a literary work, and it is natural they could not write using a dry (dull) language. They could not have known the thoughts of the SS-men who had been working in the camp, but they could use the vast archive materials (by the way, Tomin is a historian) concerning other camps and trials in this case."[33]

After expanding on the father-son relationship in the family, Lev suddenly reverted again to historical knowledge:

> He also remembered and often heard about the city and the house where they had lived. Kremenchuk was then a significantly Jewish city (about thirty-two thousand Jews) with narrow, twisty alleys, and severe poverty reigned there. . . . Later memories assailed Pechersky further: memories of Rostov, where they had to start all over again, linked one image with another. He remembered people from near and far. Why, one might ask, did they suddenly leave a place where they were well established? The answer: frequent blood-libels and innumerable other accusations, which led to pogroms.[34]

Lev vividly described the pogrom of 1919 in Ukraine when he spoke of the fate of Pechersky's father: "Aaron Pechersky decided to flee from the Ukraine to wherever his feet would take him, and that is how they fell into Rostov-on-Don."[35] The passages that follow provide us with valuable insights that we have no reason to doubt, except that the story of the Pechersky family is interwoven with the story of the Lev family in order to give us a wider historical picture. Lev tried to point out that Ukraine was not a good place for Jews to live; he himself came from a family of Byelorussian refugees who had fled to Rostov. When the Pechersky family arrived in 1915, people were adrift from World War I, later joined by those who had tried to escape from pogroms. There was no way back. People knew what happened in the regions further to the west, where the fate of Jews seemed a sequence of endless destruction. As David Roskies puts it:

> The Russian Civil War was a catastrophe for the Jewish communities of the Ukraine; estimates of killed Jews vary from 50,000 to 200,000 and many more thousands were mutilated, raped, and robbed. The situation in Ukraine was worse than elsewhere since the country plunged into chaos after 1918 when the region became a battlefield for conflicting forces of Bolsheviks, Ukrainian nationalists, anarchists, local partisans and White Guards. Some scholars consider the Jewish pogroms of 1918–1920 as a prelude to the

Holocaust, and some have even referred to this period as the 'Holocaust of Ukrainian Jews.'[36]

The scale of anti-Jewish action was indeed staggering: according to rough estimates, between 1918 and 1920 approximately 1,500 pogroms took place in 1,300 different places.[37] The first documented attacks on Jews in Kremenchuk started in April 1918, when Jews were beaten; this was followed by a discussion in the city council about how to end the violence. Some days earlier, the Jews had tried to negotiate by offering to pay.[38] The physical attacks came from members of Ukrainian military units—*haydamaks*, named after the seventeenth-century anti-Semitic Haydamak movement—who arrested, brutalized, and sometimes killed Jews in the town and its surroundings.[39] In December of that year, a group of Ukrainian haydamaks surrounded the buildings of Jewish clubs and labor unions and arrested approximately sixty people. These events were just a prelude for what happened in 1919, when the territory of Ukraine plunged into complete lawlessness.

In February 1919, the Jews of Kremenchuk were a target for pogroms when the forces of the infamous Symon Petliura entered the city. His name still scares many of those who left the region as a result, and he is part of the collective memory of their offspring. From that moment, the number of pogroms and robberies perpetrated by Ukrainian soldiers increased dramatically. However, in Kremenchuk at that time, local Jews were able to avoid pogroms by gathering huge ransoms.[40] Unfortunately, the aggressors were less interested in such a peaceful solution later that year. In May and August of 1919, Kremenchuk experienced two large pogroms enacted by two different forces: anti-Bolshevik units of Ataman Grigoriev—a former Bolshevik commander who turned against the Bolsheviks—and units of the Armed Forces of Southern Russia, headed by General Anton Denikin, a famous leader of the anti-revolutionary White Movement. The largest pogrom in Kremenchuk occurred in May, when the Cossacks of Grigoriev moved into Krukovo, the Jewish suburb of Kremenchuk. From there, Grigoriev's troops moved into the city, surrounding and plundering Jewish houses. The first murders started on May 13, and the pogrom peaked on May 14. The next day, a unit of armed Russian workmen was able to stop the pogrom, and six days later the city was occupied by the Bolshevik (Red) Army.

The second pogrom was related to the capture of the city by the Whites, who reconquered Poltavskaya province from the Bolsheviks in August 1919.[41] While this pogrom was "milder" than the first one, it is often viewed as more tragic. The Jewish community had received the White Guard with open arms since they promised to restore the rule of law. However, they never intended to do that for the Jews, since they assumed that the Jewish population was in favor of Bolshevism and was therefore collectively responsible for resistance against them. In some cases, Jews were taken as hostages in order to save White hostages who were imprisoned by the Bolsheviks.[42]

The widespread accusation at that time—"You are guilty because you are a Jew"—served to restore pre-revolutionary anti-Jewish regulations, such as

34 *Jews in a Post-Revolutionary World*

restrictions on freedom of movement. When the Whites began to lose the Civil War, the pogroms intensified. For several reasons, these pogroms were different from those in the pre-war period: there was massive involvement of soldiers and the public; there were rapes and cruel tortures. The aim was the total destruction of Jewish communities. Still, the violence in Kremenchuk was relatively limited compared to the pogroms in many other places, such as Kiev, Smela, Cherkassy, and Fastiv. In Kremenchuk, a union of Jewish Soldiers was created, consisting of 1,000 men.[43]

The pogrom in Kremenchuk started on August 9 with the entrance of the Whites into the city; Cossacks were allowed to plunder local Jews for three days.[44] The real pogrom lasted for five days.[45] Officers participated actively in the pogrom along with ordinary soldiers, and the few officers who tried to stop the robbers were harassed by their own men. Soldiers soon received assistance from local gangs. Jews were cruelly beaten; girls and women were raped by gangs, often in front of their husbands. It is assumed that in the course of the pogrom at least several hundred victims were raped.[46]

Further to the East was Rostov, a town with a booming economy that had certainly witnessed dramatic persecutions of Jews in 1905. The town had become a major commercial center with a large Jewish community that was generally more open to secularism and more distant from the dominance of the strict Orthodoxy of Kremenchuk. During World War I and the Civil War, Rostov had sheltered many refugees. There was now reason to go back there, and this feeling was reinforced by a cultural climate that seemed much better for Jews.

A Dangerous Trek Through Chaotic Territory

The Pechersky family traveled from Kremanchuk to Rostov-on-Don, which is quite a distance. The two towns on the periphery of the Soviet Union are in different countries: Ukraine and Russia. The Jewish author Isaac Babel from Odessa (1894–1940) described the crowded trains as masses of people tried to escape. The Pechersky family probably was among them, and although the family left earlier, Babel's descriptions represent that chaotic world. He wrote:

> There is in the world no spectacle more cheerless than Kiev railway station. Its temporary wooden huts have for many years now disfigured the approaches of the town. On the wetboard lice chirred. Deserters, black-market speculators, gypsies lay all together in a huddle. Old Galician women urinated standing on the platform. The low sky was furrowed by clouds, sodden with murk and rain.
>
> Seventy-two hours passed before the first train left. At first it stopped every *verst*, then it got going in earnest: the wheels began to rattle more excitedly, to sing a powerful song.[47]

War, poverty, and persecution had created a flood of vagrants, wandering in all directions in search of safety and shelter. Living mostly on the street or sitting

Jews in a Post-Revolutionary World   35

down at squares and railway stations where dirt accumulated, they needed food, water, and money. It all ended up in unimaginable misery. These people were not only fleeing; they also wanted to go to a place they thought safe. By the thousands they boarded trains, which became crammed with human misery. The scale of misery also angered those who wanted to travel calmly and who were not fugitives. As a result, Jews were regularly killed or thrown out of the trains they had boarded and left for dead on the rails. But the reason could also be that other passengers were disturbed by the sheer presence of Jews, their hatred of Jews innate. Babel described how he was also thrown out; he managed to survive although he was forced to walk barefoot in the snow, getting frostbite on his toes.

We can assume the Pechersky family also took one of these trains in the middle of chaos, although we cannot be certain. They crossed the 500 kilometers through Poltava Province and the industrial region called the Donbas, which has become a metaphor for bare land and large mines, to Rostov-on-Don, the capital of Rostov Province across the eastern border with Russia. The 500-kilometer journey must have taken days, and the Pechersky family must have confronted unbelievable conditions. They were part of a large group of hungry vagrants; they might have slept on the platforms of railway stations, which was a common ordeal. Rostov might have appeared a better place, but it was not a safe place. There as well, everyone seemed at war with everyone.

In an important monograph about this Ukrainian-Russian borderland, Hiroaki Kuromiya has described the region the family had to pass through.[48] Eastern Ukraine was a mining-industry territory, dirty and poor. People were not cultivated as they had been in Kremenchuk. It was considered dangerous to be there. In these lands a civil society did not exist, partly due to the mine owners' amazing cruelty toward the population. When the Nazis arrived two decades later, they did not have to introduce sadism; it already existed there. The sadism was random and physical, punishment bringing about a slow and painful death. There was no longer "good" or "right"; there was just survival. Random killings and torture from genocidal politics, ethnic purification, and conflicts among minorities were a part of life in that area since well before World War I and the Russian Revolution. One can assume it was a dangerous journey, especially in these chaotic times. One needed contacts and money. It is very likely that the family did have some reserve funds.

The whole region was the theater of that immense wave of international dislocation across borders generated by World War I and by the war between the Reds and Whites after the Russian Revolution.[49] The ensuing massive displacement sharpened social, economic, and national antagonisms. In attempting to establish order, the authorities made a distinction between "core" and "peripheral" or "alien" populations. As Barin and Gatrell argue: "All set store by collective endeavor, yet insisted that some categories of population could never be part of the collective."[50] In this process the Jews remained aliens, though many made an effort to assimilate fully into the new post-revolutionary world, rife with slogans about equality and a better future. They hoped to succeed and to become equal citizens, but they never had a real chance. It was a world of anti-Semitism and

36   *Jews in a Post-Revolutionary World*

prejudice, and any politician could appeal to these feelings of hostility. While the lives of many Jews changed dramatically, their marginalization remained.

Life in a New Town: Rostov-on-Don

In Rostov-on-Don, Pechersky's father found work as a lawyer, as he had done before. The family consisted of four brothers and a sister. They did not share the poverty that was normal among refugees, and they had a relatively comfortable life. They were integrated, they spoke Russian, like 82 percent of the Jews in that town,[51] and their future seemed good. Aleksandr attended school and wrote later that "music and theater were the most important things in the world to me."[52] In his memoirs, he mentions finishing the seventh year of elementary school and music school,[53] although it is unclear what kind of training the latter offered. At age seventeen he began working as an electrician at the locomotive repair works; in his free hours he played the piano, and he directed some amateur performances in the last years before the war. He also worked as an accountant, rising to the rank of vice chancellor of the Finance Institute. Aleksandr was a member of the Communist Party, but we don't know when he joined. It was a normal trajectory to join the Communist youth organizations and to become a party member in one's early twenties.

Some people I spoke with who had known Pechersky told me that he had believed in the new world the Soviets claimed to create, a world where it no longer mattered where you came from or if you belonged to a cultural minority. In this spirit, in 1933, probably when he finished his service in the army, he married a Don Cossack woman, Lyudmila Vasilyevna (the daughter of Vasily Zamynetzky), a beautiful and well-known actress. Such marriages between Jews and non-Jews were not uncommon. But Cossacks and Jews had been enemies for centuries, and hostilities between Jews and Cossacks were part of the history of the region. A good Communist would claim that the obsessive hatred between the groups was part of the past. People could live assimilated Russian lives; they wanted to be equal, just like others. The couple had a daughter, Eleanor (Ella),[54] who still lives in Rostov-on-Don, where I met her in the summer of 2013.

The mythology surrounding Pechersky presents him as being formally educated, although he did not finish school before starting work, nor did he attend a university, contrary to what many memorials and websites suggest. However, seven years of schooling was a lot for that time, and that he was able to attend school for so long was one of the advantages of the new Communist regime.

Pechersky's friends described him as kind, both soft-spoken and outspoken; he had a natural charisma. He was not an intellectual in the formal sense; he was a well-bred man who behaved in a pleasant way and was involved in the artistic world of his town, which he loved. Since he was married to an actress who made her career in the theater, he was familiar with the artists' and musicians' circles. Several photographs depict Pechersky playing in amateur theatricals, and he attempted to compose music. He loved to direct theater and to work with amateur artists. However, stories about his career and my conversations with many people give no indication that he had ambitions to become a professional artist. His disposition toward life and art should be viewed as the expression of a young Communist Jew in Rostov-on-Don, where, like everywhere in Russia, theater plays were an expression of modernism and the new times. To understand this requires a look at the political and cultural position of Jews in this city in the 1920s and 1930s.

Figure 1.3 Aleksandr Pechersky acting in a theater in Rostov-on-Don in the 1930s
Source: Photograph courtesy of Ladychenko.

38   *Jews in a Post-Revolutionary World*

The Pechersky family belonged to the masses of Jews who fled east to escape the conflicting parties and warlords in Ukraine only to face war again.[55] Rostov-on-Don was a modern, industrial city at the juncture of three railways that became a battlefield of the Russian Civil War (1917–20). The city was marked by violent clashes between the revolutionary Bolshevik Red Army and the White Guards, the loose confederation of forces that fought the revolution. Both sides recognized the strategic importance of the bitterly contested city, with its central position in the network of railroads. Rostov-on-Don changed hands six times, as Brian Murphy describes in his study of Rostov and the Russian Civil War,[56] for which he relied heavily on the observations of the British journalist Rhoda Power, who lived in Rostov at the time.[57] Power noted that prejudice against Jews was widespread among all classes in southern Russia despite the "new times" announced publicly. Officially Jews had equal rights, and even before the Civil War a small stratum had slowly been allowed to enter professions such as medicine and law. (The Pechersky family was an example.) At the bottom of the social ladder were the masses of Jewish refugees who had flooded into Rostov since the outbreak of the war. In 1926, the 26,323 Jews living there found livelihood as employees (21.1 percent), independent artisans and salesmen (7.6 percent), and workers (6.1 percent). The workers were mostly sewers and tanners.[58] Some sources number the Jews in Rostov at 27,039 in 1939 (about 10% of the population).[59] Presumably most of the others were originally employed as small tradesmen or lived in poverty, and would become industrial workers.

Knowledge about the history of Rostov and the Jews of Rostov is fragmented and mostly a matter of local Russian historiography.[60] During the Civil War that raged in the territory that later became part of the Soviet Union, all sides killed Jews.[61] After the Red Army took over the city soon after the revolution, many Jews who believed in a better future joined the administration.[62] But according to the historian Oleg Budnitski, the idea that Jews chose this side of politics in order to combat anti-Semitism is itself part of the mythology of anti-Semitism. They had many reasons for making this choice, but mostly they went along with a positive feeling about change. Jews wanted to be part of the innovation that Communism seemed to promise. Indeed, people seemed to fare much better than in other nearby places. However, by outlawing of private trade and manufacturing during the period of war, Communism had weakened the economic base of Jewish life in the early 1920s and created massive unemployment.

In the early 1920s, when the Civil War had finally ended, Rostov attracted people who wanted to profit from the economic boom that was the result of the New Economic Policy (NEP), which spurred private enterprise. Technically skilled workers were particularly in demand. But soon a new persecution of Jews was prompted by a variety of religious, national, political, and other motives. Most dominant was the Communist aversion to religion, which targeted not only Judaism (Jewish culture) but all Jews, and took many shapes over the decades that followed. The persecution, often based on arbitrary grounds that masked the real motives, occurred despite a significant Jewish cohort that had joined the Communist Party, the administration, and other political bodies. Rostov historian E.

V. Movshovich argues that archival evidence of this development is difficult to find and can only be read between the lines in documents. He describes the slow elimination of Jewish culture and the rise of persecution, which targeted only Jewish organizations and networks in the beginning but soon targeted all Jews.

The first Five Year Plan (1928–33) was a blow to the Jewish economy. All attention was on massive industrialization, and the workshops and small industries where Jews worked became less important. An enormous workforce was needed, and among the groups relocating to Russian cities were Jews from the shtetls and towns who sought new educational and employment opportunities in the rapidly expanding urban industrial centers.

In his excellent study A Century of Ambivalence, Zvi Gitelman describes how young Jews abandoned traditional Jewish life for the excitement of new Soviet industrial cities.[63] Indeed, from the revolution forward, the Jews faced ambivalence: a world of equality and toleration of other cultures, where differences of nationality and culture would be ignored, was attractive; but participation in that world implied giving up Jewish culture and tradition, which could not be done without risking a loss of identity. In this sense secularization was also oppressive. Moreover, Jews were never truly considered equal, and in the existing climate they became a major target of persecution. Gitelman wrote that during and after the revolution, the Luftmentshn had been indeed "productivized," becoming white-collar workers, technicians, teachers, cultural and artistic workers, and engineers. Those who wanted to succeed would have to adapt.

According to Gitelman, "the overwhelmingly urban Jewish population was in a good position to take advantage of the vocational and educational opportunities the new economic program had opened up."[64] By the late 1930s Jews were well established in the working class and in managerial and professional groups. Under Communism, Gitelman says, Jews made new contacts with non-Jews, and as a result, they realized that Yiddish would not bring them very far. Jews visited Russian theater, listened to classical music, and read books unknown to them before. Some became officers in the Soviet Army. Pechersky's trajectory fits well in this pattern, similar to what has been described by Elissa Bemporad who studied the Jews of Minsk. However, in this town for decades the organization of Jewish workers in the Bund had created a specific cultural atmosphere that did not exist in Rostov. In both cases there was an image of what a Soviet Jew could be and how such a person should behave, which assumed assimilation.[65]

Modern research with data on the Jews of Rostov-on-Don is scarce. This kind of cultural historical research was rarely done in a society in which writing or speaking about Jewish culture was taboo only two decades ago. Nevertheless, specialists have assured me that there is no reason to assume the city followed any pattern different from other places. The politics of assimilation had an enormous cultural impact, which Gitelman beautifully depicts in a quote from a Soviet émigré who believed in internationalism: "We thought there would no longer be any differences between Jews and others, and we were proud to have friends of all nationalities."[66] But the disappearance of minority status that the Bolshevik leadership proclaimed went hand in hand with attacks on Jewish cultural life.

40 Jews in a Post-Revolutionary World

Status became a pretext to stigmatize, and the prejudice toward the Jews, with all its anger and hatred, did the rest. Early in the 1920s, Jewish cultural and religious leaders and institutions were attacked, and some months after the death of Lenin, and in the following years, 3,000 persons were arrested and accused of Zionism; of these, 156 were exiled from Rostov-on-Don.[67] It was a major attack on Jewish culture and Jewish leadership.

After Lenin's death in January 1924, Stalin became more and more powerful; by 1929 he had got rid of all his rivals. Historians agree that he hated Jews, and attacks on Jews started almost immediately. Under Stalin's leadership persecution replaced marginalization;[68] Jewish immigrants, who were treated with hostility because they were poor, were condemned in the press as parasites who harbored hidden anti-revolutionary sentiments.[69] *Shuls* (synagogues) and other institutions were closed, and the Jewish cultural world was narrowed.

Isaac Babel portrayed the ensuing disappointment in his descriptions of the community, people, and culture of his native *shtetl*. He pictured the impossibility of being anything other than a Jew, although many ignored the ambivalence and clung to optimistic Communism. This is also the theme of Mary M. Leder's fascinating autobiography, My *Life in Stalinist Russia*.[70] Leder's parents immigrated from the United States to the Soviet Union and lived in Birobidzhan, in the Jewish Autonomous Oblast in the Russian Far East where in 1934 the Communist leadership aimed to establish a Jewish homeland. Leder managed to live and work in Moscow, and married a man from Rostov-on-Don, where the couple moved in 1940. Although she initially believed in Communism, she was disappointed to be classified as of "Jewish nationality." Despite her atheism and her belief in Communism, she was ostracized as a Jew. At first she blamed her American origin, but she slowly discovered that she belonged to the wrong minority.

The only possibility for advancement seemed to require relinquishing the Jewish cultural world and Aleksandr Pechersky was among the many who sought to so. How much he suffered from prejudice before the war we will never know. His fate during the war made him more a Jew than he probably ever imagined. Pechersky's generation was confronted with the instrumental political use of atheism, which made it impossible to be an observant Jew or even culturally to belong to the Jewish world. Although the Great Purges of 1934–39 were by no means directed only at Jews (Jews were also among the persecutors, and many of them belonged to the Soviet administration), the outcome defined openly being Jewish as a deviation from the correct Marxist-Leninist line.

We can assume that Pechersky's mental world was similar to that of many other young Russian Jews. He did not speak Yiddish (which might have helped to bridge the language gap with Polish-speaking inmates during the 1943 uprising), and according to friends and family and his writings after the war, he believed in a Communist future in which all humans would be equal. To understand this world better, I examined several interviews recorded by the Shoah Visual Foundation in the 1990s and stored in Los Angeles, in an archive that contains thousands of interviews with Shoah survivors. I tried to find interviews with working-class people who could talk about being a Jew in the 1920s in Rostov-on-Don. The collection is accessible in several places worldwide, including Budapest, where the organizations' representatives helped me to transcribe several of the Rostov interviews and others.[71] The survivors interviewed in that project had become more conscious of their Jewish roots and culture as a consequence of the Holocaust, but in earlier times they would have denied there was any distinction between Jews and non-Jews. Some of them were scared during pre-war Stalinism, but not particularly because they were Jewish. They said they knew they were Jewish, but it was not something they talked about. The authoritarian state was felt, but as youngsters they had tried to go along with the tide. They had lived, but the real rip tide had not yet come.

Interviewed in 1988, Rebecca Brodyanskaya (born January 29, 1924) remembered her time as a girl growing up among non-Jews: "All my life I have lived and worked mainly with Russians. I cannot say much. There is no special feeling about it."[72] Watching and listening to the video, I was wondering what kind of toleration of Jews had existed in Rostov-on-Don. What did it mean to be a Jew? Of course there is no simple answer. When asked if she celebrated Jewish holidays, she said she did not know any Hebrew, though her mother did. Her major concern was that her aunt had immigrated to the United States, which made the family potentially suspect. Her mother spoke Yiddish, but the rest of the family spoke Russian, and all communication was in Russian. The neighbors were not Jewish, and although another Jewish family lived in the same apartment house, they were not special friends.

Brodyanskaya described how she was excluded when she tried to find work and when she had a job, and she was uneasy telling people she was Jewish. As a member of the pioneer movement, she dressed in a dark skirt and a white blouse and vowed loyalty to the fatherland and to Communism. She participated in parades and demonstrations, but did not remember them very well. After the war, when she was older, she experienced the exclusion of the Jews. As was the case with all Jews, her life was totally interrupted by the war and was never the same.

Tanha Otherstein, another citizen of Rostov, said in an interview that the synagogue felt safe until the arrival of the Red Army. Although he had Russian friends, he vividly remembered the negative attitude toward Jews.[73] He kept his distance from Communists, but did not feel any hostility toward them. His friends were mainly non-Jewish Russians. Tesya Liulyeva also had few memories of the pre-war period, except for the arrest of her brother and the anxiety she felt when five or six men suddenly invaded the house to pick him up.

In contrast to the strong memories of the post-1945 period, the surviving images of childhoods spent among Russian friends and neighbors contain vague memories of being different. Even the Great Terror of the late 1930s remains vague, and the interviewees were too young to make a distinction between the various stages of Communist policy and economy. They were just children belonging to families of lower-income groups. Does the horrendous suffering during the war make memories of the world before that time homogenous? I would even argue that the difficult trajectory "from death to life," as interviewee Iakov Krut phrased it,[74] overshadowed any negative pre-war experiences. But maybe they

42   *Jews in a Post-Revolutionary World*

just did not belong to those who suffered under forced collectivization, and the famine was much worse during the later period of German occupation. During my earlier research, I found that only after hours of expressing the enormous pain of losing families and loved ones during the Shoah are surviving Jews inclined to talk about their experiences before that time. The interview format of the Shoah Visual History Archive does not allow the time span one often (but not always) needs. Their interviews also follow a protocol that does not allow interviewees to meander widely among their memories. The interviews are much more eyewitness accounts than oral histories of trauma.[75]

War Comes to Rostov-on-Don

In September 1939, the Soviet army crossed the Polish border and in a few days occupied western Belarus and western Ukraine. In violation of the Molotov-Ribbentrop non-aggression pact of 1939, Germany attacked the unprepared Soviet Army on June 22, 1941. When the Germans crossed the borders of the Soviet Union that had been established by the treaty, many Jews sought to flee to the east, although a large number of Jewish families feared that conditions beyond the Urals, where the authorities wanted to deport the Jews, would be very hard. There was no guarantee families could stay together. Indeed, conditions proved extremely hard, but many who stayed in Rostov, which would be occupied by the Nazis, suffered an even worse fate. Among those who fled, many died from hunger and exhaustion, but they escaped the mass slaughter of the Shoah. In general, historians assume that more than 500,000 Jews joined the Red Army.[76] But many others did not trust the Soviets' atheism, and some even believed that the Germans would be more civilized.

The major aims of the German march east, called Operation Barbarossa,[77] were to destroy Bolshevism, use Soviet territory to expand German farming, and through colonization of the terrain make a profit from existing industries and from those that would be built later. They headed for the oil reserves of Baku on the Caspian Sea. The German invasion was enormous (three million soldiers) and was carried out along three major axes. During the purges of 1937–38, the Red Army had lost many senior commanding officers, which is one of the main reasons why at the beginning the Germans seemed to be winning the war while the Soviets reorganized. Later, Soviet industry would provide thousands of new tanks and planes. During those first months there was no good strategy; there was no other way to stop the invader but by sending thousands of soldiers to the front. Many were not trained. In the beginning of the "Great Patriotic War," the Red Army was defeated, and no obstacle seemed to prevent Germany from conquering Moscow in November 1941. The Soviet defenses did not hold, and hundreds of thousands of Soviet soldiers were captured.

The war was a military as well as ideological conflict, and the latter legitimized cruel behavior toward civilians, prisoners of war, and the Jews. Rostov-on-Don was where the German retreat began in 1941, the first major German withdrawal, and the city was also where most of the Pechersky family were killed. In Rostov, hunger was immediate, as Josif Golba described in an interview in 2000. With

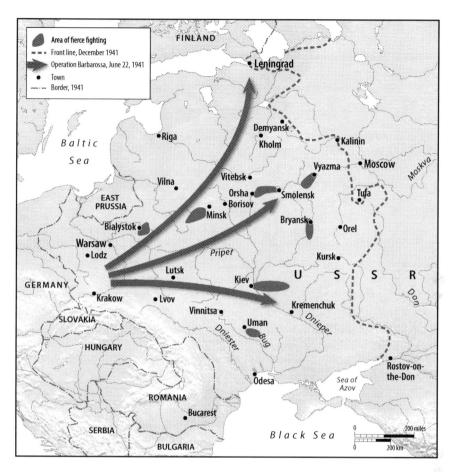

Map 1.2 Operation Barbarossa in 1941
Source: Map produced by Isabella Lewis.

the Germans fast approaching, there was a severe bombardment, and rockets lit up the night sky.[78] Rostov-on-Don was a stronghold of the German army on its way to the Caucasus, and German soldiers occupied the city several times, during which they relentlessly persecuted and killed thousands of Jews; 27,000 Jews were buried in the mass grave in the city at Zmievskaya Balka. The commemorative plaque that used to read, "The largest site of mass killings in the Russian Federation of Jews by the Nazi invaders during World War II" was rewritten in 2004 to read "mass killing by the fascists of captured Soviet citizens." In 2013 the text was restored to its original version.

Yuri Dombrovsky, the chairman of the Holocaust Memorial Board of the Russian Jewish Congress, saw this revision as a sign of progress in Holocaust commemoration efforts in the former Soviet Union. "For many decades, under the

44 *Jews in a Post-Revolutionary World*

Communists' rule, the state denied the Holocaust," he said. Although some Jews were dissatisfied that the text did not contain the word Holocaust, Dombrovsky says he believes "it's the only possible solution."[79]

American author Paul Hughes described the German withdrawal in his famous fictional trilogy *Retreat from Rostov*, in which he depicted the population's daily struggle and the insurgency against the Germans with graphic violence.[80] As a witness of the first major German retreat, Hughes intertwined the suffering of those who lived in Rostov, where many houses were destroyed and random killing became normal, with romantic scenes in the snow and experiences of love suddenly interrupted by revenge, punishment, and death. Hughes portrayed a struggle against evil in which killing anyone responsible for the evil was accepted as normal and even good.

Pechersky had spent his adolescence in Rostov-on-Don as an assimilated Jew. It had been a pleasure for him to participate in the cultural life, and one could argue that he belonged to the cultural elite. It had been a good choice of his father to go there and stay there, and not to keep traveling as many refugees had done. The family had settled, and the narrow world of Jewish life in Kremenchuk belonged to the past. In the newly created Soviet world, there was a collective future. Later, emancipatory ideals would feel the backlash of the rise of Stalinism with its ensuing purges, when Jews became an easy target, more than any other group.

I suppose that in Rostov-on-Don, a town far away from the Kremlin and far from national politics, one could hope to adapt and to hide among the mass of a new kind of citizen. While the Jewish cultural world was attacked everywhere, one could still try to be a common worker. Pechersky was protected by belonging to the working class and by emanating the culture of the new Soviet citizen. He was so "Russified" that when he was later a prisoner, he could even hide for a long time the fact that he was a Jew. There is no reason to believe he was less safe than an average resident of his town. He was a theater director with a reasonable standard of living, partly provided by his non-Jewish wife, whose extremely successful career protected him. Like so many young men, he left behind the protection of that world when he went off to the army. After the war he returned to a destroyed town where the Jews had been killed, as in so many other places the Germans had occupied. The Jewish community was decimated, and, as elsewhere in Europe, persecution had created a new kind of identity in which the memory of the catastrophe that had overcome the Jews was dominant. Despite building up a new existence, trauma would remain and would be aggravated by the kind of world Stalinism would bring about. The world around Aleksandr Pechersky had changed forever.

Notes

* Permission was given for the use of material from "The Routledge International Handbook on Narrative and Life History" Aleksandr (Sasha) Pechersky (1909–1990): In Search of a Life Story, 318–331.

1 Zvi Gitelman, *A Century of Ambivalence: The Jews of Russia and the Soviet Union, 1881 to the Present* (Bloomington: Indiana University Press, 1988; reprinted 2001); Mordechai Altshuler, *Soviet Jewry on the Eve of the Holocaust, a Social and Demographic Profile* (Jerusalem: Ahva Press, 1998).

2 For this history, see Arno Lustiger, *Stalin and the Jews* (New York: Enigma Books, 2002).

Jews in a Post-Revolutionary World   45

3 Nora Levin, *Paradox of Survival: The Jews in the Soviet Union Since 1917* (New York: New York University Press, 1988), 121.

4 Lev Simkin, *Полтора часа возмездия* [Half an Hour of Retribution]. (Moscow: Zebra, 2013), 34–35: "From 1931 to 1933 after school I served in the army" (letter from Pechersky to Valentin Tomin, 16 April 1962). In the central archives of the defense minister there are documents dating Pechersky's term of service from September 1931 to December 1933, when he was demobilized as "senior clerk—junior leader."

5 Nanci Adler, *Keeping Faith with the Party: Communist Believers Return from the Gulag* (Bloomington: Indiana University Press, 2012).

6 Timothy Snyder, *Bloodlands: Europe Between Hitler and Stalin* (New York: Basic Books, 2010).

7 Ibid., vii–viii.

8 For two examples of the extensive debate on this book, see Dan Michman, "Bloodlands and the Holocaust: Some Reflections on Terminology, Conceptualization and Their Consequences," *Journal of Modern European History* 10:4 (2012): 440–446; and Darius Stola, "A Spatial Turn in Explaining Mass Murder," *Journal of Modern European History* 11:3 (2012): 299–305.

9 Stola, "A Spatial Turn," 304–305.

10 www.yahadinunum.org, P31, January. The archive uses only first names.

11 Patrick Desbois, *The Holocaust by Bullets: A Priest's Journey to Uncover the Truth Behind the Murder of 1.5 Million Jews* (New York: Palgrave Macmillan, 2008).

12 For excerpts from the trial, see Eliezer Leoni, ed., *Wolozin, the Book of the City and of the Etz Hayyim Yeshiva* (Tel Aviv: Yizkor Book Project, 1970), 576.

13 USHMM file RG00602503, 3–4.

14 Yitzhak Arad, *The Holocaust in the Soviet Union* (Jerusalem and Lincoln: University of Nebraska Press, 2009), 137.

15 See Gitta Sereny, *Into that Darkness: From Mercy Killing to Mass Murder* (London: Pimlico, 1974), 119–131.

16 Peter Black, "Foot Soldiers of the Final Solution: The Trawniki Training Camp and Operation Reinhard," *Holocaust and Genocide Studies* 25:1 (2011): 1–99.

17 P. Molokiv-Zhurskiy, M. Nechaev and S. Rozdestvenskiy, *Кременчук (короткий довідник)* [Kremenchuk: A Short Handbook] (Kremenchuk: Kremenchuk Association of Local History, 1929).

18 I am deeply indebted to Mykola Makhortykh, at the time a Ph.D. student at the University of Amsterdam, for information about the Jews of Kremenchuk and references to the literature.

19 Oleg Budnitskii, *Российские евреи между красными и белыми (1917–1920)* [Russian Jews Between the Reds and the Whites, 1917–1920] (Moscow: ROSSPEN, 2005), 14.

20 Pipes Richard, "Catherine II and the Jews: The Origins of the Pale of Settlement," *East European Jewish Affairs* 52 (1975): 14–17.

21 Budnitskii, *Russian Jews*, 16.

22 Dimitrii Vyrskiy, "Єврейський погром у 1905 року у Кременчуці" [The Jewish Pogrom in 1905 in Kremenchuk], *Historical Journal* 2 (2006): 110–117.

23 Jonathan Dekel-Chen, David Gaunt et al., eds., *Anti-Jewish Violence: Rethinking the Pogrom in East European History* (Bloomington: Indiana University Press, 2011).

24 Budnitskii, *Russian Jews*, 286.

25 Eric Lohr, *Nationalizing the Russian Empire: The Campaign Against Enemy Aliens During World War I* (Cambridge: Harvard University Press, 2003), 14.

26 Budnitskii, *Russian Jews*, 291–298.

27 Michael Lev, *Sobibor* (Jerusalem: Gefen Publishing House, 2007), 576.

28 Ibid., 101.

29 Ibid., 103.

46 Jews in a Post-Revolutionary World

30 Altshuler, *Soviet Jewry*, 89–103.

31 Michael Lev, "Kimat a Legende," *Sovetish Heymland* 2 (1964), Moscow.

32 Valentin Tomin and Aleksandr Sinelnikov, *Vozvrashchenie nye zhelatelno* [Return Is Undesirable] (Moscow: Molodaya gvardia, 1964).

33 Letter Aleksandr Pechersky to Reuven Ainsztein, nr. 5, 12 February 1965. YIVO.

34 Lev, "Sobibbor," 105.

35 Ibid.

36 David. G. Roskies, *Against the Apocalypse: Responses to Catastrophe in Modern Jewish Culture* (Cambridge: Harvard University Press, 1984), 138.

37 Budnitskii, *Russian Jews*, 275.

38 Elias Heifetz, *The Slaughter of the Jews in the Ukraine in 1919* (New York: Thomas Selzer, 1921), 30.

39 Elias Tcherikower, *История погромного движения на Украине 1917–1921 гг. Антисемитизм и погромы на Украине 1917–1918 гг.* [The History of the Pogrom Movement in Ukraine in 1917–1921: Anti-Semitism and Pogroms in Ukraine in 1917–1918] (Berlin: Ostjüdisches Historisches Archiv, 1923), 274–276.

40 Heifetz, *The Slaughter of the Jews*, 39; 1.5 million rubles was mentioned.

41 Joseph Schechtman, *Погромы Добровольческой армии на Украине* [The Pogroms of the Volunteer Army in Ukraine] (Berlin: Ostjüdisches Historisches Archiv, 1932), 101.

42 Ibid., 40–41.

43 Heifetz, *The Slaughter of the Jews*, 126.

44 Nokhem Shtif, *Погромы на Украине. Период Добровольческой Армии* [The Pogroms in Ukraine: The Volunteer Army Period] (Berlin: Vosto, 1922), 56.

45 Lida Milyakova, *Книга погромов. Погромы на Украине, в Белоруссии и европейской части России в период Гражданской войны 1918–1922 гг.* [The Book of Pogroms: The Pogroms in Ukraine, Belorussia, and the European Part of Russia During the Civil War in 1918–1922] (Moscow: ROSSPEN, 2007), 219–222.

46 Schechtman, *The Pogroms of the Volunteer Army*, 314; Milyakova, *The Book of Pogroms*, 221; Heifetz, *The Slaughter of the Jews*, 111.

47 Isaac Babel, "The Journey," in *Red Cavalry and Other Stories*, trans. Peter Constantine (London: Penguin, 1994), 80.

48 Hiroaki Kuromiya, *Freedom and Terror in the Donbass, a Ukrainian-Russian Borderland 1870s—1990s* (New York and Cambridge: Cambridge University Press, 1998).

49 Nick Baron and Peter Gatrell, "Population Displacement, State-Building and Social Identity in the Lands of the Former Russian Empire, 1917–1923," *Kritika: Explorations in Russian and Eurasian History* 4:1 (Winter 2003): 51–100.

50 Ibid., 100.

51 Altshuler, *Soviet Jewry*, 275.

52 *Jewish Electronic Encyclopedia* (in Russian), lemma Aleksandr Pechersky.

53 See the Polish edition of 1952 mentioned by Bruder, *Hunderte Solcher Helden*, 30.

54 Evgenii Veniaminovich Movshovich, "Aleksandr Pechersky, Leader of the Uprising in the Sobibor Death Camp," in *Очерки истории Евреев на Дону* [Essays on the History of the Jews in the Don Region] (Rostov-on-Don: ZAO Books, 2011), ch. 18: 320–324.

55 Brian Murphy, *Rostov in the Russian Civil War 1917–1920: The Key to Victory* (London and New York: Routledge, 2005).

56 Murphy, *Rostov in the Russian Civil War*, 2.

57 Rhoda Power, *Under Cossack and Bolshevik* (London: Methuen, 1919).

58 Movshovich, *Essays*, 110.

59 "lemma Rostov-on-Don," *The Yivo Encyclopedia of Jews in Eastern Europe*, www.yivoen cyclopedia.org/article.aspx/Rostov-on-Don.

60 Movshovich, *Essays*.

61 Budnitskii, *Russian Jews*.

62 Nora Levin, *The Jews in the Soviet Union Since 1917: Paradox of Survival* (New York: New York University Press, 1988).

63 Gitelman, *A Century of Ambivalence*, 108.

64 Ibid.

65 Elissa Bemporad, *Becoming Soviet Jews, the Bolshevik Experiment in Minsk* (Bloomington, IN: Indiana University Press, 2013).

66 Ibid., 111, citing one of his own interviews.

67 Movshovich, *Essays*, 111.

68 Ibid., 106.

69 Ibid., 107.

70 Mary M. Leder, *My Life in Stalinist Russia: An American Woman Looks Back* (Bloomington: Indiana University Press, 2001).

71 I am grateful to Andrea Szoni who organized access to this resource. In Los Angeles, Dan Leshem and Crispin Brooks translated as many interviews as they could in a short time.

72 Rebecca Brodyanskaya, interview Shoah Visual History Archive USC, nr. 44288. Interviewed by Evgeniya Litinskaya in Donetsk, Ukraine, 8 May 1998.

73 Tanha Otherstein, interview. Shoah Visual History Archive USC nr. 31823. Interviewed by Sergey Shpagin in Taganrog, Russia, 25 May 1997.

74 Jakov Krut, interview. Shoah Visual History Archive USC nr. 5009. Interviewed by Maria Lackman in Ashkelon, Israel, 10 October 1995. 1186 #83.

75 Stephen M. Sloan and Marc Cave, eds., *Listening on the Edge: Oral History in the Aftermath of Crisis* (New York: Oxford University Press, 2014).

76 Yitzhak Arad, *In the Shadow of the Red Banner*.

77 Christian Hartmann, *Operation Barbarossa: Nazi Germany's War in the East 1941–1945*, translated from German (Oxford: Oxford University Press, 2011); David Stahel, *Operation Barbarossa and Germany's Defeat in the East* (Cambridge: Cambridge University Press, 2009); David M. Glantz and Jonathan House, *When Titans Clashed: How the Red Army Stopped Hitler* (Lawrence: University of Kansas Press, 1995).

78 Iosif Golba, interview. Shoah Visual History Archive USC 51345. Interviewed by Marianna Salz in Columbus, Ohio, USA, 24 October 2000.

79 JTA, *The Global Jewish News Source*, 17 December 2013; several other Jewish periodicals also mention this.

80 Paul Hughes, *Retreat From Rostov* (London: Random House, 1943; reprinted Columbia: University of South Carolina Press, 2011).

2 A Trajectory of Misery
The Army and Imprisonment

This chapter will follow Pechersky's life after he left Rostov and was conscripted into the army in 1941, and will continue with his trajectory as a Russian soldier and his deportation to Sobibor. He was serving near Vyazma in Belarus, where the Red Army attempted to halt the German advance to Moscow, when he was taken prisoner. He was one of many, since during the first months of the war, the Red Army was powerless and could only draw upon its immense reservoir of soldiers. All conscripted soldiers were summoned to join. In the first six months of the war, 4.4 million Soviet soldiers were killed.[1] Yet losses were always compensated with more troops from the east.

Pechersky's imprisonment in occupied Belarus was an extremely difficult and dangerous period that lasted one and a half years. His time in Minsk came to an end with his deportation to Sobibor in Poland, the last in a line of horrendous places he passed through. He did not know what awaited him there, nor that deportation meant a journey to an almost certain death. He did not know that if a person was assigned to be part of the labor force of the camp, it was sometimes possible to survive due to the fact that the Germans needed a stable force of skilled workers for construction and for many other tasks.

In Pechersky's testimonies concerning his war experience (deposited in Moscow in 1944), two important themes emerge. Without doubt, he focused primarily on the revolt in Sobibor, but there is no indication in the transcript that the inmates were Jewish, as his testimony was censored by representatives of the state. In his many other testimonies and reminiscences, he also paid considerable attention to what happened on Russian territory, concentrating on his terrible fate in Minsk. Since the Russians were not really interested in conditions in a Polish prison camp apart from the heroic endeavors of Russian soldiers, and as his accounts were produced in Russia, there were good reasons to concentrate on his ordeal on Russian territory.

His time in Minsk seems to have traumatized him more than his experiences in Sobibor, which ended with a successful escape. He could only survive Minsk because of his physical strength and because "luck" was on his side: he was fortunate not to become a victim of the random shootings carried out by the Germans or to succumb to the other cruel ways of killing that the Germans so frequently employed.

Pechersky arrived in Sobibor following a year of life-threatening conditions in Minsk, conditions he shared with hundreds of thousands of Russian POWs captured in the early stages of the war. Both Jews and Russian POWs faced almost certain death at the hands of the Germans, but their victimization differed in horrifying ways. While Russian POWs were ambushed or taken on the battlefield, Jews were targeted as a result of the racist Nazi ideology. This meant that the identity of the Russian soldier was less fragmented; he knew that capture and imprisonment were part and parcel of war, whereas the Jews were imprisoned solely because of who they were or were thought to be. One can surmise, therefore, that because Pechersky was captured as a soldier defending his country with pride, even if he was also a Jewish victim (although he managed to hide his Jewish identity for quite some time), he derived from there the inner strength not to give up, and he believed in agency. Still it remains difficult to understand how Pechersky was able to survive amid all the threats to his life and stay psychologically strong under conditions that would cause most people to abandon hope, personality, and identity. Simply to stay alive was a sign of enormous resilience, since for many inmates, death meant a welcome end to suffering and dehumanizing treatment. This does not imply that suicide was a real option, but to stay alive was a daily struggle.

It was the objective of the Germans to exterminate as many Russian soldiers as possible, not by killing them directly but through gradual starvation and exposure to inhuman conditions. In fact, most Russian POWs never reached concentration camps but perished en route. The starvation of the population was also part of the Germans' long-term plan to occupy the Soviet Union.[2] The Germans never intended to feed their prisoners or the populations of occupied territories, even if at moments there was no shortage of food.[3] The "dangerous population" living in occupied Belarus was to be destroyed, and the Communist politics of the region eliminated. According to Nikolaus Wachsmann, a British specialist of the history of concentration camps, "Hitler and his generals were obsessed with Soviet commissars; among all the enemies they saw lurking in the east, the commissar was one of the fiercest, an almost mythical figure."[4] The "empty" land resulting from the German policy meant new *Lebensraum* (land to make a livelihood) for German farmers to implement modern agriculture, which was imperative if the food shortage was to be eliminated.

In addition to Pechersky's rank, being a Jew also increased the danger he was in. German camps were places of death, and Pechersky survived several German POW camps where more than 80 percent of the inmates died. As a Jew he had been thrown into a cellar where only a few survived; after that he was a prisoner in Minsk, where random killings carried out for the amusement and diversion of the guards were the norm. Pechersky was apparently able to survive all of this mentally, and he even managed to develop friendships with strangers in Sobibor. Here he collaborated with veteran prisoners who had sometimes been there for over a year, drawing on their extensive knowledge of the camp to help him plan an escape. In a mere twenty-two days he organized the uprising in Sobibor and took all the necessary steps to implement his plan. Did he derive strength from the resilience of the post-Revolution generation full of hope for a new dawn and a new humanity? Did that hope enable him to believe in a future even in the face of the daily threat of death? It is possible to gain some insight into how he survived, but we will never be able to grasp the reasons fully.

50   *A Trajectory of Misery*

By his own account, Pechersky played only a modest role in the revolt and claimed to have acted as anyone else would have done. He said repeatedly that he was not the hero people thought he was; he had been a mere soldier defending his country against barbarism, acting as any soldier who had survived fascist atrocity would have done. He thought collective action had been crucial, and he believed in togetherness. In a letter to Reuven Ainsztein discussing the admiration of a journalist, he stated: "In my letter I asked him not to make of me a God, because in the conditions of the concentration camps, especially one like Sobibor, surrounded by minefields and a water ditch, one person could not organize an uprising and help the entire camp to escape. Only collective struggle and international friendship can win."[5] The letter is dated 1972 and is phrased in the language of Communist newspeak; his letters were censored at that time.

Like many Soviet soldiers, he believed that Communist values were worth fighting for and he did so with enthusiasm. We know that many others who did not share this conviction were forced to fight as well. But he always wrote and spoke very positively about the defense of Mother Russia. It was a duty he never doubted. The reality was something else: regardless of their convictions, the battle became a nightmare for all soldiers. There was no leadership, and soldiers were forsaken and left behind on the battlefields by their retreating comrades. The freshly installed Soviet supreme command had not expected a German attack and had no clear idea how to stop the swiftly advancing German army. They had no real military strategy. The Germans advanced and the war seemed lost.

In her book *Ivan's War: The Red Army, 1939–45*, Catherine Merridale describes the common fate of the Russian soldier.[6] As a subordinate in a mandatory hierarchy, every soldier was cannon fodder; the only resistance the Soviets could offer to the well-trained and well-organized enemy was to launch wave upon wave of new and often badly prepared soldiers. Merridale and other scholars have documented extensively the German capture of 2.5 million Russian soldiers in the first five months of the war. Life as a soldier meant not only the threat of being killed on the battlefield but also the political surveillance that permeated Stalinist Russia, which included a real danger of betrayal, condemnation, and eventually prison or death.

The War, 1941

In many Russian towns and villages, important announcements were made on loudspeakers located on the public square. As people gathered to listen, the authorities were able to judge people's reactions to their announcements. It was in this way that Deputy Premier Vyacheslav Molotov's announcement by radio of the German invasion at noon on June 22 was disseminated:

> Citizens of the Soviet Union! The Soviet Government and its head, Comrade Stalin, have authorized me to make the following statement:
> Today, at 4 a.m., without any claims having been presented to the Soviet Union, without a declaration of war, German troops attacked our country,

attacked our borders at many points and bombed from their airplanes our cities Zhitomir, Kiev, Sevastopol, Kaunas and some others, killing and wounding over 200 persons. Air raids by enemy planes and artillery bombardment were also launched from bases in Romania and Finland.

This unheard-of attack upon our country is a perfidy unparalleled in the history of civilized nations. The attack on our country was perpetrated despite the fact that a treaty of non-aggression had been signed between the USSR and Germany and that the Soviet government most faithfully abided by all provisions of this treaty. The attack upon our country was perpetrated despite the fact that during the entire period of operation of this treaty, the German Government could not find grounds for a single complaint against the USSR as regards observance of this treaty.[7]

Soviet citizens were not told about the scale of the disaster and the chaos on the front, and during this time patriotism and belief in Communism persisted and even became stronger. At that time no one knew what the people or army would do in such an unexpected situation. As Merridale writes:

The truth about people's mood in that first week is still hard to unravel from the web of propaganda. No one, not even the NKVD, could measure the relative strength of patriotism and panic, anger and mistrust. No one could predict what the crowds would do. One fear, that there would be a run on stocks of food and fuel, proved accurate.[8]

Communist ideology permeated daily life, and even though the Great Terror (1937–38) was past, people were still controlled through a culture of suspicion and betrayal. The authorities worried about the degree of panic that could develop as hundreds of thousands made their way to the east while the Red Army withdrew behind the Dnieper and the Daugava Rivers. Meanwhile the Soviet government moved industries from the west to regions beyond the Urals, as far as Central Asia and Siberia and to the Caucasus. Nearly six hundred large factories and at least fifty thousand smaller units with sixteen million workers were removed from the reach of the enemy. But many had to stay and were left at the mercy of the German occupiers.

We can assume that Communist propaganda was no longer effective because Communist slogans were replaced by patriotic propaganda; People were told Mother Russia had to be saved. The war became known as "The Great Patriotic War," and the headline of *Pravda* announced "Death to the Fascist Invader." The political atmosphere became even more suffocating because there was always the possibility of being indicted for suspicion of treason. In order to control the chaos, everyone was spying on everyone, and political surveillance became even more widespread than before, especially in the army. These were exceptional times, and despite the fear of random political persecution, people followed orders and remained hopeful for the future. Fascism was deemed to be the worst of all evils, as for years Russians had been told there was nothing worse than

52   A Trajectory of Misery

Nazism. In the minds of the Russians, there had always been a foreign aggressor that could invade Russian, and now Soviet, territory and destroy Soviet society. Only, since the Molotov-Ribbentrop Pact signed two years earlier on August 23, 1939, had this changed. Molotov, in his speech given immediately after the invasion, emphasized patriotic love for the homeland:

> This is not the first time that our nation has had to deal with an attack of an arrogant foe. At the time of Napoleon's invasion of Russia our people's reply was war for the fatherland, and Napoleon suffered defeat and met his doom. It will be the same with Hitler, who in his arrogance has proclaimed a new crusade against our country. The Red Army and our entire nation will once again wage victorious war *for the fatherland, for our country, for honor, for liberty.* (emphasis in original)[9]

Numerous scholars of the Soviet Union in World War II have stressed the sudden transition from a Communist to a patriotic emphasis in Soviet propaganda. The war became not simply a defense of Communism, about which many Russians felt uneasy, but a patriotic struggle against a feared and hated enemy. Russians heeded this propaganda and, as Merridale writes, "twenty years of meretricious talk, of communist jargon, had furnished Soviet patriots with an impressive stock of wooden phrases. The younger generation knew no other language for this kind of thing."[10] The younger generation did not hesitate to join the war, believing the official narrative by the leadership that a Soviet victory was only a matter of weeks away.

But there would be no quick victory. This was only the beginning of a war that would last for years and in which millions of soldiers and civilians would be killed, slaughtered on an unknown and massive scale. Russia was not prepared for war; the Red Army lacked equipment, munitions, transport, and food; worse, there was no long-term military strategy. Volunteers with no military training sacrificed themselves by the thousands in the conviction that Nazism was worse than Communism and that a common Soviet soldier had no chance of survival under Nazism.[11]

For Jews and non-Jews alike, it was clear that capture and imprisonment by the Germans meant torture and a painful death. Most deaths occurred between June 1941 and January 1942, when the Germans killed an estimated 2.8 million Soviet POWs, either by summary execution or by letting them die from starvation or exposure. When young men became soldiers, they had no other choice but to try to survive by fighting hard to stay out of the hands of the invader. Their motivation was self-preservation, first of all, but they also believed in their mission to defend what they thought to be a better world.

Pechersky was conscripted on the first day of the war and was immediately sent to the front with the rank of second lieutenant.[12] Because he served in the regimental headquarters he was promoted to technical quartermaster, a rank equivalent to first lieutenant. In a desperate attempt near Vyazma (Smolensk Oblast) to stop the German advance to the east, the retreating Red Army managed to

A *Trajectory of Misery* 53

halt the Germans but at an enormous cost: the casualties totaled 218,000, with 90,000 killed or missing and another 700,000 taken prisoner. It was here, in October 1941, during the Battle of Moscow, that the Germans surrounded and captured Pechersky's unit in the *kotel*.[13] Pechersky described his capture:

> In the first days of October 1941 the Germans managed to break through the defense near the city of Vyazma. In a whirlwind attack they moved forward hundreds of kilometers.
>
> The 596th howitzer regiment of the 19th Army [Pechersky's regiment] was fighting its way out of the encirclement. In one of the battles, the commissar of the regiment, Mikhail Petrovich Tishkov, was badly wounded in the belly. The political instructor of the 4th battalion, Comrade Pushkin, and eight soldiers, me included, were charged with the commission to carry the commissar out of the encirclement. Several times our group tried to fight through the line of fascists. Cartridges were nearly exhausted. In one of the battles the commissar Tishkov and one of the soldiers were killed by the fascist running fire. We managed to withdraw and take our slain comrades to the forest.
>
> In the evening before dark we buried the commissar and the soldier in a trench and put two soldier's helmets on the hillock. Several times our group got into an ambush. We could not enter any village to get some food. In deserted trenches we found cartridges and at that moment, notwithstanding our hunger, they were more precious to us than bread. Weakened by starvation and without cartridges, we got into an ambush and we could not escape from it. The most terrible thing happened—imprisonment.[14]

Following his capture, Pechersky spent time in Belarus until his deportation to Sobibor. The Nazis, fearing local resistance in occupied Belarus, where they were alien invaders and easily lost in the vast moors and forests, implemented a harsh occupation and committed many atrocities. Controlling Belarus was essential for the German army if it wanted to open a route to Moscow; but the vast lands could not be controlled, and as the war progressed, growing resistance increasingly hindered their advance. Frustrated, they vented their fury by massacring entire villages; the Germans felt free to kill. The Belarus Slavs, like all Slavs, were considered *Untermenschen* (people of an inferior race) by the Germans. In addition, the Germans were convinced that all Russians were Marxists, which Hitler claimed was a Jewish doctrine.[15]

Historians have described the policy of the Wehrmacht in the occupied Soviet territories such as Belarus as the deliberate murder and starvation of civilians.[16] Anti-partisan warfare was confused with "hunting Jews," a license for the regular practice of random slaughter.[17] The history of the cruelty of the German occupation of Belarus is little known in Western academia, and even in Belarus itself, historical research based on comparative local studies is only in its infancy. Although every place the Germans occupied in Russia shows us examples of the worst of German cruelty, in the case of Belarus one can argue that the people there suffered more than anywhere else.[18] According to Waitman Wade Beorn,

54   *A Trajectory of Misery*

who published a major study of the Wehrmacht's genocide in Belarus, 700,000 Soviet POWs were murdered or starved, and between 500,000 and 550,000 Jews and 400,000 other civilians were killed.[19]

Not a Step Back! Order 270

The Soviet Supreme Court granted the Soviet army the power to punish deserters. The notion of "deserter" included any soldier who did not fight to the death or was taken prisoner by the Germans. Falling into the hands of the enemy was considered treason and was punished with death, the Gulag, or long imprisonment. This fate awaited hundreds of thousands of POWs since the infamous Order Number 270 of 1941 even abolished the idea of the possibility of becoming a POW. Although there is no hard evidence, Stalin allegedly said, "There are no prisoners of war, only traitors." Anyone attempting to surrender would be killed, and their family members deprived of any state welfare or assistance.[20] The only choice for soldiers was to fight or die.

According to Merridale, "Not a step back!" was to become the Soviet army's rallying cry. Every man was told to fight until his final drop of blood. "Are there any extenuating causes for withdrawing from a firing position?" soldiers would ask their *politruks* (political commissars). Handbooks would prescribe that "the only extenuating cause is death." "Panic-mongers and cowards," Stalin decreed, "must be destroyed on the spot." Any officer who permitted his men to retreat without explicit orders was to be arrested on a capital charge. All personnel were confronted with this new sanction, which included that the guardhouse was too comfortable to be used for criminals; in the future, laggards, cowards, defeatists, and other miscreants would be consigned to penal battalions.[21]

To be caught was even a deadlier threat: the German atrocities toward the Russian POWs deliberately ignored all international regulations. Very soon, Russian soldiers knew well what would happen if they were caught, because many had witnessed the atrocities inflicted on others.[22] There were stories all around; soldiers had escaped and they talked. The prisons were visible for those who ventured to approach and observe, and information gathered by curiosity was eagerly used by Soviet propaganda. Before Operation Barbarossa began in 1941, the leadership of the Wehrmacht had decided that Soviet prisoners taken during the upcoming campaign would not have the protection of international and customary law. Orders issued to subordinate commands suspended the German military penal code and the Hague Convention, the international agreement that governed treatment of prisoners. In March 1941, Hitler issued the so-called Commissar Order, clearly spelling out the goal of the coming war in Russia. The coming conflict was to be "one of ideologies and racial differences and will have to be waged with unprecedented, unmerciful, and unrelenting hardness." The order also instructed Hitler's subordinates to execute Soviet commissars and exonerated soldiers of any excesses. "Any German soldier who breaks 'international' law will be pardoned," Hitler stated.[23]

Conditions in German POW camps were horrendous. Without shelter or sufficient food for the hundreds of thousands of imprisoned men, POWs were forced to walk hundreds of miles to a dulag (*Durchgangslager*) or transit camp. Often they were given no food or water on a regular basis. In a 1992 interview at Yad Vashem, the commemoration site and archive in Jerusalem, Sobibor survivor Simion Rozenfeld described the conditions in the first camp of his internment:

> They kept some 100 thousand POWs there. They didn't give us anything to eat in that camp till about the fifth day of our stay in that camp . . . [The camp] was just a field, with machine guns at the corners. There was no fence at all, only those machine guns put in place, and that was it. They didn't give us any food. One of those days I stood up and began to yell: "I can't see anything, help me, I've gone blind!" I had become blind from undernourishment, from malnutrition. I was yelling, help me! All of a sudden someone came up to me and slipped something into my hand. I felt it was a lump of sugar, I put it in my mouth and the sugar already started to dissolve; I began to see again. I wanted to look at that man, who gave me that lump of sugar, but I couldn't see him; there was no one around.[24]

Pechersky's Trajectory: Vyazma, Borisov, Minsk, Stalag 352

When Pechersky was captured near Vyazma and imprisoned near Smolensk, his life was immediately at risk. Not only was he a Russian officer and a POW, but he also was a Jew, which meant immediate execution. He could hide his Judaism, however, since early in the war racial research was not very thorough. An official Russian document stated that until the spring of 1942, the Germans had only interrogated prisoners and asked if they were Jewish, and we can assume that many assimilated Jews answered "no" to this question.[25] Pechersky remained in the western part of Belarus for seven months and attempted unsuccessfully to escape in May 1942 with four others. He was moved to a prison camp at Borisov, seventy kilometers from Minsk, where he continued to hide the fact that he was a Jew.

Borisov had a long history of Jewish residents, and after German troops occupied the town on July 2, 1941, a ghetto was formed. Extreme density of population and unsanitary conditions caused outbreaks of infectious diseases. The first punitive actions had occurred in Borisov in August and October 1941, when the Nazis shot approximately 7,000 Jews, and the liquidation of the ghetto began on October 20, 1941.[26] As Historian Leonid Smilovitsky reported:

> Early in October 1941, in a northern city suburb near an air field, prisoners of war dug two broad and deep holes in a ravine. In celebration, a banquet in honor of the German army was arranged in a dining room on the market square on October 19. When Obersturmführer Kraffe arrived, Stanislav Stankevich, the burgomaster of Borisov, declared that in some hours "the major Aktion" will begin.

56 *A Trajectory of Misery*

On the morning of October 20, Jews were transported in trucks or marched in columns to a ravine fifty meters from the holes the prisoners had dug. According to Stankevich, they were forced to undress and lie face downward in the holes "like sardines" to save space. The supply manager of the police substation, Joseph Majtak, brought vodka for the policemen before they started their "work." Any who were not killed immediately in the ensuing gunfire were buried alive. The bodies were covered with a thin layer of soil through which blood flowed into streams and to the Berezina River. The mass grave was covered with unslaked lime and an additional layer of sand. On those two days—October 20–21, 1941—7,245 Jews were executed.[27]

Near Borisov were also a dulag (prisoner transit camp) and Stalag 382, both of them places of mass murder.[28] Information about these camps is sparse, but officers were most likely sent to the stalag. As was often the case with the German handling of prisoners, the administration was poor because of the sheer numbers of prisoners.

Many camps were similar to those described in *The Complete Black Book of Russian Jewry*, a collection of eyewitness testimonies, letters, diaries, affidavits, and other documents on the activities of the Nazis against Jews in the camps, ghettos, and towns of Eastern Europe. Renowned Soviet authors Ilya Ehrenburg and Vasily Grossman compiled the *Black Book*, first published in 1944, although numerous documents were censored from the original manuscript.[29] Grossman, whose mother was murdered at Berdichev in Ukraine, became known as the Chronicler of the Jewish Catastrophe.[30] However, in the post-war Stalin era, writing about Jews became less acceptable than was the case at the end of the war, when recounting the fate of the Jews was used to show the enemy's barbarity.[31] The *Black Book* was heavily censored and much of its contents vanished. A complete text was not available in English until 2002, when an American translation was printed.[32]

In his testimony in the *Black Book*, former POW Sheinman told of his capture on October 27, 1941: "On that day my ordeal in fascist camps began. As a Soviet citizen, a battalion commissar, and a Jew on top of it, I was a prisoner marked for death." At that time, the Germans were convinced they would win the war "so they did not try to hide . . . the fact that they were annihilating the prisoners." During the following winter, seventy thousand people died in the Vyazma hospital and camp for POWs where Sheinman was held. Prisoners were forced to work beyond their strength, and "people were housed in half-demolished buildings without roofs, windows or doors." Many froze to death.[33]

After his capture, Pechersky was ill for seven months with epidemic typhus, which is transmitted by lice and may recur if the immune system is compromised. Epidemic typhus can bring about very high fever, and the survival rate among infected prisoners was low. Prisoners in hospitals often succumbed to hunger, neglect, and cold, not to mention random executions. Seven months is a long time to be ill, even during peacetime and when adequate medical care is available. In a letter, Pechersky said he received no medical treatment.[34]

A Trajectory of Misery   57

There were many camps where conditions were the same. In fact they were just places where the Germans wanted as many prisoners as possible to die. With the immense numbers of starving soldiers, many tried to escape, even when being caught meant harsh punishment. In May 1943, after a failed escape attempt, Pechersky was transferred to the infamous Stalag 352 in Masyukovchina near Minsk, which was described in a 1944 Russian report about German atrocities.[35] Other camps may have been quite similar:

> The whole territory of the camp is surrounded by a complex system of barriers, fortifications, and guard posts. The main link in this system is a fence, two meters in height, consisting of a double web of barbed wire, fixed to poles dug into the earth in two parallel rows with a distance of two meters between them, which in turn is filled, to a height of 70cm, with a tangle of barbed-wire rolls. In addition to this, the outer row of poles is provided with iron spikes (up to 50cm in length) turned inwards, to which additional rows of wire are tightened . . . On the outer side of this fence, guard posts were located, at a distance of about 300 meters apart, and between them pillboxes with machine-gun posts. At all angles, as well as around the gates, watchtowers (up to 18m in height) are erected, with searchlights on them. Analogous watchtowers were also located within the camp at crossroads. Some guard posts were surrounded by buffer zones out of barbed wire.
>
> This whole system of protection and its structure was in its turn bordered by a continuous buffer zone, located at a distance of 100–300m from the outer fence of the camp. The buffer zone is a wide barrier, densely interlaced with barbed wire fixed to stakes, in diameter looking like a half-circle, up to 70cm in height and up to 2m in width . . . The northern gates of the camp, leading from the railway track, form the entrance to a wide road, which cuts the whole territory of the camp from NNE to SSW into two, almost even parts: an eastern [part], intended mainly for watch teams and service rooms, and another [part] being the place of detention of the prisoners of war. Perpendicular roads and streets dissect the camp into separate quarters . . . [The first part, described as zone A] is especially strongly fortified; a threefold wall of wire barriers borders it. Here the point of intake of the prisoners of war was located, which consisted of six barracks. The windows of all the barracks are interlaced with barbed wire.
>
> [Zone C] occupied the largest part of the whole territory of the camp. The entrance to this zone is barred by gates with a guardroom and a watchtower, whose four searchlights crossed all intersecting roads with their light beams. In front of the gates there is a pillbox with a machine-gun post. Workshops, storehouses and other service structures occupied the small eastern section of this zone.
>
> The western part, with the exception of a small quarter that was occupied by structures of a servicing character (kitchen, garage, etc.), was separated for prisoners of war (8 barracks) and mainly for the sick quarters, where a few tens of thousands of people were tormented, where 50–60 people used to die

58 *A Trajectory of Misery*

over the course of a single day. According to surviving documents, during a period of no more than eight months, from October 1941 to August 1942, around 10,000 people died here, mainly from exhaustion. The sick quarters occupied a large, stone, three-story building and seven wooden barracks. Here as well, all the structures were separated from one another by fences made of barbed wire.[36]

Numerous stories told of thousands of POWs being kept behind a fence in a space so small that they could only stand up straight and not move a step. They had to urinate and defecate in their clothes, which became dirtier every day; in the winter their excrement would become plates of frozen ice that burnt the skin. More room was available only after enough had died and been taken away (which was not always the case), but the space was soon filled with more incoming prisoners. It was normal that not enough water was available, and the open-air climate in Russia and Poland could be either very hot or freezing cold with ice, wind, and snow. If the POWs had any warm clothes at all, the guards and executioners immediately stole them for themselves, leaving the prisoners in rags. In *Bloodlands*, Timothy Snyder wrote about the conditions in these camps:

> They were designed to end life. In principle, they were divided into three types: the Dulag (transit camp), the Stalag (camp for enlisted men and non-commissioned officers), and the smaller Oflags (for officers). In practice, all three types of camps were often nothing more than an open field surrounded by barbed wire. Prisoners were not registered by name, though they were counted. This was an astonishing break with law and custom.[37]

A 2004 official report of the Republic of Belarus stated that the Germans had not expected the prison population in Belarus to grow so large—as many as 500,000. The German authorities had intended to transport many of the prisoners to work in German industries that needed foreign labor, but they lacked sufficient transportation. Faced with hundreds of thousands of prisoners, the Nazis were desperate, and all they could do was to kill as many as possible. No names were asked. When prisoners reached a stalag, they were given a number and a card. But many never reached that hell and died instead in open fields and dugout holes surrounded by barbed wire. Jews were often shot immediately.

Changing Times: The Need for Slave Labor, Stalingrad, and the Germans Need to Eat

During the winter of 1942–43, the lives of Russian POWs changed dramatically for several reasons. The Russian winter engulfed the German army, which could not manage the cold. Victory was no longer self-evident, and the conquest of Moscow would certainly not be accomplished quickly. Previously, in December 1941, the German army had to retreat from Rostov-on-Don, and though the two armies had both experienced moments of defeat followed by victory, the German army suffered over a million casualties and never fully recovered from the beating it took from the Russians in the earlier winter months. There simply were not enough available men of military age in Germany to make up for the losses, nor to address the shortage of manpower in German industries and agriculture.

From 1942 on, the Soviets seemed clearly able to send waves of new soldiers from the eastern territories to the front, and these soldiers were now better equipped and trained than in 1941. After a months-long siege that killed hundreds of thousands, the German army in Stalingrad surrendered in February 1943. The Battle of Stalingrad turned the tide and the Germans were no longer on the winning side.[38] On Wednesday, February 3, 1943, a special radio announcement informed the German people that they had lost the Battle of Stalingrad. The news had a devastating impact on morale, casting an undeniable shadow of doubt on the future of Nazi Germany. A secret opinion survey taken shortly afterward by the Nazi intelligence service reported that fear that an unfavorable end to the war was possible made people look for escape.

The Nazis did not hide their defeat at Stalingrad, but proclaimed three days of *Staatstrauer* (mourning) in February 1943 throughout Germany and the many places it controlled. In her recently published diary, a girl in Minsk, Czesława Waszkiewicz, wrote on February 16, 1943, "The three days of mourning for the German troops killed at Stalingrad have been proclaimed in the city. Now the city [Stalingrad] is ours."[39] An article on the city underground published in *Vecherniy Minsk* (Evening Minsk) said, "In early 1943, in Minsk for the first time the Germans hung out mourning banners in connection with the defeat of the German forces at Stalingrad."[40]

Hirsh Smolar, a well-known resistance fighter from Minsk, told of how his partisan unit in the forest learned of the German defeat at Stalingrad:

> When the forest siege was lifted [at the end of January 1943] and we got in touch once more with other detachments . . . we learned of the victorious termination of the Stalingrad battle. It was then that the reports of our partisan scouts about the thousands of wounded, battered, completely demoralized, vermin-ridden, and half-frozen Nazi troops which passed through our region westward, became clear to us.[41]

As the Russians and their allied partisans proclaimed their victory everywhere, the world for the retreating German soldiers was turned upside down. They had survived hunger, starvation, and disease in the belief that they were fighting for a good cause, but the other side had proven the stronger.[42]

The Need for Labor Versus the Wish to Kill All Jews

Now, to address the labor shortage in Germany's war industry and to support the German economy, forced labor from prisoners and men rounded up from the streets of occupied territory was crucial if the war were to be won. Transporting

60 A Trajectory of Misery

able-bodied men and women as slaves to Germany was now preferable to extermination. As a result, conditions in prison camps improved in the spring of 1942 as the Germans realized that the prisoners were needed as laborers.[43] Although the extermination of Jews continued in other places, in 1943 the camps of Night and Fog, where people disappeared in the dark, became labor units. Everywhere houses and barracks were needed to shelter workers. At that time there were initiatives to transform Sobibor into a labor camp.

In describing the transformation of the German economy, the Swiss historian Christian Gerlach argues for a direct connection between the economic policies of the occupation and the destruction of populations.[44] Although others have contested his thesis, the consensus is that Germany could not feed both its army and the many prisoners it held. The solution was to eliminate those who could not be used for industrial or agricultural production. The extermination of the Jews had always been central to Nazi ideology, but now the question was what to do with the prisoners and those who lived in occupied territories. They were considered redundant; they ate food and used wood to warm houses and to cook. That should stop, so the villagers and farmers of Belarus were relentlessly killed on a mass scale to minimize the number of people to be supported. According to Gerlach, racist economics drove the politics of destruction even more strongly than racism. Starvation was considered by the Nazi leaders a more acceptable way to kill prisoners because the perpetrator was more anonymous. Although the Germans had freely violated the Geneva conventions regarding prisoners, they were aware that shooting or otherwise killing too many would not be morally acceptable, even to many Germans. And the stronger among the prisoners could be used to fulfill the tasks previously done by the men who had joined the army. With their help the economy might be more productive.

Also, since Stalingrad, more Germans were being captured by the Soviets, and the German leadership worried that the Red Army might take revenge. Russian Minister Molotov had warned that if the Germans continued to kill on a massive scale, the Red Army would do the same to German prisoners. Prisoners were aware of the warning; as Sobibor survivor Arkady Weiszpapir recalled, "We were told that there was a note by Molotov that the Germans are killing our prisoners of war. If this continues, we will act likewise, just as the Germans are doing. And the Germans responded, we are not going to shoot you, but you will die here of hunger. Slowly."[45]

Another component of the changing conditions on the ground during this time was the Jewish resistance. Since 1941, Jews had launched approximately one hundred uprisings inside the ghettos, including armed attacks on German personnel and massive breakouts. Weapons were smuggled into the ghettos, and fighters resisted forced deportations. The best-known revolt took place in the Warsaw ghetto in spring 1943, when Jews fought the Germans and their supporters in the streets. Many other armed clashes occurred, even inside prisons. In Minsk, the underground began in 1941, and resistance was organized well enough to provide regular escapes to the surrounding forests. An estimated ten thousand Jews fled, but of course not many survived. They were hunted down, and those who were caught were killed.[46] Many others were not able to survive the primitive conditions; holes dug in the ground were their hiding and living places in the vast woods of Belarus. These would be dirty and damp, but the idea of survival until the war was over gave them hope.

To Be Caught as a Jew

Though circumcised, Pechersky managed to hide the fact that he was Jewish for a time, which creates a sort of enigma around him. Perhaps his German captors did not expect a Jew to be a strong, technically skilled army officer. Also, there were too many prisoners to investigate all of them. For example, Josif Golba, interviewed in 2000, described his capture and imprisonment near Smolensk.[47] He said he was forced to walk to Borisov, which took his group a month. Upon arrival the Germans ordered all Jews to step forward. He was a commissar and thus took a risk by doing so. No other commissar had stepped forward, but Golba did and he miraculously survived. However, with this voluntary identification, the prisoners were not asked to show if they had been circumcised or not. Some Jews were not circumcised since their parents had adapted to Communism, so it did not have to be unmasked. The only consequence was the threat of severe punishment if the Germans found out later that a man was a Jew. Later, inspection on circumcision became more physical and the capacity to identify every Jew became more efficient. This was the procedure that Pechersky encountered when he was sent to Minsk.

According to Sheinman's testimony in the *Black Book*, "People were caught and were picked up in the streets of villages and delivered to gathering places. They picked out the Jews according to their appearance and murdered them . . . they systematically shot Jewish prisoners of war, including women nurses and doctors."[48] The testimony describes prisoners later being forced to lower their pants to show if they were circumcised in order to identify the Jews among them.[49] Another testimony in the *Black Book* also noted that many non-Jewish Russians—including doctors—helped to hide their Jewish colleagues from the Germans.[50]

The first explanation for Pechersky's survival is that he was lucky to be a very assimilated Jew whose background and looks did not identify him. He definitely did not resemble the more religious men from the many *shtetls* who had beards and sidelocks. He seemed to be simply a Russian soldier, many of whom had a dark complexion, especially those from Southern Russia or the Asian East. Another explanation is that he was physically strong and had an immense morale. He believed he was fighting for a good cause, as he reiterated many times after the war. As long as his Judaism remained hidden, he suffered the same fate as most other Russian POWs. When he tried to escape, he was deported to Minsk, where he was imprisoned in Shirokaya (Broad) Street Prison.

In his 1944 testimony in Moscow, Pechersky said his Jewish identity was discovered on August 11, 1943, in Minsk when medical staff systematically set out to discover anyone who was circumcised. Among the two thousand POWs, the

62   A Trajectory of Misery

Germans found eight Jews, who were all sent to a *padwal*, an underground cellar (sometimes referred to as a basement prison, or a *judenkeller*) inside Stalag 352.[51] Such areas are described in the last pages of the *Black Book*:

> Later they [the Jewish POWs] were sent to a special Jewish section of the Minsk forest camp. Here they were subjected to the crudest of regimes: they were fed only every other day, and the food was of a very poor quality. By spring all the Jews in the camp had been murdered or had died of hunger and illness. According to the testimony of I. K. Deryugin, Jews were also kept in a cellar in the same Minsk camp; from time to time a group of them would be taken out and shot. Typhus was rampant in the cellar. The bodies of the dead were taken out once a week.[52]

Pechersky was kept in the cellar until August 20, 1943. His testimony about what happened is recorded in a document deposed at Yad Vashem:

> On a sunny day in August 1942, a burly *Polizei* [policeman] led us, nine prisoners of war to the Minsk "Lesnoi [Forest] Camp," around the camp. We passed by long, wooden barracks filled with prisoners of war, past the administrative courtyard, the living quarters of the police. When we reached the cellar that was off to the side and evidently was constructed long ago for prisoners condemned to death, he ordered us to go down in. Twenty-four steps led to the underground cell.
>
> On this long path down to the cellar, the policeman announced to us, with a "good-natured" smile on his lips:
>
> "Don't worry, men. You are going to the entrance of Hell. Rest a bit. Think a bit. And then, one stop to Hell. There is no way out of this cellar. And you won't get into Heaven."
>
> The open door let in a flash of daylight as we came in. We hardly had time to look around at the two or three boards lying on the floor and the close stool in the corner of the cellar when the door closed.
>
> We heard the sound of the hanging lock being shut.
>
> One person rushed to grab the boards for himself, the rest spread out on the cold and damp floor.
>
> Darkness surrounded us. It was a deep cellar without any small window or air vent. The policeman was truly not without a sense of humor when he called it "the entrance to Hell."
>
> Feeling my way, moving my legs slowly so as not to touch one of my comrades lying beside me, I went up to the wall and slowly lowered myself to the ground. Stretched out my legs. Lay my hands under my head, trying to fall asleep.
>
> There was dead silence in the cellar. Everyone was occupied with his own thoughts.
>
> I was not able to sleep. The dampness penetrated your body, not allowing you to concentrate, to think over what had happened.

A *Trajectory of Misery*   63

On my right someone stirred, sighed heavily.

"What's going to happen?" my neighbor asked quietly, with a Ukrainian accent.

"You heard," I answered. "We're on the road to Hell."

"What's your name?"

"Sasha."

"Where are you from?"

"I'm from Rostov-on-Don."

"And I'm from the Donbass," my neighbor answered thoughtfully.

"What's your name?" Sasha asked.

"Boris. Boris Tsibulski"

We were silent.

"You know, Sasha, let's sleep. It's good to forget yourself for a bit."

"I already tried. I can't. I can't stop thinking."

"Well try, fly off into the clouds," Boris answered. "It helps. Sleep."

He slept a little, and when he woke up, he found the photo of his daughter.[53]

Other documents on Stalag 352 refer to the cellar as a "punishment cell" (*karzer*). As a 1944 Russian investigation into "fascist crimes" reported:

> The camp for Soviet prisoners of war, Stalag 352, also known under the name of "Forest Camp," was located five kilometers west of Minsk, to the south of the Minsk-Vilnius railway track. A *Karzer* (*Arrest-Baracke*) is a barracks made out of boards and dug into the ground. It is up to 25m in length, rising above the surface at 0.5m. It is divided into eight cells, each 3.5m in length and 2 to 4m in width. Small windows (20x40cm) are barred with barbed wire, hardly allowing any daylight to pass. The cells are absolutely empty; there is not even a bench to sit on. The prisoners were forced to spend all their time standing up, as the floor was intentionally doused with water.[54]

Descriptions of these cellars vary, but they seem to have existed also in other camps. People were sometimes able to leave messages, although the cellars in which Pechersky and Waiszpapir were kept must have been too dark to do so. As Trutnev Stepan, a former POW from Barnaul who escaped from such a place, wrote, "The walls and the doors of cells are covered with inscriptions. Let me cite one of them: 'Comrades, imprisoned soldiers and commanders, fight against the German occupiers and murderers. Soon the hour of retribution will come, when the fascist vermin will pay for Russian blood.'"[55]

Arkady Waiszpapir, whom I interviewed in Kiev in 2010, described his imprisonment in a *padwal*:

> I was in the hospital for prisoners of war, and in the hospital for prisoners of war the deputy head of the hospital appeared to be a Jew. And after that they did a full check for Jewry in the hospital. Already then I had a leg broken in

64 A Trajectory of Misery

two places . . . but both places were healing. I even worked as an orderly in this hospital. And then some seventy of us were revealed as Jews, more than half of the staff of doctors and medical attendants appeared to be Jews. And we had been put in a so-called forest camp near the hospital but now we were put in an evacuation camp, from which the prisoners of war were sent to Germany. And they put us all in a cell, an underground cell. And it was so narrow, we would turn to the other side on command. They would give us 150 grams of bread once a day and on top of that, *balanda* every other day. Well, *balanda* was . . . this brownish thing—soup with a couple of potatoes. Some would float. . . . There we stayed, when already more than half of us were dead. Suddenly we were led out and lined up and sent somewhere. It appeared, we were brought to Minsk to a camp; and well, we were deported, to this Minsk concentration camp. There was a camp for Jewish prisoners; then they were deported, and the final period there were only Jews in this camp.[56]

In his 1944 statement in Moscow, Pechersky said those who denied they were Jewish and were later discovered were whipped until they admitted their identities. When Pechersky was released from the cellar, he was taken to the Shirokaya Street Prison in Minsk, like Arkady Waiszpapir.

The American historian Polly Zavadivker has found descriptions of the prison camp that confirm what survivor Michael Treister, a former inmate, told me in 2013 in Minsk:

Prisoners inside the camp labored in workshops for shoemakers, locksmiths, and carpenters. Columns of workers were also marched outside the camp on a daily basis to construction sites and factories elsewhere in Minsk. The sources do not indicate where the products were sent or which companies used the workers, although clearly some work was to support the needs of the German Army and the Organisation Todt.

At the center of the camp was a large courtyard surrounded by barracks, workshops, and a kitchen. Soviet POWs slept in barracks with three-tiered plank beds. Jewish prisoners slept separately in buildings that were formerly used as horse stables. At one point the barracks could only accommodate one-third of the prisoners. They slept in shifts, or else pressed together while standing up. Once a day prisoners received a ladle of watery soup (*balanda*), and occasionally 100 grams of bread or pickles. POWs and other prisoners were forced to wear red badges; Jewish inmates wore yellow badges. After an outbreak of lice, the camp authorities had inmates build a steam boiler that was regularly used to delouse their clothing, as well as a large bath, where they were made to wash on Sundays.[57]

To Escape and to Resist

Pechersky and the few other survivors of the *Waldlager* were chased through the streets of Minsk to the prison with their hands above their heads. He said there were about 500 other Jews in the Shirokaya Street camp, mostly specialists in technical professions who were sent there from the Minsk ghetto, along with 200–300 Russian Jewish POWs. Pechersky was held in this prison until September 18. According to his deposition, the Jews inside Shirokaya Street were in close contact with the partisans.

The inhabitants of the prison in Shirokaya Street were in regular contact with the ghetto of Minsk which accommodated a major resistance movement. As Polly Zavadivker noted, "The geographic proximity to the Minsk Ghetto allowed prisoners in the camp to establish connections with the ghetto's underground and the Judenrat, both of which maintained ties to the partisan movement in the local forests after the spring of 1942. These connections served as a channel of moral and pragmatic support to prisoners and enabled a significant number of escapes."[58] The resistance had managed to get Sofia Kurlandskaya appointed as main secretary. She was the liaison with the resistance, and she participated in the organization of escapes to the partisan detachments and had her web of messengers. She arranged the official papers for those who carried messages. There were major escapes in 1942, as Pechersky remembered:

> In July 1942 a guide—messenger Tanya Boiko, conspiratorial name "Natasha," 17 years old, arrived from the Staroselsk Forest from a partisan group led by Feldman. Through Mikhail Gebelev, one of the underground leaders, she got in touch with Sara Levin. The latter arranged the escape of S. G. Ganzenko from the camp with the help of Sofia Kurlandskaya, and Natasha successfully brought him to the partisans. At the end of October 1942 Sofia Kurlandskaya and Blatman helped the communist Goland who was in a death cell to escape from the camp. They wrote him off as dead. Goland was taken to the Frunze partisan detachment. In January 1943 he was killed in a battle with fascists.[59]

Why did Pechersky not join the other partisans and attempt to escape the prison in Shirokaya Street? Of course, escape was hazardous and full of the dangers of betrayal and aggression, but he had been caught before and had known harsh punishment. The fate awaiting those who failed was horrific: "Fugitives who returned to the camp were stripped, doused with water, and driven into the yard. Then they were beaten with shovels and brutally tortured to death," one survivor stated.[60] In the ghetto, even women with children attempted to escape, which seemed the only chance of survival.[61] To escape Shirokaya was more difficult than to escape the ghetto, but still people tried endlessly.

Perhaps by not fleeing the prison, Pechersky made a choice in the ongoing discussion: was it better to fight inside the ghetto and resist there, or to escape and fight as a partisan?[62] Perhaps he was tired of trying to escape his fate or fearful that others would be punished, a fear that played a large role in the Sobibor revolt when he felt responsible for what might befall others. To resist collectively may have been more attractive, although he must have known there was little chance of survival.

66   *A Trajectory of Misery*

There are several stories of major escapes. One is about a larger group that was betrayed by the man who was supposed to drive the group to the partisans. Survivor Rosenfeld, who was also in Shirokaya, wrote a letter about his ordeal there:

> Autumn 1941, 7–10km from Minsk there were 70–80 thousand of Soviet war prisoners in the concentration camp. The war prisoners Jews about 235–250 men were separated from the others. We were placed in a cellar and were fed once a day. But when a German in spectacles was on duty (he could speak "loishen koidesh") we were fed twice a day. I do not know who he was or what his name was but he was a good man. We spent a fortnight in the cellar and then we were transferred to Minsk, to a newly founded concentration camp in Shirokaya Street. When we were driven to this camp there were about 100 Jews from Minsk there. The commandant of the camp was Gorodetsky. He was the son of a Russian white guard émigré who left Russia during the revolution. He was a big fellow, 2–2.10m tall, in a German uniform, and spoke Russian well. He would taunt us endlessly. He would form us, worn out and tormented, to stand at attention without caps in the yard in the rain and cold weather while he would watch us from the office. Those who could not bear it and moved or put on a cap were immediately shot. Or he would form us with a shout "Dress!" take his carabine, go to the end of the line with a shout "I'll level you, Russian swines!" and shoot along the line 2–3cm from the noses. We felt the heat of the bullets at our noses. Each time after such a leveling at least ten people were killed.[63]

In this same letter Rosenfeld told the story of a man named Blatman who tried to help the Jews. But his underground role was betrayed, and Blatman was sent to Sobibor like everyone else:

> His death was tragic. In spring 1943 Byelorussian peasants were brought to the camp. They had red patches on the back and on the breast. There were Gestapo agents among them.
>
> Blatman was preparing an escape of a large group of prisoners. And he evidently asked one of the red patch prisoners for advice which direction to move, or where there were partisans. He informed the Gestapo against Blatman. And one day, a month or a month and a half before we were taken to Sobibor, Gestapo came to the camp and Blatman with them. He was tortured but gave no one away. When we were loaded onto the cars to go to Sobibor he was in one of the cars of the train. When we arrived at Sobibor he was on his knees and it seemed he was the first to go to the gas chamber.[64]

The decision to escape was fraught with psychological hardship, and fear was a major component. Pechersky related a failed escape attempt when some Jews tried to bribe a custodian to lead them to the partisans in the forest.[65] They were betrayed, and all fifty were sent to the cellar. Survivor Arkady Waiszpapir also described an escape attempt in a letter to Valentin Romanovski:

> Apparently 25 people wanted to escape. They had agreed with the police, Ukrainians working in the gendarmerie, to be taken out of town. Rifles were kept in a bag and when they started to ship this bag on the car they were surrounded by the Germans . . . How these guys were tortured cannot be described. They were torn apart by dogs, they poured boiling water over them, they were cut into pieces of meat, and half dead, they were shot.[66]

Pouring boiling water over them and then letting people freeze in the snow was a normal punishment. Still, according to Pechersky, the Germans beat them, but they did not kill them because the people in his part of the camp were needed for work.[67] Was he aware that the Germans were reluctant to kill those who could work? If so, his idea of German politics was too rational. Despite a labor shortage, the Germans' anti-Semitism "obliged" them to commit mass murder. Could Pechersky in Minsk have known about the unimaginable killings in Sobibor, Belzec, and elsewhere? Certain things become a reality only after one has seen them.

Frida Wulfowna told me during an interview in Minsk in May 2013 that people in the Minsk ghetto knew that Jews were being killed in Sobibor. She said that people knew they should take care never to end up there. She also remembered the columns of Russian POWs marching through the streets, many without shoes and in terrible shape. She said the POWs were forced to carry stones to exhaust them. She witnessed Minsk citizens being shot when they tried to give food to the prisoners.

The Minsk Ghetto

More is known about the Minsk ghetto than about Stalag 352 or the SS Arbeitslager in Shirokaya Street as a result of the research of the History Workshop of Minsk, which has attempted to retrace the history of German cruelty in and around their town. The prison in Shirokaya Street was not in the ghetto, which has become known for its resistance movement and its close contacts with partisans not far from the town. From July 1941, Jews were confined to the ghetto, which consisted of a few overcrowded streets where they waited for deportation and certain death. The stronger ones faced the danger of escape, and some managed to reach the partisans.

In *The Minsk Ghetto 1941–1943*, Barbara Epstein paints a rosy picture of the relations between the ghetto inhabitants and the non-Jewish residents of Minsk. Since their arrival, the Germans had killed Jews, not in secret but publicly. The inhabitants were starved from the beginning, but the ghetto was porous enough that many were able to escape. The forest was near, and there was good contact with the partisans. Some people moved back and forth between them, picking

68   *A Trajectory of Misery*

up new escapees from the ghetto. According to Epstein, the underground activity was successful only because of outside help, and the good relations between Jews and non-Jews facilitated the many escapes and were themselves a form of resistance. In her opinion, the city underground organization was led by Communist ideology, with its fundamental principle of solidarity in the joint struggle across ethnic and national lines. She argues that more than two decades of Soviet rule in Minsk had fostered Jewish integration into society and strengthened interethnic ties, which became the basis for solidarity during the war. Moreover, the ideology of internationalism was perceived by the younger generation as a sign of a developed, modern society, while nationalist feelings were rather weak among the Byelorussian people. As a result, the Jews of Minsk had a secret weapon: the non-Jews of Minsk.

Israeli scholar Dan Zeits has challenged Epstein's ideas about this solidarity.[68] He argues that Epstein's book attempts at all costs to adapt her research to a predetermined thesis. For this reason, he claims, she prefers to ignore a significant number of sources that contradict the thesis of solidarity and reflect a deep cleft and distrust between Jews and non-Jews in Nazi-occupied Minsk. Both historians illustrate their arguments with moving examples of audacity and courage, while providing an image of the excessive violence and cruelty suffered by the ghetto population.

Although the argument that Epstein's book is ideological is understandable, hardly any other work is so moving, evocative, or full of empathy. She paints a world of overcrowded streets and desperate resistance, and through her interviews, we meet the survivors and learn how they were betrayed. We learn about the underground and its relationship to the distant Communist regime in Moscow that sought to dominate the partisan movement. After the war, many in Minsk were accused of collaboration with the Germans, and suspicions were raised even during the war. Indeed, those who seek to obscure the way the Communist leadership abandoned Minsk to the Germans in the first days of the war have clouded the relationship between the ghetto resistance and Moscow. Moscow delivered the population of Minsk to the enemy without a real effort to evacuate them to safe territory. Their actions were hostile to Jews and served their own self-interest. The very same people who had not done their job were returned to power after the liberation and persecuted the former leadership of the ghetto resistance. Years passed before the latter were recognized; those falsely accused were rehabilitated, and those who were sent to the Gulag were allowed to return. When I walked over the terrain where the ghetto once stood and looked at old maps, sad images came to mind.

The German historian Petra Rentrop has described the Minsk ghetto as the portal to the hell of the extermination camp Maly Trostinets. Very few books describe these places (Maly Trostinets is described in the *Black Book*),[69] and Rentrop's book in the German language is ground-breaking. Rentrop also describes the escapes to the forests. She devotes one part of her book to the special ghetto (*Sonderghetto*) for German Jews, who were separated from the local Jews. Often these Jews of German origin were moved into the homes of murdered Russian Jews. The history of these German Jews has been recounted in the *Memorial Book*, a splendid effort by contemporary German historians to deal with the past and to remember.[70] The book contains beautiful biographies, different from all that has been written about the Byelorussian inhabitants, though deeply moving and saddening.

The Prison at Shirokaya Street

Pechersky was never in the ghetto—it was not a place where POWs were sent—but he met many of its inhabitants in the Shirokaya prison and his fellow prisoners had met others. The ghetto was about three kilometers away. The people in the ghetto and in the prison knew the tide of war was turning. They knew how strong the partisans were, and they eagerly awaited the Soviet army's arrival, even when the army was still far away. Some people from the ghetto would pass through the fence and make it to the forest. Sometimes they would return for other groups they could bring to the partisans.

Polly Zavadivker describes the prison as a place mainly for Soviet POWs, with a continuous population of about 2,500 people.[71] Prisoners labored in workshops, while columns of workers were daily marched outside the camp to construction sites. Jewish and Soviet prisoners slept separately. When there were too many prisoners they would be forced to sleep in shifts or while standing up.

According to Zavadivker:

> The camp's population was systematically reduced by four methods: killing in gas vans, shooting on the camp premises, deportations to other labor and extermination sites, and death by disease, malnutrition and exhaustion. The SS began to significantly scale back the size of the camp in August 1943. Starting then, four specially equipped gas vans (*Gaswagen* in German, *dushegubki* in Russian) transported prisoners from Shirokaya Street to Maly Trostinets, the extermination camp located twelve kilometers southeast of Minsk. People died on the way by asphyxiation from gas that was piped into the vans from the exhaust fumes, and their corpses were cremated in Maly Trostinets.[72]

It is estimated that some 20,000 people who had entered the camp were killed either by being gassed or shot in the Blagovshchina Forest, near Maly Trostinets.[73]

My impression is that contacts between the partisans and the inmates were manifold but dangerous. The prisoners in Shirokaya Street were well informed, and some managed to escape. According to Pechersky, Simion Rosenfield and Arkady Waiszpapir managed to obtain leaflets printed by the resistance in the ghetto informing people about what was happening at the front and encouraging them to fight with the fascists and to accelerate the victory. These leaflets were distributed among the prisoners.

70 A Trajectory of Misery

In a personal mail to me, Barbara Epstein wrote:

> There was a connection between the Minsk ghetto underground and the Shirokaya camp. A major connecting person between the inmates of the camp and the underground movement in Minsk was Sofia Kurlandskaya, a member of the ghetto underground, who was secretary and translator to the head of the camp; as a member of the underground, her assignment was to locate prisoners in the camp who could be sent to the partizans, and to help them escape the camp and reach partisan units in the forest.
>
> (December 17, 2012)

Resistance fighter Hersh Smolar also remembered Kurlandskaya, whom he called Kurliandski: "A modest, heroic, young woman from Grodno." According to him, she was murdered during an attempt to escape.[74] In May 1942, the ghetto underground learned through Kurlandskaya that a former Red Army lieutenant, Ukrainian-born Semyon Grigorievich Ganzenko, was imprisoned at Shirokaya.[75] With the goal of supporting the fledgling partisan movement in the nearby forests, the ghetto underground smuggled Ganzenko and a few other POWs out of the camp in barrels of garbage and brought them to the Staroe Selo forest region, about twenty-four kilometers west of Minsk. The partisan squad named Ganzenko commander of the newly formed Budyonny detachment.

All the men from the ghetto who were sent to work passed through the prison, as did most of those to be deported to Sobibor or to Maly Trostinets. The Shirokaya prison operated from July 5, 1941, through June 30, 1944, as a work camp and a collecting point for deportations. The facility was a prison for those Minsk inhabitants who refused to comply with forced labor, and it was also a camp for partisan sympathizers—sometimes entire villages of families, with children. Those at Shirokaya Street who could not work were sent immediately to Maly Trostinets to be executed in mass shootings. Some never reached the extermination camp, but were gassed in transit.

In an excellent article on the history of Shirokaya Street, Natallia Yatskevich described the camp, which was established in former horse stables where 10,000 people were killed.[76] There were two large barracks, and in every crib were bunks of two floors where twelve people would sleep. In September 1943, the camp housed an estimated 2,500 prisoners who received 200 to 250 grams of bread a day and were whipped regularly. On September 18, 1943,[77] the day Pechersky was taken away, thousands of Minsk citizens were brought to the camp in reprisal for an attack on the Security Police canteen and for the assassination of Generalkommissar Kube.[78]

As Michael Treister, wrote in his autobiography:

> Right behind the gate there was a vast, asphalt square; in the depth—former cavalry barracks with three-tiered plank-beds in them, on the left a shed and, under it, piles of bricks; on the right—a service area with workshops, barracks and a kitchen. The barracks were occupied by the constant prisoners of the camp, who, in comparison with us, were aristocrats among prisoners: we

were waiting to be shot. Unlike us, they would not be killed immediately . . . The days spent in the camp were like a nightmare. We all were sheared close with a kind of shearing clippers. There were several thousand people in the camp. By day they all stood, sat, or lay right on the asphalt. Once a day we were given a ladleful of thin, rotten soup. People stood in a huge queue to the cauldron in the middle of the service area. Actually, stood is the wrong word: they were driven on past the cauldron in the middle of the service area. Some of them did not have enough time to put their tins under the ladle and were pushed further, without getting even that portion of food . . . not enough beds, waiting for their turn to sleep a few hours on the bed. Sleeping standing up.[79]

He described in graphic detail the murder of thousands of Russian POWs in Minsk:

It was the winter of the years 1941–42. I was working as a shoemaker. The column would leave the ghetto before dawn, when it was still dark, and would return to it in the evening, when it was already dark. I made use of the darkness and would sometimes remove patches and labels from my coat (they were pinned to it and not sewn). Then I would sneak out of the column on the way back to the ghetto, would hide myself in the nearest gateway, and, after the column had gone past it, I would come out and go to see my nanny Yuzya. At her place I could get warm, eat, and spend a restful night. To tell the truth, I was nagged every time by the thought of how I would get back in the column the next morning, but it would be only the next day. One morning, while it was still dark, I had left Yuzya's house and was coming to Moskovskaya Street. From there I had to go to the west bridge in order to get back in the column . . . I suddenly saw something on the opposite side of the street that looked like a heap of garbage. Several passersby were standing around, looking at it. The others turned away and went past, quickening their steps. According to my plan I had to proceed along the left side of the street, but that strange heap drew me across the road and when I came to it, it turned out to be not garbage, but several dead bodies of Soviet war prisoners, heaped one onto another. They were extremely emaciated and were dressed in overcoats and under those almost naked. Their faces were grey-yellowish, feet—wrapped in rags. Some had been shot in the breast, the others in the head or stomach. Some corpses had their eyes open and in them an expression of death agony was frozen, or perhaps it was relief of the end of the tortures. There was very little blood—they must have been too exhausted to bleed much. Some fifty meters farther I saw another such heap and then more. They lay at regular distances, all the way as far as the bridge. [He was told there were many more piles.] That night a ten-thousand column of war prisoners had been driven through Minsk. The exhausted, wounded, and sick could not keep up with the pace of the rest of the column and inevitably gathered in the tail end.[80]

In an interview in May 2013, Michael Treister told me that he went back and forth from the partisans to the ghetto, which became impossible after he was

72   A Trajectory of Misery

imprisoned at Shirokaya Street in 1943. Treister said that this prison was in fact a
death camp and the collection point from where the Jews were deported. Russian
POWs were not in the same part of the camp, but were kept separate from the
ghetto inhabitants. The prison had a stable group of workers who had hardly any
contact with those who were in transit. Soup was the only food, provided once
a day, but that was more than was available in the ghetto. Beginning in summer
1943, vans arrived in which groups of Jews were gassed.[81]

Testimonies about Shirokaya Street are hard to read because of the graphic
descriptions of horror. As former frontline soldier M. Lokshin testified to Ilya
Ehrenburg in February 1943:

> The camp was under the authority of the military field police. Brought there
> under the force of arms, 120 Jews had to dismantle several structures near
> the cavalry barracks with their bare hands and clear a space for the camp
> within two hours. They had to carry the first beams, logs, or boards that fell
> into their hands for 200 meters at a run and to lay them down sorted by type
> and size. At approximately the halfway point, the Germans would greet the
> martyrs with a dog. And they would seize and begin to beat any fellow the
> dog rushed at. And so work went on.[82]

Food and medical care were urgently needed. The ghetto had a hospital, but the
camp did not. After the German defeat at Stalingrad in February 1943, the camp
was crowded with Soviet soldiers who flooded in following the Soviet advance.
They came from Smolensk and were followed by Byelorussian political prisoners
and people from zones where partisans dominated. Previously the majority of
those at the camp had been Jews (except for the POW camp), but after September 1943 there were many nationalities and backgrounds. The Jews had disappeared to the various extermination sites.

One survivor, Lev Moiseevich, testified in 1944 regarding the sadism of the
camp guards, which he considered worse than in other camps, but the pattern
was similar everywhere.[83] Arriving prisoners were subjected to humiliating insults
and beatings, which, as we now know from psychological studies, were inflicted
to drive the prisoners to lose their identities. Sadistic contests of efficient shooting alternated with severe beatings, especially when hungry prisoners stood in a
queue for food. According to Moiseevich, many people were swollen from hunger, and he remembered the spring of 1943 as the worst moment. At that moment
conditions were so bad that people could not work, while at the same time their
work was urgently needed.

Yet the need for workers did not stop the cruelty and sadism. Former inmate
Abram Astashinsky described his ordeal:

> It was a conveyor belt of death. We lined up in the morning, and there was
> a local camp commander . . . surnamed Gorodetsky, who came with two
> sheepdogs. He would walk down the line and kill with a pistol every morning
> ten people, "for breakfast." He called this atrocity "morning exercises." Then

A Trajectory of Misery 73

appeared the German commandant Wachs, and he also killed. . . . Columns from the camp of the Jews drove to work. Everywhere nearby were many thousands of prisoners of war who died like flies from starvation, disease, and the abuse of camp police. We had to survive. We had heard rumors that in Bialystok they had burned a thousand Jewish men directly in the synagogue and that they had shot 5,000 young men in Brest. We knew what had happened to the Jews in Minsk. We had no other choice but to hope. The camp was surrounded by electric wire and many prisoners threw themselves on the wire in order immediately to end all suffering.[84]

Punishments were severe and physical. Death did not come easily, but only after tremendous suffering. In his 1944 deposition in Moscow, Pechersky described how torment was inflicted before death.[85] Former inmate Hersh Smolar wrote:

Every day a group left for the town, they were taken to work, forty to forty-five people. People died as often as stars go out early in the morning. Each waited his turn. Everyone knew that no one could leave the gate of Shirokaya, no one would come out alive. There was only one road . . . The camp inflicted on us more ordeals than hunger—we suffered from lice. They were crawling everywhere, like ants. In the winter it was the cold . . . we made a fire in the yard, boiled water, stripped naked, and threw our dirty ragged clothes into the boiling water. We quickly wrung them out and put them on again. It helped for one or two days, then it all began again. Voracious insects sucked it seemed all our blood. The daily beatings were not comparable with what tormented me so much more—an unbearable headache. It always started in the evening, and then disappeared after vomiting and terrible heartburn with acute abdominal pain. Gradually, my body started to be covered by a continuous psoriasis.[86]

In June and July 1943, the camp workshops were eliminated, and in the fall, the transport of workers to the west (to Poland and Germany) intensified. Despite the cruelty at the camp, former Commander Adolf Rübe defended himself at his trial on December 13, 1949 by saying that the situation in the ghetto was worse. Indeed, there was profit to be made from labor, but as we have seen, cruelty was all around.

In his book *Innocence in Hell: The Life, Struggle and Death of the Minsk Ghetto*, David Guy quoted former inmate Arkadi Zelikman: "The living hell of the camp at Shirokaya was far worse than any nightmare, but its inmates were men, POWs, people prepared for suffering and capable of resistance."[87] According to this account, the children and the elderly suffered the worst; for others, as long as resistance was possible, there was hope. Pechersky clung to hope, although the worst was still to come on September 18, when he and 2,000 others were pushed onto a train bound for Sobibor.

One cannot know where the personal suffering was worst; we know that our historical image is overshadowed by our knowledge of the thousands who were

74 *A Trajectory of Misery*

murdered in Sobibor. The camps and killing sites of Eastern Poland are less well known in the west, and in the former Soviet Union there have been decades of silence. Visiting the Belarusian State Museum of the History of the Great Patriotic War in Minsk in 2013, I was shocked to find that there was hardly any information about the fate of the Jews. But with the new museum recently opened (in 2014), Maly Trostinets is no longer ignored. Pechersky does not belong to the Byelorusian heritage; he was just a Russian POW, deported to Polish territory. One keeps wondering why he did not join the partisans in the woods. He had done the stunt before, several times. Indeed, he had been caught and punished.

In Minsk Pechersky had met Boris Tsibulski, who came from the region of Donetsk; Shlomo Laitman, a communist from Warschau; Aleksandr Shubaev from Dagestan; Arkady Waiszpapir and Simion Rosenfeld, who were both POWs from Ukraine; and Jefrim Livitnowski, who had belonged to a division of Cossacks. These would remain the people he trusted most, whom he relied on for many tasks to be done in preparation for the revolt.[88] The German historian Franziska Bruder has suggested that already in Minsk these men were involved in underground activities. I have not found proof of this, though she might be right. The several testimonies contradict each other, probably since they were made decades after the fact. Pechersky himself mentioned a meeting with the aforementioned Blatman, who helped him to recover by giving him a less exhausting job.[89] As Pechersky mentioned in a letter to Ainszstein, Blatman warned Leitman that "we should be ready to escape to the forest. As soon as Sofia Kurlandskaya is able to cross our names from the list, the following day we go out for firewood stacking."[90]

But it did not happen. Pechersky must have had no illusions about what was awaiting him. I suppose he did not believe that strong men who could work would be spared. But exactly for that reason he was not murdered when he was selected for work in Sobibor. Did he already plan to resist inside the camp or in the ghetto? In his letter to Ainszstein in 1965, he shared the responsibility he felt for those left behind after an escape. But that letter was written more than twenty years later. Certain questions have never been asked, while attention has been focused exclusively on his heroic role in Sobibor.

It is a miracle that he survived one of the most lethal battles in 1941 in Vyazma and later the several deadly camps in Byelorussia. He was not a "common soldier," as he liked to repeat. On the contrary, he was most uncommon in physical strength, but even more, as we shall see in Chapter 3, on Sobibor, he was dauntless and mentally strong. With this personality he managed to convince others to follow him and to join in the resistance.

Notes

1 Catherine Merridale, *Ivan's War: The Red Army, 1939–1945* (London: Faber and Faber, 2005), 6.

A Trajectory of Misery 75

2 Alex J. Kay, "German Economic Plans for the Occupied Soviet Union and Their Implementation, 1941–1944," in *Stalin and Europe: Imitation and Domination, 1928–1954*, eds. Timothy Snyder and Ray Brandon (New York: Oxford University Press, 2014), 163–190.

3 Nicolaus Wachsmann, *A History of the Nazi Concentration Camps* (London: Little Brown, 2015), 258–260.

4 Ibid.

5 YIVO, New York folder 144, RG116-Poland. Pechersky to Ainsztein, 15 February 1972.

6 Merridale, *Ivan's War*, 78–79.

7 *Speeches That Changed the World* (London: Quercus, 2014), 102–106.

8 Merridale, *Ivan's War*, 78–79.

9 *Speeches*, 102–106.

10 Merridale, *Ivans War*, 78–79.

11 Richard Overy, *Russia's War: A History of the Soviet Effort: 1941–1945* (New York: Penguin Books Ltd., 1998), 181–183; Omer Bartov, "The Conduct of War: Soldiers and the Barbarization of Warfare," *The Journal of Modern History* 64 (December 1992) [Supplement: Resistance Against the Third Reich]: 32–45.

12 Lev Simkin, "interview," www.echo.msk.ru/programs/time/1137964-echo/. Simkin is the author of "Александр Печерский свидетельствует: неизвестные страницы истории концлагеря Собибор," *Bylye Gody* 27:1 (2013). See "Death Sentence Despite the Law: A Secret 1962 Crimes-Against-Humanity Trial in Kiev," *Holocaust and Genocide Studies* 27 (2013): 299–312, which deals more generally with the 1962 trial of Kiev. See also *Полтора часа возмездия* [Half an Hour of Retribution] (Moscow: Zebra, 2013).

13 Lev Lopukhovsky, *The Viaz'ma Catastrophe: The Red Army's Disastrous Stand Against Operation Typhoon* (Solihull, UK: Helion and Company, 2013). While difficult to translate, the word *kotel* is sometimes translated "pocket."

14 Reminiscences of Aleksandr Pechersky deposited in Yad Vashem (Jerusalem), nr. 033–1052, probably 1972.

15 Michael Ellman and Sergei Maksudov, "Soviet Death in the Great Patriotic War: A Note," *Europe-Asia Studies* 46:4 (1994). The authors have made an inventory of the debate over war losses.

16 See P. M. Polian, "First Victims of the Holocaust: Soviet-Jewish Prisoners of War in Captivity," *Kritika: Explorations in Russian and Eurasian History* 6:4 (2005): 763–787, and Karel Christian Berkhoff, "The Mass Murder of Soviet Prisoners of War and the Holocaust: How Are They Related?" *Kritika: Explorations in Russian and Eurasian History* 6:4 (2005): 789–796.

17 Bogdan Musial, *Sowjetische Partisanen: Mythos und Wirklichkeit* (München: Paderborn, 2009), 378–379.

18 Waitman Wade Beorn, *Marching into Darkness: The Wehrmacht and the Holocaust in Belarus* (Cambridge: Harvard University Press, 2014). See also Timothy Snyder, "Holocaust: The Ignored Reality," *New York Review of Books* 56:12 (2009).

19 Beorn, *Marching into Darkness*, 28.

20 See also David M. Glantz, *And Their Mothers Wept* (Victoria, BC: Heritage House Press, 2007).

21 Merridale, *Ivan's War*, 135.

22 Reinhard Otto, *Wehrmacht, Gestapo und sowjetische Kriegsgefangenen im deutschen Reichsgebiet 1941/42* (München: R. Oldenburg, 1998); Christian Gerlach, "Die Ausweitung der deutschen Massenmorde in den besetzten sowjetischen Gebieten im Herbst 1941: Überlegungen zur Vernichtungspolitik gegen Juden und sowjetische Kriegsgefangene," in *Krieg, Ernährung, Volkermord: Forschungen zur deutschen Vernichtungspolitik im Zweiten Weltkrieg*, ed. Christian Gerlach (Hamburg: Hamburger Edition, 1998), 10–84.

23 Thomas Earl Porter, "Hitler's Forgotten Genocides: The Fate of Soviet POWs," *Elon Law Review* 5 (September 2013): 359–387.

76 A Trajectory of Misery

24 Semion Rozenfeld, interview for Yad Vashem archives, test 6590, rec group 3, interviewer Bedet Alperovitch, translation P. van Woerd, 1992. This was Rozenfeld's first camp, so must have been in Byelorussia.

25 State Archive Russian Federation (GARF), fond R/P-8114 op I g 965.

26 Leonid Smilovitsky, "Ilya Ehrenburg on the Holocaust in Belarus: Unknown Testimony," *East European Jewish Affairs* 29:1–2 (1999): 61–74.

27 Leonid Smilovitsky, *Holocaust in Belorussia, 1941–1944*, trans. Irene Newhouse (Tel Aviv: Biblioteka Motveya Chernogo, 2000), 163.

28 Paul Kohl, *Ich wundere mich, daß ich noch lebe: Sowjetische Augenzeugen berichten* (Gütersloh: Gütersloher Verlagshaus Gerd Mohn, 1990).

29 Katerina Clark, "Ehrenburg and Grossman: Two Cosmopolitan Jewish Writers Reflect on Nazi Germany at War," *Kritika: Explorations in Russian and Eurasian History* 10:3 (2009): 607–628.

30 Polly Zavadivker, "Blood and Ink: Russian and Soviet Jewish Chroniclers of Catastrophe from World War I to World War II," Ph.D. dissertation, University of California at Santa Cruz, 2013. See Chapter 5, "To Carry the Burden Together: Vasily Grossman as Chronicler of Jewish Catastrophe, 1941–1945."

31 Harvey Asher, "The Soviet Union, the Holocaust and Auschwitz," in *The Holocaust in the East: Local Perpetrators and Soviet Responses*, eds. Michael David Fox, Peter Holquist and Alexander M. Martin (Pittsburgh: University of Pittsburgh Press, 2014), 29–51.

32 Ilya Ehrenburg and Vasily Grossman, *The Complete Black Book of Russian Jewry*, trans. and ed. David Patterson (New Brunswick and London: Transaction Publishers, 2002).

33 Ehrenburg and Grossman, *Complete Black Book*, 532–535.

34 Letter Aleksandr Pechersky, 22 October 1959, archive Moscow.

35 *Масюковщина: Шталаг-352. 1941–1944: Документы и материалы/ Авт.-сост. Р.А. Черноглазова.*—Мн.: Издательство «Четыре четверти», *Masjukovshina: Stalag 352. 1941–1944*: Documents and Materials / M 31 Avt.-status. RA Chernoglazova. [Minsk: Four Quarters, 2005].

36 Report by O. Mazing, Senior scientific worker of the Commission to the CC CP/b/B for the history of the Patriotic War, 1944. Archive of Belarus/Minsk.

37 Snyder, *Bloodlands*, 176–177.

38 Antony Beevor, *Stalingrad: The Fateful Siege, 1942–1943* (New York: Viking, 1998).

39 *Belorusskaya Voennaya Gazeta* (Belarusian Military Newspaper), 13 August 2014, http://vsr.mil.by/2014/08/13/pisma-i-dnevniki-iz-okkupirovannogo-minska-2/. I am indebted to Israeli historian Dan Zeits for this reference and the next.

40 *Vecherniy Minsk*, 19 December 2002, www.vminsk.by/news/30/22713/.

41 Hersh Smoliar, *Fun Minsker geto* [Resistance in Minsk] (Oakland, CA: Judah L. Magnes Memorial Museum, 1966), 67.

42 Jochen Hellbeck, "The Diaries of Fritzes and the Letters of Gretchens: Personal Writings from the German-Soviet War and their Readers," *Kritika: Explorations in Russian and Eurasian History* 10:3 (2009): 571–606.

43 *Komitee für Archive und Archivangelegenheiten beim Ministerrat der Republik Belarus: Lager Sowjetischer Kriegsgefangenen in Belarus, 1941–1944* (Minsk: 2004), 6–8.

44 Christian Gerlach, *Kalkulierte Morde: Die deutsche Wirtschafts- und Vernichtungspolitik in Weißrussland 1941–1944*, 4th edn. [Calculated Murder: The German Economic and Extermination Policy in Byelorussia] (Hamburg: Hamburger Edition, 2012). See Chapter 8, "Die Arbeitskräfte Politik," 449–503.

45 Alexander Y. Stupnikov, interviewed in Poland, 28 March 2013.

46 Michael R. Marrus, "Jewish Resistance to the Holocaust," *Journal of Contemporary History* 30:1 (1995): 83–110.

47 Iosif Golna, SVF "Interview."

48 Ehrenburg and Grossman, *Complete Black Book*, 538.

49 When the hangmen of the Minsk ghetto were prosecuted, one of them, Mittman, assumed this was a normal procedure; USHMM RG00602503.

A Trajectory of Misery 77

50 Ehrenburg and Grossman, *Complete Black Book*, 542.
51 State Archive Russian Federation (GARF), fond R-8114 op I g 965, p. 152.
52 Ehrenburg and Grossman, *Complete Black Book*, 541.
53 Reminiscences of Aleksandr Pechersky deposited in Yad Vashem (Jerusalem), nr. 033–1052, probably 1972.
54 Translated by Dan Zeits, from his own material.
55 O. Mazing, Sen. Report of scientific worker of the Commission to the CC CP/b/B for the history of the Patriotic War, 1944.
56 Arkady Waiszpapir, interview with the author, Kiev, 2010.
57 An excellent article by Polly Zavadivker, "Minsk-Shirokaia Street," is forthcoming in *Extermination, Transit, and Forced Labor Camps for Jews*, vol. V of *The United States Holocaust Memorial Museum Encyclopedia of Camps and Ghettos 1933–1945*, ed. Martin Dean (Bloomington: Indiana University Press in association with the United States Holocaust Memorial Museum, Forthcoming).
58 Ibid.
59 Jerusalem, nr. 033–1052 (probably 1972), 16.
60 O. M. Arkadieva, ed., *Crossroads of Fate: From the Memoirs of Former Ghetto and the Righteous People of the World* (Minsk: 2001), 58–63.
61 Musial, *Sowjetische Partisanen*, 384.
62 Barbara Epstein, *The Minsk Ghetto 1941–1943: Jewish Resistance and Soviet Internationalism* (Berkeley: University of California Press, 2008); see Chapter 8, "Strategies of Resistance Elsewhere, The Kovno Ghetto," 258–282.
63 Letter to Rodinov, by Simeon Rozenfeld, Yad Vashem 033–1047.
64 Ibid.
65 Pechersky, letter to Valentin Romanovski, USHMM collection, Michael Lev 25/I, 1983. See also Petra Rentrop, *Tatorte der Endlösung: Das Minsk Ghetto und die Vernichtungsstätte Maly Trostinez* (Berlin: Metropol, 2011), 157.
66 Arkady Waiszpapir, letter to Valentin Romanovski. Date unclear (around 1983, tracable near to letter in note 63)
67 Deposition Pechersky1944, 154.
68 Dan Zeits, "Was Minsk Really Different?" (Professor Barbara Epstein and Soviet Internationalism), unpublished manuscript.
69 Leonid Smilovitsky, "Ilya Ehrenburg on the Holocaust in Byelorussia," *East European Jewish Affairs* 29:1–2 (1999): 61–73. The article states (pp. 66–67):

> The Trostinets death camp was established by the Nazis in September 1941, some ten kilometers from Minsk, for the mass extermination of the civilian population and Soviet prisoners of war. It was surrounded by a barbed-wire fence. Wooden watchtowers were built at each corner of the perimeter, where soldiers with searchlights stood guard twenty-four hours a day. A guard room was located near the gate. The victims were brought from camps, prisons and ghettos in Minsk and other cities in Byelorussia. They were kept in long barracks, and given bunks made out of thick, rough wooden planks in three tiers. There was no bedding and no mattresses.
>
> Mass shootings were carried out in the Blagovshchina woods. Between September 1941 and October 1943 150,000 people were killed. The Nazis then transferred the executions to the Shashkovka woods near Maly Trostinets village.
>
> Here, between October 1943 and June 1944, over 50,000 people were murdered. In all, according to official data, 206,500 people were murdered here. Trostinets death camp is fourth in the total of victims in Europe occupied by German troops. It follows Auschwitz (4,000,000 people), Majdanek (1,380,000 people) and Treblinka (around 800,000 people). In Minsk in 1995 the Trostinets historical memorial foundation issued a statement confirming that, following an examination of archival information by its staff, the number of those murdered in Trostinets was 546,000 people.

78 A Trajectory of Misery

Non-Jews as well as Jews were murdered in Trostinets. At the time of writing [1944], it is impossible to determine precisely the number of victims according to nationality, but we can say with certainty that tens of thousands of Jews from Byelorussia, Germany and elsewhere in Europe countries were murdered here. Transportations carrying Jews arrived here from Austria, Holland, Germany, Hungary, Poland, France and Czechoslovakia and were organized in Berlin, Hannover, Dortmund, Münster, Düsseldorf, Cologne, Frankfurt, Kassel, Stuttgart, Nuremberg, Munich, Vienna, Breslau, Prague and Brno.

70 Anja Reuss and Kristin Schneider, eds., *Berlin-Minsk, Vergessene Lebensgeschichten: Ein Gedenkbuch für die nach Minsk deportierte Berliner Jüdinnen und Juden* (Berlin: Metropol, 2013).

71 Polly Zavadivker.

72 Ibid., p. 3 of the not yet printed manuscript.

73 See Adamushko et al., eds., *Spravochnik o mestakh prinuditel'nogo soderzhaniia grazhdanskogo naseleniia na okkupirovannoi territorii BSSR 1941–1944 gg.* (Minsk: Gosudarstvennyi komitet po arkhivam i deloproizdvodstvu Respubliki Belarus, 2001), 49; Treister, *Gleams of Memory*, 33; Kohl, *Ich wundere mich*, 81.

74 Hersh Smolar, *The Minsk Ghetto: Soviet-Jewish Partizans Against the Nazis* (New York: Holocaust Library, 1989), 120.

75 For the following paragraph I am indebted to Polly Zavadivker who gave me a copy of her manuscript.

76 Natallia Yatskevich, "Das Lager in der Schirokaja-Straße in Minsk," in *Existiert das Ghetto noch?*, ed. Anne Klein (Berlin: Hanser Literatur Verlage, 2003), 220–221.

77 Ibid. See also: "Memories of M. L. Yamnika, Prisoner Minsk Ghetto," in *The Tragedy of the Jews of Belarus, 1941–1944*, ed. R. A. Chernoglazova (Minsk: Collection of Materials and Documents, 1997), 243–244.

78 Peter Kohl, *Ich wundere mich*, 81–83.

79 Michael Treister, *Gleams of Memory* (Minsk: History Workshop, 2011), 34.

80 Ibid., 25–26.

81 Treister, interview by author May 2013, Minsk.

82 M. Loshkin, "Letter to Ilya Ehrenburg, February 1945," in *The Unknown Black Book, the Holocaust in the German-Occupied Soviet Territories*, eds. Joshua Rubinstein and Ilya Altmand (Bloomington: Indiana University Press, 2010), 263.

83 L. Moiseevich, testimony, from State Archive of the Russian Federation (GARF), 7021–87–17a, pp. 13–15; published in Marat Botvinnik, *Pamiatniki genotsida evreev Belorussi* [Monuments to the Genocide of the Jews of Belorussia] (Minsk: Belaruskaia navuka, 2000), 137–139.

84 Abram Astashinsky, "interview 13 February 2008," http://iremember.ru/partizani/astashinskiy-abram-isaakovich/stranitsa-2.html.

85 State Archive Russian Federation Fond (GARF) R-8114 op I g 965, p. 153.

86 Hirsch Kantor, "Letters to a Deceased Brother," in *Crossroads of Fate: From the Memoirs of Former Ghetto and the Righteous People of the World*, ed. O. M. Arkadieva (Minsk: 2001), 58–63.

87 Guy David, *Innocence in Hell: The Life, Struggle and Death of the Minsk Ghetto* (New York: Guy David, 2004), 151.

88 Ainzstein, "Jewish Resistance in Nazi-occupied Eastern Europe," 414.

89 Lev Simkin, *Полтора часа возмездия* [Half an Hour of Retribution], 17.

90 Manuscript 1972, Yad Vashem 033–1052, 36.

3 Sobibor Through the Eyes of Survivors

Much has been written about that grim deserted place hidden in the moors of eastern Poland, Sobibor. As survivor Esther Raab said when I interviewed her, "the reality of the camp was fear." Killing and death were arbitrary; no one knew who would be murdered next, where or why. People arrived there from many parts of the world after days in freightcars. Suddenly doors were opened. Dazed by daylight, the prisoners immediately heard shouted commands, and the beatings would start. For many from the west, the confrontation with extreme physical violence was new; for those who came from the ghettos, it was a confirmation of doom; and for many it was unexpected. Everything needed to be done fast; speed was imposed to aggravate the panic and anxiety. From the moment people left the train, they were outlaws without any rights. They had no name, no legal status, and no civil rights; they were degraded to the status of animals to be slaughtered. Resistance seemed pointless, while the terrible stench of burning and rotten flesh that permeated the air took their breath away. While at first sight the railway station seemed friendly, what happened next made people aware that behind the rosy image of the forester's house, the first building they would see the moment they arrived, there was a world of violence and death. Still, most people believed that if they worked hard, the strongest among them would survive.

This black comedy was maintained with Oberscharführer Hermann Michel giving a welcoming speech, wearing a white coat to give the impression that he was a doctor. He would announce to the Jews that before starting to work, they would have to bathe and undergo disinfection to prevent the spread of disease. After undressing, the captives were taken through *die Schlauch* (the tube)—a passageway three to four meters wide and 150 meters long, which the SS men in the camp cynically referred to as the *Himmelfahrtstraße* (Ascension Street, or the Road to Heaven). One SS man led the way, and five or six Ukrainians at the back hastened the captives along. Once undressed, there was no time to think; as soon as people were naked, real physical abuse was unleashed in the form of biting dogs, beatings, and unimaginable violence.

The revolt of Sobibor was a result of the shifting tide of the war and the slow victory of the Red Army, which meant that the Germans needed new and more labor. The Germans wanted to transform the camp into a productive unit that could serve the needs of German strategy. As I have described in Chapter 2,

80   *Sobibor Through the Eyes of Survivors*

the irrational killing of Jews was no longer the most productive strategy, since killing all Jews became problematic in a country that lacked industrial labor due to sending nearly all able-bodied men to the front. However, there was not enough food to feed all the laborers. Already early in the war the dilemmas were acute. As American historian Timothy Snyder writes: "One relevant calculation became Jewish productivity versus Jewish consumption of calories. At moments when food seemed more pressing, Jews were killed; at moments when labor seemed more urgent, Jews were spared. In such a dark market, in which Jews were nothing but economic units, the general tendency was towards extermination."[1] Snyder's argument is primarily about the food needed by the Germans, but as we have seen in Chapter 2, by 1943 labor was even more important. In both cases we can see how the German policy toward Jews was never the result of a closed argument but always the result of considerations involving various political and economic factors. Again and again there were new conditions, and with the advance of the Red Army decisions became more and more ad hoc. The Germans wanted to build a new zone at the camp to store and recycle Russian weapons, and for this they needed strong men. This was the result of Himmler's decision in July 1943 to transform Sobibor into a concentration and forced-labor camp that would support German industry and the war effort.

The Prisms of the Narrative

This chapter will focus on the world of Pechersky in the camp and on how he began to organize the uprising. It is important to keep in mind that the camp consisted of many worlds. None of the inmates had an overview of all that happened, and even many Germans did not know. People were aware that there was killing and burning, but many did not know that there were gas chambers, and if they had known, they might have been unable to imagine such horror. Immediately after the uprising, Sobibor was razed, so we have no other way to write its history than on the basis of the testimonies of those who survived the revolt and of the perpetrators who had to defend themselves in court.

Documents made on the basis of testimony are never a straightforward source, and memories change over time. They may seem inaccurate since they contain personal interpretations of evidence stored in the brain, which have adapted and changed. In a letter written in 1965, Pechersky mentioned that he was aware of the shortcomings of memory: "Could we, the former prisoners, count how many towers with machine guns there were? The camp was surrounded by towers, moreover the third camp, where the gas chambers were situated, had its own towers. We had no right to move around the territory of the camp. That is why the information is so contradictory."[2]

Through many survivors' written autobiographical accounts and interviews, I have learned that survival was a combination of luck, fate, and the mental strength not to give up. In most of the narratives, those told to me personally and other accounts stored in archives, the story of the revolt and escape was intertwined with the periods afterward, when the escapees were on the run and when

Sobibor Through the Eyes of Survivors 81

they finally found safety. All writing on Sobibor must be read with awareness that the lens is fragmented by various personal perspectives. People who have described the camp can only look back through the prism of what happened to them after the revolt, while we know that part of the story they tell now is the narrative of other survivors and historians. There is no authentic story about Sobibor, and let us keep in mind: none of the inmates knew what was happening on its vast territory; access to many places was forbidden, and the Germans sought to keep the massive killings secret. Therefore, any description of the camp is bound to be partial, to which other stories have been added, and anyone who makes use of narratives about what happened there must be aware of the impossibility of mastering the total picture. Still, from the many statements we are able to build an image.

Pechersky's strength is not contested; the amazing story of his strength and his survival have been retold many times. We have to admire how he managed to stage such a courageous endeavor in only twenty-two days. In Chapter 2, I wondered how he could have survived Minsk; but to have stayed alert and active in the world of Sobibor is an even more serious proof of unimaginable psychological strength.

For the story of Pechersky's arrival and his initial period in the camp, I have relied mostly on two of the many eyewitness accounts. The first can be found in the aforementioned book of testimonies of Sobibor survivors, as told to Holocaust historian Miriam Novitch, published in 1980.[3] My second source is a 1956 Dutch translation of Pechersky's deposition given in Polish to the Jewish Historical Institute in 1952.[4] The Dutch translator of this account noted that this testimony was probably the only information about Sobibor from that time, apart from Red Cross deportation lists.[5]

However, the uprising was reported in 1943 in *The Voice of Warsaw*, an underground journal.[6] Here and there, I have drawn upon Pechersky's unpublished memoirs from 1972 and several documents he wrote or testimonies he gave, such as a testimony of 1974, when he acted as a witness at the trial of Hubert Gomerski in Hagen.[7] He had to testify in Moscow since he was not allowed to leave the Soviet Union. The resulting document was heavily censored by the KGB.[8]

The most extensive early description of Sobibor is an account in Russian written by Pavel Grigoryevich Antokolsky (1896–1978) and Veniamin Alexandrovich Kaverin (1902–89). This text was published in Russia, and it became a well known and contested document. Much later the text was reprinted in *The Black Book* and made available to English readers.[9] Antokolsky became famous for his writings about the Jewish ordeal during the Holocaust. He became an easy target for later anti-Semitic actions during the time when, according to the dominant ideology, there had been only an anti-fascist fight against the Nazis and special attention to Jews was unwelcome. All who had suffered or had been fighting were homogenized under the name of Soviet civilians, and a special status for cultural or religious minorities was not accepted in the frame of the politics of the time. During the anticosmopolitan campaign after 1948 (which will be discussed in a later chapter) Antokolsky was charged with being a Zionist and a bourgeois nationalist.

82   Sobibor Through the Eyes of Survivors

One important source for the descriptions in *The Black Book* is a deposition from Selma, who met her future husband, Chaim Engel, in the camp. He was Polish, and she was Dutch, and they would become a well-known couple among the survivors of Sobibor. Selma worked in the storehouse where the victims' luggage was sorted, cleaned, and sent to Germany.[10] When I interviewed her in 2010, we spoke a long time about the emotional weight of this kind of work. She had sorted children's clothes and found jewelry, diaries, and letters. She knew the people these objects had belonged to had been murdered, and she felt distressed. It was a privilege to meet her again in 2011. She was one of my interviewees for the project "The Long Shadow of Sobibor," carried out with the support of the Sobibor Foundation in the Netherlands. Wijnberg and Engel escaped the camp together and survived a rough itinerary that ended in New Jersey. Engel had been part of the central group that planned the revolt, and he had protected Selma during their flight.

From the start, survivors were eager to tell the world what they had seen, since, like many survivors of other camps, they believed that testimony was the only way to tell the world what had happened there. Selma Engel's earliest public account of what happened in Sobibor was published on September 22, 1944, in *Amigoe di Curacao*, a journal published in the Dutch colony in the West Indies. This publication pre-dates the liberation of the Netherlands in May 1945. Another early testimony on which *The Black Book* was based is that of Ber (Dov) Moiseevich Freiberg given in 1946.[11] These two testimonies were very early in time. Freiberg's descriptions are graphic, as if only by narrating in this style would he be able to convince his readers. For example, he recalled, "The Gestapo in the camp often kicked children and split open their skulls. They set dogs on defenseless people, and the dogs were trained to tear people apart."[12]

Probably already in 1945 (or maybe 1944), he had testified in Chełm.[13] He described how it had taken him three days to get to Sobibor from Minsk, and he was in the camp for one year. What really happened in the gas chamber and how people were killed, he never saw, although he had been present at the undressing of those who were bound for the gas chamber. The leader of the underground, Leon Feldhendler (like many inmates, Freiberg called him Baruch), had told him about the gassing. Baruch was informed since he had spoken with one of the guards. In his testimony, which was the basis for his autobiographical account published in 1988, Freiberg described the process of killing. According to him, once people understood what was awaiting them, they preferred to try to kill themselves by throwing themselves into the barbed wire. Terrified, they tried to die in a way where they knew what kind of ordeal awaited them.

While some knew about the relentless cruelty of the Germans, no one really knew the details of the gassing except for those who cleaned the gas chambers afterward. These men had no contact with other inmates or with the outside world. In order to prevent the "enemies of the Reich" from knowing about the crimes committed in Sobibor, these men were replaced regularly. Replacement is a euphemism for the fact that, after a few weeks, all the workers working in and around the gas chambers were killed. Those burning the dead met the same fate.

Sobibor Through the Eyes of Survivors   83

The second part of the *Black Book* article on Sobibor is devoted to the revolt, and here Pechersky is at the center of the account. Despite his centrality, the reader does not learn very much about who this man really was or about his feelings. In the interview with Novitch, Pechersky was more emotionally present while he told the story about how he left Minsk to go to Sobibor. The information in the text is very similar to his 1952 deposition. In both texts, Pechersky related that the day of departure began at 4 a.m. in Shirokaya Street. His words convey the misery:

> It was still dark. We had to appear at the *Appelplatz*. In this nightly darkness, we were standing with our shabby belongings waiting for our ration of 300 grams of bread for during the trip. On the square people were swarming, no one dared to say anything; frightened children clung to the skirts of their mothers. It was even more silent than usual, though now no one was flogged; no one was doused with boiling water; there were no sheepdogs.
>
> Commander Wachs, who played with his whip, asserted, "Later they'll bring you to the railroad station. You are going to Germany to work. Hitler will graciously give life to those Jews who in honestly want to work for Germany. You will travel together with your families, and you can bring a few pieces of luggage." . . . On our way to the railway station we passed the ghetto. When they saw us they started to throw bread and other food in our direction.
>
> Part of the large column was people from the ghetto who had been ordered to go to Shirokaya Street the day before. We heard shouts of farewell, crying and wailing. Everyone knew what could happen to us in the near future. Seventy of us were crammed, men, women, and children, into a boxcar. There were no plank beds or benches. There was no question of sitting or lying down. Sometimes one could sit for a moment. It was even hard to stand up. The doors were not opened; the cracks in the blackened windows were sealed off with barbed wire. We did not receive any food, nor anything to drink. No one was allowed to leave the wagon, not even when one needed to go. Four days we were traveling, and we did not know where the train would take us.[14]

This brief impression makes one shiver. The exhausted and doomed inmates of the ghetto, located not far from the Shirokaya prison, saw their loved ones leave to an unknown place in the half-light of early morning. Many had seen people deported to Maly Trostenets, the camp nearby, where they knew gas vans were killing people with their exhaust fumes. But this time the column was moving to the railway station. Where would these people go, and what did the Germans mean by being sent to Germany? No one knew. We are not able to imagine their sadness and despair. To this column of people, the stragglers of the ghetto threw food to show their solidarity and their love, food they themselves needed so much.

Pechersky described how the Russian soldiers left the prison in Minsk as part of a transport of 2,000 people. The train ride from Minsk to Sobibor was long and

84   *Sobibor Through the Eyes of Survivors*

was done in an overcrowded freight car: "In September 1943, we were told that Jews would be transferred to Germany, but that families would not be separated. At 4 a.m., a silent crowd left Minsk, the men on foot, women and children in trucks. We gathered at the railway station where a freight train awaited us. Seventy people were crowded into a boxcar, and after four days we reached Sobibor. We stopped during the night."[15]

According to another survivor, Boris Taborinski, who was on the same transport but in a different freight car, the train ride took four days, and passengers had to endure a fifth night in the car before they were all unloaded. In a 1984 deposition in Donetsk, he said, "Our physical condition was bad."[16] In fact, many died during the trip, and the prisoners began to realize that their fate was sealed.

Eighty Russian Soldiers and a German Miscalculation

Once they arrived in Sobibor, the Germans selected eighty Russian POWs to be kept alive in order to work. This decision would become their biggest mistake, for they had admitted to the camp an extremely hostile group of soldiers who were used to military discipline, had a military command structure, knew how to handle arms, and could obey orders. They were also extremely motivated to fight against fascism, which they viewed as an absolute evil. They were proud to be fighters. As Pechersky put it: "The arrival at the camp made a great impression on the older prisoners; they knew well that the war was going on, but they had never seen the men who were fighting in it. All these newcomers could handle weapons!"[17]

The unloading of the Jews who were to work at the new building site of the camp went smoothly, with no violence. The eighty men easily found their way. Pechersky stated, "In order to maintain the fable [that] Sobibor was a work camp . . . we were sheltered in Camp I, which is where the housing barracks were. There were barracks for men and for women."[18]

> The others were sent in the opposite direction. We know now . . .
>
> Simion Rosenfeld, who became one of Perchersky's close friends, testified in Tel Aviv in 1992 about his early morning arrival at Sobibor:
>
> We sat there 'til 2 or 3 p.m. [Then] . . . three men came up to us. Two were carrying a can, the third, pillow-cases. They came and gave us a lump of bread and a glass of coffee each—this was what we should have had in the morning. We talked with these older inmates. "What kind of camp is this, where are we?" . . . We began to ask where our comrades were, as there had been 2,000 men in the transport. They looked east; smoke was already going up there. "Look," they said, "that's your comrades." And they told us that this was a death camp and that people were rounded up in the shower rooms in batches of 300. Instead of water, gas would come out and they would choke and then be burnt. This here was Sobibor camp, a death factory.[19]

The next morning Pechersky and his group were sent to Camp IV, where they had to build new barracks. He said, "When I became a member of the underground

Sobibor Through the Eyes of Survivors   85

resistance, I was transferred to the joinery, which was in a barracks in that part of the camp." But his descriptions of the camp are not precise and detailed, since, as he said during his 1974 deposition in Donetsk, he was in the camp only twenty-two days. Therefore, he did not have more than a brief experience of the violence of the perpetrators who at that moment were on trial in the German town of Hagen. He did not know the larger picture. Understandably, most memories and depositions contain examples of bestial cruelty and do not provide much information about daily life in the work camp. People lived there, and from their corner they would witness unusual violence. They were not experienced in survival in a world where life and death had become totally arbitrary, and the feeling of fear is dominant in a fog of traumatized memories that haunts them forever. They were upset and terrified, and after the war the traumatization would be transformed from fear to rage and indignation. This violence had become the major theme of a horror movie that began inside their heads.

The Russian POWs arrived the day after a group of Dutch prisoners had been killed as punishment for a failed plan to escape. Thus, new laborers were needed to do their work. There was a need for strong men to carry heavy loads. The eighty Russians who were chosen would become a driving force behind the resistance that until that moment had been scattered and thus ineffective. The underground movement was set up by Polish inmates. The major person among them was Leon Feldhendler, who prior to his deportation to Sobibor had been head of the *Judenrat* (Jewish Council) in his village of Żółkiewka, in the region of Lublin in German-occupied Poland. He was the son of a rabbi and had arrived early in 1943. He was put to work in the provisions warehouse and sometimes had to help out in the *Bahnhofkommando* that was responsible for unloading the trains. Leon Feldhendler was murdered after the end of the war in 1945 in Poland, presumably by Polish anti-Semites.[20]

The Germans thought that the Russians would have the disadvantage of not being able to speak Yiddish or Polish, and therefore they would not be able to contact the partisans surrounding the camp, nor would they be able to find support if they managed to escape. Speaking only Russian, they would live in linguistic isolation. But the Germans did not realize that some of the Russians also spoke Yiddish, and several Polish inmates understood Russian. More importantly, the Germans underestimated the power of the Soviet military hierarchy, which required orders to be executed. Several Russians said later that when Pechersky ordered them to kill, they did not question his command but simply obeyed. In the impressive documentary by French Filmmaker Claude Lanzmann, *Sobibór, 14 octobre 1943, 16 heures*, survivor Yehuda Lehrer is asked if he had ever killed before. His answer is "no." Lerner was not a Russian soldier. But he had no doubt that he had to do so, and so he obeyed.[21] They also wanted to die with dignity while defending themselves against murder.

Pechersky's report to the Jewish Historical Institute on his arrival in Sobibor continues: "The doors opened, and facing us was a poster: *Sonderkommando Sobibor*. Tired, hungry, and broken, we left the wagon. Armed SS officers stood there and *Oberscharführer* Gomerski shouted, 'Cabinet-makers and carpenters with no families, forward!'"

86 *Sobibor Through the Eyes of Survivors*

At first sight Sobibor was set up as quite a rustic place. In sunny weather people could indeed be deceived that they had landed in a countryside where they had to work. But that deceptive veil was soon lifted. In his testimony to Novitch (as well as in other stories), Pechersky related:

> Eighty men were led into the camp and locked in a barracks. Older prisoners informed us about Sobibor. We had all fought in the war and suffered in labor camps, but we were so horrified about Sobibor that we could not sleep that night. Shlomo Laitman, a Polish Jew from Sheroka [Pechersky's spelling], was lying at my side. "What will become of us?" he asked. I didn't answer, pretending to sleep. I couldn't get over my reaction and was thinking of Nelly, a little girl who had traveled in my boxcar and who was, no doubt, dead already. I thought of my own daughter, Elochka.[22]

Pechersky provided factual information about his arrival, life in the camp, and the uprising. Only in this passage did he describe his anxiety and wonder how he could face the death of others; that, and especially the killing of children, would keep him busy for the rest of his life. Only indignation would replace the sadness expressed in the passage above, and the indignation would be transformed into an accusation of cruelty.

Though romanticized, this 1952 document is the most authentic of the early statements. By the time of the Novitch interview more than twenty years later, historians were familiar with Sobibor, and the story had become more formalized. Survivors had spoken with each other; they knew the histories that were told by the others. By then Sobibor had been staged for an imaginary audience that needed to be convinced and to whom knowledge should be passed on. I doubt if Pechersky realized that first night that Nelly was dead. It is clear from many testimonies that some time was needed for people to make a connection between their knowledge about the massive killings and a state in which they were able to accept that people they had known personally had been murdered immediately. That he thought of Elochka is understandable, especially since his desire to see Elochka again was a tremendous incentive to survive. During his entire imprisonment and service in the army, he managed to keep a photo of Ella with him; it's a photo of a young father with a small child. It was shown to me when I visited Rostov-on-Don.

An Unimaginable Crime

The gas chamber was beyond imagination. Thus people kept wondering what had happened to the thousands who were led away. During the interview mentioned in Chapter 1, conducted in 1984 to prepare for a film documentary of Sobibor survivors, Pechersky was asked whether prisoners knew about the gas chambers before they came to Sobibor. He said, "Of course we did not know what happened there, but we knew how they dealt with people and that they killed, we were very aware of that. We believed we would be able to escape during the ride, but we did not manage."

Sobibor Through the Eyes of Survivors 87

Even in the camp, it was difficult to grasp the scale of the crime. Novitch's book includes an account by Hershel Zukerman, who said, "The gas chambers were so well camouflaged that for 10 weeks I believed that my fellow prisoners who came with me were in a labor camp."[23] Zukerman worked in the camp kitchen where food was prepared for the part of the camp where the gassing took place. Ukrainian guards would come to fetch the soup, and Zukerman said he placed a note in a dumpling asking what happened there. He got a reply hidden under an empty mess tin warning that people were gassed, but when he told some inmates about it, they decided to keep the information to themselves so as not to upset others.

Survivor Dov Freiberg stated:

> There were guys who collected the clothes from their transport. And one of them even found the clothes of his own kids. When he pulled them out in some courtyard from a pile that was there outside, he turned to a German . . . He asked him, "Why are the clothes of my kids here?" And he answered, "You don't have to be afraid. All the women who get here are dirty, and they all take their clothes off and go to take a shower. And when they come out of the shower, they get new clothes. Clean, new clothes. And there, in the middle of the forest there are trains. They get on the train and travel."[24]

According to the 1956 translation of Pechersky's deposition, the weather was quite warm when the eighty selected Russian inmates were sent to a long barracks with bunk beds. Others from the transport remained behind the fence, and Pechersky said he never saw any of them again. The men sat down together outside the barracks and talked about their homes and close members of their families. Although Pechersky had not received a single message from his family, he had convinced himself that they had all been evacuated, and therefore he assumed they were safe. He was approached by a Yiddish-speaking Jew whom Pechersky could not understand. He left the conversation to the others and sat down in silence. But he remembered a horrific moment:

> Suddenly I saw grey clouds of smoke, which were coming in our direction and dissolved on the horizon further away. There was an awful smell in the air. I asked what was burning. The Jew warned me not to look. "The bodies of the comrades who arrived with you today are burnt there." I felt a nausea coming up.[25]

Soon after, the Russians decided they had to escape. From the first week on, Pechersky started to make coded notes in undecipherable handwriting.

The Sobibor Facility: Accounts of a Death Factory

There are so many descriptions of Sobibor and the atrocities that occurred there that rehearsing them here may not be useful. Many accounts are repetitive, and the Sobibor narrative has become more uniform over time. The survivors

88   *Sobibor Through the Eyes of Survivors*

have listened to stories of other former inmates; they have spoken at collective remembrance events, combined stories, and added others' tales to their own. Still, despite the passage of decades, the fates of individuals shine through. I was bewildered to listen to these accounts in 2009–10 and to discern diversity among the similarities in the many audio-visual archives collected over a period of seventy years. From many corners, I got a glimpse of the enormous crimes committed in the camp and the underlying state of perpetual terror and violence that left psychological and physical scars.

Slowly, the massive killing of people who arrived integrated into the daily life of the inmates. Some took two weeks to adapt; others described becoming hardened or a steady adaptation to a survival strategy of not thinking and following orders as much as possible. There was no choice; any failure would be punished by beatings, torture, or death. A life-threatening situation could arise when an SS soldier did not like an inmate's face or if a prisoner was simply in the wrong place. The threatening sense that no one knew officially what happened in other places throughout the whole camp aggravated the many anxieties. Everybody observed only from a small corner. But the inmates heard stories and got information while sitting together in the evenings when the long workday was over—evenings that could be disturbed at any time by German or Ukrainian guards who enjoyed interrupting them with violence and torture. New sadistic and deadly games could be invented at any moment, and inmates were at the mercy of their captors. They had to obey when ordered to dance, to imitate animals, and to perform sexual acts, because refusal meant being sent to the gas chamber.

To keep the death camp operating, many jobs had to be done. Victims had to be unloaded from the trains and undressed; their clothes, properties, and shoes had to be packed. One commando shaved the women's hair, and a special group cleaned the gas chambers and burned the bodies. In addition, the workers had to be fed, and the soldiers needed someone to maintain their households. The standard of living of the Germans and their helpers was high, as compensation for being far from home and doing an unsavory job. They also were allowed informally to examine the personal property of the victims and to take what they wanted. We should never forget that the massive killing of Jews also was accompanied by massive collective and individual robbery by the perpetrators.[26]

The highest official and commander-in-chief was Gustav Franz Wagner, who was feared for his cruelty and known for his loud voice. Even the SS men shrank at his shouting. He oversaw the unloading of the trains and ordered the men and women to separate. As survivor Kalmen Wewryk wrote: "Many mothers didn't want to leave their children, so Wagner gave an order to the SS men and Ukrainians standing near him. They ran over and started to rip the children out of the mothers' hands. The children were crying; some of them felt what was in store for them; others were simply terrified of the monstrous murderers."

He also described how the inmates were sheltered:

> We slept on bunks of rough wood, made out of logs. There were four levels of bunks, and three to four Jewish prisoners slept in each bunk. At night

Sobibor Through the Eyes of Survivors 89

people, some of them, deranged and at the end of their sanity, were biting, scratching, tearing, and clawing at each other. I heard many cry from hunger; others shrieked and moaned. The door was locked at night, so little pots were brought as toilets. There was no light at all in the barracks—fire was strictly forbidden—and hundreds of us were packed in there. It ended in a mess, which was punished with beating.[27]

According to Wewryk, the camp authorities kept what was really happening a secret from the Jewish camp workers, although word was passed on secretly. People also were alarmed by the stench. Many kept the illusion they could survive. Wewryk said, "You could tell most Jews one thousand times what was really going on there and they wouldn't believe you. People believe what they want to believe, or hope to believe—anything but the truth, if that truth is horrible enough."[28]

The camp was compartmentalized and, alas for those of us who want to know more about the experience, only the perpetrators were allowed to roam the grounds, and not even all of them. The introduction to Novitch's book includes a description of the camp that she deduced from the stories told to her, which has not changed very much over the years. But the secrecy around the camp and its destruction after the uprising have created a debate among historians and archeologists about the exact locations and numbers of victims. No one doubts the killings there (except a lunatic fringe of negationist historians), but there are contradictions, which are partly rooted in the fact that personal testimonies have been used as "proof" or "evidence" in court because no other information was available. The maps that Pechersky and other inmates drew differ from those made by the Germans who were sentenced by various courts in several trials. But because inmates were not allowed to enter the whole camp, they had to work from partial memories. One can quibble about whether the path between Camp II (undressing) and Camp III (killing) was straight or curved, but these discrepancies matter little to our understanding of the world Pechersky and other prisoners entered after being unloaded from the train.

Who Speaks? First-person and Other Narratives

Apart from earlier and fragmented documentation, Novitch's book is the first to focus systematically on survivors' experiences using testimonies as a source. For many reasons, she was right to do so: there was hardly any information on the experiences of survivors, and the accounts that did exist were spread over Polish reports and newspapers. The most important Soviet accounts were written early on by authors who later fell into disgrace with their government. Articles in official Soviet newspapers were censored and automatically suspected as distortions. More reliable articles appeared in the Yiddish monthly magazine *Sovetish Heymland*, which published parts of Pechersky's memoirs in Moscow in 1973.[29]

Novitch's objective was to document the Jews' resistance and the uprising. She wanted to counter the idea that Jews had merely been victims who had allowed themselves to be slaughtered. Her goal is understandable in the context

90 *Sobibor Through the Eyes of Survivors*

of post-war Europe. Archives had not yet been opened; documentation was often disorganized and unavailable to researchers, left in cellars and on shelves under Communist "protection." Until then (and later), Jews figured as sad figures in court proceedings, where they were permitted to testify only according to juridical procedures. Often attacked by questioning judges and attorneys, they could end up in the position of having to defend themselves.

The most informative books were written much later, such as Yitzhak Arad's 1987 work that placed Sobibor in the context of the Reinhard camps and opened up academic study of the topic.[30] The 1993 book by Dutch historian and survivor Jules Schelvis stands out with its detailed lists of the Dutch who were deported to Sobibor.[31] His book also is the first study to combine personal history with a new kind of historiography in which the subjectivity of personal experience is no longer shunned. Schelvis told me in 2010 that he wanted to know his own place in history and to which cohort of victims he belonged. He was able to find the deportation lists, which have tremendous historical value. Indeed, the administration of the deportations from the Netherlands was so thorough that we still have all the names. (I also found my grandparents' names there and the names of many other members of my family.) Finally, in 2008, German historians Wolfgang Benz and Barbara Distel devoted part of their book on the concentration camps to Belzec, Treblinka, and Sobibor.[32] These books were different from the published autobiographies. Previously, in trials and testimonies, the history and layout of the camp had been described, but what happened was told in different contexts and with different plots. These were books based on historical research and written by people who wanted to go beyond the personal accounts.

Pechersky often described events he could not have known when he was inside the camp, so he must have heard them later from others and interwoven them into his own experience. This problem arises in all such eyewitness reports by survivors. Memories were told many times to audiences with the help of highly personal accounts, but by the time they were published as books, the authors had interwoven their own personal trajectories with other tales. For instance, the book by the youngest survivor, Thomas Blatt—subtitled *A Survivor's Report*— is rife with events he could not have witnessed.[33] Blatt's book is a warning, an accusation, and an effort to tell the world, and is not written in the first person. Nevertheless, such stories are a source of knowledge and allow us to glimpse a world beyond civilized imagination. They are documents of mourning, sadness, and anger. I became again aware of the depths of these accounts when I interviewed Regina Zielinski, who was living in Australia, where she lectured and witnessed in schools. In our 2011 interview, she said this about Sobibor:

> I don't actually know where to begin, but . . . the month of December is a very, very sad month for me, because on the 20th of December we were taken from our slave labor camp, Staw, to a place we didn't even know where we were going, but when we arrived it was Sobibor. . . . We never knew about Sobibor. The whole transport was on a horse-drawn wagon. It was about 700 people of us from the slave labor camp. And when we arrived in Sobibor . . . it was

almost night time—because the days are so short in wintertime in Europe—and the camp was lit like daylight, and a lot of loudspeakers were playing. When we arrived we all had to get off . . . the wagons, [and] they segregated the men and the sons and . . . the women and their daughters. . . . There was a podium there and a very tall SS man was standing on the podium, and he asked who can knit. And my mother pushed me out and she said, "You are a good knitter; step out . . ." There [were] about 12 . . . or 13 of us who stepped out saying that we can knit. And I said to my sister, "How about you?" She said. "I'll stay with mum, because we might be assigned to different work."[34]

Zielinski's account was a sad description of her own history. For hours she went on, talking in a very gloomy, soft tone. The story she told of her brother impressed me: When it was clear their carts were taking them in an unknown direction, her brother said to their mother, 'Mum, let's say goodbye to the night, because we won't see the daylight.' Daylight would never come and therefore there would be no new night. The wording comes from a Polish expression. It means that the world has turned into darkness. Zielinski has retold her stories in many schools, but her words still convey the desperation of those thousands who were forced to walk the same path.

The Camp: A Place of Violence and Death

The Sobibor camp had three parts. First was the forward camp (*Vorlager*) where the entrance gate, the railway ramp, and lodgings for the SS and Ukrainian guards were located, and Camp I, which accommodated those prisoners who were selected to work and where the workshops were located. Camp II was where the majority of the arriving Jews were received. It included the camp area where prisoners were undressed and their property stored for transport to Germany, and where they entered the "tube" connecting the camp to the area where they were murdered. Halfway through the tube, the women's hair was shaved off. Once they had entered Camp II, families did not get a chance to say farewell, although they might meet again inside the gas chamber. Some SS lived in Camp II in a kind of forester's house that was thoroughly fenced off from where the victims passed.

Survivor Dov Freiberg described how fast the separation happened. He and his family wished to leave the crowded, filthy train as soon as possible after the long journey. When they jumped out, they encountered a threatening situation:

Germans in green uniforms, and Ukrainians in black uniforms, whips in their hands, urged us forward. We came to a small gate. On the other side stood a German and a Ukrainian, quickly separating those who entered—women and children were sent to one side and continued to walk straight, men to the right. I walked to the right with my uncle, with the men, and all this happened so quickly that we didn't have a chance to react, to say anything to one another. No one realized exactly what was happening; why were they separating us, to what purpose? The men were instructed to sit on the ground

92   *Sobibor Through the Eyes of Survivors*

in a long-roofed barracks. From where I was, I could see a long line of women and children continuing on their way and disappearing as they left the courtyard. It was early evening. The barracks filled with people. We sat crowded next to each other, in shock, not understanding what was happening. Where had the women and children disappeared to? Perhaps they were on the other side of the courtyard?

Their inquiries received no response. All night they sat in the silence—there were no crying children, where had they gone? The next day Freiberg was chosen to work. His fellow workers told him their job was to gather garments. Someone recognized the clothes of his wife and children, and supposed that people had undressed and walked naked to another place. Freiberg said, "We were gripped by fear. Could it be that they were killing everyone? But we had not heard any shots or explosions."[35] This lack of information about what was happening was a recurring theme in the various eyewitness accounts by Freiberg, of which there are quite a few. In an interview for the Shoah Visual History Archive, he said he heard an engine started, some generator, but he did not know why.[36]

Jules Schelvis wrote, "No one knew what to expect on arrival at camp Sobibor. Even the Polish Jews had no idea, certainly not in the early days."[37] However, Sobibor was known not to be a "normal" labor camp. Schelvis said when he arrived, "We wondered what had happened to the baby in our wagon and to the people unable to walk; and what about the sick and the handicapped? But we were given no time to dwell on these things, and, besides, we were too preoccupied with ourselves."[38] He had no chance to say farewell to his wife Rachel: "Suddenly [she] was no longer walking beside me. It happened so quickly that I had not even been able to kiss her or call out to her."[39] Schelvis was in Sobibor for six hours before being sent away to work, and would search a lifetime for what happened to his people and others from the trains that had left the Netherlands.

The third area, on the northwestern side, was Camp III, which included the extermination area, gas chambers, burial pits, and barracks for the guards and the Jews employed there. Camp III was surrounded by barbed wire, and watchtowers stood at the corners. Unlike in other camps, the area around Sobibor was mined, which resulted in many deaths during the uprising.[40] Sobibor was located on the railway between Chełm and Włodawa, with a special track leading to the camp. From the platform where the freight cars were unloaded, most people were chased to Camp II, but the elderly, the ill, children, and others who were immobile were taken directly to a ditch where Ukrainian guards, supervised by the Germans, shot them with machine guns. It was ironically called the "Lazaret"—a quarantine hospital in English.

Despite the shouting and the violence of their reception at Sobibor, some victims—especially Western Jews—believed they would simply be allowed to wash and dress in clean clothes, and then would be sent to work. Upon their arrival, Western Jews were instructed to write postcards to be sent home. These messages were intended to pacify the inhabitants of the Nazi-occupied Western countries. This was especially the case in the early months of the camp. Prior to having their hair cut off, some of the women asked their "hairdressers" not to cut their hair too short. They supposed the cutting was needed for delousing, but they wanted to be pretty again as soon as possible.

And Then . . .

For everyone, the last moments before entering the gas chambers were always violent: victims were chased, naked, to their deaths. Killing was not enough; some Germans enjoyed torturing the terrified people who by then realized they would be eliminated. Naked prisoners were beaten, scolded, shot at, and attacked by dogs. The turmoil and chaos were intended to give the frightened victims no time to think and to drive them forward.

Polish and Russian Jews were treated more violently than Western Jews. Indeed, in 1942 some Dutch Jews had arrived by a normal passenger train. They were better dressed and gave the impression of wealth and assimilation. But after writing the deceptive postcards they were ordered to write, they suffered the same fate as the other Jews. In a few hours, they were part of the smoke. Certainly by 1943 Jews from the East, who had suffered violence and cruelty in the ghettos and camps, could not be deceived about what was in store for them. The Germans felt physically threatened by people coming from the trains; they could not be fooled and sought in turn their own ways to fight their executioners. After Stalingrad, people knew the Germans were losing the war, and they would do anything to survive until the day the German domination would end. This gave them the courage to stage insurrections.

With a shortage of trains and an immense number of Jews to be killed, the transports on their way through Europe stopped regularly, and sometime hours of waiting ensued. It added to the suffering inside the carriages, where no water and food were provided, and people would slowly pass away from exhaustion. During the winter, many would not arrive at the camps alive. They froze to death. Survivors' memories abound with violent scenes. Kurt Ticho, whose memoirs were published by the museum in Włodawa in 2008, related one experience that took my breath away. Assigned to empty the arriving wagons, he described what he saw when the door was opened:

> We were confronted by a tragic and almost surreal sight. Nude corpses lay on the blood-soaked straw of the cattle cars . . . Atop the decaying bloated bodies stood live, naked people. We tried to lift the corpses to remove them from the cars, but their skin slid from their bodies. They had been dead for some time. We had to put sand on our hands to grasp and carry them to the camp's small railroad that would take them to Camp III for cremation.
>
> Seeing the few who still were alive was even worse than looking at the corpses . . . A distinguished-looking couple, both in their 30s, stepped off. The man was tall, handsome, and well built, with a neat, short black beard. The woman was statuesque. They, like everyone else in the transport, wore no clothing. The woman had blood on her thighs, probably from menstruating.

94 *Sobibor Through the Eyes of Survivors*

Holding hands, the pair walked slowly, with unbelievable dignity, pride and tranquility, toward Camp III, where they would be shot and cremated. I shall never forget the power of this heartbreaking scene: a silent, yet forcefully contemptuous protest against Hitler and his cowardly executioners.[41]

In a deposition made probably in 1945 in Chełm, Samuel Lerer described equally shocking scenes:

> Following the liquidation of the Warsaw ghetto, they brought in a transport that was completely full of naked women, men, children, and also, in several wagons there were dead [bodies]. What the cause of their death[s] was, nobody told [us]. All of the dead were swollen, with outstretched tongues. They mobilized all of the workers in the camp to unload this unit, which numbered forty-something wagons. The dead were placed in the gas chamber [probably, he meant the crematorium]. I shall never forget the picture of how, in one of the wagons, there remained a dead woman with a cut-open stomach. Alongside of her lay a one-year-old child who played with the [dead woman's] intestines.
>
> As soon as people were crammed into the gas chambers, the doors were closed. The people yelled before they suffocated. They struggled to survive. Mothers tried to protect their children, and slowly people choked to death.[42]

The painful process of asphyxiation took fifteen to twenty minutes, as the gas masters peered through a small window to ensure that everyone was dead before the bodies were burned. In the beginning the dead were buried, but when the smell became unbearable and the Germans sought to hide their crimes, they found that burning was more efficient. Later, burning was done in specially designed crematoria, which Ticho witnessed.

A Prisoner in Sobibor

Asked in an interview about his contacts in the camp after his train from Minsk arrived at Sobibor, Rosenfeld said, "Those were camp inmates, who had lived there for seventeen months." He said he had already met Pechersky in Minsk. Pechersky arrived in Shirokaya Street much later than Rosenfeld, who was there since 1941. Rosenfeld said, "He stood out. He was tall, handsome, and sang beautifully." Rosenfeld said any signs of Perchersky's rank as a lieutenant were no longer visible, although others have said he was still recognizable as an officer. I am inclined to believe Rosenfeld for two reasons: first, we may assume that after nearly two years of imprisonment, his clothes had become filthy rags; second, enemy officers were usually shot, so hiding his rank would have been extremely important. According to Rosenfeld, Pechersky not only sang beautifully, but he also told beautiful stories, and was quite an educated person: "The older camp inmates, who had been there for seventeen months, began to observe us in order

Sobibor Through the Eyes of Survivors   95

to find out with whom they could start something. They noticed Pechersky and understood that he was an officer. They organized an underground committee and involved him."

The group from the Minsk camp numbered about eighty to eighty-five people, but Rosenfeld said about twenty were marched to Camp III to replace some who had been shot. They would be used for the tasks around killing and the cleaning of the gas chamber. Thus, he said, "In our camp some sixty or sixty-five Soviet POWs were left. . . . Pechersky's group was in the northern camp, uprooting the woods there."[43]

Pechersky may have stood out among the Russian soldiers as better educated, but others in the camp were also well educated. Pechersky's most important ally was Leon Feldhendler, a cultivated man. Others included Josef Duniec (born December 21, 1912), who had studied chemistry and migrated to France, and Simcha Bialowitz (also born in 1912), who was a pharmacist. Of course, many at the camp had less education, and some, like survivor Toivi Blatt, arrived too young to have received much education at all. The underground resistance movement, which had been created during the past year, had not yet been able to organize coordinated action, and they lacked a leader.

The morning after their arrival, the newcomers arose at five o'clock; at five-thirty, the counting was done, and the column left at six for the northern camp, with the Russian POWs in the lead.

Pechersky mentioned that as many as fifteen of the workers were caned twenty-five strokes as punishment. To be caned was a serious matter. Some would be able to get up afterward; others would be so covered with blood and bruises that they were taken away to the so-called hospital (the "Lazaret"), which meant they would be murdered. On September 23, Pechersky started a diary written in code describing the days' events and making notes about the camp and its custodians.

In the fourth camp, the cries of the Jews driven to the gas chamber could be heard. Throughout his memoirs, Pechersky talked about his shock:

> In the fourth zone, Germans forced us, eighty people who arrived with the last train, to build some huts. That area was located not far away from the third zone, where people were killed, and I could hear the screams and the crying. And I could hear shots killing people. The Germans tried to hide those screams and to prevent the camp population from knowing what was happening inside.[45]

Pechersky told Miriam Novitch that geese were used to camouflage the noise of the victims. Once, he said, when a convoy had just arrived, "We heard a terrible scream from a woman, followed by children wailing 'Mother, mother!' And, as if to add to the horror, the honking of geese joined the human wailing. A farmyard was established in the camp to enrich the menus of the SS men, and the honking of the geese covered the shrieks of the victims."[46] Prisoners were charged with

96 *Sobibor Through the Eyes of Survivors*

driving the geese so their calls would hide the groans and cries of the dying and those awaiting their fate would not hear them. According to testimony from surviving prisoner Eda Lichtman, when one of the geese became ill, Shaul Stark, who had been assigned to care for the geese, was whipped to death. He died crying for revenge.[47] Pechersky said that at one stage he was so shocked he started to tremble: "No, we were not scared, we were overcome with a hostile feeling of helplessness. There we were looking on and we could not help the women and children."[48]

The Other Side: Experienced Perpetrators

When Pechersky arrived, Karl Frenzel was commandant of Camp I and also supervised the work done by Jewish prisoners in Camp II and Camp III, where the killings were carried out, as did commander Erich Bauer. Frenzel had the closest contact with the inmates, and through his network of informants, he knew what was happening on the work floor. In his 1952 statement, Pechersky expressed his repugnance. Pechersky stated that Frenzel was "a German asshole, very well-dressed, wearing gloves, smile on his lips, ice-cold eyes."

There is a famous story about Pechersky chopping wood and his confrontation with Frenzel. On September 26, a Dutch Jew was unable to chop a tree trunk because he was too weak and could not see well. Frenzel beat him severely, and Pechersky, who stood nearby, stopped working to look away. Frenzel ordered Pechersky to finish the Dutchman's work in five minutes or he would be caned twenty-five times. With tremendous effort, Pechersky managed to finish the task, and Frenzel offered him a package of cigarettes—a precious reward. Pechersky refused, later saying, "I could not; physically it was impossible to accept a gift from such an individual." The refusal felt like the right thing, and some sources have said that Pechersky would also refuse food, because "he was not hungry." Some part of the story is probably true, but it is also part of the Pechersky mythology.

The Russian author Lev Simkin wrote, "Unfortunately, judging by publications, nobody who survived Sobibor could not recall the episode with the tree trunk." While preparing his book *Escape from Sobibor*, Richard Räshke spoke with many Sobibor survivors, and nearly all of them displayed skepticism about the story of Pechersky's confrontation with the SS men. I asked Mikhail Lev (see Chapter 1) if the story was true, but he did not give me a direct answer. Instead, he thoughtfully replied, "There was in Pechersky something theatrical."[49] Michael Lev (as he was called in Israel) loved Pechersky and was hardly able to say anything unpleasant about him. His later life was devoted to the memory of the leader of the revolt. But he could not swallow this story.

However, Simkin did recognize that it is difficult to determine whether the story actually took place or something entirely different occurred. But surely something happened, and Pechersky managed to draw attention to himself within a week of his arrival. As the Germans and Ukrainians were busy unloading trains and sending people to the gas chambers, Pechersky was making a mental map of the camp. Once the winter snows began to fall, fleeing would be much harder because the escapees' tracks would be more visible, he noticed. At that time, Pechersky's closest friend was Shlomo Laitman, the previously mentioned communist who had taken refuge in Minsk in 1939. According to Pechersky, Laitman had authority in cases of conflict.

The inmates had to be careful to act in total secrecy. They were controlled all the time, and at this stage of the war the Germans feared resistance, especially with the help of the partisans. Of all these Germans, the most hated was Gustav Wagner, about whom the historian of Sobibor Marek Bem wrote:

> The most feared and hated figure of the camp personnel was Gustav Wagner, the non-commissioned officer addressed by his equals as '*Spiess*' ('*Sergeant*'). It was he who created a formidable penal commando (*Strafkommando*). Wagner was not only the most brutal but also the most cunning and the most intelligent SS man in Sobibór. He made regular inspections of the prisoners' barracks. Indeed, he even had the prisoners remove the barracks' floor planks to check whether they had hidden there any weapon or whether they were digging a tunnel to prepare an escape. He was always very observant. Unlike the other SS men, Wagner was completely unpredictable, and sometimes he would beat prisoners for no earthly reason.[50]

The camp workers had more to do with the hated Karl Frenzel, an expert in killing who was later sentenced to life imprisonment. He was responsible for Camp I and was in charge of labor. He was a daily nuisance, and one did best to avoid him. A loyal party member, Frenzel had applied for special service in the military through his SA unit, but instead was assigned to Action T4, the Nazis' program to kill people with disabilities. Frenzel reported to Columbus House in late 1939, where he and other T4 recruits (as the unit was called) were checked for political reliability and then shown a film on the supposed degeneration of the disabled. He worked first in the laundry, then as a guard at Grafeneck Castle, and later at the Hadamar Euthanasia Center. His experience in killing disabled people would prove useful later in the extermination camps.

Indeed, the massive gassing of people at Sobibor was only part of a larger policy to isolate and then destroy Jews. When Pechersky arrived, the systematic killing had found a script as the result of years of experimentation. The authorities knew what kind of people to select to supervise the task, and over the years they had created a cohort of willing helpers. Later research into this group revealed a network of people who supported each other, and friendships developed among those with whom they could share their secret. For a long time, the larger public was not ready to know and accept killing on such a massive scale, and when they were, the facts had to be kept secret because Germany was losing the war. The network was called T4.[51]

In September 1943, the *Gauleiter* of Vienna, Odilo Globocnik, who had started the Belzec extermination camp, was in charge of Sobibor. Top officials of the

98 *Sobibor Through the Eyes of Survivors*

T4 program had visited him, and he probably initiated the disguising of the gas chambers as shower rooms, proposing to exterminate Jews in assembly-line fashion. The gassing facilities that Globocnik established at Belzec used carbon monoxide, as the T4 program had done, and were designed by T4 program veterans assigned to Globocnik. Pechersky later testified against Globocnik in Donetsk. Experimental killings were carried out from the beginning of April 1942.

Pechersky summarized how the Germans behaved in the camp: "With their boots they stepped on babies; they beat them on their heads; they incited mastiffs against humans; animals tore large pieces of meat from the human bodies. If one of us became ill, he was immediately finished by the Hitlerites."[52] He described one instance in which the emission of gas in the packed gas chamber failed to start, and realizing their fate, the desperate victims destroyed the door in an attempt to escape. But those who managed to get outside were shot by the SS.

Men from Ukraine trained as guards for the camps in nearby Trawnik helped the SS.[53] These non-Jewish POWs had been forced to choose between life and death; life meant being trained in cruelty and becoming a helper in guarding and killing the Jews and others sent to Sobibor.[54] The underground resistance doubted if these Ukrainians could be involved in a possible escape. Sometimes there was close contact, because some of the Trawniki prisoners also hated the Germans. (In Chapter 4, I describe them wrestling with this dilemma.) Like all desperate people, the Trawniki men were afraid and tried to perform well in their captors' eyes, which meant exerting extreme violence, as they tried to make as much profit as possible and improve their lives. In this world, violence was rampant and death was close at hand. The degree of violence and the massive factory of death was shocking to the Russian soldiers. Every day trains arrived with thousands to be murdered, and those inmates unloading the trains had to immunize themselves against the sufferings of others, in the knowledge that any hesitation would lead to their own deaths.

Not Only Jews, But Mostly Jewish Victims: Mythologies

There were probably also non-Jews killed in Sobibor, since there are several reasons to assume that Sobibor was a place where not only Jews were killed. From early on, the Jewish survivors wanted it to be recognized that they were victims of racial politics. They had done nothing wrong and were picked from their houses and neighborhoods to be deported and murdered. In the former Communist world the specific suffering of Jews during the war was a taboo subject, so they could not speak out, nor were they heard in a world where all experiences were enveloped in the tale of the Great Patriotic War of the Soviet people who stood up collectively against barbarism. In this discourse, all fates were homogenized, and the Jewish victims became civilians persecuted like many others. This was the case in Russia and Poland.

In a 2009 interview, survivor Thomas Blatt told me that many Polish nationals especially had not come to terms with the way their country had stolen goods from Jews and helped to kill them; they had not come to terms with history. As he said: "The Poles didn't want the Jews. The Jew was a competitor in business and many aspects. So . . . I want to say it plainly: They were happy that their dream, Poland without Jews, [was] finally coming true. So they [say] 'til now, many Poles do, that one good thing that Hitler has done is they cleaned up Poland from Jews." Blatt described visiting Sobibor in the 1970s when signboards made no mention of the extermination of Jews. Rather, he said, "They speak of Czechs— so many Czechs they killed, so many Poles were killed—it was difficult to find a sign that described the killing of Jews."[55]

The reaction was that survivors, and a new kind of memorial culture close to the survivors, emphasized the killing of Jews, and, ironically, the deaths of non-Jews faded away. In the Minsk archives, where several historians have studied the deportation trains to Sobibor, the assumption is that non-Jews were also on the trains. Samuel Lerer stated in 1945 that "gypsies" were killed in Sobibor.[56] During hearings in Kiev regarding the lawsuit of 1962, Pechersky testified as an eyewitness: "It should be noted that not only Jews arrived at Sobibor. Several Russians arrived . . . with our car and they were also exterminated in the gas chambers. Such cases happened in other troop trains, because in the work camp near Minsk we were kept together with the Russians."[57] Lerer mentions that several Polish prisoners arrived blindfolded, and we can assume they were partisans operating in the surroundings.[58] There were three hypothetical reasons to mention the inclusion of non-Jews: first, it can well have been the case; second, the narrator included them for political motives, seeking to not over-emphasize the Jewish experience; and third, people of mixed Russian-Jewish origin were often listed as Russians in documents. I assume there were also non-Jews, but we don't know how many.

Psychological Survival and the Russian Soldiers

Since this is a chapter about Pechersky and his survival, I want to mention the resilience with which he survived psychologically. Not only Pechersky, but all those involved in the uprising, withstood the psychological terror aimed at stripping the inmates of their personal identity. Not all inmates were eager to join the rebellion, and several refused to escape; they felt safer staying behind, since they lived in the conviction that all those who fled would be caught. But for many there was optimism in the bonding with each other, strengthened by the knowledge that the Red Army was coming nearer. The arrival of the Russian POWs changed the psychological mood of the inmates, many of whom had managed miraculously to survive for more than a year in the camp. Wewryk, who wrote about the early days after the Russian POWs arrived, has described the effect of the arrival of the Russians. He admired Pechersky and said that without this hero, he would not have survived:

> The Germans had succeeded in depriving us of our self-image as human beings, with the dignity that that entails. That was why the revolt . . . [that] came later was so important. Whether we would live or die, we would at least regain our dignity as human beings.
> Many times big transports of Jews arrived from Russia. These Jews were unlike their Dutch or German brothers in that they knew where they were

100   Sobibor Through the Eyes of Survivors

going. They had no illusions, so they resisted. They would throw themselves on the Germans when they were unloaded from the trains, and they had resisted before they were caught. So, after a while, the Germans instituted a "refinement": the Jews in the Russian transports were moved completely naked to Sobibor. They undressed them to make their escape more difficult; being naked, those Jews couldn't conceal weapons in their clothing. Some tried to bolt from the unloading ramp and fight the SS, but without weapons their cause was utterly hopeless.

That I am alive today to write this memoir is [because of] an event that took place in September 1943: the arrival at Sobibor of Aleksandr Pechersky (Sasha). Sasha, a Soviet-Jewish prisoner-of-war, had been shipped to Sobibor from a Minsk work camp. He was an educated man, and had been an officer in the Red Army. When his transport came to Sobibor, the Germans asked if any of the prisoners were "*Schreiners*" or "*Tischlers*" (carpenters or cabinet-makers) and Sasha, a tall man, said that he was a carpenter. Although he knew nothing about carpentry, he saved his life by lying at that moment. The Germans took him and some others out of the mass of arriving prisoners doomed to death, and threw them into our barracks. Sasha had thrown away his officer's papers and insignia, because had the Germans known that he was a Soviet officer they would have disposed of him immediately. The Germans killed educated people and officers first, with the political commissars.[59]

Several testimonies mention a kind of psychological resistance, which was a sign that the prisoners did not want to give in and believed that soon the Germans would be defeated. The guards and SS men knew that their days were numbered. Sometimes attempts to escape were successful, and even the thought of this possibility restored people's identities, which the Germans so eagerly wanted to destroy. As Sobibor survivor Esther Raab said in an interview for the U.S. Holocaust Memorial Museum:

We were so deep in the woods that nobody could even know that something was going on there. So, we started thinking about an uprising and about revenge, and I think that kept us going. Although it was a silly thought, . . . that gave us the courage to survive, to do, because we planned, we planned. The plans weren't worth much, maybe five cents in the beginning, but we planned and we saw ourselves outside, and we saw all the Nazis killed, and this kept us going.[60]

During that same interview Raab recalled talking with Feldhendler, the other leader of the revolt and a major organizer of the underground movement, about a planned escape:

He said there must be a way. And we tried, we started planning, and going to a meeting, where only a few went because you had to be very careful. . . . Coming back, you felt like you're doing something, you're planning something, you're trying something. If you'll succeed it would be wonderful. If not, you'll get a bullet in the back—it's better than going to the gas chambers. I promised myself I'll never go to the gas chambers. I'll start running, I'll start—do they have to waste a bullet on me? And we started organizing and talking, and it kept us alive again, you know, that maybe we'll be able to take revenge for all those who can't.[61]

Raab's friend Zelda Metz told Novitch: "We all wanted to escape and to tell the world about the crimes of Sobibor. We believed that if people knew about it, Nazi Germany would be wiped out. We thought that if mankind knew of our martyrdom, we would be admired for our endurance, and revered for our sufferings."[62]

Marek Bem described how life in the camp was completely isolated from the outside world, not only in a physical sense, but also emotionally:

> According to the survivors, for the prisoners the past now seemed so distant that they had the impression that it had simply never existed. They were exhausted physically and mentally, and thus lived on instinctively. They knew they could die at any moment, and they even hoped that this would be so. At the end of each day, the prisoners were amazed to realize that they were still alive. Their health kept on deteriorating; they were beaten every single day. Nonetheless, they somehow knew how to cope. For example, while laboring, survivors' statements say, they kept a watchful eye on the German who happened to be supervising them on that particular day. Any time the German turned his back, they stopped doing anything, but when he looked back at them, they started working fast and energetically. In this way, they avoided a flogging.
>
> Most of the prisoners suffered also because they felt alone and lonely. However, even in such tragic circumstances, people managed to make friends, later betrayed them, fell in love with somebody and then walked out on them, like in real life. Post-war accounts speak of a famous case of a Jewish prisoner, a barber, whom the Germans tolerated due to his exceptional professional skills and abilities.[63]

Despite all the killing, many in the camp survived and managed to rebuild a life where ties, friendships, and emotions existed. There were evenings with singing and even sometimes dancing. Such "normal" daily behavior prevented the disappearance of the personality, and the stories about camp life and emotional ties are a miracle. Yet amazingly little research has been done into this kind of mechanism for survival. Although life had become arbitrary, there was still some semblance of the world the inmates had known before. That world of long ago had been a world of decency and morality, of mutual help, comradeship, and love. That story is seldom told, and it is not a story that in its lack of sparkle is welcome in a world that is outraged by the immensity of the crimes and wants to convey it. In *The Survivor: An Anatomy of Life in the Death Camps*, psychologist Terrence Des Pres explained,

> Primarily survivors stress the negative side of concentration camp existence because their accounts are governed by an obsessive need to "tell the world" of the terrible things they have seen. This determines not only the kind of

102   *Sobibor Through the Eyes of Survivors*

material they select to record, but also the emphasis they give it. As a witness the survivor aims above all to convey the otherness of the camps; their specific inhumanity. . . . Acts of care and decency seem so out of place in the camps that survivors themselves are perplexed. . . . What impressed survivors most indelibly were death, suffering, terror, all on a scale of magnitude and monstrosity not to be faced without lasting trauma . . .[64]

Still, survivors' accounts regularly include small deeds of courage and resistance, of help and mutual care, but in the larger picture, the image of viciousness and death grows to such enormous intensity that all else—any sign of elementary humanity—pales to insignificance.[65] Des Pres argues that once the will to live had been regained, it was constantly undermined by chance and despair.[66] Those who survived were the ones who could resist the moral and physical mechanisms of disintegration.[67] The basis for this resistance was the ability to mobilize positive values of life against the fear of death common to all human beings.[68] The individual's capacity to preserve essential values allowed for a distance between the self and experience. Des Pres argued that survivors maintained this distance by means of exceptional detachment, an idea that psychoanalyst Bruno Bettelheim has attacked, warning against the idea that survivors were exceptional people.[69]

Pechersky remembered vividly that everything was done to destroy the prisoner's personality. According to him, not to give in to the destruction of one's personal identity was a form of resistance. Suicide, or to give up and thus to be killed, was an option many considered. To resist the drive for death in Sobibor was difficult and challenged the destructive character of the camp, where one had to be constantly on guard. At any moment, random punishment or killing could be administered without warning. Some custodians were delighted to torture and kill, especially when they were in a bad mood. To avoid beatings, flogging, attacks by specially trained dogs, and worse, the best strategy was to keep to one's self and not draw attention.

Human Bonding and Hope for a Better World

Still, Pechersky managed to find friendship, loyalty, and solidarity; he was able to inspire others and to act not only for himself but for the collective. As Austrian psychiatrist Viktor E. Frankl wrote: "Everything can be taken from a man but one thing: the last of the human freedoms—to choose one's attitude in any given set of circumstances, to choose one's own way."[70] For inmates who were totally at the mercy of the whims of their torturers, a sense of inferiority and subsequent loss of identity was common. But according to Frankl, inner strength determines whether one will overcome suffering and survive. One important asset is having a goal, which, if not resistance, is certainly a vision of life after the camp and in the future.

In the scarce literature, we can find some factors that could have made a difference, but predominant is what psychologist Hilde O. Bluhm, in her studies of the mental and psychological hardware needed for survival, called the anarchic power of accident.[71] While Frankl pointed to inner strength and proof of one's own experience, Bluhm looked for individual defenses in her systematic study of twelve autobiographical accounts of camp survivors. She noted that the first days after arrival were the hardest—the initial shock, the unexpected, and the change to a regime of terror. According to Bluhm, at the moment of the first selection, some were more fit for survival than others. For those who could get through the first weeks, the chances of survival rose rapidly.[72] But inmates needed additional mental energy, which meant, she wrote, "they had to withdraw from other, non-vital, functions, particularly from those which maintained contact with the outer world." All attention was shifted to the self. Bluhm cited a statement from Ernst Wiechert's autobiography:

> It was the sensation of an ever-growing coldness that spread gradually from deep within until it filled his entire being. It was as if the life he had lived up to now, and his world, was freezing to numbness in this chill. As though he was gazing through a thick sheet of ice at distant things. And in this distance moved the noiseless and unreal spirits of his past: the people he had loved, his books, his hopes and plans . . . he felt a crack running through God's image, a crack that would not ever heal.[73]

Frankl described this state as apathy—the mental regime shifted to a kind of mental emergency. Bettelheim called this mental state "depersonalization."

Most important, Bluhm described the role of a group leader and a group ideal that represented a substitute for the father, who exercised a remarkable influence on others. Pechersky became such a person. His friends indeed felt they were responsible to him—that they had to report to him and listen to him—and doing so made them feel better, even protected. It gave strength, as Bluhm wrote:

> Belonging to a political group whose ideology was strictly opposed to Nazism, taking part in its secret activities in the camp, managing to keep up the connection with group members outside the camp—these were some of the most important object relations the prisoner was able to maintain. Such activities allowed a certain amount of emotional discharge in a socially approved way . . . increasing its chances to act in harmony with its old ego-ideals.[74]

Shamai Davidson was a major Israeli therapist who studied the mechanisms of survival in a concentration camp.[75] He died in 1992 and his work, posthumously edited by Israel W. Charny, is the most extensive study of how the prisoners of the Germans could have survived at all. Pechersky and other Russian POWs fit his image amazingly well. According to Davidson, preserving human awareness and a sense of self was crucial; these could be stimulated by human reciprocity. As he put it: "Interpersonal bonding, reciprocity, and sharing were an essential source of strength for adaptation and survival of many of the victims. Apart from limited opportunities for the starving inmates to share their sparse food rations, it was their interpersonal support that sustained their motivation to carry on with the struggle to live."[76]

104   Sobibor Through the Eyes of Survivors

Little systematic study has been done of social bonding in concentration camp life, but Davidson noted that bonds between people were crucial. As we have seen, Pechersky had such bonds with his fellow POWs from Minsk. He knew that at some point the war would end, and he had learned that he had to stay together with his friends. The Russians were a group; they helped each other, and deference to the officer was part of the group interaction. Davidson also concluded that such groups often had a collective political or religious orientation.[77]

During the preparations for their revolt, the Russian POWs' bonds were strengthened, since secrecy was the only way to succeed. In later stages of the preparations, other inmates helped to hide Pechersky and took care that he got easier work so he would be more or less invisible to the Germans. This measure allowed him the space to plan systematically. He relied on some loyal Russian friends and others, including Feldhendler, who had become convinced that fighting was the only option. Individual efforts to escape had failed, and as a Russian soldier, Pechersky wanted to fight the enemy. He was amazed that a revolt had not yet been organized.

Above all, the Russians were a circle in themselves, with an identity averse to fascism, a common language, jokes, and pride. They would challenge the Germans' peace of mind, as Pechersky told Novitch in his 1956 testimony:

> October 10: I saw an SS officer with his arm in a sling. I was told it was Greischutz, back from his leave. He had been wounded in a Russian air raid.[78] Tsibulski proposed: If Frenzel orders us to sing, we shall greet Greischutz with the song of the aviators, singing aloud! Excellent, we'll sing aloud today! And so it happened. Oberscharführer Frenzel counted us speedily and ordered departure. The Russians had to sing. Tsibulski blinked in our direction and we sang, "We Soviet men able to do great deeds. . . ." And when we left the gate, we marched and sang: "Higher, ever higher our birds will fly. . . ." Our aviators march song had offended Greischutz immensely. Excited, with blood-shot eyes, he ran to us and started to lash out . . . We bowed to avoid the beating, but we did not stop the singing.
>
> On September 28, one week after I arrived at the camp, I knew everything about the hell of Sobibor. I was informed of the exact place occupied by the personnel, the guards and the arsenal.[79]

Later, during preparations for the uprising, Pechersky became acquainted with Luka, the daughter of Germans who had fled to Amsterdam, and according to what he and others have written, their relationship may have been close, but apparently it was not a sexual affair. She guarded the rabbits the Germans liked to eat. She had seen naked people passing through the *Schlauch* since there was an opening between the wooden shelves and branches, and she told Pechersky about it. Luka has been described as an eighteen-year-old woman from Holland, but she was actually a German, whose real name was Gertrude Poppert-Schönborn. She was born on June 29, 1914 in Dortmund, Germany, so when Pechersky met her, she would have been twenty-eight. Still, he described her as eighteen years old, and perhaps we'll never know if this was really her. Some authors and film-makers have romanticized their relationship. Most mention Luka and her usefulness in the preparations for the revolt. More than two years had passed since Pechersky had left his family, and he did not know what had become of his wife. What is certain is that he enjoyed sitting with Luka and that he found some consolation in her friendship, which was a sign of his wish to live. When the revolt started she gave him a shirt, which he kept during the remaining years of the war and which is still part of his heritage in Rostov-on-Don. Indeed, there were examples of some people in the work camp who fell in love, which was another part of the fight against dehumanization.

The Tide Turns

When Pechersky arrived on September 18, the Germans were losing the war. Trains through Belarus and eastern Poland were crowded with masses of wounded soldiers on their way to treatment in Germany, and this was a kernel of hope for the Russian soldiers' morale. They had seen the wounded, and they knew they had to outlive the war. For the Germans, there was no longer any safe place. If they sought respite at home, they found their German cities were being bombed daily, and destruction and scarcity were the rule. As we saw, the tide was turning. There was hope for the prisoners to survive, and they wondered how fast freedom would come. Would it be in time? Would they survive?

In their turn, the German guards knew about the massive death and starvation of German soldiers in Russia. The *Ostfront* (Eastern front) had changed from a place of victory into a field of defeat, slaughter, and starvation. They did not want to be there, so they continued their duty in the camp, as did the Ukrainian guards, all in the hope of surviving.

To be a guard in Sobibor was relatively safe, and certainly less dangerous than the massive slaughter on the Eastern front.

Notes

1 Timothy Snyder, *Black Earth: The Holocaust as History and Warning* (London: The Bodley Head, 2015), 201.
2 Aleksandr Pechersky to Reuven Ainszstein, 12 February 1965, YIVO New York folder 144, RG116-Poland.
3 Miriam Novitch, *Sobibor, Martyrdom and Revolt* (New York: Holocaust Library, 1980).
4 *Report to the Jewish Historical Institute Warschau, January—June 1952.* Willem A. Maijer translated this work in 1956 for the Rijksinstituut voor Oorlogsdocumentatie. He knew the story from the Polish Jew Henryk Lewy, who had lived in eastern Amsterdam, probably in the Jewish neighborhood.
5 NIOD dossier 804.
6 *Voice of Warsaw*, 16 November 1943, publication of the Warsaw Committee of the Polish Workers' Party (N73/82, 16 November 1943), information on the uprising of Jews in Sobibor, which also reported that the liquidation of the camps proceeded very quickly. The original of this handwritten document bears the stamp of Yad Vashem and Numbers M-141 file 191 20.

106   *Sobibor Through the Eyes of Survivors*

7 In 1948 Gomerski was sentenced to life in prison, and was released in 1972 because of poor health. In 1974 he was sentenced to another fifteen years.

8 *Protokol Witness Statement 17.07.1974*, authorized translation from Russian to German, available at the Netherlands Institute for War Documentation, collection Jules Schelvis, nr. 804.

9 Ehrenburg and Grossman, *The Black Book*, 487–500.

10 Ad van Liempt, *Selma, de vrouw die Sobibor overleefde* (Laren: Verbum, 2010). See also: Ann Markham Walsh and Saartje (Selme) Wijnberg Engel, *Dancing Through Darkness: The Inspiring Story of Nazi Death Camp Survivors, Chaim and Selma Engel* (Portland, ME: Dunham Books, 2012).

11 Dov Freiberg, *To Survive Sobibor* (Jerusalem: Gefen Publishing House, 1988). I have used the English translation dated 2007. Julian Hirszhaut, YIVO, New York, RG 104 Series I | Sobibor, 25 July 1945 (or maybe 1944).

12 Ehrenburg and Grossman, *The Black Book*, 489.

13 Hirszhaut, YIVO, n.p.

14 Novitch, *Sobibor*, 89–90.

15 Manuscript Aleksandr Pechersky, 1972, Yad Vashem.

16 *Translation of Eyewitness Account of Boris Israelewitsch Taborinski*, Donetsk, 14 March 1984, deposited at the Netherlands Institute for War Documentation, nr. 804.

17 Novitch, *Sobibor*, 91.

18 Deposition 1974, German translation, 3–4.

19 Interview Semion Rozenfeld, Yad Vashem archives, test 6590, rec group 3, interviewer Bedet Alperovitch, translation P. van Woerd, 1992.

20 We will never know with certainty because he was shot through the door of his apartment. Generally it is assumed that he was shot by right-wing Poles. Isaac Kowalski, *Anthology of Armed Jewish Resistance 1939–1945* (New York: Jewish Combatant Publishing House, 1985), 245.

21 Paul Gomberg, "Can a Partisan Be a Moralist?" *American Philosophical Quarterly* 27:1 (1990): 71–79. Gomberg surveys the ethical questions that arise in such cases.

22 Novitch, *Sobibor*, 90.

23 Ibid., 107.

24 Interview Dov Freiberg, SVF 7829, cassette IV.

25 *Report to the Jewish Historical Institute Warschau*, 5.

26 Jan Tomasz Gross and Irena Grudzinska Gross, *Golden Harvest: Events at the Periphery of the Holocaust* (New York: Oxford University Press, 2012).

27 Kalmen Wewryk, *To Sobibor and Back: An Eyewitness Account*, ed., transc. and trans. from the Yiddish by Howard Roiter (Montreal: Concordia University, 1999), 61.

28 Ibid.

29 See Franziska Bruder, *"Hunderte solcher Helden": Der Aufstand jüdischer Gefangener im NS-Vernichtungslager Sobibor* (Münster: Unrast, 2013); also the writings by Valentin Tomin and A. Sinelnikov, *Vozvrashchenie nie zhelatelno* (Moscow: Molodaya Guardia, 1964), which are well known and of an earlier date. Their articles are more fiction than history.

30 Yitzhak Arad, *Belzec, Sobibor, Treblinka: The Operation Reinhard Death Camps* (Bloomington: Indiana University Press, 1987).

31 Jules Schelvis, *Sobibor: A History of a Nazi Death Camp* (Oxford and New York: Berg Publishers, 2010).

32 Wolfgang Benz and Barbara Distel, eds., *Der Ort des Terrors: Geschichte der nationalsozialistischen Konzentrationslager*, 9 vols. (München: Verlag C. H. Beck, 2008).

33 Thomas (Toivi) Blatt, *Sobibor: The Forgotten Revolt* (Issaquah: H.E.P., 1996).

34 Interview with Regina Zelinski by Selma Leydesdorff, Adelaide, December 2011.

35 Dov Freiberg, *To Survive Sobibor*, 192.

36 Interview Dov Freiberg, SVF 7829, cassette III
37 Freiberg, *To Survive Sobibor*, 66.
38 Ibid., 76.
39 Ibid., 77.
40 Novitch, *Sobibor*, 24.
41 Ticho, *My Legacy*, 106–107.
42 RG 720—Julian Hirszhaut Papers, File 260, YIVO Institute for Jewish Research Archives (New York, NY); testimony of Lerer, Shmuel; p. 6 appears on the file but it is actually p. 5.
43 Yad Vashem file 03 6590 3740257.
44 If tomorrow war comes, if the enemy attacks
If dark forces come up,
All the Soviet people, like one man
Shall rise for the free Motherland
45 Testimony Pechersky, 1972.
46 Novitch, *Sobibor*, 91–92.
47 Ibid., 56.
48 Letter, NIOD file 804_19_0004, *Für sie kann es keine Vergebung geben.*
49 Simkin, *Half an Hour of Retribution*, in his chapter "Myths and Bread" (71–79), deals extensively with the way this story has been passed on. It was used in Soviet literature; it fit the ideology of that time. Perhaps some of it is true, but because the story was used ideologically to bolster the idea that the Soviets had a higher morale than others, we should be careful to believe it all.
50 Bem, *Sobibor Extermination Camp*, 115.
51 Sara Berger, *Experten der Vernichting: Das T4-Reinhardt Netzwerk in den Lagern Belzec, Sobibor und Treblinka* (Hamburg: Hamburger Edition, 2013).
52 Pechersky 1956 in translation, 16.
53 For the organization of the camp, see Arad, 32–34.
54 Peter Black, "Foot Soldiers of the Final Solution: The Trawniki Training Camp and Operation Reinhard," *Holocaust and Genocide Studies* 25:1 (2011): 1–99.
55 Interview Thomas Blatt, Warsaw, 15 December 2009.
56 RG 720—Julian Hirszhaut Papers, File 260, YIVO.
57 *EXAMINATION RECORD, City of Kiev, 11 August 1961, Investigator of the Investigation Department of KGB of USSR*, First Lieutenant Loginov interrogated as a witness.
58 RG 720—Julian Hirszhaut Papers, YIVO, n.p.
59 Kalmen Wewryk, *To Sobibor and Back*, 92.
60 USHMM 1992, interview Esther Raab, RG-50.042*0023, interview by Sandra Bradley.
61 Ibid.
62 Novitch, *Sobibor*, 131.
63 Bem, *Sobibor*, 187.
64 Terrence Des Pres, *The Survivor: An Anatomy of Life in the Death Camps* (New York: Oxford University Press, 1976), 98–99.
65 Shamai Davidson, "Human Reciprocity Among the Jewish Prisoners in the Nazi Concentration Camps," in *The Nazi Concentration Camps* (Jerusalem: Yad Vashem, 1984), 555–572.
66 Des Pres, *The Survivor*, 90.
67 See also Bruno Bettelheim, *Surviving and Other Essays* (New York: Knopf, 1952), and Ernst Federn, "The Terror as a System: The Concentration Camp; Buchenwald as It Was," *Psychiatric Quarterly Supplement* 22 (1948): 52–86.
68 See Selma Leydesdorff, "The State Within the State: An Artisan Remembers His Identity in Mauthausen," *Studies on the Audio-Visual Testimony of Victims of the Nazi Crimes and Genocides* 10 (2004): 103–117.

108 *Sobibor Through the Eyes of Survivors*

69 See for the long debate about the mechanisms for survival: Lawrence L. Langer, *Versions of Survival: The Holocaust and the Human Spirit* (Albany: State University of New York Press, 1982).
70 Viktor E. Frankl, *Man's Search for Meaning* (London: Random House, 2004), 75.
71 Hilde O. Bluhm, "How Did They Survive? Mechanisms of Defense in Nazi Concentration Camps," *American Journal of Psychotherapy* 53:1 (1999): 96–122, here p. 98. The original study was made in 1948.
72 Ibid., 100.
73 Ernst Wiechert, *Forest of Death* (New York: Greenberg, 1947), originally published in German, 101.
74 Ibid., 119.
75 Shamai Davidson, *Holding on to Humanity* (New York, London: NYU Press, 1992).
76 Ibid., 123.
77 Ibid., 133.
78 Novitch, *Sobibor*, 93.
79 *Report to the Jewish Historical Institute Warschau*, 30–32.

4 Resist and Tell the World*

Sobibor was sealed off from its immediate surroundings geographically, but the camp was not isolated from the rest of the world. The hordes of people transported by train came from all parts of Europe, many of them from Poland and Byelorussia. They brought news: about the defeated Germans in Stalingrad and the victory of the Red Army; about the sadness in the ghettos of Poland, France, Holland, and Byelorussia; and about the suffering and slaughter of Jews. Many knew about the ghetto uprising and the ensuing slaughter in Warsaw, since most ghetto fighters who were not shot immediately were transported to Treblinka and Sobibor to be killed in the gas chambers of Operation Reinhard. All these events and news about the progress of the war seeped through to the inmates of the work camp. The inmates hoped they would make it to the end of the war and be free again. But many doubted.

In addition to news that came with the new arrivals, messages were sometimes passed on by Ukrainian guards who feared severe punishment if the Germans were defeated and therefore wanted to discuss or negotiate their uncertain futures. One way to negotiate was to cheat the Germans and help the Jews. Another reason they wanted to help Jewish inmates was that the prisoners who sorted the goods that belonged to new arrivals were sometimes able to steal liquor and much-needed food. They also found money, which they used to bribe the guards. Some Ukrainians started to talk to the inmates and no longer beat them as much as they were expected to do. Some even became friendly. In turn, the workers learned about bold Jews who had jumped and escaped from the trains, and there were stories about others who had resisted. Ainzstein mentioned that of the two thousand Jews from Jasinówka deported to Treblinka on January 25, 1943, about three hundred escaped by jumping from the train. Although they were betrayed by the local population, fifty-eight survived. The authorities were disturbed that nearly all the young men had jumped.[1] It was clearly not unusual to get out, and this was why the Germans forced people to undress before they boarded the trains.

The workers and inmates knew that the Germans were scared. But random and irrational killing went on. Most of the Germans were in the camp because they did not want to fight on the Eastern; they preferred to witness and help with the murdering of Jews. They no longer felt safe, especially when General Reinhard

110 Resist and Tell the World

Heydrich, who felt so confident that no harm could come to him that he regularly displayed himself in an open car in Minsk, died from the effects of an assassination attempt in Prague in June 1942. At that time such an assault was an unusual and unexpected event, but times were changing. Many of the Germans knew they were committing crimes they did not want to be held accountable for. The secrecy surrounding the camps was their ally, but they feared that punishment would come. The euphoria had waned, and the fear of a day of reckoning and feelings of guilt began to seriously hinder them.

Often the SS men had been or were still religious, or they had religious families and wives who would object to inhumanity. They could not talk openly about what they were doing. In her book *Into that Darkness*, Gitta Sereny looks at the psychology and history of Franz Stangl, the former commandant of Treblinka and later of Sobibor. One of Sereny's many interviewees was Stangl's wife, who said that she had learned accidentally about what happened in the camp. She had been upset when she learned that her husband had joined the Nazis in 1938. As she told Sereny: "What I believed in happened to be the Catholic Church; it was the Church of my country and I was brought up in it. But mainly I just believed in God. And to think—oh, it was a terrible blow, just a terrible blow. My man . . . a Nazi . . . It was our first real conflict—more than a fight. It went deep."[2] For weeks she could not be near him, and life became very difficult.

When she was informed that her husband was in Sobibor, at first she was happy that he was not at the front. He seemed safe. When she went to visit him in Sobibor, she did not know what happened there. She was lodged in nearby Chełm, where she was alarmed by the sexual abuse of two Jewish girls at night by the owner of the house. She was relieved when she could move with her children to a fish hatchery. One day a man called Ludwig came with friends to buy fish, and she recalled:

> Ludwig came up to me—I was in the garden too, with the children—and started to tell me about his wife and kids; he went on and on. I was pretty fed up, especially as he stank of alcohol and became more and more maudlin. But I thought, here is he is, so lonely—so I must at least listen." He told her "it was dreadful." She asked him to explain what was so dreadful, and first he told her they did all this for the Führer. He also said: "Can you imagine what would happen if the Jews ever get hold of us?"

Learning from him about the mass killings, she was amazed and shocked. Crying, she started to walk to Sobibor to confront her husband and hold him accountable for what she could not tolerate.[3] He argued that his job was only administrative, which in the end she accepted. There are so many stories of wives who went on to support their husbands, thinking there was no other possibility.

Safety and stability no longer existed for the Germans. A year later, an even more shocking event for the occupying forces was when Wilhelm Kube, a senior official of the Reichskommissariat Ostland with the rank of Generalkommissar for Weißruthenien (Byelorussia), was killed by a time bomb in his mattress

(September 22, 1943). It felt as if one was not even safe at home. Such events made it clear to the German military that the violence against them would never stop, and the warfare on the ground would become increasingly threatening since it was everywhere. The revenge for the killing of Kube was random, as thousands, mostly non-Jews, were murdered. The news about Kube's death and the story of brutal reprisals against the citizens of Minsk arrived with the trains. Later, information about the liquidation of Belzec reached Sobibor, also by train, and this became the major reason for the revolt. The story goes that in late June 1943, the prisoners had to stay in their barracks when a new transport arrived. They heard gunfire and yelling, and they then found out that the transport had come from Belzec. In the clothes of the victims was a warning that the laborers had been promised work and would be transported to another work camp. The prisoners of Treblinka brought with them food and vodka. They had trusted the authorities who had been so generous to provide this all for a "trip to Germany." In a note hidden in the clothing there was a message saying, "If this is a lie, you should know that death awaits you, too. Don't trust the Germans. Take revenge for us."[4]

When the group of Russian soldiers arrived, many prisoners were already convinced that the fate of the workers of Belzec would also be theirs. The prisoners knew that Germany had been defeated at Stalingrad, and they wanted to see the liberation and the Germans chased. Many had seen trains packed with wounded German soldiers being sent back to Germany, because these trains passed through city centers where the railway stations were usually located. They were convinced that the Red Army would win the war, although they knew it would take more time. Unfortunately for them, it took another year. The German soldiers feared that since the German army had not followed the Geneva Convention in their treatment of POWs, they could expect harsh repercussions if their side lost. They were scared of the Russians, who they had been told for years were savage and not human. The Germans had reason to be scared, because both parties avenged cruelty and death with cruelty and death.

Partisans and Resistance in Poland and Byelorussia

By 1943, Byelorussia and Eastern Poland had become major battlefields for a tenacious fight between partisans and occupiers; this was the kind of fighting we now call guerilla warfare. The Germans were chased by partisans in the vast woods and feared to go there. They took revenge on villages, and in the confusion they assumed that farmers and others who were unwilling to collaborate with them were Jews. Massacres were common, and the hostility against Germans was growing. No longer did Germans venture at night outside their protected areas. The same was the case around the Polish town of Lublin and in the dense woods of Eastern Poland.[5] The region around Włodawa, close to Sobibor, became known for its underground help to Russian POWs. It was a small town near the Bug, the river that marked the border.

112   *Resist and Tell the World*

But why, wondered the inmates, did these people not come to help them? Were the stories about the strength of the partisan army true? Pechersky wrote in his memoirs how he responded to the women in the women's camp who asked him if the rumor that there were partisans was true: "The Germans, for instance, would not leave Minsk in fewer than ten vehicles, armed with machine guns and hand grenades."[6]

Many ghettos had connections with the partisan movement. The best-known history of a ghetto that resisted the killing is, of course, that of Warsaw. However, in terms of connections with the partisans, Minsk was more important, and this town has gone into history as a place from which, with the help of the underground, thousands of people escaped to join the partisans in the forests.[7] Even when it was possible to go, not everyone fled; some were convinced that Germany urgently needed Jewish labor (the required number was supposedly one million people early in 1943), which was in contradiction with the massive slaughter taking place at the same time. The choice open to Jews was to flee or to believe in the story of survival by labor. The inhabitants of several ghettos hoped to be useful to the German economy.[8] Some Jews thought they would be spared if they worked, but others did not think work would save them. The latter group was right, but not everyone tried to escape.[9] At that time, the ghetto was considered by the Germans to be a hotbed of potential anti-Nazi actions. For Jews, there was only confusion about how to survive murder attempts.

The Germans were puzzled by their persistent defeat in the East, while they were also faced with uprisings by Jews and non-Jews all around them; they were no longer the masters of the world. They knew they were operating in countries that were hostile and no longer as easy to dominate as they had been just after the outbreak of the war. By 1943, Jews were defending themselves in ghettos and camps, while in the forests Germans could operate only in groups or under heavy guard.

The atrocious killing could not be kept secret; it was visible in the streets of towns and villages. For instance, in November 1942, during one of the "resettlements" of Jews from the Chełm ghetto, witnesses claimed that among the people forcibly gathered in a square at Kopernika Street was a large group of so-called Gypsies. They were placed at the front of a column that set off on a march toward the railway station, where they were to be loaded onto a train destined for Sobibor. The witnesses related that many of the Jews and Gypsies resisted and were shot on the spot. Their dead bodies were left lying on the square until they were carried away in horse-drawn carts by some Jews from the ghetto.[10] It was no longer an easy task to deport people. Life in occupied territory had become risky for the Germans, who were attacked fiercely by people who had nothing to lose.

Between 1941 and 1943, underground resistance movements developed in approximately 100 ghettos in Nazi-occupied Eastern Europe, especially in Poland, Lithuania, Byelorussia, and Ukraine.[11] Their main goals were to organize uprisings and outbreaks from the ghettos, and to join partisan units in the fight against the Germans. The best known of these was the spring 1943 uprising of the Warsaw ghetto, which ended, after heroic fighting, with mass deportations

Resist and Tell the World   113

to Treblinka and Sobibor. Some of the deportees landed in the labor camp of Sobibor; most had been gassed. But there were so many revolts, like those in the ghettos of Białystok in August 1943 and in Tarnow in early September of that year.[12] Reuben Ainsztein has documented many of these in detail.[13]

The killing continued, and 1943 saw a worsening doom in Eastern Poland. In his coverage of the war for the *Red Star* (*Krasnaya Zvezda*), Vasily Grossman described horror he could hardly digest.[14] He, who so much wanted to see his family back on occupied territory, expressed his amazement when he arrived in Treblinka:

> Can we find within us the strength to imagine what the people in these chambers felt, what they experienced during their last minutes of life? All we know is that they cannot speak now . . . Covered by a last clammy mortal sweat, packed so tight that their bones cracked and their crushed rib cages were barely able to breathe, they stood pressed against one another, they stood as if they were a single human being. Someone, perhaps some wise old man, makes the effort to say, "Patience now—this is the end." Someone shouts out some terrible curse. A holy curse—surely this curse must be fulfilled? With a superhuman effort, a mother tries to make a little more space for her child: may her child's dying breaths be eased, however infinitesimally, by a last act of maternal care. A young woman, her tongue going numb, asks, "Why am I being suffocated? Why can't I love and have children?" Heads spin. Throats choke. What are the pictures now passing before people's glassy dying eyes? Pictures of childhood? Of the happy days of peace? Of the last terrible journey? Of the mocking face of the SS man in that first square by the station: "Ah, so that's why he was laughing . . ." Consciousness dims. It is the moment of the last agony . . . No, what happened in that chamber cannot be imagined. The dead bodies stand there, gradually turning cold. It was the children, according to witnesses, who kept on breathing the longest.

Furious, Grossman continued in a realistic style:

> After twenty to twenty-five minutes, Schmidt's assistants would glance through the peepholes. It was time to open the second doors, the doors to the platforms. Urged on by shouting SS men, prisoners in overalls set about unloading the chambers. Because of the sloping floor, many of the bodies simply tumbled out of their own accord. People who carried out this task have told me that the faces of the dead were very yellow and that around seventy percent of them were bleeding slightly from the nose and mouth; physiologists, no doubt, can explain this.[15]

Grossman was psychologically devastated when he arrived in destroyed Treblinka in 1944 as a war correspondent with the Red Army.[16] With his coverage he helped to make the revolt of Treblinka known to the world. But he did not write about the two other camps of Operation Reinhard, Belzec and Sobibor,

114 *Resist and Tell the World*

which by then had been razed to the ground. He went to nearby Majdanek, which was also a labor camp, not only a death camp. Grossman stressed to his audience that it was Jews who had been killed in Treblinka, but that message was not welcomed by the Soviet authorities.[17] Grossman was part of the army, and the war was still going on, so he had to adapt and could not write more about the Jewish fate. He continued in the following years and disagreed with the party line and official history. We may therefore assume that Grossman did not withhold knowledge but probably did not know about the revolt of Sobibor, although he was generally well informed, and instead mentioned uprisings in lesser-known camps like Koldczewo and Janowska Street in Lvov.[18] The story of Sobibor would come after many more years and would be published by others.

Partisan groups came in many shapes: some were units of fighters; others created camps that sheltered threatened Jews and defended them against possible German attacks. The best known of these was the so-called family camp of the Bielski brothers in Byelorussia.[19] This camp contrasted with the partisan units that would only accept male fighters; here women were also sheltered, and Jews who did not have weapons were also welcomed. Such camps were not only fighting units but also hiding places, protected by those who could handle arms. The Bielski brothers kept the camp going from mid-1942, and although there were many misfortunes, more than a thousand people at the camp were liberated at the end of the war.

In *Fugitives of the Forest*, Allan Levine describes the options available to those who escaped from the ghettos. They could join a fighting unit affiliated with the Red Army, or they could join a more independent unit. They could opt for a family camp, where non-combatants were also admitted. In a later chapter 5 on partisans, I will return to some camps and groups, and the variety of camps and hiding places in the vast forests of Poland and Byelorussia. The independence of the partisan groups made the Soviet leadership of the partisans in Byelorussia suspicious, which often led to anti-Semitism when the leadership felt that there were too many Jews in a unit. Those who fled in Poland also had to fear the Polish partisans of the AK army (Armia Krajowa), which was infested with hostility toward Jews. Levine quotes a report stating that "our units are now forced to fight on two fronts. The underground leadership [the AK command] is organizing units whose role is to wipe out the communist gangs, prisoners of war and the Jews." The report complained that these AK soldiers did not attack Germans. Levine also noted that when such groups met a lone Jew, they would kill him, but they refrained from engaging in combat. They were afraid to be provocative. The soldiers of the AK knew that Jewish groups would fight back.[20]

Reaching the partisans did not mean safety. Once arrived, the danger of betrayal was added to the harsh and unsanitary living conditions, hunger, and exposure to the severe climate of that part of Europe. People often lived in shelters dug out of the ground, which were cold and damp. To get there, one had to pass unknown and sometimes hostile villages and roads and meet people who could betray you. Some people might hate Jews, while others might be angry with

Resist and Tell the World   115

the Jewish partisans because of food confiscation, and still others might want to make a profit through betrayal.

The Russians—Experienced Fighters Arrive

The inmates of Sobibor had applauded the arrival of the Russians, since the group with Pechersky consisted of Jewish soldiers who knew how to fight. As survivor Kalmen Wewryk wrote: "They had military experience. They knew all about guns, bullets, etc. They would not be squeamish about hand-to-hand combat." Like all inmates, Wewryk was very impressed by Pechersky: "He radiated an air of command and control."[21] Also, the camp was surrounded by partisan groups, and there was sometimes an expectation that these groups would come to help and attack the Germans. The group of German guards was small. There was contact between the Ukrainian guards and partisans; these guards themselves had often been POWs. Some of them hoped to escape. Zelda Metz told Novitch during an interview about how rumors had spread that partisans had tried to liberate the camp.[22] Later, the inmates were told that bandits had attacked.

In most narratives about the events, the arrival of the Russian group overshadows the fact that there was already an underground organization in the camp, under the leadership of Leon Feldhendler. As we will see, without his network Pechersky would not have been able to connect with the people who could help and protect him, or to gather so much information. It was Feldhendler who decided that Pechersky should be a central figure in any future escape or revolt, since all such previous attempts had failed. The Polish Jews, of whom Feldhendler was one, were accustomed to sabotage against the Germans, and they had found ways to support each other in a network to survive. They knew that Jews elsewhere would fight back, even when death was almost certain.

Some of the survivors I interviewed in 2010–12 acknowledged the strength of the Russian soldiers, but others repeatedly stressed how important the Polish underground had been. Examples also abound in the interviews with Polish inmates conducted for the Shoah Visual History Archive. One example is the testimony of Samuel Lerer, who argued that Feldhendler was the most important leader, and said of Pechersky, "He needed us more than we needed him."[23] Lerer also said, "We wanted to escape but we had no place to go."[24] Another survivor, Dov Freiberg, was of the same opinion. According to him, Polish Jews had knowledge about electric wiring and telephone lines.[25] Esther Raab suggested the same when I interviewed her in 2010, but this was not during an official interview, and Feldhendler was a member of her family. When she was interviewed in 1997, she was explicit in stating that the planning for an escape had started before the Russians came.[26]

Wewryk wrote the following of Feldhendler: "One of us, Leon Feldhendler, the son of a Rabbi, had been in Sobibor for close to a year. The transports to Sobibor had virtually stopped and Feldhendler figured that the camp and every single eyewitness-prisoner would be wiped of the face of the earth. He had organized a

116   *Resist and Tell the World*

team, composed largely of shop chiefs, and they were plotting to escape from the hell that was Sobibor."

Feldhendler was excited about the military experience of the Russian POWs and wanted to find out who this "Sasha" was. Pechersky had escaped the gassing by saying he was a carpenter, which he was not. He confessed this to the underground organization. Since the Germans rarely visited the workshops, the organizers were able to cover up for him. He promised that he would work on a plan.

Wewryk continued:

> Sasha got to know us very well, because he made it his business to know as many prisoners as he could. He wanted to find out who the squealers were. He set a task for himself: to study Sobibor as methodically as he could. Action would come later. We were all very impressed with this Sasha. He radiated an air of command and control. Since Sasha spoke no Yiddish, Feldhendler communicated with him via an intermediary, Laitman, a cabinetmaker who worked in our shop. He was originally from Warsaw and had been shipped to our camp from Minsk work camp where he had met Sasha and had become a friend.[27]

Pechersky studied the camp methodically and tried to map what was going on secretly in Camp III. In his 1984 interview for the movie by Dunya Breur and Jules Schelvis, Pechersky told how, in the beginning, he was confronted with the inmates' plan to escape:

> We were working on that idea. The revolt was a later idea. I understood very well that it was impossible to flee from the camp. There were minefields around, there were two hundred and fifty Ukrainian guards, and we were six hundred prisoners. Statistically that is one guard for two prisoners, if we don't count the German officers. The minefield was fifteen meters wide and the ditch around it was filled with water. It is even impossible to think you can escape. My major goal was to kill fascists, those who had killed people themselves. And maybe fifteen or twenty people would be able to escape.[28]

He did not believe in a future success, but he did not tell this to the others.

Not Slaughtered Like Sheep

In a study of the historiography of the resistance of Jews against the Germans, historian Michael Marrus argues that after the war the accusation was made, by resistance fighters themselves, that the Jews had gone to their deaths "like sheep to the slaughter." For more than fifteen years after the liberation of Europe, professional historians scarcely touched on the subject. Writing on resistance, like writing on the Holocaust in general, was mainly the work of those who had experienced it first hand: participants in the struggle against the Nazis whose anguished writings were published after the war, and survivors

Resist and Tell the World   117

who recounted their experiences with the special authority that their suffering accorded them.[29]

Very few historians tackled this subject, partly because the Jews of Europe were still trying to digest what had happened and to rebuild their lives. In her book on the Eichmann trial, Hannah Arendt described how the prosecutor, Gideon Hausner, kept asking the witnesses why they had not protested and had boarded the trains.[30] Arendt had deplored such questions, arguing that they were cruel and silly. The Jews had behaved as many non-Jews would have done. According to Marrus:

> Her point was that Jews had been the victims not of an indelible non-Jewish antipathy, but rather of a totalitarian ethos that threatened the entire world. In her view, Jews were as susceptible as anyone else to be sucked into the maw of a totalitarian system and to end up collaborating with it. Those who resisted, however, were her heroes. Youthful Jewish rebels in ghettos, she insisted, had to struggle constantly against the established Jewish leaders of the *Judenräte*. Many of the resisters, she noted, were tortured to death after their capture by the SS.[31]

Marrus juxtaposed Arendt with Raoul Hilberg, the eminent historian of the Shoah, and wrote:

> In Hilberg's view the Jews' failure to resist—which he defined broadly as opposing the perpetrator—was one of the striking features of the destruction process. "The Jews were not oriented toward resistance," he contended. "They took up resistance only in a few cases, locally, and at the last moment [. . .] They avoided 'provocations' and complied instantly with decrees and orders. They hoped that somehow the German drive would spend itself." The Jews' reluctance to attack the perpetrators stemmed directly from the Jewish past—'a two-thousand-year experience.' "[O]ver a period of centuries the Jews had learned that in order to survive they had to refrain from resistance."[32]

Over the years, the meaning of resistance has been expanded to the many ways in which Jews survived spiritually and maintained their cultural and religious life, as well as a quality of life, under the worst conditions.[33] Yehuda Bauer, the dean of research on the history of the Shoah, has argued that not taking up arms did not mean giving in to the Germans.[34] He and other Israeli historians has proposed the Israeli term *amidah* to define a resistance that included non-armed resistance.[35] There is the following striking example about Sobibor:

> One Polish Jew struggled hard against being forced. The Jew no longer believed the lies he was being told. When he got out of the car, he scooped up two fistfuls of sand and then turned to Karl Frenzel, the SS man, and said: "You see how I'm scattering this sand slowly, grain by grain, and it's carried

118   *Resist and Tell the World*

away by the breeze? That is what will happen to you; this whole great Reich of yours will vanish like flying dust and passing smoke!" The old man went along with the whole convoy, reciting "Hear, O Israel" [a prayer to be said as one's last words]; and when he said the words "The Lord is One," he turned to Frenzel and slapped him with all his might.[36]

James Glass argues that spiritual and moral resistance was meant to transcend a trusted frame of mind; remaining collaborative seemed to be a better guarantee of life, and resistance was a big step to take. Traditional ways of acting supported the morale of many inmates, so why take one step beyond what was conceivable? Soup kitchens and mutual help had prevented mass starvation in the ghettos; they gave agency and made life valuable. People felt togetherness, and it preserved their identity.[37]

Interestingly Marrus argues that "to refute contentions of Jewish passivity, historians of Jewish resistance frequently point out the absence of such revolts, at least until the very end of the war, among Soviet prisoners of war—young men with military training who were subject to treatment at times as murderous and brutal as that meted out to the Jews."[38]

Resistance in Sobibor: To Die With Honor

The story of the revolt of Sobibor does not need such a refined discussion on resistance and revolt. However, it remains a marvel how the story developed from small efforts to escape into collective action. The first answer lies in the fact that everyone in Sobibor knew that others would be punished if there was an escape (or escape attempt). This collective responsibility had been experienced time and again, and people were reluctant to try, even if they had the opportunity. They felt responsible, given that the repercussions had become unpredictable. For example, as a punishment every tenth man was killed, regardless of who the person was. The Germans simply counted. Thomas Maher has analyzed how much the immediate threat of being killed forced the inmates to act collectively.[39] Still, as we shall see, the Sobibor revolt was threatened until the very last moment by individual actions, and the threat of German revenge made a successful revolt unlikely.

More than anything, Pechersky was convinced that the inmates had to fight for themselves and should not wait for the partisans. Up to that moment, the prisoners had high expectations of liberation by groups in the forests around Sobibor.[40] Perhaps with their help they could survive, they thought. There was uncertainty if they would be alive the near future if they stayed in the camp, since the transports were less frequent, and fewer trains arrived. This was life-threatening because their lives depended on keeping the death factory going. The cold of the winter was coming and no one looked forward to it. If the ground was covered with snow, it would become more difficult to escape. But the low tide in the arrival of transports also created less work, so prisoners had more time to sit together, to talk, and to worry. News about the destruction of Treblinka made it more urgent to do something. It was clear that if they stayed passive, everyone would be killed.

Maher has argued that despite the life-threatening situation the prisoners were in, they had some agency over their actions and decisions.[41] As we shall see, there was distrust from those who feared they would be left behind if a small group managed to escape. Anyone who studies the revolt takes sides, argued Paul Gomberg in a somewhat philosophical article entitled "Can a Partisan Be a Moralist?"[42] Reading about Sobibor and listening to the stories, we develop a state of mind in which we want the prisoners to defeat their captors. Although the rest of Gomberg's article deals with philosophical questions, his title invites us to consider the ethical side of the revolt. Even though what happened was self-defense combined with revenge, many survivors hesitated to participate in premeditated killing. Most of the inmates came from a cultural world in which killing someone was beyond their imagination. Others thought it was not the moment to be moralistic; some wanted revenge, which was more obvious for those prisoners who had been Russian soldiers and were accustomed to warfare. They had had to kill before.

Learning to Fight and to Kill

Jews learned to be violent and to fight back. All over the occupied territories, Jews resisted against the violence of the Germans. The resistance in Sobibor is rooted in a world in which Jews began to defend themselves and where they did fight. It was a new kind of agency to them; in the past they had negotiated and used money to avert disaster, but physical combat was new. Endless compromises seemed to fail now; there was no negotiation.

According to Ainsztein, when prisoners who had just arrived in Sobibor staged a protest, they were shot immediately. This happened more and more frequently, since Polish and Soviet Jews no longer believed that they had been transported to a work camp. Ainsztein described the growing resistance and efforts to escape. From the beginning of 1943, the arrival of trains from Poland and from the East was met with automatic weapons. The people who left the trains were immediately surrounded by a large group of armed soldiers.

The inhabitants of the nearby village of Włodawa revolted against repression on April 30, 1943. They attacked the SS men and the Ukrainian guardsmen. All of those involved in the revolt died in the gas chambers of Sobibor, including the non-Jews. The region around Włodawa was known as a place where Russian POWs could find shelter. Further away, in the forests of Polesie, rather large Soviet units were operating.[43] The partisans were worried about attracting large numbers of Jews, because they assumed many Jewish fugitives would prompt more German Jew-hunting.

The Germans were so scared of the Jewish resistance that when the survivors of the Warsaw uprising arrived in May 1943, they were forced to undress before they went into the trains.[44] The Germans believed that the prisoners would not resist or jump from the train if they were naked. People did fight, indeed. In

120 *Resist and Tell the World*

September 1943, the ghetto of Minsk was annihilated. The Jews who arrived from there threw stones and bottles at the guards, resulting in a serious fight. There were women who refused to undress, did not want their hair to be cut, or did not want to be separated from their children. In such cases, a rather irrational and cruel punishment followed: the SS slowed the stream of gas so the victims would experience more agony. It was irrational, since no one would know about this punishment. Was it just revenge? Or did they try to calm their own fears by being cruel? The story did survive, however, making those who committed these crimes appear even more barbarous. The Germans became reckless when they met resistance. Some newly arrived Jews tore the money they had with them to pieces to make it valueless.

Marek Bem, a historian of Sobibor, stated that for some prisoners the only form of protest was suicide. This irritated the Germans, who felt they had a monopoly on the killing of Jews.[45] According to Bem:

> During the court trial held in Hagen, Karl Frenzel was charged (Indictment No. 22) with having issued, on a morning between May 1942 and October 1943, an order to take one of the dying prisoners, who had slashed his wrists at night, from his barracks to the courtyard where the daily roll-calls were held. Next, Frenzel rebuked the dying man sharply, lashed him with his whip and shot him in the presence of all the gathered Jews. Drunk with his glorious feeling of absolute power, he shouted out to them that no Jew had the right to take his or her own life—true Aryans alone had that power.[46]

Ainsztein provided many such examples and demonstrated the untrustworthiness of the image of Jews who went like sheep to the chopping block.[47] Even near or inside the gas chamber, the protests did not stop. The Germans shot some women who refused to go inside. Once, when the diesel engines malfunctioned, a group managed to open the doors but did not manage to escape. Near the crematoria in Camp III, Jews tried to revolt several times and tried to escape, according to survivor Moshe Bahir.[48] One boy escaped from the camp in 1942, with the aim of telling the world about what was going on. Telling the world was crucial, as Zelda Metz said to Novitch: "We thought that if mankind knew of our martyrdom, we would be admired for our endurance, and revered for our sufferings."[49]

In Camp III some Jews managed to cut the iron wires and escape. They were then betrayed to the Germans. Late in 1942, two prisoners escaped through a tunnel they had dug. In December 1942, two women got out with two guards, according to Ainsztein, or accompanied by inmates, according to Krakowski.[50] They were armed with guns, but were caught and killed. The point is not whether the escapees were guards or prisoners, but that the revolt of Sobibor needs to be seen against the background of many efforts to escape and resist. Contacts between Jews and the guards became more and more common.[51]

As a result, during the winter of 1942–43, some men, mainly from Lublin and Warsaw, managed to organize a nucleus of resistance. The core activity was to listen and tell about broadcast messages in which the German defeat was announced

Resist and Tell the World   121

and discussed. Morale was also boosted because Ukrainian guards showed the inmates newspaper clippings about German defeats. However, any attempts to oppose or escape were smothered by the principle of the prisoners' collective responsibility. As Krakowski correctly wrote: "Any unsuccessful attempt was paid for not only with the lives of those who took part in it, but also with the lives of other prisoners. In addition, the success of one group of prisoners (an escape for example) usually led to the death of others left behind." Krakowski continued: "All of these factors—unlimited terror, inhuman living conditions, the principle of collective responsibility, the death sentences for civilian accomplices, and the complicated system of barriers, and watches—almost nullified the chance of organizing resistance, particularly armed action."[52]

Indeed, no one thought of taking the weapons from the Germans, nor did the idea of killing them come to their minds until the Russians came. The nucleus of resisters could think only about escape by tunnel. Alas, no one knew how to smuggle arms into the camp, and the idea of taking them from the Germans did not cross their minds. But there were many weapons inside the camp.

Organizing an Escape

During the summer of 1943, the inmates of Treblinka staged an uprising that had as its main goal to inform the outside world about the mass exterminations. Since the camp was built in 1941, the resistance had existed for some time and consisted of mutual aid, escapes, and spontaneous actions. Some had managed to flee Treblinka and had even warned the Warsaw Ghetto and its Jewish underground organization. As early as September 1943, the first reports of what had happened in Treblinka had been received in Warsaw.[53] The organization of the resistance in Treblinka had tried to buy arms from the Ukrainian guards and to steal them from the storehouse. Although the revolt was not successful, around twenty prisoners did escape and survived until the end of the war. Some who had survived but were caught were sent to Sobibor, and the prisoners unloading the train found passengers, former inmates of Treblinka, with broken arms and legs. One kapo, Cepik, found a notebook with a description of the uprising of Treblinka.[54]

During that same summer of 1943, a tunnel was dug in Sobibor. Unfortunately, the exit ended in a minefield surrounding the camp. There the digging caused an explosion, and the idea of digging a tunnel was given up. Small acts to defy the Germans are mentioned in many sources. For example, Krakowski mentioned that on April 30, 1943, newly arrived victims attacked the SS men when they saw what awaited them. Later that year, Jews from Minsk attacked the SS guards. There were many small efforts to escape; people tried continuously and showed their anger. Though the Germans and their Ukrainian helpers always won and punished the prisoners with random killing, they became increasingly scared. Sometimes a guard was killed. The accounts of Ainsztein, Krakowski, and Bem all give examples of such events. In 1943, Polish Jews were no longer allowed to work outside the camp, for example, or to be employed in woodcutting or the construction of new barracks. Every time someone escaped, the result was

122 *Resist and Tell the World*

counter-measures and revenge taken on those who had nothing to do with the "misdeeds." When two tailors escaped in July 1943, twenty other inmates were shot.

The most creative plan was one by Dutch inmates who intended to poison all the Germans in the camp. They worked in the kitchen and involved Jews working in the pharmacy. With small quantities of poison put aside, they would accumulate enough. Simcha Bialowicz, the pharmacist involved, told me about the plot when I interviewed him in 2010 in Holon, Israel.[55] Betrayal of the plan led to all of the Dutch Jews being shot. Other plans varied from arson to blowing up the canteen, for which the inmates had collected twenty grenades. These initiatives were reported to the Germans, sometimes by other Jews who feared they would be killed in reprisals.

It was not only the Jewish inmates who were a threat to the Germans; some of the Ukrainian guards hated the Germans as much as the Jews. When the Red Army advanced, the guards made several efforts to flee. They also formed a link with the partisans in the surrounding woods and talked with them about a possible assault on the camp. They staged one attack on the northern side in an effort to obtain grenades and ammunition.[56] The result was that the prisoners had to gather on roll-call. Again it was the Dutch inmates who had staged the effort, so all of the Dutch from Camp IV were killed. Their places and the need for their labor would be taken by the Russian POWs.

The Germans were aware of the possibility that Jews and Ukrainian guards might collaborate. Although the Jews did not trust the guards, they did reach an agreement in July 1943 for the purpose of penetrating into the armory and escaping together after destroying the main gate. Bem stated that there were various scenarios for this revolt.[57] The descriptions in the testimonies indeed vary, but the main intention was to escape. Bem also quoted the testimony of Eda Lichtman, who confirmed that the Germans could leave the camp only with armed protection.[58] They had to participate in manhunts and search in the forest for partisans. Eda was working in the laundry and noticed that the Germans came back extremely dirty, black from smoke and covered with blood.

In his book on Sobibor, former inmate Jules Schelvis described the effort to escape by the *Waldkommando* (Forest Command) on July 27, 1943. The group was looked after by three SS men. The group of workers usually consisted of about forty men, half of whom were Dutch. There were a few Ukrainians to guard them. Since it was a very hot day, two prisoners were allowed to fetch water. The Ukrainian guard who had gone with them was found dead. In the ensuing chaotic moments, fourteen Polish Jews escaped. Many were recaptured quickly. As a result, the surviving Polish Jews were brutally tortured and shot in front of the other inmates as a warning against any similar future efforts.[59] This story can be found in many other sources.

Just before the uprising, Jews transported from the Minsk ghetto attacked the SS and were killed on the platform with the help of machine guns. That same month, prisoners at Camp III who worked near the gas chambers dug an underground passage from their barracks to the other side of the fence.[60] The historian Krakowski mentioned that besides the underground organization there were secret

Resist and Tell the World   123

groups, sometimes numbering ten people, who planned escapes, sometimes with the help of Ukrainian guards.[61] He writes, "These small groups were an obstacle to Pechorski's [*sic*] and Feldhendler's central organization and made it imperative to organize all the underground activities in the camp into one organization."[62]

Co-operation between the mainly Polish underground in the camp and the Russian soldiers was crucial. Yitzhak Arad stresses that it was decisive.[63] The Polish group was experienced and knew the camp and various conditions, while the Russians provided military know-how and leadership. Apparently social meetings in the women's barracks provided a cover for meetings of the underground. Any individual action or any action or escape by a small group would risk retaliation against many.

The escape would be a united effort, and there was no time to lose. Krakowski described how Shlomo Laitman and Boris Tsibulsky tried to convince Pechersky to escape when they heard women screaming. At that moment the Germans were busy unloading a transport and gassing Jews. They wanted to kill the Germans with the axes they had to use for their work. Pechersky said, "Maybe we can get away from here. But what would await the others? If we flee, we have to do it with everyone; no one can stay behind. Some of us certainly will lose our lives, but those who are saved will take bloody revenge." Tsibulsky (who was named Kalimali in the camp) said, "You are right, but we cannot postpone it for too long. The winter is coming and traces are visible in the snow."[64] Pechersky answered that they had to trust him; he was making plans, and he made them swear not to talk to anyone. He would tell them what to do later.

As Pechersky wrote, he was very close at the time to Shlomo Laitman, a Communist from Warsaw who had spent years in jail. They knew each other from Minsk. Pechersky described Laitman as small and slender guy, with deep eyes and a pronounced nose. He was well trusted by others. Together, Pechersky and Laitman had investigated several escape possibilities in order to reach the partisans. But now they needed to develop the idea for a mass escape, which needed thorough preparation.

In his deposition of 1952, Pechersky described the camp and said that every part was surrounded by iron wire. He immediately had started to map the camp. Within a few days he knew the camp and understood how it functioned. On September 28 he was invited to the women's barracks under the pretext of a romantic encounter. Shlomo told Pechersky the girls wanted to meet him. The man who had invited him was known by the name of Baruch; it was Leon Feldhendler. The women's barracks were more relaxed than other places. Pechersky described them as reinvigorating, a place where one discussed science, literature, and the contradictions of being human. Here he met Luka, who had seen naked people being chased to the gas chambers. She felt powerless.

At the women's barracks Pechersky and his fellow Russian soldiers found 150 women and girls from several countries. They were all interested to know about the front, and they put forward many questions. The Russian soldiers told about how the Germans had lost the battle for Moscow and how they were defeated at Stalingrad and that the Red Army had reached the Dnieper. They told how scared the Germans were in Minsk, and how the Germans always traveled in

124   *Resist and Tell the World*

convoys of at least ten heavily armed cars. Shlomo translated into Yiddish. The Russians were asked why the partisans did not attack the camp if their units were so strong and numerous. The answer was that the partisans had their own tasks.

On September 29, at 6 a.m., the inmates were collectively abused by being made to unload bricks for new quarters. There were beatings; anyone who could not keep the pace was whipped. All six hundred prisoners (men and women) had to run with between six and eight bricks. Anyone who dropped a basket was caned twenty-five times. Anyone who paused was horsewhipped. The unloading had to be finished in time for a new transport to enter the compound. Afterward, eighty men were directed to the North Camp, where Pechersky had been assigned work on a small barracks. Because there were only five guards at that moment, some inmates wanted to escape. Pechersky warned that escape from there was not easy, and he was worried about what would happen to the stragglers. He convinced them that an escape needed better preparation and told them he did not want to participate.

That evening Feldhendler told Pechersky that his appearance in the women's barracks had made an enormous impression. Feldhendler was convinced that the Germans needed their labor, and that some might survive because of this. Pechersky started to discuss the situation regularly with Feldhendler. The secrecy of the mass murder created a practical problem, as it meant the Germans would never allow anyone to talk about Sobibor. Therefore, one could assume that everyone would be killed, and the secret would be erased with their bodies.

Feldhendler had already been in the camp for about a year. Pechersky was amazed that he and the underground organization had not tried to stage a large escape, and he criticized Feldhendler for this. In response, Feldhendler said that they had thought about it, but the inmates did not know how to act. Therefore, Feldhendler asked Pechersky to head the escape. He trusted him as a Soviet citizen and soldier. "Please accept the task! Tell us what to do and we'll obey. I understand you don't trust me, you are right, we met too recently. But we have to agree; on behalf of the group I say we trust you! Please start."[65]

Pechersky was charmed by the prudent, honest, and serious face of Feldhendler. Feldhendler knew which parts of the surroundings were mined, since the prisoners themselves had dug the holes. Shlomo would become Pechersky's intermediary and interpreter. He mediated when Pechersky and Feldhendler met again on October 7. They played chess, during which time they were able to talk; in particular, they discussed how the guard was organized. Feldhendler was well informed and passed his knowledge on to Pechersky. They also discussed possible trustworthy allies in Camp II. The idea was to dig a tunnel, and they scrutinized the parameters. The plan included the removal of twenty cubic meters of earth. The challenge was to hide the ground that was brought out. The work had to be done in the dark and would take from fifteen to twenty days.

Naum Plotnitsky, a Polish inmate had arrived in the camp early in 1943. He testified about how he met Pechersky:

> One day a group of Jewish prisoners of war arrived from Russia. Around thirty to forty of them were selected for the construction group. In the evening in

the barracks, a man came up to me who had just arrived with this group. He asked me where I was from. And I also asked where he was from; he came from Minsk. He found out from me that I am from *Lunintsa*. He invited me to meet again the following day. And we met again. He asked me how long I had been in the camp. I told him that it had been more than a month. He asked me to stop in the barracks where the tailors worked.

Several days after we had become acquainted, he drew me into an underground organization that he organized and led. His name was Sasha. Later, after the war, I found out his full name: Aleksandr Pecherskii [sic]. The underground organization met a day later. He gave out assignments, preparing people for an uprising. There were women in the group too.[66]

For the story of the uprising I have made use of the translation of a Yiddish version of Pechersky's reminiscences published in *Der Emes* in 1946 that was later translated and updated by Yuri Suhl.[67] The story is known to many, but I will tell it again. The text of 1946 is similar to the one in *The Black Book* and is often used for reference. Pechersky describes how he and his friends mapped the camp over a period of a few days. The text focuses on explaining why the group chose the difficult road of collective resistance and is a self-justification. Pechersky tells how another group wanted to escape at a moment when there were fewer guards than usual. Someone told him this and he reflected: "So irresponsible a step could only bring harm. I tried to convince the fellow why it should not be done. 'It is easy to say,' I said, 'But the guards are not bunched together in one group. You kill one and another will open fire on you. And with what will you cut the wire fence? And how will you cross the minefield? If you should tarry for just a few minutes the Germans will catch up with you. Perhaps some of you will succeed in breaking through, but what about those who work in the barracks?'" He was convinced they would be shot. He was convinced that with good preparation there was more chance of success, and he refused to join in the outbreak.[68]

During a private conversation, Feldhendler warned that some inmates were convinced that some Jews would be spared by working hard. He called them fools. At the same time, realizing the Russians wanted to escape, he was worried for those who stayed behind. He was convinced that as soon as the Germans became aware that escape was possible, they would worry that the secret of the camp would become known to the outer world. According to Feldhendler, that would bring about the total liquidation of the camp. Pechersky wondered during this talk why the others thought he would escape and tried to finish the discussion. He was cautious.

Not Mass Escape but Revolt

On October 7, Pechersky gave a sign to Feldhendler that he wanted to talk to him since he needed more information about the guards. At that moment, a week before the revolt, they were still discussing the possibility of digging a tunnel eighty centimeters deep. A complication was that they needed to hide the earth that would be dug up, which could be done but would take twelve to fifteen days.

126   *Resist and Tell the World*

Pechersky was worried that the time between 11 p.m. and dawn would not be enough for six hundred people to crawl through the tunnel, one behind the other, unnoticed. He was worried that people would start fighting to be first. He was also worried that some would not join, believing they would be spared by work.[69]

Pechersky proposed to attack the German officers. In the meantime, he wanted to collect as many as seventy sharp knives and razors to provide the inmates with weapons. He also wanted to be assigned with Shlomo to the cabinetmaker's shop, from where he could observe what was happening. They discussed the possible inclusion of kapos. The men were assigned to their places on October 8, and in the evening they received the first forty sharp knives from Feldhendler.

The next day, some Jews were severely whipped, and that night eight people were ready to escape. It seemed the only solution. They had asked Tsibulsky (Kalimali) to join. The idea came from a man named Grisha, who had been one of the whipping victims that morning.[70] Grisha invited Pechersky to come along too. He wanted to cut the wires near the badly lighted latrines. Pechersky asked him if he had thought about the people who stayed behind—they would be killed immediately—and offered him a place among the leaders of his own escape plan. Pechersky promised to assign him to a prominent position in the revolt he was staging. Grisha refused, and there was a quarrel. Then Pechersky told him preparations were in an advanced stage and that he wanted everyone to escape. The general plan would be undermined by the small group putting in an effort now. If necessary, Pechersky would kill Grisha. A strong man was posted near the latrines that evening to watch out for anyone who wanted to get out.

On October 11, new arrivals resisted going to the gas chambers and were shot. It was a warning that everyone would be killed anyhow, and the retaliation was made known to the inmates. The next day, a Dutch woman did not allow her husband, who was ill, to be led away to be gassed together with everyone else who was ill. She attacked the Germans and joined her husband in going to the gas chamber while she shouted to the Germans that they were murderers. That evening in the cabinetmakers' shop, a meeting decided to include Kapo Brzecki and to collaborate with some kapos. At that moment, Pechersky unfolded his master plan to kill many Germans efficiently in a very short time. The killing of German officers had to be done by Soviet POWs selected by Pechersky personally. "It is clear that such a task must be entrusted to people of courage and resolution, people who will be firm and unwavering. One moment of vacillation, one failure, and we're all done for," he said.[71]

Kapo Brzecki would start by killing four "Hitlerites" who were working there. From then on, no one would be allowed to leave the camp; those who made any noise would be silenced or killed. Immediately after, telephone lines were to be cut and the killing of officers in Camp I would start by inviting officers to the workshops, where they would be executed.

According to the plan, a little later it would look like inmates were lining up for work, and this column of inmates would move toward the exit. An attack on the arsenal would follow, with an attack on the guards to come later. Pechersky was eager to fight once the Russians had weapons in their hands. The underground

Resist and Tell the World   127

group knew that on October 13, a number of SS men would not be in the camp. Most importantly, Gustav Wagner would also leave. As Dutch survivor Schelvis, who used material from the Hagen trial of 1966, wrote, Wagner had been in favor of killing all the Soviet POWs, but Frenzel "had argued that he needed them in Lager 4."[72]

The escape was to start at 5 p.m., after dark, but at 10:30 that morning a group of SS men arrived from Osowa, where they had been guards. While the inmates worried that these men had to come to reinforce the guards, it turned out they had come for eating and drinking. The revolt was postponed. The SS men returned to Osowa that night, and on the eve of October 14, the older people said prayers: it was Yom Kippur, the Day of Atonement. Some inmates told them, "Better pray for Sasha to help you." They answered, "We are praying to God to help Sasha."[73] This is probably an apocryphal story that was later invented.

On October 14, as had become normal, no transport arrived. This was crucial, since the chaos of a new transport would have made the revolt impossible. Pechersky described the day as a clear and sunny one. The knives had been distributed, along with a number of hatchets. Anyone who needed warm clothing had received it. *Unterscharführer* Berg was, as expected, at the tailor's shop at 4 p.m. for the fitting of a uniform he had ordered. Fifteen minutes later, the chief of the camp guards would come for the same reason.

I now follow Pechersky's own words from 1946 and combine them with later historical research. Pechersky was assigned to the cabinetmaker's shop, and from its window he could see the whole yard of Camp I. Shlomo Laitman worked in the nearby barracks with a selected group of twenty men. "All the men who had to carry out assassinations worked with Shlomo that day." They had all received a personal assignment from Pechersky. The first one was Subaiev. Pechersky described how they shook hands silently when he left. Tsibulski had been his friend since the cellar in Minsk. He got the most difficult task. Together with others, he had to go to Feldhendler, who was in Camp II. They had to take hatchets, and Tsibulski had to use one to deliver the first blow. "It'll have to give courage to all others. If any of the other fellows going with you gets scared, put another in his place. No one should be compelled to do this."[74] Boris (Feldhendler) replied that Pechersky should not worry; he was convinced that all were awaiting the signal. The whole proceedings were interrupted because one of the kapos, Brzecki, was unexpectedly transferred to Camp IV and could not fulfill his task.

One of the other inmates, Szmajzner, who was very well trusted, had managed to obtain three rifles wrapped in a blanket after threatening two young inmates with a knife and forcing them to collaborate by smuggling the rifles through a window. He gave the rifles to Pechersky, who recognized them as Russian-made. Szmajzner wanted one for himself, which initiated the first conflict about the possession of arms.

At 4 p.m. the revolt started. The first SS member, Nieman, was killed after being told he had to try a new coat. Nieman was expected at a barracks. Subaiev did the job and the body was shoved under the bed. He reported this to Pechersky, at which point there was no turning back. The next German entered the

128   *Resist and Tell the World*

tailor's shop and never came out. A short moment later, the chief of Camp III entered the shoemaker's. While he was trying on new boots, and during a seemingly friendly conversation, Arkady Waiszpapir used the hatchet. Later he was asked if Pechersky had asked him to kill. He replied: "He did not ask, he ordered. We were soldiers. In such conditions, anyone could understand that orders had to be followed. He told us what needed to be done, and I did it; I did not think. He told me to go with Lerer to the workshop. We were sent to liberate the camp, so we went." He thought the role of Pechersky was special. He noted: "He was a pleasant person. His looks were pleasant and dauntless acts bound him with people. That was his major strength during the preparations for the escape—he created solidarity among a diverse group of people. They differed not only in ideology and language, but also had different convictions."[75]

Just before 4:30 p.m. the telephone and telegraph cables were cut. Tsibulsky announced that four Germans had been killed in Camp II, which was under the "command" of Feldhendler. From this point on, no one was allowed to leave until the sign was given to lead everyone to the main gate. Pechersky wrote that just before this sign was given, he saw Luka for the last time. He ordered her to dress in a man's clothes, comfortable enough to endure a long stay in the woods. She embraced him, but as Pechersky wrote, "This was not the moment for gentleness. 'Take yourself in hand at once,' I said with all the sternness at my command. 'Aren't you ashamed of yourself? A daughter of a Communist! Go change your clothes. When you hear the signal, you'll come and take your place by my side. Don't you trust me, Luka?'" He told her this was the only way to stay alive. "We must not perish, because we must take revenge." She came back a moment later and gave him a shirt that she said would bring him luck. Sasha never saw Luka again; apparently she did not make it.

Things did not go as smoothly as planned. A kapo warned one of the German officers not to enter a barracks; inside, another German was killed by Shlomo Laitman. Pechersky wrote, "It was time to give the signal, but Franz [Frenzel] was still alive and his whereabouts were uncertain. The situation became more chaotic but was still successful." They decided to give the signal for the revolt. People started to arrive from all sides. Seventy men, mostly Soviet POWs, were at the forefront of a column that should be led to the main gate. The group was joined by people who were totally surprised and could not adapt or act. A column from Camp II also approached to join. "Shaken by the unexpected scene, they began to scream. One prisoner was on the verge of fainting. Another began to run blindly, without any direction. It was clear that under these circumstances it would be impossible to line up the people in an orderly column. 'Comrades, forward!' I called out loud. 'Forward!' Someone on my right picked up the slogans: 'For our Fatherland, forward!'"

Pechersky described how the Jewish inmates united and people shouted "hurrah!" But the attack on the arsenal failed, and bad luck came when the inmates were met with automatic gunfire. Most people ran for the central exit: "Trampling the guards, firing from the several rifles in their possession, hurling stones at the Fascists they met and blinding them with sand, they pushed through the gate

Resist and Tell the World   129

and made for the woods."[76] Another group made their way through the barbed wire. They had to cross the minefield, where most of them perished. Pechersky chose another way through the wire fence, near the officer's house, assuming there were no mines there. Shooting was going on around him. "And there we were, on the other side of the fence! On the other side of the minefield!" There was just one barren strip of land to pass; they ran. This was quite a sober description that mentions revenge and the fatherland.

Myth and Reality in Stories about the Revolt

Mythologies are unavoidable in such moments. According to Dutch historian Schelvis, the Russians shouted, "Forwards, Pro Stalina! [sic]"[77] Survivor Philip Bialowicz described the scene in the following words:

> Leon and Sasha realized what must be done. Immediately they jumped on top of a table at the front of the yard and called out to everyone:
> "Brothers! The moment of destiny has come. Let us rise and destroy this place. We have little chance of surviving, but at least we will die fighting with honor. If anyone survives, bear witness to what happened here! Tell the world about this place."
> I quickly promised myself that, yes, if I survive the next moments, I will fulfill Leon and Sasha's wishes; I will tell everyone beyond this forest about this cursed place and its brave prisoners.[78]

Thomas Blatt, another survivor, has his own memories of Pechersky. He wrote:

> Jumping on a table, he made a short speech in Russian, his native language. This was not the heroic pep talk heard in war films. His voice, clear and loud so that everybody could hear, was composed and slow. He told the prisoners that most Germans in the camp had been killed. There was no turning back. A terrible war was ravaging the world and each prisoner was part of that struggle. He reminded everybody of the power of his motherland, the Soviet Union, and promised that dead or alive, they would be avenged, and so would the tragedy of all humanity. He repeated twice that those prisoners who by some miracle survived should forever be a witness to this crime. He ended with a call: "Forward Comrades! For Stalin! Death to the fascists!"[79]

Survivor Kalmen Wewryk also mentioned Stalin—"Hoorah Na Stalinya!"—and, as he stated: "Stalin was our God then; every Jew looked for Stalin as his savior. First one man, then twenty men, and finally many, many others shouted: 'Hoorah Na Stalinya!'"[80]

This invocation of Stalin was also part of the story that Philip Bialowitz told me in an interview in New York on April 9, 2010. Memories change and are stored in different ways in the mind after so many years. In Philip's memory, over the years Pechersky had become more Communist. The story was taken over by Schelvis

130 *Resist and Tell the World*

in his book on Sobibor,[81] but Stalin is also in Pechersky's testimony of 1952 for the Polish Historical Commission: "These proud slogans fell like thunder in the death camp." He described how they united all Jews from many countries. But in this version the table on which he had jumped is absent. I personally doubt the table story. No soldier who has a clear mind would climb up on a table where he could become an easy target for the Germans. I don't doubt that people shouted and yelled. During the revolt, many were shot, lost their lives, or were wounded by mines and bullets. In the following days, the Germans started an enormous search for Jews who had escaped. The executed SS men are named in the messages of the authorities in Lublin sent to the higher command in Krakow.[82]

Marek Bem summarized the conditions that led to success. According to Bem, the members of the resistance movement had good jobs and good positions. They had the opportunity and the time to focus on the planning. Also, he argues that the German idea of collective responsibility reduced the number of escape attempts. As he wrote: "many prisoners even claimed to have prevented other prisoners from escaping from the camp during the time leading up to the revolt."[83] He said it was a paradox that the principle of collective responsibility worked to the benefit of the resistance group. He argued that the guards paid less attention to the prisoners because they assumed "that the prisoners themselves would keep an eye on each other." Another asset was the presence of a strong leader with the ability to organize and maintain the resistance movement.

The main uncertainty regarding a possible escape was that people had nowhere to go. As survivor Kalmen Wewryk described:

> On two occasions, I could have escaped. A big forest fire broke out near Sobibor and they took us to put out the fire. The Germans said that the partisans had started the fire. The smoke was very thick. I was sent to get some sand. I was half a kilometer away from the main group of prisoners; the smoke covered everything and the area was heavily wooded. I wanted to take off and run, but then I had qualms. Where could I hide? They would start a massive search for me because they didn't want the 'secret' of Sobibor to get out. How far could I run before I tired? Remember, I was weak. And, curled up in some hole, could I *really* fool the dogs they would bring in?[84]

On another occasion, he was with four others alone with a Ukrainian guard, since the others were negotiating about a sale of vodka. He suggested killing the guard, but the others refused. According to Wewryk, many Jews did know how to escape because they had been the builders of the camp, so they knew the wiring of the electrified fence.

I would like to add my observation to the explanations of why the revolt was successful. The factors Bem notes do not mention the military discipline within the Russian group. People were ordered to resist, and they were used to accepting orders if there was one person from whom orders were accepted. In those circumstances people were prepared, and they dared to take risks. They knew they had nothing to lose. But people do not automatically manage to be organized in such

Resist and Tell the World 131

conditions; there must be a will, and there must be hope. Pechersky was able to hide his serious doubts about their possible success, except among the Russian soldiers.

In 1980, and he repeated this in later years, he said, "I did not take revenge. I fought for my Motherland as a soldier, not as a murderer." This seems exaggerated, but there is also some truth in it. In all their acts, the Russians behaved like soldiers, and they formed a group. Philip Bialowitz described a conversation with his older brother Simcha: "I know we can count on the Soviet soldiers to carry out their assignments. But what about the other prisoners?" he said. "They aren't soldiers. They have no training or experience in killing." They agreed that Polish Jews might not be able to kill. "We'll rely on the Soviets as much as possible," Simcha said.[85]

Twelve Germans were killed, but even more important, the Germans were in panic and were scared. Frenzel reorganized his group, and his primary concern was that the partisans would use the chaotic situation to attack the camp in order to free the prisoners who had been left behind. He was not sure if the uprising was the result of collaboration between the prisoners and the partisans. Whoever was found in the camp was detained in the barracks. Frenzel contacted his superiors, who immediately sent commandos (*Einsatzcommandos*) to conduct a thorough search of the camp. They killed those Jews who were not yet confined. Protective measures were taken against a partisan attack. It slowly became apparent that some Ukrainian guards were missing, although most of them had been fighting with the Germans. There was some debate about whether the Jews who had remained in the camp should be executed immediately. But the Jews were needed to do the labor.

I have followed Marek Bem in all this, and I have used his figures. According to him, on October 14, 1943 there were five hundred Jews in the camp, of whom one hundred and eighty-four did not manage to escape. Forty-one prisoners were killed during the uprising, and one hundred thirty were killed later. The fate of thirty-two others is unknown. In the end, *fifty-eight* survived the war. In the months to come, there would be regular clashes between the Germans and the Jews who had escaped. Arad mentions how the Germans were upset, which was reported to Berlin. The search operation lasted for four days.[86] The escapees bore a secret no one was supposed to know.

The common fear among the prisoners was to be caught by the Germans. As survivor Dov Freiberg said: "The most important thing was that we didn't fall into the hands of the Germans again. That was the worst thing that could happen. Nobody believed that we could run away."[87] To see the Germans killed was a joy, but the escapees did not know where to run, and they ended up having another ten months to survive. According to survivor Thomas Blatt, the weeks following the escape were terrifying. There was a major force searching for the prisoners, and special attention was given to roads leading to the East, where the Bug River formed a natural frontier. Bridges were guarded, and guards stood at the crossroads. The camp itself was closed immediately and demolished with the help of Jews from Treblinka. It took the workers a month to do the job. The last Jews

132   Resist and Tell the World

were executed by bullets on November 23. The population who lived around the camp immediately began to search for gold and valuables.[88]

Pechersky ran out of the camp while bullets were flying everywhere around him. He made the first hundred meters and then reached an open field, where one could still feel the eyes of the persecutors, so he tried to run faster and faster. As long as he was in the open field, bullets could reach him. It was different in the forest, and he finally reached the shadow. "I stood still for a moment," he wrote, to "get my breath back and I looked backwards. Exhausted and with their last strength, people proceeded and they reached the trees. But where was Luka and where was Shlomo?" By 1952, Pechersky knew that the majority of the prisoners of Camps I and II had managed to escape, but many had fallen in the open field before they reached the trees. "We decided not to stay in the woods, and we split into several smaller groups who went in different directions. Polish Jews chose to head in the direction of Chełm; they spoke the language and they knew the region. Those of us from the Soviet Union marched to the East."

Pechersky understood the problems of those who did not speak Polish or Russian. Carefully he tried to create more distance from the camp. "By the sound of the bullets we could orient ourselves. Where the shots came from was the location of the camp." These shots slowly abided and, by the time evening fell it was silent. Pechersky was with Tsibulski and Waiszpapir.

Pechersky and his men decided to try to reach Russian partisans or territory controlled by the Red Army. This was logical, as in Polish territory their language would betray them; if they crossed the Bug River, Russian would be more common. They met Shubaev, who gave them a message from Shlomo Laitman, who had been wounded and could not reach the safety of the forest. According to Yiddish author Michael Lev, Laitman had sent a message to his friend Sasha: "We should repay them, not with tears but with weapons!"[89] At one point he had no longer been able to continue, and he asked to be shot. Since Michael Lev spoke so often with Pechersky in later life, we can trust this story, even though Lev's book is fictional. He gave such statements in Rostov much later. In 1952, Pechersky mourned the loss of his loyal friend. He had felt closer to him than to the others. As Pechersky said in 1952 his testimony for *Jewish Resistance*: "Bright insight, his calm, courage, and self-sacrifice strengthened me in the most difficult moments of life." In all his memories, he said that he wondered what had happened to Luka.

Pechersky proposed walking throughout the night, so the escapees moved in single file, with Waiszpapir bringing up the rear. He forbade the men from smoking or speaking and made them keep together. If the first one threw himself on the ground, everyone else should follow the example. Panic should be avoided. They sometimes met other escapees, and at one point found a larger group. They were now fifty-seven people and approached the railway as dawn came. They had to invent ways of hiding during daytime and chose low bushes and had to camouflage everything and to lie down as if dead and not make a single sound. There was a slight drizzle. The men started to map where they were and found that they were not far from a forest. Planes flew above their heads throughout the

Resist and Tell the World   133

day, but they were not discovered. When night fell, they met two people who had tried to cross the Bug. These men told them that Luka was heading in the direction of Chełm. Pechersky then said that the group was too large and it would be impossible to feed such a large group, so they split into smaller groups. A group of nine men would try to reach the Bug and to cross the river, but they failed.

While I do believe it was a wise decision to split from the larger group and to walk on with those speaking Russian, the story is more complicated and maybe less beautiful. Of course, the first objective was to reach the Red Army. Every Russian soldier knew that POWs were going to be punished, and fighting well could reduce the sentence. Thomas Blatt describes how Pechersky announced to the other inmates that a small group would go on a reconnaissance mission. They also collected money to buy food. Only one rifle was left with the larger group that waited, but as Blatt explains, they felt they would be abandoned by their leaders. Indeed, they waited in vain. "We had lost hope. Despite his promise, he had defected. They had taken our money and guns and left. Or had something happened to them? We were now without leadership or firearms, except for one rifle."[90] Blatt went on to describe how quarrels started and more strong men left, leaving the weaker and older ones behind.

Much later in 1980, Blatt visited Pechersky in Rostov. He admitted he would never have been alive without the organizer of the revolt. But he wanted Pechersky to explain why he had abandoned the larger group of inmates. He wrote:

> Without question, the rest of the survivors and I considered Sasha a hero, and we all agreed that if it had not been for him, no Jew would have survived Sobibor. Even so, I had troubling questions to ask.
>
> THOMAS: "In your memoirs, you summarized your departure in the forest from the rest of the escapees with a few sentences. 'We realized that it made no sense to continue together in such a large group; therefore, we divided into small units, each going its own way.' You know, Sasha, that faith kept me close to you. After your speech, just before the escape, I lost you for a while to meet you again by the barbed wires, and then lost you again, only to find you in the forest. I was with you until your departure and I see it differently."
> Sasha's eyebrows came together as he gazed at me piercingly.
> THOMAS: "Sasha, don't take this the wrong way, please. Because of you I am here alive. Because of you, many of us have families, children, and grandchildren instead of finding our end in Sobibor. If you lived in the West, you would be admired by untold thousands. I just want to know: Why didn't you organize a partisan group of us?"[91]

Pechersky explained that he considered himself a soldier and he had learned that small units had a greater chance of surviving. He was not able to tell people that he had to leave them. They would have followed him. "What can I say, you were there. We were only people. The basic instincts came into play. It was still a fight

134   *Resist and Tell the World*

for survival." He denied he had known about the money, he was not able to oversee all that happened. And those who had arms did not give them up.

Shame and Guilt in Testimonies

There is shame and guilt in all narratives, also in the narratives of survivors. These lead to distortions. In his book Thomas (Toivi) Blatt includes a long story about Pechersky, saying he was thrown in prison for many years. He also described how Pechersky said he did not seek revenge, but fought for the Motherland as a soldier. His admiration for Pechersky made him write this way, and in 1980 he wanted the world to understand how much he wanted recognition for the heroic role of the leader.

Many of the testimonies are rooted in the ways narrators have constructed the stories they tell the world. These are monuments of time and place. In the former Soviet Union, certain stories were not told, as was explained to me by Aleksey Vaytsen in Ryazan (see the Introduction). Aleksey told me how, until the late 1990s, he had been unable to talk about his experiences in Sobibor. Therefore, the story of Jewish suffering was closed, as Aleksei called it. He was not certain what would have happened if he had talked about such forbidden subjects.

When I interviewed Esther Raab in New Jersey in 2010, there were long periods when the camera was not on. We needed a calm moment. Esther had worked in the quarters of the Ukrainian guards as a cleaner. That is why she recognized John Demjanjuk, who was standing trial in Munich at that very time. She said that any woman who had been forced to be very close to a man would always recognize and remember him. There was reluctance on both sides. I was too shy to ask what she meant; the pain was too visible on her face. Now we can only guess, even though sexual behavior with a Jewish woman was considered to shame the Aryan race and would therefore be punished. There was a lot of forced sexual contact between Germans and Jews, but Demjanjuk was from Ukraine and did not belong to the superior race either.

Interviewing survivors of the revolt, I encountered feelings of shame and guilt that were so deeply repressed and so much the result of trauma that everyone I asked refused to talk about it. In fact, the subject was avoided in nearly all the interviews I have listened to and all of the videos I have seen. There was a consensus that everyone should have been able to escape, but the people in Camps III and IV never got that chance. No one tried to open a door for them, and so the men in charge of the most filthy and obnoxious jobs—the gas chambers and the crematoria—never had a chance. No one can convince me not to think for a moment about those killed that very same night and the following day.[92]

Notes

* Permission was given for the use of material from Yuri Suhl, *They fought Back*, (New York: Shocken 1967), 47–51.
1 Reuben Ainsztein, *Jewish Resistance in Nazi-occupied Eastern Europe* (London: Paul Elek, 1974); in German as *Jüdische Widerstand im deutschbesetzten Osteuropa während des Zweiten Weltkrieges*, trans. and ed. Jörg Paulsen (Oldenburg: Bibliothek und Informationssystem der Universität Oldenburg, 1993), 85. Page numbers refer to the German edition.

Resist and Tell the World 135

2 Gitta Sereny, *Into that Darkness. From Mercy Killing to Mass Murder* (London: Pimlico, 1974), 47.

3 Ibid., 134–137.

4 Blatt, *"From the Ashes"*, 113.

5 Shmuel Krakowski, *The War of the Doomed, Jewish Armed Resistance in Poland, 1942–1944* (New York and London: Holmes and Meier Publishing, 1984).

6 Yuri Suhl, *They Fought Back: The Story of the Jewish Resistance in Nazi Europe* (New York: Shocken Books, 1967), 20.

7 In her book on the Minsk ghetto, Epstein mentions the number of 10,000 (Epstein, 260). Besides Epstein, "The Ghetto of Minsk," see David Meltser and Vladimir Levin, *The Black Book with Red Papers*, Cochesville, Maryland: 2005, 1–93.

8 Rachel L'Einwohner, "Leadership, Authority and Collective Action," *American Behavioural Scientist* 50:10 (June 2007): 1308, which mentions that everyone who became a leader was a political activist.

9 Shalom Cholawsky, *The Jews of Bielorussia during World War II* (Amsterdam: Harwood Academic Publishers, 1998), 53–57.

10 Bem, *Sobibor*, 160.

11 See also: Jacob Apenszaik and Moshe Polakiewicz, *Armed Resistance of the Jews in Poland* (New York: American Federation for Polish Jews, 1944). On p. 69, the book mentions a massive uprising in Lublin.

12 Ibid., 70–74.

13 Reuben Ainsztein, *Jewish Resistance*, passim.

14 Vasili Grossman, *With the Red Army in Poland and Byelorussia*, trans. Helen Altschuler (London and New York: Hutchinson and Co., 1945).

15 Ibid., reprinted in: Robert Chandler et al., eds. and trans., *The Road: Stories, Journalism, and Essays* (New York: New York Review of Books, 2010), 116–162.

16 David Shneer, *Through Soviet Jewish Eyes: Photography, War and the Holocaust* (New Brunswick: Rutgers University Press, 2012), 171.

17 Ilya Ehrenburg, "Nakanune," *Pravda*, 7 August 1944. Antoni Rutman and Samuel Krasilhik, "Fabrika Smerto v Sobibure" [The Death Factory in Sobibor], *Komsomols'kaia pravda*, 2 September 1944.

18 Grossman, *With the Red Army*, 6.

19 Peter Duffy, *The Bielski Brothers* (New York: Harper Collins, 2003). This and other family camps are described by Nechama Tec in *Defiance* (New York: Oxford University Press, 2009).

20 Allan Levine, *Fugitives of the Forest: The Heroic Struggle of Jewish Resistance and Survival During the Second World War* (Guilford, CT: The Lyons Press, 1998), 41–42.

21 Kalmen Wewryk, *To Sobibor and Back*, 93–94.

22 Novitch, *Sobibor*, 130.

23 Interview Samuel Lerer 23.3.1995–13.4.95, Segment 25, Shoah Visual History Archive.

24 Ibid., Segment 4.

25 Interview Dov Freiberg, Shoah Visual History Archive, 134.

26 Interview Ester Raab, New Jersey, in USHMM, 22.6.1997.

27 Wewryk, *To Sobibor and Back*, 92–94.

28 Jules Schelvis, *Ooggetuigen van Sobibor* (Amsterdam: Ambo, 2010), 178.

29 Michael R. Marrus, "Jewish Resistance to the Holocaust," *Journal of Contemporary History* 30:1 (January 1995): 85–86.

30 Hannah Arendt, *Eichmann in Jerusalem: A Report on the Banality of Evil* (revised and enlarged edition, New York: The Viking Press, 1965).

31 Marrus, *Jewish Resistance*, 87.

32 Ibid., referring to Raul Hilberg, *The Destruction of the European Jews* (New Haven: Yale University Press, 1961).

33 James M. Glass, *Jewish Resistance During the Holocaust: Moral Uses of Violence and Will* (Houndsmill and New York: Palgrave Macmillan, 2004).

136 *Resist and Tell the World*

34 Yehuda Bauer, *They Chose Life: Jewish Resistance in the Holocaust* (New York: American Jewish Committee Institute of Human Relations, 1973).

35 Yehuda Bauer, *Rethinking the Holocaust* (New Haven: Yale University Press, 2002), 130.

36 Novitch, *Sobibor*, 157, testimony Bahir.

37 Glass, *Jewish Resistance*, 21.

38 Marrus, *Jewish Resistance*, 104.

39 Thomas V. Maher, "Threat, Resistance and Collective Action: The Cases of Sobibor, Treblinka and Auschwitz," *American Sociological Review* 75:2 (April 2010): 252–272.

40 See also Albert Nirestein, ed., *A Tower from the Enemy: Contributions to a History of Jewish Resistance in Poland* (New York: The Orion Press, 1959), 314.

41 Maher, "Threat," 267.

42 Paul Gomberg, "Can a Partisan Be a Moralist?" *American Philosophical Quarterly* 27:1 (January 1990): 71–80.

43 Shmuel Krakowski, "The War of the Doomed," 26–27.

44 Ainsztein, *Jewish Resistance*, 215.

45 Marek Bem, *Sobibor*, 245.

46 Ibid., 246.

47 Ainsztein, *Jewish Resistance*. This is the thesis of his book

48 Novitch, *Sobibor*, 148.

49 Ibid., 131.

50 Ainsztein, *Jewish Resistance*, 216; Bem, *Sobibor*, 245.

51 Ainsztein, Ibid.

52 Krakowski, *The War of the Doomed*, 236–237.

53 Ibid., 239.

54 Ainsztein (this is the NIOD manuscript typescript), 420.

55 See: *The Long Shadow of Sobibor*, 2010.

56 Ainsztein, NIOD manuscript 419–420.

57 Bem, *Sobibor*, 254.

58 Ibid., 257, referring to the *Zentrale Stelle der Landesjustizverwaltungen*, Ludwigsburg Archives, case file 45 Js 27/61, file ref. No.208 AR-Z 251/59, Holon, Israel, May 1959.

59 Bem, *Sobibor*, 260, 261; see also Schelvis, *Sobibor*, 193.

60 Krakowski, *The War of the Doomed*, 245.

61 Ibid.

62 Ibid., 246.

63 Arad, *Belzec, Sobibor, Treblinka*, 310.

64 Jewish Historical Institute 1952, 12.

65 Ibid., 22.

66 Statement, Naum Iankelevich Plotnitski, 16 June 1980, Yad Vashem no.03, file 4123.

67 Yuri Suhl, *They Fought Back: The Story of the Jewish Resistance in Nazi Europe* (New York: Shocken Books, 1967), 47–51.

68 Ibid., 21.

69 Schelvis, *Ooogetuigen*, 24.

70 Bruder, *"Hunderte Helden,"* 38. Grisha was known as Gregori according to Bruder, although neither she nor I could find further information about him.

71 Suhl, *They Fought Back*, 32.

72 Schelvis, *Sobibor*, 154.

73 Suhl, *They Fought Back*, 35; *Report to the Jewish Historical Institute Warschau*, 41–42.

74 Suhl, *They Fought Back*, 34.

75 Schelvis, *Ooggetuigen*, 151.

76 Suhl, *They Fought Back*, 37–40.

77 Schelvis, *Ooggetuigen*, 165.

78 Philip "Fiszel" Bialowitz, with Joseph Bialowitz, *A Promise in Sobibor: A Jewish Boy's Story of Revolt and Survival in Nazi-Occupied Poland* (Madison: University of Wisconsin Press, 2008), 119.

Resist and Tell the World 137

79 Thomas (Toivi) Blatt, *Sobibor, the Forgotten Revolt: A Survivor's Report* [Issaquah: H.E.P., 1996], 86.
80 Wewryk, *To Sobibor and Back*, 200.
81 Schelvis, *Sobibor*, 168.
82 Letter Lublin, 15 October 1943: various letters from the *Kommandeur der Ordnungspolizei im Distrikt Lublin* on 14 and 15 October 1943 to *Offizier vom Dienst, Krakau*. In the same letters it is clear that some of the Ukrainian guards fled to the partisans, in these letters called "bandits." Copies of these letters were sent to me by Dariusz Pawłoś, Chair of the Commission for Reconciliation between Poland and Germany. Russian State Archive GARF f r-r-7021, op 115, D8 l 161–162.
83 Bem, *Sobibor*, 276.
84 Wewryk, *To Sobibor and Back*, 73.
85 Bialowitz, *A Promise at Sobibor*, 110.
86 Arad, *Belzec, Sobibor, Treblinka*, 338–340.
87 Interview Dov Freiberg, Shoah Visual History Archive.
88 Blatt, *The Forgotten Revolt*, 98–102.
89 Lev, *Sobibor*, 135.
90 Blatt, "From the Ashes," 220.
91 Blatt, *The Forgotten Revolt*, 133–134.
92 Bem (*Sobibor*, p. 297) mentions that there were probably 184 prisoners who did not escape or were not able to do so. In fact, he is the only historian who devotes some lines to them.

5 After the Escape
Life With the Partisans and the Red Army

What should they do next and what steps could they take, now that they had fled from the camp? How could they avoid capture? They rightly assumed that a major search for escapees had been launched. Of course they wanted to reach the partisans, and it is very likely they were worried about the anti-Semitism in some of the partisan groups, especially the Polish. Pechersky had warned the inmates before the revolt that they could not count on help from the Polish partisans near the camp. It was clear they had to reach territory where the Russian language was spoken in order not be recognized as foreigners.

Before their deportation to Sobibor, when they were still in Shirokaya Street in Minsk, they had been informed about what was happening in the partisan movement near Minsk, since there was contact with the ghetto and with the partisans. We can assume that the small group around Pechersky knew that the leadership in Moscow wanted to control the partisan movement and that their struggle for this control led to disagreements among various partisan groups. They must have known that, in most partisan groups, Jews were low in the hierarchy. While some Soviet groups accepted Jews as fighters, many others refused them.

News of the revolt did reach Polish newspapers, but the news about Sobibor was hidden from the Soviet-oriented partisans and the Red Army because the special suffering of Jews was an unwanted story. The fate of Jews was seldom covered by the Soviet newspapers, especially after 1943, because the leadership was afraid that too much support for Jews would help the Nazis in traditionally anti-Semitic territory where Jew hunting could be used in their favor.[1] According to the dominant Soviet ideology, Jews had to look and behave like everyone else, and if they wanted to be integrated into the partisan struggle they had to give up their Jewish identity. They should stop claiming they were special. The biggest compliment was when a Jew was told he did not resemble a Jew.[2]

It was mid-October, and winter was coming, so they needed a shelter where they could hide and be protected. They realized that in most places they would not be welcome. The small Russian group was left alone; they had no road map for what could or should happen next; there was no historical example, nor a best way. Intuition and good luck, based on military skills, were all the escapees could hope for. The revolt had been unique, the act of a bold brain full of imagination and the result of meticulous planning. Pechersky had learned from the failed

After the Escape 139

escapes he had witnessed in Minsk and elsewhere, and he knew the danger of treason if too many people were informed about a possible break-out. Pechersky mentions an attempt by a group of fifty people who had accumulated weapons to organize a mass escape from Shirokaya Street. Everyone was told about the plan, which was too many people, and the plan was betrayed. By the time he was taken to Sobibor, he clearly knew how easily such efforts could fail.[3] In Minsk there had never been a plan to attack the guards. The acts of resistance in Minsk were mostly efforts to escape, and there were some cases of sabotage. Only in Sobibor had the inmates accepted that perhaps all they could do was kill some of the German and Ukrainian guards without much hope for their own survival. In most cases, those who had managed to escape from the Shirokaya Street prison in Minsk and had reached the partisans had been well informed, and they were guided by the information of thousands who had already left the ghetto. The walls of the prison and the ghetto seemed impenetrable, but they were porous. Partisans returned regularly to guide new groups of Jews to the forests. The walls of Sobibor were much higher and thicker and surrounded by a minefield, so the Germans felt confident that no one could pass.

The small group of Russian inmates had no one to go to; no one was waiting for them, and their flight would take them first into dangerous Polish territory with partisans who were known to be hostile to Jews. More to the east, across the Bug river, was Byelorussia, where the language was a Russian dialect. They had information from prisoners who had worked in forced labor camps near Sobibor. Some of these men who were too weak or too sick to work were sent to the gas chambers in Sobibor. They would arrive and had a brief chance to speak with the inmates and to warn them. The guards could also talk about the partisans; sometimes there was even regular contact between the two. Some guards wanted to escape to the partisans in case Germany lost the war, and therefore they would try to make contact with partisans nearby. Maybe by changing sides they could avoid punishment, they believed. Another source of information was the farmers living in the villages around Sobibor. They passed on news from the front and would even warn if the front and, with it, the Red Army were approaching.

In the forced labor camps and in the villages near Sobibor, people were well aware of the hostility of many partisan groups to Jews, especially those who belonged to the AK (Armia Krajowa, the Polish national resistance). The escapees, conscious of such dangers, hoped to reach "safe" territory and to find information about the partisans, preferably under Russian command. As Arkady Waiszpapir told me, they assumed that Russians would treat the POWs better, even if they were Jewish. It was only twenty-two days since they had been taken away from Minsk; therefore up until September 18 they had good information about where the partisans could be found. But the distance to Minsk was about 500 kilometers. To go to the western and nearby part of Byelorussia seemed the best option, and the escapees had probably heard about the wide woods and forested moors where so many had fled.

As we have seen, the Russian group consisted of trained soldiers who accepted the hierarchical command of the army, which enabled them to act as an organized

140 *After the Escape*

unit. More important, they had taken the rifles with them when they left the larger group. Many partisan groups considered rifles a condition for acceptance in their midst. Pechersky automatically became the leader, as had always been the case. In 1946 he noted, "My group consisted of nine people—we headed east with the polar star as our compass. The nights were starry. Our first aim was to cross the Bug. To do that we had to find the proper place and the proper time. In quiet, deserted hamlets we obtained food and received vital information and directions. We were warned which places to avoid.[4] We were told quite a number of the fugitives drowned while crossing the river."[5] Either they were shot while swimming to the other side or they perished in the very icy water. Some could not swim.

They were lucky to get food at all. The people they approached were intimidated by the armed men and did not dare to refuse their request for food. Although what they received was never enough, they could survive. Hunger would become a major threat to all who escaped; it was an enemy as relentless as the danger of being caught by the Germans, who indeed had launched a massive manhunt. The revolt had come as a surprise to the Germans, as Marek Bem notes in his book on Sobibor.[6] In the following paragraphs I will follow Bem's book, which is based on an impressive range of sources available in Poland.

The Germans despised the Jews so much that they felt invincible, despite all the resistance in and around the camp. As a result, what had happened during the uprising was beyond their imagination. They were afraid of the partisans when they went in small groups to the forest and preferred to travel in convoys. When they were in a group, they could defend themselves if partisans attacked. But the idea of such a massive resistance of hundreds of people and the ingenuity of their revolt was beyond anything they could have foreseen. In their hubris the Germans had forgotten that the Jews had nothing to lose and would therefore fight for any small chance to survive. Every inmate taking part in the revolt had realized that many people would die, and they had only hoped that at least some would escape to tell the world what was happening. The Germans had not realized that the Jewish prisoners wanted the world to know of the horrendous crimes that had been committed. The message to the world became their assignment. They had also failed to see how dangerous it was to admit the group of Russian soldiers into Sobibor. They became scared in the ensuing chaos where a few German soldiers could no longer dominate the mass of furious people. Clearly, before they started to hunt in the forests, it would be necessary to find out who and how many prisoners were left in the camp, and to find out if there was a threat from their side. It was soon clear that the majority had managed to escape.

Most of all, Karl Frenzel worried that the escapees would bring partisans into the camp and that they would come back to liberate the other prisoners who had stayed behind. Since the telephone lines to the camp had been cut, Frenzel had to use the telephone and telegraph at the Sobibor railway station. Once the initial panic was over and some control of the situation had been restored, Frenzel went to the railway station to warn various branches of the SS and to ask for reinforcements. A military intervention seemed unavoidable because of the feeling that danger was everywhere. Two squadrons of soldiers arrived on the evening

After the Escape 141

of October 14. The Jewish prisoners who had stayed in the camp were locked in their barracks; those who were still in Camps III and IV were shot immediately.[7] That night some Jews returned voluntarily to the camp. They realized they did not know how to survive, and they had no place to go.

The next day the nearby forest was combed in the search for prisoners, especially in the stretch between Włodawa and Chełm. The manhunt lasted until October 21. Afterward, several groups of inmates from other camps, mainly from Treblinka, were brought to the camp for its liquidation. They had to dig deep trenches, because in the heat of the summer the corpses would swell and the sand covering them would rise. The mass graves were not good enough, and they had to start over again to dig still deeper pits.[8] The last group of these "auxiliaries" was shot at the beginning of December 1943. In July 1944 the Red Army arrived. In the meantime, local residents had started to dig up the earth in search of valuables. Marek Bem quotes from an interview he conducted in April 2011 with Jan Dolińkski, who told him how eager people from the surrounding villages were to dig for gold in Sobibor. When Dolińkski arrived, he found the ground torn up. He said that each time he went to the camp, there were about one hundred people digging. They used sieves to find pieces of gold and precious stones. Utensils such as children's combs were not valuable enough for them. "Everything on that yard was dug up—everything, be it a stone, a branch or a stump." Dolińkski mentioned a man from Włodawa who went there with a metal detector so that nothing would be overlooked.[9] This story is confirmed by an interview conducted by Yahad-In Unum in which the interviewee tells how much gold came from the camp while it still existed. There was always barter, and the gold was mainly used to buy enormous quantities of vodka.[10]

On October 19, a meeting of Germans in Cracow had agreed that there were real problems with security in the camps in Eastern Poland. According to those attending the meeting, the presence of Jews in all possible types of camps presented a threat. The order to liquidate Sobibor followed immediately. Bem wrote: "The unprecedented uprising and mass escape in Sobibor was used by Himmler as a pretext to commence the final stage of the 'Final Solution' within the General Government area. Despite the ensuing debate over whether to use Jews as free labor force or not, Himmler sealed the fate of the Jewish camps only a few days after the Cracow meeting. His instructions were quickly forwarded to Cracow."[11] The Sobibor camp would cease to exist; all traces of it were to be destroyed, and the so-called Operation Harvest Festival would then conclude Operation Reinhard. Operation Harvest Festival became one of the largest cases of mass murder, wrote Bem. Between November 3 and 4, all the Jews in Lublin and in the Majdanek and Trawnik camps were killed, and the same happened at the Poniatowa camp the following day. More than 42,000 people were slaughtered in two days.

Pechersky learned later that the Germans had raised a great alarm on the same evening as the revolt. He was told that on October 16 a special division of excavators had arrived and destroyed all the buildings and guard towers. They pulled out the pillars of the barbed wire, loaded them on vans, and took them away with the bulldozers that had excavated the pits for the ashes of the burnt corpses.

142   *After the Escape*

They also took the transport of wagons on which there were still corpses and the diesel engines that had operated the flow of carbon monoxide. They even killed the geese that were kept to make noise during the gassing of Jews to conceal the screams of the victims. Frenzel had selected Pechersky for his personal special moment of sadistic killing, as he said later. He wanted to force Pechersky to kill the other Russians before being slaughtered himself. We shall never know how Pechersky would have reacted, but we might expect resistance. In the end no one would have survived.

Memories of Survival after the Escape

All of the escapees had a very hard time surviving after Sobibor in hostile territory, and it was difficult to find their way back to normal life. The men of the Russian group were strong and managed rather well. The others survived by enduring tremendous hardships. There were no longer any Jews living in the Polish villages and *shtetls* near Sobibor whom they could fall back on for help or food. Poles in the countryside had become scared to hide Jews; others just hated the Jews since they believed that the Jews had murdered Christ. Some thought the Jews were politically with the Communists and hated them for this reason.

While the first days had felt for these inmates like rescue and freedom, the escapees now faced a new ordeal that occupied a prominent place in their memories during the interviews I conducted with them. Many of the autobiographies mentioned in Chapter 1 are devoted to their hard life after the camp experience, when survival was never taken for granted and their perilous situation called for ingenuity. People had to hide and live in holes in the ground; they were betrayed and delivered to the Germans. Only a few were treated with generosity. They suffered and were robbed of their last possessions, while the gold and valuables they had managed to smuggle with them during the escape were dwindling. Interviews conducted with them by others during the many decades after the end of the war depict these lonely survivors, hungry and cold, being chased away and on the run.

They also wrote about it. "I was free," said Dov Freiberg. "There was no barbed wire surrounding me. There was no morning roll call." But in freedom, no one knew where to go. In the camp, Freiberg and others had heard about partisans in the forest. But where were they hiding? How could they find them? Where was a shelter? And how could they find their way home when there was no home or destination? After wandering for a long time through the woods, Freiberg and his group had been convinced they were thirty or forty kilometers away from the camp, but it turned out they were again near Sobibor.[12] They had apparently been walking in circles. The forests were a labyrinth of small roads.

When the fugitives met Polish partisans, they were often robbed of their rifles, and several of them were killed. Freiberg's group wandered for three weeks; they were sometimes chased away, and sometimes helped with some food. The group had started out with more than twenty people but had shrunk to three men, who by accident found other escapees. Together, the seven tried to make a life in a bunker under the ground. Their relative calm was disturbed when they were

After the Escape 143

robbed by Polish peasants who also murdered several of them. During the next attack by Polish farmers, the opening of the bunker was blocked by the aggressors. They could barely liberate themselves and free themselves from their prison where they were waiting for the Germans, to whom the peasants would reveal the location. In the end, the few who remained alive eventually found shelter and passed the winter while waiting for the Red Army.

Kalmen Wewryk, a Polish survivor, was also with Pechersky when the revolt began. He wrote that Pechersky had a compass, while Pechersky himself wrote in 1945 that he had been guided by the stars. Pechersky seemed to know something about the area, wrote Wewryk, and he would point the direction. It is almost as though he had informed himself while he planned the escape. He led the group for days and nights. The group would sneak into hamlets and beg for food. When the peasants saw how many hungry men were in the group, they got scared and would grudgingly hand over bread. The peasants also told them there were special German squads looking for the fugitives. The group tried to get as far away from Sobibor as possible. Wewryk described how Pechersky became nervous by the behavior of some who did not follow his orders, such as those who, unlike the Russian soldiers, did not walk in single file and would talk when he had asked for silence. After the Russians left, the number of people in the group Wewryk belonged to diminished. More and more people left the group.

With Shloime Elster, Wewryk continued to walk: "So the days and nights passed. Shloime and I became more and more disconsolate and depressed. We were haunted by fear, consumed with hunger, weakened and filthy."[13] He and Elster had been the oldest of the group, which made the other members consider them a burden. They were not given an equal share of the food. Exhausted and weakened by hunger, they had a hard time preparing hideouts for the night, and they could not work as quickly as the others. Wewryk confronted the group with their selfish attitude, and he warned they would be captured as a result of their greediness, which included the consumption of large quantities of alcohol. After a while he decided to leave them because he thought staying in such chaos was suicidal. After some hesitation, Shloime followed him. When they knocked at the door of a house, they met a Ukrainian. He seemed friendly but had an axe behind his back, so they had to run. By late October Wewryk had managed to reach Chełm and sought out a business friend to whom he had entrusted merchandise. He asked for a piece of bread. The former friend shouted, "You scum, if you don't leave immediately I will call the Gestapo to come and get you!"[14] In the coming days he met distrust, hostility, and coldness. When he reached another man he had worked for in the past, the man knelt and begged him to go away.

Wewryk hid in a forest and, as he wrote, "I had one big problem—my thoughts. I could not control what I was thinking, and I spent many hours in my dug-out, thinking and remembering the life I had before the war. The faces of my loved ones, now gone, flashed before my eyes hundreds of times, and their voices echoed and re-echoed in my ears."[15] He ended in a ruin filled with excrement. The bad smell would keep people away, he thought, and therefore he felt safe. When he begged at the house of one woman, she called him *Diabel* (Devil), even though

144   *After the Escape*

she had known him well in earlier times. He hid in a haystack, from where he grabbed food from a nearby house, but his footsteps were traceable in the snow. He ended in a hole in the forest he had dug out, always in danger and always hungry. His major fear was that he would become too weak to run in case people found him or to search for food.

All he wanted was to find the partisans. He wrote: "A man alone was nothing— a Jew alone was even less than that—but with a partisan group a man had half a chance. Or a quarter of a chance. In any case, being a partisan would be a vast improvement over my present forlorn state. And it was bitterly cold by now."[16] According to him, the peasants knew the partisans since they had to hand over food to them. But they refused to tell him where they were. When he asked for shelter and food, he was caught and tied up with ropes. He waited to be delivered to the Germans. He had no hope, but managed to gnaw through the rope and to run. Later, he was alone in the forest again, living on berries. He was hungry and lost his strength. In the end, after having been hunted for weeks by Polish farmers keen to collect the bounty for handing over Jews to the Germans, and in desperate physical condition, he reached the partisans. He had been betrayed and nearly killed several times; he was cold and undernourished, and probably would not have lived much longer. The partisans he finally encountered were official "Soviet" partisans who did not trust his story. Who was this man who had suddenly turned up from the woods, and was his story true? He talked about a camp they did not know about. As was routine, he was questioned extensively, but he was eventually taken into the group and became a partisan.

When I interviewed Selma Engel (Wijnberg) in 2010, the major part of the interview was about her life after Sobibor. Of course she had talked about the camp many times, but she liked to focus on the way she had to live afterward and how she had done so. She also made me realize that the disappointment that occurred after leaving the camp was easier to talk about than the chaotic story of the revolt when she had followed the mass of prisoners. Her story of the escape was framed in a standard way: she had not known it would happen, but she joined in and ran. But what happened afterward, when she was exhausted and the situation seemed hopeless, was even more traumatic. Selma had managed to stay together with Chaim Engel, a Polish man and former soldier, whom she met in Sobibor. He had protected the young woman from Deventer, a provincial town in the Netherlands, and the fact that he spoke Polish had been an asset. They got married after the war.

Chaim, who was active in the underground movement of the camp, had foreseen that he would have to bribe people, and he had been smart enough to stuff his pockets with gold and diamonds, and had even collected dollars. He had acquired these treasures from the possessions of Jews who had arrived in Sobibor with the transports and had been gassed. Indeed, Chaim had anticipated that he and Selma would need money to buy a place to hide and to survive. They could profit from their wealth, and it would save them. But the possession of valuables was also a danger, since there was always a chance that gold and money would be a reason to be robbed and killed.

After the Escape   145

Selma said:

> We walked and we walked and we walked and we were at the end of a little town. . . . And Chaim knocked on the door and asked if we could spend the day there. That man said "yes." Chaim gave him a twenty-dollar bill, a golden bill, and we stayed there, in the attic . . . When the evening came, we started walking again. . . . And we walked and we walked. . . . I think we did so for ten days. . . . We had nothing to eat . . . we slept in the woods . . . and at night we walked. Not in open fields but in the woods most of the time.

She continued:

> Two persons arrived on a wagon and they asked if we would like to go with them. Chaim said "yes." So Chaim went in one wagon and I went in the other wagon. They spoke Polish to each other and said, "We are going to kill them. For sure they have money." Chaim said to me, "Selma jump," so we jumped. I jumped and he jumped. And then we walked further.[17]

They had been walking only at night, but further away from the camp they started to walk during the daytime.

They were not welcome, and when Selma knocked at a door to ask for a glass of water, a maid opened the door, and "a woman was sitting next to the fireplace, knitting. And she said 'no'! and she closed the door. Later we walked at night, guided by the stars." The daytime visibility was too dangerous. Where should they go? Chaim decided to connect with his former employer, who was a safe contact. They were turned down and continued their search for shelter. "After ten days we were, you know, exhausted." The couple reached a farmhouse, and Chaim asked if they could stay overnight. They were directed to the barn by a farmer who wanted to help and who guided them to his brother's farm, which was more isolated. For the next nine months Chaim and Selma were confined to hiding in an attic they could not leave; they did not get much food, and sometimes they did not even get water. The attic was hot, dirty, and filled with flies, and perhaps twice they were allowed to wash. All the time the two of them were alone, sometimes with only rats for company. Selma got pregnant while they just waited and watched the storks that had settled on the chimney. They had nothing else to do. But when the storks left, the farmers superstitiously thought their departure was an evil omen, so they had to leave.

After a period in Chełm where they waited for the Red Army and met other Sobibor survivors, the couple landed in the Netherlands, Selma's native country. But Chaim's nationality was Polish, and even though he did not want to return to Poland, the couple was not allowed to settle. In an extremely bureaucratic way, Chaim was not admitted to the Netherlands. He was expected to return to Poland and was denied Dutch refugee status or future citizenship. The couple left for the United States. For all these years, Selma has remained angry about the way in which they were again chased away, since to live together in the Netherlands was not possible.

146   *After the Escape*

Regina, another survivor I interviewed in Adelaide in 2012, had a less coarse story about life after the escape. She managed to pass as a Christian woman who had lost her papers. In Lublin she managed to get new ones, and she traveled westward to Germany, where she was employed as a nanny in a family near Frankfurt. She cheated her employers with her new identity. No one could have thought she was a Jew while she had volunteered to work in Germany. She survived the allied bombings and managed to avoid betraying her true identity. She swallowed her tears and hid her despair, but near the end of the war she had a nervous breakdown and lost her will to be strong, as she called it herself. She suddenly realized she did not know where to go when the war ended and that she had nobody to go to.[18] She had pretended to love the child she had to care for, but it had all been part of the theater she had to stage. Lonely, she ended up in a camp for displaced persons where she met her future husband, a non-Jewish Polish soldier.

The fact that she found shelter, could hide, and was nourished does not mean she was less traumatized than the others I interviewed. She lost her family in Sobibor, and when she spoke with me in Australia, she told me she had lost herself as well. Regina did the "job" of a survivor in Australia, lecturing at schools and at public performances. She was hindered by the fact that she suffered from terrible kidney problems, which originated in the war. I was impressed with this woman putting such an effort into telling her story; during the interview, she tried to break away from the standard narrative she had usually told.

Although she failed to do so and started her standard narrative, it was still impressive. It came through during moments and exacerbated the pain and tension. She talked about how she had been transported on a cart to Sobibor. Before, she had been working in Staw, a slave labor camp. She said:

> Staw, there's another name for it, but it's too long; that was a very big slave labor camp. Because there were all the Jewish people from the ghettos, from all around Siedliszczki, from Chełm, you name it, you know those are little places around a bigger city; all the Jewish people were gathered in that particular camp. There in Staw, a lot of them died of hunger and sickness. There wasn't enough food, everything was rationed, and it was so cold and we had to dig trenches to straighten a river. First in the ghetto and, when that was finished, we were taken to Staw to do the same thing—to straighten a river—and the winter was coming. We went to Staw on the 22nd of October 1942. We were only two months there and then the 20th of December we were taken to Sobibor.

At Sobibor she lost all her family, except for a cousin. She continued:

> While we were on the way to Sobibor, my youngest brother was still on the wagon with mum, my sister, and a lot of other women. There was a crossroads; one road went to Chełm and the other one was going to Włodawa. We turned to the left, towards Włodawa. It might have been half an hour later that we were driving through very big forests. The Germans were on each

side, riding on horses and watching us so that no one would escape. When a couple of young people escaped, the Germans stopped the transport, went into the forest, shot them and brought them back and told us that the same would happen to anyone who wanted to escape.[19]

Staw was also the camp where Esther Raab had been sent for forced labor. She arrived there with her mother and brother. The mother was older and weaker than Esther, and she worried that she would burden her children. She assumed she would not make it and wished for her children to survive. After some weeks she went herself to the Germans and asked them to kill her. I guess that my interview with Esther was one of the last she gave. She had problems expressing herself. The regret about her mother never dwindled. She said:

We had to protect my mother from going to work, because she wasn't able to work, or to walk miles in a day. I'm making it a short story: my mother felt that in order to make it easier and to give us less responsibility to take her away into the woods so they wouldn't take her to work . . .

(And my mother didn't want to be a burden to the two of us.) So she went to the police and asked to be shot. And they did her the favor. She felt that the two of us, or perhaps just one, would survive. And they shot her. We buried her there. Because we went to work and they got her; I mean, they didn't get her, she went in. And they threw her at the edge of the woods and when we came back we buried her. Not that we ever found her remains.[20]

They performed the Jewish ritual for a funeral; for instance, they said kaddish (the prayer for such occasions). The death of her mother was only the beginning, since for Esther worse was yet to come in those very long months during which she was hiding after the revolt.

Forever Traumatized

When I interviewed the survivors of Sobibor and sensed their loneliness, I was overcome with empathy. They had all found their way back to life and had become socially successful. But they remained traumatized for the rest of their lives, and the story of the revolt is so painful because many of the people they knew and were close with had been shot or killed by mines during the revolt. They had run for their lives, but there was a massacre, since their friends were killed in the minefields. The memory of those who did not survive haunted them, as was the case with Toivi (Thomas) Blatt, who said in 2009:

Analyzing the past, I'm still in [Sobibor]. And in my dreams. And in the pain, and in my dreams I become scared and the dreams are very real. No wonder when I wake up . . . finally . . . eh and I have eaten breakfast I want to go back to bed. Because the dreams, although I sleep well, they . . . are finishing me. And when I get up, eat a little, I want to go back to bed.[21]

148 *After the Escape*

I fear that the traumatization of the Sobibor inmates is worse than in the cases of the many survivors of other German camps whom I have interviewed over the years. (I have interviewed survivors of Auschwitz, Dachau, and Mauthausen.) They were also alone, certainly, but in a different way. I keep wondering if this extreme loneliness is due to the fact that the existence of the Reinhard camps was not known to the world. Maybe the fact that the world had not acknowledged the existence of these camps, and that the survivors had to fight to make their existence known and spread the word, made them suffer more. I wonder if those lonely months in hostile eastern Poland were even more fatal. They were liberated from the camp, but the real fight for survival started then. No one can answer such questions.

Further to the East, to the Territory Controlled by the Red Army

The story of the Russian soldiers who made their way to the east is no more accommodating than those already described. Although the soldiers were young and strong, they had to survive partisan life and later had to engage in armed combat. More important, they knew they would be considered traitors to the Motherland, and they knew they would be punished. This knowledge is not traceable in the memoirs and letters written by the survivors; they did not write or speak about it openly, since it was dangerous to do so. People were spied on all the time. Every Russian soldier who had been a POW knew this was the case. The knowledge of such a harsh political ordeal was formally deployed to prevent the defection of soldiers. Even worse was the fate of those men who gave up fighting during combat. They could be executed on the spot. Those were the rules, but what happened in reality was much more arbitrary. All the POWs had seen atrocities on the battlefields, and they had been told what was in store for them if they dared to surrender.

Before they reached the border of Byelorussia and while they were trying to cross the Bug River, the Russian soldiers must have felt lost in a country where they did not speak the language and where the people they met were hostile and potentially dangerous. As long as they remained in Poland, they were foreigners, and Soviet soldiers were not popular. They were wandering in unknown territory, heading for a home that probably no longer existed. They did not know who in their family was still alive, and they did not know what kind of punishment would be waiting for them. They knew only that they would be punished.

During the day, the small group of Russians remained hidden in the woods, and at nightfall the men entered small hamlets in search of food. The group wanted to cross the Bug, but German guards made a safe crossing impossible. After some days they came to a house where a light enabled them to see into a room through an open window. A young man with an unbuttoned shirt wearing baggy peasant pants was sitting at the table. Near him was an old man. There was also a crib with a baby in the room and a woman rocking the crib. When they asked if they could enter, they got an answer in Russian. The hosts covered the window and offered the men a seat. The escapees tried to find out where to cross the river,

After the Escape 149

knowing that the shores were heavily guarded. Pechersky asked where the river was shallow and could be crossed. The hosts said they did not know where this was the case, and said they were not allowed to go near the river. In the end, the young man admitted he knew where the river could be crossed and he said:

> I won't take you all the way to the river. You'll find the way. You must bear in mind, however, that the shore is heavily guarded. There was an escape from a camp not far from here where people were turned into soap [*sic*]. Now the Germans are searching every nook and cranny for escapees. Go. If you make it, it's your good luck and I wish it to you from the bottom of my heart. If you fail, please don't destroy me.[22]

They were provided with bread and the old man blessed them with a cross. They passed over the river by wading from stone to stone, said Arkady Waiszpapir. Pechersky wrote in his unpublished memoirs of 1972: "This happened on the night of October 19–20, 1943. Once again we were on Soviet soil. Although these parts were still occupied by the Germans, the air, it seemed to us, was different here; it was fresher. And the roads, the trees, the sky were more familiar, friendlier." On October 22, the group made contact with partisans in the area of Brest. Pechersky continued: "In one of the villages we met partisans of the regiment named after Voroshilov. We and a group of the partisans were ordered to carry wounded partisans across the Pinsk-Brest railway to the partisan airfield in the village of Svaryn in the Brest region (about 100 km east of the Bug)."

But transporting the wounded was not enough. They were assigned the major partisan task of disturbing the transport between Germany and the front. So, as Pechersky writes: "Once they had crossed the railway, the partisans put explosives under the rails. We went away less than a kilometer and saw a train as it turned out with Germans, which was blown up. The surviving fascists got out of the carriages and started rapid fire to both sides of the railway. Our group lied down. After firing, we moved further and safely carried the wounded to the village of Svaryn."

Every member of the group of escapees was admitted to the partisans, and the story goes on:

> All our men were admitted to the regiment named after Frunze, while Plotnitsky and I joined the regiment named after Shors. Both regiments belonged to the Brest partisan unit. We were assured that we should not worry about Boris Tsibulsky because he was staying in the partisan zone and in case of danger he would be taken away. From the rumors we learned in April 1944 that Boris Tsibulsky had died of croupous pneumonia.[23]

But they were in danger until the last moment. At the meeting dedicated to the sixty-fifth anniversary of the Sobibor revolt, Waiszpapir said:

> We got to the Frunze regiments and spent several days there. Then we were told, "We do not need Jews. Go east, join the army and fight there." We went several kilometers east and were assaulted by the patrol group of the same Frunze regiment. We were laid down on the ground and they took our weapons

150   *After the Escape*

(Pechersky, Shubaev and I had pistols) and told us "now you may go," and went away. We continued our way and suddenly met the supply transport of the Stalin brigade. This brigade [named after Stalin] consisted of several regiments, including the Frunze regiment. This supply chain was procuring food for partisans. We arrived at the brigade that had horse carts. Pechersky and Shubaev went to the command and we were divided. There was a Jewish group in the Schors regiment. Pechersky and Naum [Plotnitsky] were sent there. Naum was sent there because he was a butcher and they needed a butcher.[24]

Naum Plotnitsky wrote about the episode:

When we were half a kilometer from the Bug, Pechersky gave me an assignment to find the shallows of the river, to walk it through, and to return. I walked it through and returned to the group. Together with the group we crossed the Bug. After crossing the Bug we met a platoon of the Frunze [named after a hero of the civil war in Russia] partisan detachment. After the Frunze detachment we were in the Schors [named after another hero of the civil war in Russia, the name is spelled this way] detachment.

I fought for six months until the partisan detachment rejoined the Red Army. With the Red Army fighting heavy battles, we passed Zhabanka [a village in Poland], the army took Brest, and so we went along the Bug [here he is mistaken, it must have been the Vistula] right to Warsaw.

It is unclear whether the two stayed together. We know how Plotnitsky continued his journey. He did not mention whether he was punished, but went on to say:

I was shell-shocked and wounded in my left hand. I was in the hospital, then again at the front, got to my regiment. Through battles we took Gdynia, from Gdynia we went to the Oder where we met Americans on the Elbe. I finished the war on the Elbe in the Second Byelorussian front, 38th Guards Division of the 110th Guards Regiment holding the Order of the Red Banner.[25]

It was mandatory for the Russian escapees to join brigades that were part of the resistance controlled by the Soviet Union, and, by doing so, to make a first step toward joining the Red Army. The escapees probably understood that this was better than joining an independent group surviving in the forest. Having served in the army and in battle, they knew that it was better to adapt to political control than to try to escape it. They knew that all newcomers to these groups had to prove their good will and their value as Soviet citizens in order to redeem alleged past crimes, whether real or imagined. But the men of Slavic background were more important than others in the partisan group. Kenneth Slepyan, who studied "Stalin's guerillas" (as he called them), argues that the hierarchy established among partisans foreshadowed their later position. Jews were lowest in the hierarchy; they were despised, and there was prejudice against them. It was suggested they were not good fighters.[26] The same pattern can be seen after the war, when Jews again were low on the social ladder. Pechersky had no other option

After the Escape 151

than to go through this difficult trajectory in a world that would reject him and his role during the coming decades. He probably just wanted to go home when the war was over. He had managed to keep the photo of his daughter.

Of course, the revolt was known in the region; people told each other the story. The name of Aleksandr Pechersky was passed on from hamlet to hamlet, and people praised his leadership. The myth of the Russian officer and his heroism started immediately. There is an eyewitness account of someone who had seen the effort of the Russian group trying to cross the Bug. The story is connected to the news about the uprising. The account is from the memories of Ben-Zion Bluestein and is written in Hebrew.[27] In 1943, Bluestein had been a partisan in the Brest area. The following paragraph was found and translated by the Israeli historian Dan Zeits:

> The operation zone of our partisan unit, named after Zhukov, included the triangular area between Malorita, Domachevo and Brest and extended to the banks of the Bug River. In October 1943, after the revolt in the Sobibor death camp, the commander of the rebels, Aleksandr Pechersky, managed to cross the Bug into our area. He came to our unit and asked if he could join as a fighter. The unit command didn't admit him and sent him to the formation headquarters for investigation.
>
> We heard from him some details about the uprising of the Jewish prisoners in the Sobibor camp, and were proud to hear about the losses inflicted on the German and Ukrainian guards and, most importantly, that hundreds of Jews had been able to escape. He stayed with us for quite a short time and had no chance to tell us in detail what kind of camp it was.

The narrative is interwoven with tales of other resistance in the camp, and the following paragraph refers to the escape by people of the so-called wood command in Chapter 3[28]:

> After we had learned the Pechersky story, I was told by Abdu Aliev, the second in command of our unit,[29] that a few months before he was with his men in the vicinity of the Sobibor death camp. Every day they saw a group of Jewish prisoners, escorted by the German guard, going to the forest to cut wood. A group of Jewish prisoners who managed to attack the German guards and escape from there came to the area occupied by partisans and asked to join them. Because the Jews were in poor physical condition and had no weapons, the partisans refused to admit them. The Jews wandered in the forest like shadows, without food or shelter, and it is doubtful that they managed to survive in the hostile environment.

What happened in Sobibor was also transmitted by other escapees, as the story continues:

> Several weeks after the appearance of Pechersky, a Jewish couple, a man and a woman, also Sobibor camp survivors, came to our unit. They told us that

152   *After the Escape*

they had worked at various jobs there and had escaped during the uprising. For weeks they were wandering from place to place at night, and by day were hiding from their pursuers, until they came to us. The man gave the unit commander a valuable gold pocket watch, made in Schaffhausen, and he agreed to admit them as workers in the partisan camp. We heard from them about the tortures, murder in the gas chambers and cremation, but we thought they were exaggerating. How is it possible to kill hundreds of thousands of people by gas? . . . It just seemed impossible.[30]

Indeed, the story of the gassing was amazing. It upset people and was a horror beyond imagination. The cruelty of the Germans was known, but to kill in an industrial way!

Communist Policies in Byelorussia

This is exactly the kind of disbelief the fugitives would face during the rest of the war, even among the partisans. Everywhere they were met with hostility; people could not imagine what had happened. According to a manuscript by Meilech Bakalczuk recalling his time with the partisans, the Jewish partisans complained a lot about how Jews were treated, even in his own detachment where there was a large Jewish presence.[31] This is the manuscript of a partisan who, despite his staunch belief in Communism, gave a rare insight into what actually happened, and he felt he had to be honest about it. But there was more: in 1943 most of the partisan units in Byelorussia were controlled by Moscow.[32] Panteleimon Ponomarenko, a communist from Byelorussia, had been appointed as director of the central staff of the partisan movement, and he managed to expand the centralist politics.[33] In September 1942, only a year earlier, the command of the partisan movement had issued a warning against Jews who claimed special victimhood for Jews. Such Jews were German agents, according to the document. In September of 1943 a warning had been issued that 200 Jewish girls infected with venereal disease had been sent to the partisans to spread the disease, which was already rampant. Jews were also a danger since they were suspected of poisoning wells.[34]

Jews often arrived without weapons and were in poor health. They were deemed unable to endure the hardships of partisan life, and many thought they were cowards. However, the lust for revenge among those Jewish men whose families had been shot meant they could be used in the fight against fascism. Thanks to a serious effort on the part of the leadership in Moscow, more and more Jews were admitted.[35] As the influence of Moscow grew, Jews became more safe from random killing; but there was still a consensus that it was risky to accept too many Jews. The feeling was that doing so not only stimulated the German hatred but also that too many Jews would make the locals, who were presumed to hate Jews, even more hostile. The result was that Jews, if admitted, were often given the most dangerous jobs. Apart from joining the fighting partisans and staying in the semiformal camps to receive Jewish refugee families, many small groups of Jews tried to survive in the forests. They were not fighting the Germans but had just escaped.

As we have seen, when the Russian soldiers first met the Voroshilov Brigade, they started to part ways. Waiszpapir was sent to the Frunze battalion; he was from Ukraine and was highly suspect because he was the child of an "enemy of the people." His father had been murdered during the Great Terror in the late 1930s.[36] Such a background stuck to a person. The Vorishilov partisans represented Soviet interests in the region and followed the NKVD (secret service) directives in numerous revenge actions. Traitors were supposed to be everywhere. Pechersky, with his Communist background and his merits on the battlefield, plus his knowledge of how engines worked, turned out to be useful for their policies in an offensive that aimed to block the railroads over which trains from Germany found their way to the battleground.

Partisans Under the Control of Moscow

Revenge actions were taken not only against the Germans, but also against other partisan groups that were dissident or did not follow the guidelines from Moscow. At the beginning of the war, the partisan movement had been a loose collaboration of escaped POWs and soldiers who were left behind when the Red Army withdrew and seemed to be defeated. Jewish refugees and villagers who disagreed with the German occupiers had joined forces in a variety of ways. They had developed their own military tactics, and they had various ways of dealing with the refugees who crossed their paths. Newcomers could be considered as additional strength, but they could also be considered a nuisance since they needed food.

Some partisan groups only accepted men who could fight or men with weapons, refusing elderly refugees, women, and children. Others thought it was their duty to give shelter to all who were threatened. The family camps of the Bielski brothers are perhaps the best known of these in Poland,[37] while around Minsk the Zorin partisans were actively receiving Jewish refugees. By 1943, when Pechersky joined them, the partisan movement in Byelorussia had been reorganized and subordinated to the leadership in Moscow. Partisan warfare had been centralized, and they formed an organized army parallel to the Red Army, although they were not so well equipped.[38] They lacked munitions and other necessities for fighting, and had a hard time staying alive. Their organization was the result of Moscow's effort to establish central command directed by the Stavka, the highest military leadership, presided over by Joseph Stalin.

The fight for ideological and military control by Moscow permeates the history of the partisan struggles in Byelorussia. The NKVD (secret service), SMERSH (a counter-espionage organization separate from the NKVD), and GRU (foreign intelligence main directorate) had started training a special group of future partisans (effectively, Special Forces units) in the rear and then dropping them into occupied territories. Candidates were chosen from among volunteers from the regular Red Army, the NKVD, and Internal Troops, and were mostly elected with a preference for Soviet sportsmen. Behind the German front lines, these groups were to organize and guide the local self-established partisan units. Radio operators and security officers were essential members of each group since, according

154 *After the Escape*

to the commanders in Moscow, amateur fighters could not be trusted with these tasks. Partisans belonging to the ranks of the NKVD (secret services) were given sufficient munitions, and the party organization was enormous and successful.[39] There are many descriptions of how Soviet society, and especially the army, gradually became a web of groups who spied on each other.[40] On the front and in the army, everyone feared being accused of treason. The discipline was grim because it was a major task to send untrained soldiers to fight and to prevent them from withdrawing. Anyone who was caught dropping his weapon was shot on the spot; and if more soldiers were needed, they were sent back into the battle with a warning.

A structure was imposed whereby the organizations controlled one another, so that members of the NKVD spied on members of SMERSH, while SMERSH spied on the NKVD and did counterintelligence; they were formally separate organizations, and there was also the NKGB for secret police and counter-intelligence. Each had their agents in the Red Army, where insubordination was found among both the guilty and the innocent. The frontline needed to be watched, and whoever gave up the fight or panicked was considered a traitor. Even "heretical comment" was forbidden; only praise was allowed.

By 1943 Moscow had established contact with most partisan groups.[41] In December 1943 all detachments had radio contact and air support. Provisions were flown in on safe airstrips. Undercover agents were dropped into the western parts of Byelorussia.[42] Indeed, the partisan army had almost become a normal army. Coordination of the partisan struggle was the responsibility of Panteleimon Ponamorenko (chief of staff), an enigmatic man who followed the Communist hard line but at times would defend Jewish existence in the woods. Party propaganda was everywhere, and there were even locally edited journals that combined information on the war with political education. Partisans were expected to attend meetings in which the Red Army and Stalin were praised.

Life as a Partisan

There is a lot of romanticism about partisan life, with the image of a lonely fighter standing up against the evil of fascism, glorifying the men who defended noble values with their own lives. These ideas still exist and are used in various political ways.[43] A visit to the Belarusian State Museum of the Great Patriotic War in Minsk taught me a lot about the glorification of these men and women. But life with the partisans was not romantic; it was tough and dangerous. In many ways life was filled with violence. Anyone caught by the Germans was killed, with the execution often done in public to set an example and serve as a warning. The most common methods were death by hanging or being shot, preferably while others were watching. A painful death was one way to deter possible future partisans. For the Germans the fight against partisans was often mixed with raids to hunt for Jews hiding in the forests. For the Germans, during these late days of the war after Stalingrad, there was no room for subtle distinctions. They were scared, they were losing the war, they were filled with hatred, and they did everything they were told to do.

After the Escape   155

Lodgings in the forests were often no more than holes in the ground, which did not offer enough protection against the hard climate of the region, with its icy winters and steaming hot summers. Of course, such places lacked even elementary sanitary conditions. The floor was usually earth, and the stench of mold permeated the living quarters. Too many people were living too close to each other, and food was often only what the forest offered.

As one former partisan, Meilech Bakalczuk, wrote: "We endured intense cold and hunger living on raw mushrooms and berries. The situation changed when we managed to get a revolver and some rifles."[44] This enabled them to confiscate food and fuel. Bakalczuk admitted that they had confiscated food and clothes from peasants. The material situation improved after the German defeat in Stalingrad (1943), when the partisans received the supplies they needed to build roomier bunkers, equipped with ovens and sometimes with wooden floors. His description is of the lands of Polesia, near Pinsk, which is the region where Pechersky's battalion was active.

The partisans were often badly nourished and prone to infectious diseases. Their resistance was undermined by a lack of vitamins, while lung infections and abscesses were part of daily life. The wide moors and wet forests were a breeding place for mosquitoes and vermin. Most fighters complained about gingivitis and skin diseases caused by lack of hygiene. Most disturbing was the chronic lack of salt, which led to symptoms of exhaustion and mood changes. Despite all this, the units were expected to be able to move quickly and cover large stretches of terrain.[45] The winter of 1943–44 was extremely cold, especially in January.[46] The men were aware that there was often no help for those who were wounded, despite enormous efforts to move groups of wounded with the aid of many airstrips where planes from Moscow could land. But these were the lucky ones; many wounded men were left to die in the woods or slowly succumbed to illness or injury.

A Culture of Mistrust

Since there was a massive influx of newcomers, especially as the Red Army drew nearer and no one doubted that they would win the war, there were always suspicions that the newcomers were German spies. There were many reasons for such mistrust, and indeed some newcomers had been sent by the Germans. There were all kinds of stories about the ways the Germans organized espionage; for example, they were believed to have set up a training school for Jewish spies in Minsk.[47] Of course, this seems more like an expression of distrust than what really happened. Stricter control of newcomers was needed. At the same time, such necessary control could easily become oppressive since, at this moment of the war and under Stalinist rule, everyone and every action could be suspect.

Communist suspicion became a second attitude intertwined with political control. As on the battlefield, political control and betrayal were everywhere, which was confirmed by the double structure with which Moscow tried to dominate and unify these groups of men roaming in the forests and moors. A new kind of power was held by the commanders of the units, whom the historian Slepyan

156   *After the Escape*

referred to as "Little Stalins."[48] In the Red Army, surveillance was everywhere; it was embedded in the structure of multiple control. Military action was inseparable from the fight for political purity, which was an eclectic alternation between confirmed political loyalty and discretion. All this was endured under the harsh conditions of war and the coarseness of partisan existence.

Moscow failed to gain complete control of the bands of fighting men adrift. The forests and moors were a world without laws, where alcohol consumption was enormous and civilized behavior was rare.[49] Some commandants were known and feared for their licentious actions. These rough men thought they had no other choice than to take clothes from villagers if they needed clean ones. It was not only the German "collaborators" who were forced to "donate" such items, as the mythology about the partisan struggle would have us believe.[50] The relationship with the population of Byelorussia was precarious, and there was often outright hostility toward the ever-demanding partisans.[51] Indeed, the population of Byelorussia did not adhere massively to the ideology of Communism, and, though often hostile to German deeds of revenge, they were not eager to give away their desperately needed scarce possessions.

In 1943 it became the official policy of the Russian headquarters that Jews who tried to escape fascist aggression should be supported. Clearly Pechersky benefitted from these politics. On July 3, 1943, Stalin issued an order that imposed a tough structure and obedience on the partisan units. The order did not mean that cooperation between Jews and non-Jews became harmonious immediately. Hostility and distrust remained, but it was no longer officially sanctioned. Still, Jews were no longer robbed so often of their weapons. Therefore, for Pechersky and his men it was better to reach a partisan brigade with a significant Jewish presence; Voroshilov was one such brigade.[52] It is unknown whether it was Pechersky's explicit wish to reach this battalion. He was heading east, but how much was this brigade his choice? Did he know from his time in Minsk that it was prudent to go to them, since they were a major center of power? The partisan movement in the Minsk region comprised thousands of Jews, and there were many brigades. I surmise that he knew what he wanted. He had been a fugitive before, and he had spoken to partisans who had been caught. We can assume that he was not naïve and that he knew and perhaps feared the situation in which he might land. But one could also argue that the Jewish escapees looked like tramps and would only choose their direction intuitively.

The Schors Battalion

From the Voroshilov group, Pechersky went to the Schors battalion (sometimes spelled Shchors or even Chors, due to the different ways in which the Cyrillic alphabet is transcribed). His name is found on the list of Jewish Partisans in Byelorussia.[53] The list does not mention Sobibor, but it does indicate that Pechersky arrived "from captivity"; the same list reports next to the name of Aleksey Vaytsen that he came from Sobibor, so not mentioning the camp was probably not conscious politics. According to documents in the archives of Minsk, Pechersky

After the Escape　157

had been active in the region of Brest and belonged to the Schors unit where he was assigned to Sikorski's headquarters. Sikorski was the commander of a sabotage company and was credited with the exploding of eighteen enemy trains. He was also secretary of the Brest-Litovsk District Committee of the Communist Party.[54] The Schors partisans operated in the forests of Polesia in southwestern Byelorussia where thousands of Jews who had fled the ghettos and camps of southern Belarus found shelter in the moors and forests. The area known as the Polesian Plain was a vast and impenetrable terrain where guerillas could thrive. In the west is the town of Brest-Litovsk, and further west is the Bug River and the frontier with Poland. The companies in this battalion were numbered 51 to 54. In his overview of the Jewish partisan struggle, the Israeli historian Arad noted that the growing number of Jews in the 51st Company made non-Jews and their commanders leave to join other units.[55] The 51st was the best armed.[56]

Pechersky spent time with the 51st Company until the Red Army arrived. He had joined the Schors Battalion on December 1, 1943, and it was noted by the administration that he was not a Communist Party member, which is surprising given that he was indeed still a member of the party.[57] His profession, according to his military papers, was "Head of an artistic amateur performance group, his nationality is: Jewish. His salary had been 700 rubles a month. He left the partisans to join the Red Army on April 25, 1944." In the archive in Minsk, I read that Pechersky was mostly involved in the sabotage of trains. Trains and railroads were targeted, and in 2016 the records of two of his acts of sabotage were found in the archives, both on the Brest-Moscow line, in February 1944. There was damage to the equipment of the enemy.[58] In 1944 the partisans even managed to stop all transport between Minsk and Vilnius.[59]

Indeed, preventing German material and soldiers from reaching the Eastern Front was a major task for the partisans, as was preventing food and supplies from reaching the Germans fighting at the front. In his memoirs, V. E. Andreyev, the major general and former commander of the partisan unit, provides more information. He wrote about the period before mid-1942, when the Schors battalion was dissolved. In the spring of 1943 the battalion was reinstated. Andreyev described how in the Schors unit most people were members of the Communist Party. The commissar Pilkovsky was a famous organizer well known for his love of music and dancing. Indeed, the partisans would dance, sing, and drink. At such moments there was comradeship.

The Schors battalion was a Communist unit with many Jewish fighters. The number of Jews was probably one of the reasons why it was dissolved.[60] After the battalion was started again in 1943, there was no formal distinction between Jews and non-Jews in the group. All were citizens of the Communist state, where minorities were assumed to be non-existent in the dominant discourse, and their existence was downplayed. Living conditions improved for many partisans during the spring of 1943, but the arrival of so many newcomers was a concern for the leadership. These refugees needed shelter, but it was also mandatory to check their credentials.[61] That was certainly true, but it was also a mechanism for spreading mistrust.

158   *After the Escape*

Joining the Red Army

The control continued when the partisans met the Red Army, where Jews, like everyone else, had to undergo a so-called filtering process in prisons and camps. There were about one hundred filtering camps where former POWs were systematically examined and interrogated, since they were suspected of treason and contacts with the enemy. We know now that many were sent to the Gulag without being found guilty or even without a trial; suspicion or denunciations were sometimes enough. To avoid a sentence of being shot or sent to the camps in Siberia, prisoners could sometimes opt for service in a penal battalion. There is a description by a lieutenant who had been taken prisoner by the Germans because he had been wounded in battle. He wrote:

> I was sent to a screening camp and from there to a construction battalion. In the screening camp all the Russians [i.e., POWs] had to appear before a commission of the NKVD. A detailed interrogation took place. How and why did you get to Germany? Why didn't you join the Partisan movement? Where and with whom did you work in Germany, and so forth. Beatings were frequent.[62]

From 1942 onward, following Order 227 mentioned in Chapter 2, the penal battalions (*shtrafbats*) increased in number. These were units of punished soldiers created in an effort to prevent panic and retreat, as had been the case when the Germans attacked the Soviet Union; they were meant to ensure obedience. Many soldiers had fled in panic from the battle when there was no hope of stopping the attack. While unauthorized retreat by individuals meant immediate execution, escaped POWs who had fallen into German hands alive were also sent to these units. In fact, any Soviet citizen who had lived in territory occupied by the Germans was now considered "untrustworthy," "ideologically suspect," and "likely to have been influenced" by contact with the world outside the Soviet Union. They were stripped of their rank and medals and sent directly from the squalid German POW camps to the Russian Gulag prison camps in Siberia.

Penal battalion service in the infantry was the most common use for the *shtrafniki* (soldiers in the penal battalions) and was viewed by many Soviet prisoners as tantamount to a death sentence. They became cannon fodder and were often used to clear minefields. Penal battalions were administered and commanded by field units who considered the *shtrafniki* as a worthless subspecies of soldier, useful only for absorbing the heavy casualties that would otherwise be inflicted on a more worthy Soviet unit. The *shtrafniki* were often sent into battle unarmed or with sticks to mimic rifles.[63] The penal battalions were also used for the construction of roads, railways, and waterways.[64] There are descriptions of what happened with the *shtrafniki*. Rupert Butler quoted one letter from a soldier of the Wehrmacht:

> One feature of Soviet attacks was the numbers involved. One day, during the retreat [from Kursk in 1944] we found out how these were obtained.

After the Escape 159

Apparently, as we withdraw, the Red Army reoccupies the area and rounds up all adult civilians, men and women alike. They are formed into makeshift workers' battalions and then sent into attacks to make up weight and numbers. It does not matter that these conscripts are untrained, that many are without boots of any kind, and that most of them have no weapons.

He continues:

I saw other attacks which were preceded by solid blocks of people marching shoulder to shoulder across the minefields which we had laid. Civilians and army punishment battalions alike advanced like automata, their ranks broken only when a mine exploded, killing and wounding those around it.[65]

Pechersky was arrested and sent to a penal battalion—and became part of the storm rifle troops. Approximately one-third of the officers who had been in captivity were sent to such battalions.[66] According to Michael Lev, the storm battalion to which Pechersky was sent had been established near Moscow. We can read in an official document:

Pechersky Alexandr Aronovich after staying in the occupied territory was checked-up in the special-purpose camp of NKVD N 174
from June 25, 1944 till July 10, 1944.
After the inquiry he was sent to Podolsk RMC (*regional military commissariat*).[67]

While he was assigned there, Pechersky met the commander of the battalion, Andreev, about whom we know very little. He had attracted Andreev's attention because he stood out from the rest of the penal soldiers by his appearance and behavior. They managed to speak in private, so Andreev learned the story of the revolt.[68] He was greatly impressed by the news about Sobibor, but even more so by the revolt. Andreev took the political risk of sending Pechersky to Moscow and entrusting him to establish contact with the official committee for the investigation of the German-fascist atrocities. He told him to "tell everything to Alexei Nikolayevich Tolstoy."[69] Tolstoy was a prominent person in literary circles who wrote novels that were much read and praised. Though he was an influential man, he was known not to be a blind apparatchik.

Tolstoy was a member of the "Extraordinary State Commission for Ascertaining and Investigating Crimes Perpetrated by the German—Fascist Invaders and their Accomplices, and the Damage Inflicted by them on Citizens, Collective Farms, Social Organizations, State Enterprises and Institutions of the U.S.S.R." This commission was responsible for investigating and collecting material that confirmed the crimes and losses caused by the invaders. According to its own data, 32,000 commission staff members took part in the work and around 7,000,000 Soviet citizens participated in the collection of material and evidence. In the U.S. Holocaust Memorial Museum in Washington, I had the opportunity to view some of this material. Most of it is barely readable, and the copies are of

160   *After the Escape*

poor quality. The amount of material is beyond belief, but as so often with such sources, someone must find ways to order it if we want to use it systematically as a historical source.

Pechersky certainly testified before the Extraordinary State Commission, and his testimony is preserved in the state archive in Moscow.[70] The available document was written down by someone else, since it is not in his handwriting. In all likelihood it was written by the secretary, who, like everyone, was under strict political control. The word "Jew" appears in this document, in contrast to the book Pechersky wrote in 1944–45 (see Chapter 3). There would have been no other way to talk about Minsk, when the Germans discovered some prisoners were Jewish. We should keep in mind that this is a narrative about Russia (Minsk) and not about Sobibor.

In 1944 Pechersky actively approached the State Commission after he saw a report on Majdanek, the labor camp near Sobibor. At that time he was still in hospital (name: Lenin), 100 kilometers from Moscow, where he would meet Olga. He wanted to testify immediately, and signed as the head and organizer of the revolt in the camp Sobibor. Around that time he also sent a letter to Colonel L. N. Smirnov, who was later assistant prosecutor for the USSR at the Nuremberg trials.[71]

Fortunately, Pechersky was also able to transmit the story of Sobibor to Antokolsky and Kaverin, who wrote an essay about the Sobibor revolt that was published in the monthly literary magazine *Znamya* (Banner) in 1945.[72] It is logical that Pechersky never wrote about his time in the penal battalion. What happened there was a public secret, and it was dangerous to admit to having been in these units, although every Soviet citizen knew about them.

Kaverin listened to Pechersky and published a report entitled *Uprising in Sobibor* based on his testimony. This report was included in the aforementioned *Black Book*, which means it did not become an official public document for decades. Pechersky was promoted to the rank of captain and received a medal for bravery for fighting the Germans as part of the penal battalions, not for his role in Sobibor.

Back in Rostov-on-Don after the War

Pechersky was discharged after a serious foot injury. In the hospital near Moscow, he was nursed by his future wife, Olga Kotova. After the war ended he returned to Rostov-on-Don. In Alexander Marutyan's documentary film *Arithmetic of Freedom* (2010), Pechersky's daughter Ella spoke of how she and her mother had believed her father was dead.[73] She and her mother had been evacuated to a small town near Stalingrad where her grandmother lived. Her mother had gone back to Rostov-on-Don, and after the liberation Ella joined her there. Her mother had been the lover of a German officer and was later accused of collaboration. When I spoke with Michael Lev, we agreed that many women had such affairs not out of love, but because they wanted to save themselves and their children. He regretted that his judgment of her had been very harsh, and he asked me to include this milder opinion, which he genuinely held in 2012.[74]

After the Escape   161

Ella and her mother had received a letter from Moscow that her father was dead, but they later received a letter from a hospital he had been transported to near Ryazan in Szurow, where he had been found by a journalist. They started to send each other letters. In these letters to his wife and daughter, Pechersky described what had happened in Sobibor. When he had recovered, he returned to Rostov-on-Don. Ella described in a moving way how she had been at school when he suddenly appeared. He returned to a town that had been destroyed by the German occupation and by the fighting. His mother had also survived. His new love was Olga, so Ella lived with her mother, his first wife, nearby. And for a time Pechersky had two wives. This was not unusual and was ascribed to wartime conditions. The people I spoke to admitted that this was the case, but they preferred to be silent about it.

Pechersky's name became known when an article appeared in the journal *Red Star* (*Krasnaia Zvezda*) in 1944, followed that same year by an article in the journal *Komsomolskaya Pravda*.[75] Pechersky's book was published in 1945. He was home and he wanted to restart his life as the hero of Sobibor, the man who had led all those people away from the camp and revealed the secret the Germans had wanted so much to keep. Their massive crime was now open, in the public domain. He had survived punishment for having been a POW; he had been able to blow up trains and to fight. He had been part of those partisan units that were under the political control of Moscow and, although punished, he had survived. Liberation had brought new dangers, punishment, and threats. We can wonder whether Pechersky still believed in Communism or in his earlier ideals. As with so many, this might have been the case. In the coming years, his Jewishness, the reason why he had landed in Sobibor, would be more and more denied by others. But without acceptance of the fact that Jews had suffered more than other minorities, and without acknowledging the existence of the death factories built especially for Jews, his heroism could never be understood. The murders that took place would lose their special place and drown in the midst of all those who had died on Soviet territory.

Pechersky had expected a world that would recognize him as a leader and a hero. He also wanted to return home. But Rostov-on-Don was devastated, and while he took care of his wife, he was now in love with Olga. He managed to get her to live with him, but life was poor, the apartment small, and they were confined to one room. This was not exceptional during the first days after the war when many lived in poor conditions. But what shook him is that he became a war veteran in a world where what had happened to the Jews did not exist. Russia had won the war, and officially the suffering had been intense for all Soviet citizens. Pechersky wanted to spread the news about Sobibor, but he was not able to do so. The wish to tell the world about the Jewish resistance had been a major incentive to survive, as was the with most survivors, not only in the case of Sobibor. It was a way to deal with their massive trauma, and with that, survival seemed to make sense. In the years to come he would be disappointed when the public space was denied to him, even at moments when it was obvious that he should testify, as was the case at the Nuremberg trials. The silence imposed on all POWs would also become his mental prison.

162   *After the Escape*

Notes

1 Slepyan, *Stalin's Guerilla*, 210–211.
2 See also David Shneer, *Through Soviet Jewish Eyes: Photography, War and the Holocaust* (New Brunswick and London: Rutgers University Press), 2012.
3 Garf, State Archive of the Russian Federation Fond R/p 8114, op I g 965.
4 Suhl, "They Fought Back", 43.
5 Former partisan Meilech Bakalczul mentions this in his unpublished manuscript deposited at Yad Vashem, "A Record of Partisan Activity 1942–44" (series no. 033), originally named *The Revolt in the Forest*, written around 1960 or even a little earlier, 10.
6 Bem, *Sobibor*, 277. Bem's work is based on Polish sources and on Jules Schelvis' book on Sobibor.
7 Ibid., 281.
8 Unpublished manuscript Pechersky 1972, 102–103 (Yad Vashem, and Moscow).
9 Bem, *Sobibor*, 293.
10 Yad-In Unum 31P.
11 Bem, *Sobibor*, 288.
12 Dov Freiberg, "The Forests Autumn 1943-Summer 1944," *To Survive Sobibor*.
13 Wewryck, *To Sobibor and Back*, 106.
14 Ibid., 112.
15 Ibid., 115.
16 Ibid., 123.
17 Interview Selma Engel Wijnberg, Brandford, CT by Author 2010.
18 Also Andrew Zielinski, *Conversations with Regina* (Włodawa: Muzeum Pojeziera Leczyńsko-Włodawskiego, 2008), 159.
19 Interview Regina Zelinski by the author, December 2012, Adelaide.
20 Interview with Esther Raab by author 13.04.2010.
21 Interview with Toivi Blatt, 2009, Warsaw.
22 Suhl, *They Fought Back*, 44.
23 Vilensky et al., *Sobibor*, 90–97.
24 Ibid.
25 Plotnitsky testimony Yad Vashem, 103.
26 Kenneth Slepyan, *Stalin's Guerillas*, 228.
27 Ben-Zion Bluestein in Hebrew-*Ben-Zion Bluestein, a Partisan and a Combatant. The biography of a Holocaust survivor from Belarus*, independent publication, 1996, courtesy of Dan Zeits.
28 Ibid.
29 According to Dan Zeits, it was most probably Migdar Abdullaev, then the second-in-command of the Zhukov unit.
30 The chapter of the book by Bluestein published in "*Masua*", *Yearbook of the Holocaust and Heroism*, No. 23 (April 1995), 86.
31 Bakalczuk, *A Record of Partisan Activity 1942–44*, 147–148.
32 Zeev Barmatz, *Heroism in the Forest, the Jewish Partisans of Belarus* (Ramat Gan: Kotarim International Publishing, 2013).
33 Arad, *In the Shadow*, 174.
34 Irena Cantorovich, "Jews and Non-Jews in the Partisan Movement in Belorussia," *Moreshet, Journal of the Study of the Holocaust and Antisemitism* 11 (2014): 98–144.
35 Musial, *Sowjetische Partisanen*, 396.
36 Interview Waiszpapir, 2010, Kiev.
37 Nehama Tec, *Defiance* (New York: Oxford University Press, 2009).
38 Musial, *Sowjetische Partisanen*, 227.
39 Ibid., 279.
40 Rupert Butler, *Stalin's Secret War: The NKVD on the Eastern Front* (London: Pen & Sword Books, 2010).

After the Escape 163

41 Slepyan, *Stalin's Guerillas*, 123.
42 Butler, "Stalin's Secret War," 66.
43 David R. Marles, *"Our glorious Past": Lukashenka's Belarus and the Great Patriotic War* (Stuttgart: Ibidmen Verlag, 2014).
44 Bakalczuk, *A Record of Partisan Activity 1942–44*, 5–6.
45 Musial, *Sowjetische Partisanen*, 341–344.
46 Bakalczuk, *A Record of Partisan Activity 1942–44*, 244.
47 Slepyan, *Stalin's Guerillas*, 250.
48 Ibid., 238.
49 Musial, *Sowjetische Partisanen*, 350–352.
50 Ibid., 279.
51 Ibid., 357, 370.
52 Ibid., 311.
53 Inna Gerasimova, Viacheslav Selemenev and Jack Kagan, *We Stood Shoulder to Shoulder: Jewish Partisans in Byelorussia 1941–1944* (Bury St. Edmonds, Suffolk: Arima Publishing, 2010), 272. There is also an edition in Belarus published in Minsk.
54 Arad, *In The Shadow*, 313.
55 Ibid., 308.
56 Robert W. Thruston and Bernd Jonowetch, *The People's War: Responses to World War II in the Soviet Union* Champaign: University of Illinois Press, 2000.
57 BSSR (Belorussian Soviet Socialist Republic) Identity Card N 171286 NARB LA5339 014, Minsk.
58 www.sb.by/obshchestvo/article/nepokorennyy.html. Website in Belarus
59 David Meltser and Vladimir Levin, *The Black Book with Red Papers* (Cochesville, MD: Viapress, 2005), 107.
60 Hans Heinrich Nolte, "The Jewish Shtetl of Slonim," in *The People's War: Responses to World War II in the Soviet Union*, eds. Robert W. Thurston and Bernd Bonwetscch (Urbana and Chicago: The University of Illinois Press, 2000), 44–45.
61 Slepyan, *Stalin's Guerillas*, 276.
62 Rupert Butler, "Stalin's Secret War," 175.
63 Life in these units was filmed in a television series, "Штрафбат," in 2004, which should be viewed in a very critical way.
64 Butler, *Stalin's Secret War*, 63.
65 Ibid., 110.
66 Vilensky et al., *Sobibor*, 128.
67 Podolsk is not far south of Moscow.
68 Vilensky et al., *Sobibor*, 128.
69 During World War II, he served on an Extraordinary State Commission that "ascertained without reasonable doubt" the mass extermination of people in gas vans by the German occupiers. His work in the investigation of atrocities committed in the Stavropol region was recognized by Soviet prosecutors during the Nuremberg trials, where he served as an aide to the Soviet prosecution. Documents have been published in Soviet Government Statements on Nazi Atrocities (London and New York: Hutchinson & Co. Publishers).
70 Garf, State Archive of the Russian Federation Fond R/p 8114, op I g 965.
71 Letters of 2.sept 1944; 23.10.44 from Pechersky sent to me by Dariusz Pawłoś, chair of the Foundation for Polish-German Reconciliation, Warschau The document is deposited in the archive.
72 *Znamya*, N 4, 1945.
73 Simeon Vilensky et al., *Sobibor*.
74 Interview Michael Lev by the author, Rehovot 2013.
75 I am greatly indebted to Leonid Teruchkin for "The History of Sobibor and the Fate of the Participants in the Uprising," a conference paper given in 2014 in Warsaw.

6   Return to Rostov

Spreading the Word About Sobibor

It was as if he had not returned to the place he had left; in fact, only the name of the town was the same. Rostov-on-Don lay in ruins, and the citizens had to build a city with a new structure, a new social environment, and a new political and cultural life. Material conditions were extremely hard for those who lived there and for the thousands of newcomers. Some dug holes in the ground; others found shelter in the ruins of destroyed houses. Despite overcrowded conditions and food shortages, more and more people needed to be fed and sheltered, since the population of Russia was on the move, with peasants migrating to the city to enter schools and work in the factories. Many demobilized soldiers settled there as well, and they also strove to survive and create a future.[1] Malnutrition and hunger (1946–48) were rampant, culminating in a famine in 1947. People were needy; it was common knowledge, however, that the members of the Communist Party were better fed.

The "Politics of Reconstruction" was based on the assumption that Rostov had been a successful industrial hub, and according to the Fourth Five-Year Plan (1946–50), the pre-war industrial level had to be surpassed in the near future.[2] Nonetheless, earlier revenue levels were never attained, and in order to survive, many people fell back on the informal economy of corruption and the black market. Rebuilding industrial capacity was made a political priority. Officially, the "Reconstruction" of the city was a collective task for all the inhabitants, but it would take years before the average resident saw better times coming.

According to the research of Jeffrey W. Jones based on archival sources in Rostov-on-Don, during the years after the war the town's management was chaotic, and there was no rule of law. Those who had not been evacuated at the beginning of the war but had stayed behind were accused of collaboration, because they had been in contact with Germans, even if they had stayed only for purposes of survival, for instance while negotiating to obtain ration cards. Rostov-on-Don was occupied twice—for a little more than a week in November 1941, and again from July 28, 1942 to February 13 or 14, 1943—making a variety of survival strategies necessary.[3] For example, all party members had been ordered to evacuate; therefore, those who had not done so were suspected of treason after the war. Others who had burned their party membership cards, fearing that the Germans would arrest them, were considered traitors. Accusations of collaboration were interwoven with clashes between various factions in the city, particularly within the Communist Party. While some argued for the expulsion of all "collaborators," others realized that there had been so many that it would not be easy to replace them. According to the Communist leadership, working for the Germans to secure one's own survival was no excuse, and such behavior was called collaboration. To make the confusion worse, several "collaborators" were shielded by nepotism.

As Amir Weiner has argued: "The severity with which passivity under occupation was regarded was hammered into the rank and file by the refusal to redeem this offense even by means of a belated contribution at the front."[4] Those who had lived out the years of occupation for the war's fate to be decided were also punished. Punishment could vary from the Gulag to imprisonment or expulsion. Sometimes it was a threat that never disappeared.

There was no legality, there were only informal rules. Large groups of the population no longer believed the Communist rhetoric that concealed incompetence, rivalry between factions, and outright corruption. From the outset it was clear there would be a new elite.[5] Material hardships aside, people also needed to rebuild their personal lives. Most had lost friends and family members, and some were adrift without anyone to rely on. However, traumatization was not part of the language of that time, nor was the daily mourning conceptualized in such a psychological way. Mourning family members was a private event, while in public people were expected to be proud of death during their struggle to defend the "freedom of communism" and their motherland against barbarians, and there was no language capable of describing the massive loss of life. The widespread assumption of the existence of trauma is very much a part of western culture. In her book *Death and Memory in Russia*, which describes extreme violence, the anthropologist Catherine Merridale noted: "The idea of psychological damage— mental distress, trauma (a central theme of Holocaust writing)—is something that most Russians reject. Even psychologists and doctors have their doubts, and for many of the older ones . . . the concept is entirely strange."[6] But trauma did exist, as Merridale wrote: "Almost no family was unaffected, some by war, some by hunger, exile or epidemic, some by continuing political repression—the arrests and the shootings did not stop—some by the accumulated exhaustion of successive losses and emergencies."[7] A politically sanctioned frame for commemoration soon arose and lies started at once, accompanied by total silence about the Jewish losses.

The Jewish community in Rostov-on-Don had been decimated: from numbering 27,039 in 1939, or 5.4 percent of the population, they declined to 2.7 percent in 1959 (there are no data for the years in between). Twenty thousand Jews had been evacuated to the east.[8] The town had changed and had lost the cultural world of Judaism, which had been so much a part of its pre-war life. Nevertheless, one was not supposed to speak about what had happened to the Jews. It was common knowledge, though, and as elsewhere throughout Europe, people had to integrate this knowledge with the sharp rise in anti-Semitism at the end of the war.

166   *Return to Rostov*

Jews were not the only minority suspected of not embracing Russian values and the Soviet system: the large minority of Cossacks, which included the family of Pechersky's wife, became another target of suspicion. Furthermore, the loyalty of returning POWs was questioned, for they had inhaled the air and the culture of the West, and any of them could thus have become spies. Sleeping with the enemy or befriending them, as Pechersky's wife had done, was considered despicable, since loyalty to one's husband was tied to the ideology of loyalty to the country.[9] She had been involved with a man from the "other side," and though we might now be inclined not to judge too harshly a mother who protected her daughter in this way, it is difficult to expect such neutrality from a man who had suffered so much. Later Pechersky felt responsible for the mother of his daughter—and when she became ill, he and Olga took her into their house and nursed her. Most of his family had been evacuated with about 20,000 other Jews at the beginning of the war when the Germans invaded the Soviet Union, and now they also returned.

Pechersky had fallen in love with Olga, as I mentioned earlier, and soon he managed to convince her to join him in Rostov-on-Don where they started to live as a couple. He was traumatized and fought against his uneasiness and nightmares by committing himself totally to the dissemination of public knowledge about Sobibor. Within a short time, he found an office job at the place he had worked before the war. In the years to come, he would change jobs several times, ending up in a factory where he became a representative of the executive committee. He was filled with hope that he would be able to spread the word about Sobibor, and he was convinced people would listen. As he said in 1984 to Jules Schelvis and Dunya Breur:

> The main goal in my life after the war, the main goal and independent of wherever I would work, was that I was busy with a lot of public work, that is, lectures among the city's population. Among students, in institutes, in military divisions, in factories, in businesses, I could speak in public more than a few times, (for example, there was such a factory Rostelmash) and in each workshop I spoke three times. I would travel to other cities in order to speak, and I was invited to Moscow, where I was on stage and also in Kuybyshev and in many cities. For television I was interviewed about three times, even once for Moscow television, and for the television stations of Rostov, Makhachkala, and Kuybishev. I was interviewed on radio; I spoke on Rostov radio about three times, on Moscow radio twice. I was on the radio in Israel. Here in the Soviet Union, my radio talks were recorded and then sent to Israel, where they were broadcast on "The Voice of Israel." In Czechoslovakia and Romania, in 1945, when my small book was published, excerpts were read on the radio. My lectures and interviews with schoolchildren, those that I recorded, add up to about 700 performances.[10]

He wanted to convince his listeners how hard he had worked, how much he had exhausted himself, and said: "Now we're only talking about the recordings;

Return to Rostov   167

there's much I didn't record. I continued to speak in public, even though the doctors forbade it because they feared for my nervous system, until I indeed collapsed. And now for two or three years already, I do not give talks, because I simply can't do it. I simply can't do it, I am getting spasms and don't talk about all the issues." He no longer had the energy. He was over seventy years old by then, but more important, he had suffered too much.[11]

Pechersky related the above to Dunya Barnes and Jules Schelvis during their preparation for the documentaries preserved under the name "Sobibor interviews" at the NIOD in Amsterdam. At that time, he was watched closely by the KGB (the secret police of the former Soviet Union). There was a serious risk of persecution if one spoke out against the official ideology that dominated all discourse.

There Were No Jews, Only Citizens

During the early years after the war, Pechersky was frequently invited to speak, and he received many letters of praise from all over Russia. I asked his granddaughter Natasha/Natalya if he had ever spoken about the fate of the Jews. She was convinced it was a topic he had never touched upon in his public appearances, nor at home.

The official attitude toward the Sobibor uprising was ambivalent: Soviet ideology always tried to play down the specifically anti-Semitic aspects of Nazi policy, presenting Nazi Germany as a mortal enemy of all humanity, regardless of ethnic or religious identity. Lukasz Hirszowicz has argued that in Soviet historiography, the revolt of Sobibor has been represented as carried out by Russian POWs: "their Jewishness was either heavily blurred or completely forgotten."[12]

Pechersky was presented in textbooks as an ordinary Soviet officer, which he was. But there was no mention that he had led a revolt of Jews. He was a public person, but he was accepted only if his Jewish background was obscured. The fact that Jewish soldiers among the Soviet prisoners of war were treated differently from non-Jews never received attention, although it was never openly denied. It was simply ignored. Soviet writers whose works dealt with the war were encouraged to depict the sufferings and heroism of all peoples and not to focus on this "narrow" Jewish aspect.[13] There was certainly no separate recognition of Jewish partisans or Jewish soldiers—everyone was a citizen of the Soviet Union.[14] Research into the Jewish participation and the relatively high numbers of Jews in the fight against the Germans would begin only long after the fall of Communism, and research challenging the diminution of the Jewish role, while growing in Russia, is still marginal.

Changing Times and the Rise of Anti-Semitism

After returning home, Pechersky joined the group of veterans in charge of retelling the heroic struggle of the "Soviet people against the barbarous invaders." According to this narrative, the millions who had died were all victims of

168 *Return to Rostov*

fascism. This tale was intended to hide those who had fallen at the hands of the authoritarian Communist leadership, or as a result of military mismanagement as at the start of the war.[15] The war had reinforced Stalin's political grip on millions of Soviet citizens, and all public utterances were scrutinized, weighed, and fraught with consequences.

The tale of the "Great Patriotic War" was the vehicle by which the traumatized Soviet society was supposed to come to terms with its painful past. It was part of the mobilization of the country and the unification of its people when the Cold War with the West began. Stalin was at the center, and his heroism was intertwined with words glorifying the reconstruction. No one could avoid the cult of personality around Stalin. Speakers visited schools and factories and reiterated the way the Russian army's patriotism and Stalin had together overcome evil. "The resistance against the fascists and the revolt of Sobibor" could easily be integrated into this narrative without ever mentioning the fate of the Jews. During the first post-war years, the Soviet government was keen to establish good official relations with the Jewish community. So Pechersky seemed safe, and he needed time to heal. Large bundles of letters were addressed to the Pechersky family in Rostov, written by people who were fascinated by what had transpired.

Below is an excerpt written down by a crew that came to Rostov as late as 1984 to film Pechersky. In response to a girl who asked him to name the most active members of the resistance organization, he declined to name them and replied:

> All the members of the committee were active; otherwise, it would have been impossible. There would have been no need to organize; we could just have sat and done nothing. Or just raised our hands to vote. We did not behave that way. There were not only words, but actions. I consider those members who were the first to risk their lives by killing Germans the major protagonists of our victory.[16]

The children wanted to know more about what he did after the war. He replied: "After the war I was demobilized. I had been wounded and spent time in the hospital. I worked in the higher financial institute, where I administered financial affairs for the rector. After that I worked for a long time in a factory, for about 20 years, and at the age of 69 I retired."[17] Unemployment was not mentioned. He was also asked whether he was a Communist, and replied that no, he was not a party member.

Children wrote letters to him, like the girl who asked: "Tell me, is it true that you were at the Sobibor death camp? Don't take offence at my question, I don't want to offend you. You know, it's somehow hard to believe that there was a war and millions of people died."[18] He used to appreciate this question. When Dunya Breur mentioned it, he replied: "An intrusive thought irks me constantly: is it worth it to stir up the past? Is it necessary? Is it worth it once again, with pain in one's heart, to remember the difficult years of the Second World War, a war that played out so tragically for the millions of people of not only the Soviet Union but of many countries of Europe?"

Figure 6.1 Aleksandr Pechersky teaching at a Russian school in 1962
Source: Photograph courtesy of Natalya Ladychenko.

But he felt the need to warn about fascism, since he felt that fascism was again a threat: "The Fascists are not yet dead; they have once again arisen, and some of them are openly nurturing delusional ideas about a campaign to the East."[19] In 1972, when this letter was written, Jews could no longer be mentioned publicly, and the tide had turned. The attitude toward Jews changed quite soon after the war, as historian Zvi Gitelman and others have noted.[20] At first, the hostile language of the leadership seemed directed mainly against "excessive" nationalism, most of all in Ukraine; but there soon followed accusations about Yiddish writers' preoccupation with Jewish history and Jewish themes.

The Crackdown on Jewish Culture

A campaign was launched against ties and contacts with people abroad, especially in the West, and against tendencies that came to be called "bourgeois nationalism" and "cosmopolitanism" that were predominantly associated with Jews. *Cosmopolitanism* would become the main accusation—first against Jewish intellectuals, and later against the whole Jewish population.[21] After some years these pejoratives would be linked with accusations of Zionism. As Amir Weiner noted, Russia needed to be purged and purified from hostile influences[22]

170   *Return to Rostov*

Anti-Semitism had been part of the daily experience of Stalinism before the war, but it was given a new dimension even though Jews had made serious efforts to take part in the fight against fascism. In 1941, two leaders of the Jewish Labor Bund had suggested organizing a Jewish committee against Hitler, but the idea was not accepted immediately, and the initiators disappeared after having been summoned to attend a formal meeting. This initiative, though it slumbered, led to an appeal to Anglo-American Jewry to financially support the anti-Hitlerite policy of the USSR. In 1942, the Jewish Anti-Fascist Committee (JAC) was formed in order to raise political and financial support for the war effort against Germany among Jewish communities in the West.[23] The JAC also supported Yiddish authors, and the committee, which even started a Yiddish newspaper, would become the only official Jewish institution. It was therefore at the center of Jewish cultural and national aspirations. Jews wanted to be recognized as a nationality like other minorities in the Soviet Union.

In 1943, the Committee sent their chairman Solomon (Shloyme) Mikhoels, famous as the director of the Moscow Jewish State Theater, together with the Yiddish poet Itzik Fefer to the United States to solicit foreign support. They traveled all over North America to raise funds, even as far as Canada and Mexico. They were enthusiastically received by large Jewish audiences, and together with American political allies (i.e., members of the Communist Party in the United States), they praised the USSR for the elimination of anti-Semitism. While they loyally used the Communist language of that time, their popularity and the cheering crowds irritated Moscow. On January 13, 1947, Mikhoels died in Minsk under what were called "tragic circumstances." Everybody knew he had been killed, but it was made to look like an accident. Mikhoels had been speaking openly about the fate of Jews during the war and pleaded for the creation of monuments to commemorate the victims of fascism. In the following months a campaign of widespread arrests began, and state subsidies for Jewish institutions were suspended.

Mikhoels' death heralded the beginning of the aggressive repression of Yiddish culture. The JAC was dissolved in 1948, and the last Yiddish publishing house was closed that same year. From 1948 to 1953 the Jewish cultural world was destroyed, and people were arrested on various grounds, such as bourgeois nationalism, slander against the USSR, and espionage. "Jewish nationalism" was violently condemned in the official daily *Pravda*, with accusations that Jews were alien to Russian culture and were unpatriotic, since they were not rooted in Russia. As a result, Jews no longer ventured out into the streets and cut off their relations with friends abroad. The Stalinist night worsened and seemed to last forever.

Nevertheless, Jews still manifested themselves: in September 1948, Golda Meyerson (Meir), who later became prime minister of Israel, arrived in Moscow as the head of the first Israeli delegation to the Kremlin. The State of Israel, which had existed for only a few months, had been swiftly recognized by the Soviet Union, and Jews in Moscow were excited about her arrival. Enormous crowds gathered in front of Moscow's main synagogue to see her visit the morning

Shabbat service. The Jewish masses repeated this emotional reception in larger numbers some weeks later for the Rosh Hashanah and Yom Kippur services. Golda Meir was escorted through the street with shouts of "Next Year in Jerusalem!" The uncontrolled character of these events frightened and angered the authorities, who perceived them as a threat. To them these events represented "disorganization" and seemed "uncontrollable." The Jewish masses needed to get back in line, and therefore the elimination of their intellectual leadership was urgent—particularly the containment of the JAC leaders. In 1952, twelve Yiddish authors were executed, including Itzik Fefer, and during the same period many prominent members of the Jewish cultural elite were arrested, journals were closed, and the assault on Jewish cultural life was stepped up.[24]

A better-known case of aggression toward Jews was the "Doctors' Plot" of 1953, when nine Jewish doctors were accused of the medical murder of two leading Soviet politicians. In addition, they were suspected of plotting to kill important military figures. Such evil against the Soviet Union was proclaimed to be the result of close contact with foreign intelligence services. Vigilance and the rooting out of enemies of the people meant a stronger anti-Jewish policy. At the zenith of the Cold War, people started to avoid Jewish doctors, Jews were labeled "poisoners," and a vicious anti-Semitism engulfed the cities as well as the countryside deep into the provinces.[25]

Stalin died in March 1953, and the accusations against the doctors were dropped, but the anti-Semitic campaign was not over. It was fed by anti-Jewish feelings that were, and still are, deeply rooted in Russian culture. However, for some time there was hope that the worst was over. People came back from exile, they were released from prisons, and, after being "rehabilitated," they got their homes back. The new tide brought some relief. The "thaw" of these years under Nikita Khrushchev did not include the (marginal) restoration of Jewish life and its cultural institutions, as a blind eye was turned toward popular anti-Semitism. In Khrushchev's speech to the Twentieth Congress of the Communist Party, which condemned the crimes of Stalin, he also criticized what had transpired during the Doctors' Plot; however, the way the Jews had been harassed was never mentioned.

Pechersky lived far away from the intrigues of this policy, but he knew the people involved and no Jewish author could escape the negative of that time. In the coming years, Jews would lose many of their positions in the Soviet political system, but some amateur Jewish cultural performances were still allowed. Only in 1957 did a harsh campaign against the Jewish religion begin, which led to the destruction of much Jewish religious life. This time it was not only the Jews who were persecuted; the offensive was against all religions, but the attack on Judaism was the most virulent. As Zvi Gitelman noted, these attacks were spread not only in the Russian language, but also in Ukrainian and Byelorussian, stimulating more widespread prejudice against Jews in a larger part of the Communist world.[26] As he wrote, Jews "were no longer seen as equal members of society, but as a tolerated marginal group, excluded from much of the mainstream and at best relegated to sectors where they could make some particular contribution and not harm the overall Soviet cause."[27] In 1961, under pressure from abroad and

172   *Return to Rostov*

through the efforts of a few surviving Yiddish cultural activists, a Yiddish literary magazine, *Sovetish Heymland* (Soviet Homeland), was established in Moscow under the auspices of the Union of Soviet Writers. Despite tremendous efforts, the review served chiefly as window-dressing for the pacification of Jews outside the Soviet Union.

Coping with Stalinist Anti-Semitism in Rostov-on-Don

These developments all influenced the commemoration of the war, and they help one to understand how the sufferings of Jews received so little attention. In places where the slaughter of Jews had been massive, the authorities could not and did not want to avoid recognition of the cruel deaths of "innocent citizens."[28] But even in Babi Yar—a ravine near Kiev where more than 100,000 Jews had been slaughtered—the dead were Sovietized or denationalized into innocent citizens of no particular ethnicity.[29]

Like everywhere else, the Jews of Rostov-on-Don had come home. With tremendous effort, they kept Jewish religious and cultural life going. In the beginning, just after the war, there was a place for such Jewish cultural life. In the archives of the Shoah Visual Foundation, there is, for instance, an interview with Iakov Krut, who recalled the joy of Jews meeting again in Rostov and finding each other alive:

> In 1948, a Jewish dramatic group I have mentioned before reappeared. They staged a musical play by Sholom Aleichem called *The Big Lottery* [in which a poor tailor, Soroker, is told that he has won 200,000 rubles in the national lottery. His world turns upside down, as does the life of Ettie his wife and Beilke his adored, unmarried daughter, who is suddenly besieged by suitors. Events reel out of control until it becomes clear that Soroker hasn't won the lottery after all. In the end, the tailor returns to his previous state; S.L.]. The news that this famous piece would be performed spread in the city. The group of artists was established in the large Palace of Culture of Rostelmash [a large manufacturer officially of agricultural equipment; S.L.]. And so this play *The Big Lottery* was staged nowhere but in the official theater for musical comedy. The house was full. You can imagine the great feeling that you are again among Jews. It was such an elation, a wonderful feeling. And when according to this play Shimele Soroker, a tailor, or as we say, a *kapsn* for seven generations, won 200,000 and the orchestra started playing, all the spectators were dancing on the balcony. Thus I wrote a short story about this. At that moment of *tsores* (grief) and *mazl* (happiness), they were dancing, embracing one another.[30]

Was Pechersky involved in this event? Did he attend? We only know that his relationship to the Jewish cultural world remained distant. He wanted to be heard and to be accepted, and perhaps he feared the consequences of being seen among the dancing Jewish crowd. In the 1930s nearly all Jewish cultural, social, and educational institutions had been closed, and avoidance of all that was linked to religion or minority culture was part of the everyday life of young Jewish Communists.

For information about Pechersky's life in all the years that followed, we have to rely heavily on the memories of his family and friends in Rostov. One of the best sources is the movie *The Arithmetic of Freedom* (2010) by the Russian film-maker Alexander Marutyan. We met in 2015, and since his film is based on years of historical research, I checked much of my information with him. He had interviewed Ella, Pechersky's daughter, whom I also interviewed. My other major informant was Lazar Lubarsky, who was a neighbor of Pechersky and had tried to help him for about ten years. Michael Lev was also interviewed at the end of his life.

Talking about the years after the war with Dunya Breur and Jules Schelvis in conjunction with the release of their film, Pechersky said:

> I was working. I got a job right away at the financial institute. Actually, I didn't get a job; I had been working there before the war, and immediately after my discharge I was invited to the position of deputy director for the institute's daily affairs. Why? Well, buildings had to be rebuilt. Seventy percent of the city was destroyed, the very center was destroyed, and the institute was actually in the center. Later on, I would change jobs, and in the end my health became such that I went to work in a machinery construction factory, in the conveyor department. I was a representative of the executive committee of the Kirov District—that was our district—I was representative there. I always cared a lot about social work. I would lead amateur clubs again, after the war as well as before the war.[31]

It looks like the story of a busy man, but in fact, in these years life was monotonous and controlled for everyone. All this time Pechersky was not recognized as he deserved to be, and his speeches in schools were his only distractions. Lazar, his friend and helper, told me that letters kept pouring in, making the task of spreading the word about Sobibor ever larger. People wanted to know; they wanted to verify rumors they had heard. As Lazar remembered:

> Some friends we had in common introduced us, because I could help him with the translation of his correspondence in Hebrew, in Yiddish, and a little bit even in English. He didn't know these languages, and he corresponded with Yad Vashem and with kibbutz Lohamei HaGeta'oth, the kibbutz that kept the memory of Jewish resistance alive. I met him in the middle of the sixties.[32]

Lazar helped me in 2012 to sort out what was true from all the stories going around on the web about imprisonment and being persecuted. The following tale has been confirmed both by the family in Rostov and by the film-maker Marutyan.

174   *Return to Rostov*

In 1945, after the war ended, Pechersky had returned to Rostov, and later an incident was created around him. Lazar explained:

> Just because he was a Jew, he was working for a musical theater selling tickets. It was a time of repression against the Jews. They created a campaign against him while he worked in this musical theatre, and Sasha Pechersky became a victim of Stalin's policy against the Jews. He came to Rostov, he wasn't recognized as a hero, and he found work selling tickets. It was simple work. And as the campaigns began against the Jews, they made up stories about him and imprisoned him for a few days, but they didn't charge him as a criminal. So he was freed but couldn't find work for two years. And after two years someone gave him a job making frames for embroidered portraits, for a miserable salary. And this job he did until Stalin's death.
>
> He was a very poor man. He had one room in a flat shared with two other families. You know, this was the Soviet regime, the Soviet conveniences. The Soviet conditions of life were that in one multi-room flat lived several families. So he lived with two families, he had only one room, and he lived on what Olga Ivanova earned from her jobs.
>
> By the time Stalin died he was already forty-four or forty-five years old. He had no official profession and it was too late to learn one. He found a job in a machinery factory as a simple worker for a miserable salary, for sixty rubles a month.[33]

Lazar praised the man he had met and befriended: "First of all, he was very polite. He was interested in culture, in music, in theatre. He used to read . . . art, fine literature. He was, as I told you, very polite, but he was very afraid of the Soviet regime."

As Pechersky's daughter, Ella, recalled in Rostov in 2013:

> So we lived a very poor life. As soon as he came back, he went to work in this financial and economic institute. But in 1947, he was invited to work in the theatre of musical comedy.
>
> He was invited as an administrator of the theatre. But he could make very little money, and at that time the whole theatre was still destroyed. So that was a very difficult time, not only for us, but for all the people in the country.
>
> Before 1984 it was very difficult, all we could get was just bread and potatoes. And after the reforms of 1984, some other kinds of products—like sausage, for example—appeared in the grocery stores. So of course we were not rich, but still we had some food to eat and . . . father didn't like to remember about the war and especially to tell us, to tell me as a child about the war, to speak in the family about the war.[34]

The couple got married officially only about twenty years before he died. Olga made a little money, and friends helped them to survive, some by bringing them potatoes, others by bringing them groceries.

As Natalya Ladychenko, his grand-daughter, recalled:

> It was a very hard period for the whole family after the war. Because of hunger and starvation there were a lot of problems in the family. It was difficult even to survive. That's why he didn't want to . . . speak much about the war, about even more difficult times. He wanted somehow to . . . support his family and to help them to forget all the difficulties.
>
> In 1947, he was invited to the theatre of musical comedy as an administrator of the theatre. And that was the time when everything was against the Jews everywhere. So they blamed him for some dishonest actions with tickets. At that time, music and musical comedy theatre were quite popular, and they blamed him for selling tickets not in a proper way and they even sent people to their home to search for something at home, and they searched for something in the theatre; of course they found nothing, and moreover, when they came home to search for something, they were shocked to see how poorly they lived.
>
> They wanted to discharge him from the job and especially from the Party. And in order to discharge him from the Party, they needed to have a case against him and to prepare to bring this case to the court. The court session in fact didn't happen. But the fact that the papers were prepared for the court was enough. After that, it was impossible for him to find a job. Finally, around 1952, he found a job in this frame workshop, where they made frames for pictures.[35] He had been out of work for five years.

To Reconnect With the Other Survivors

The first of the Russian survivors to conduct a search for Pechersky was Aleksey Vaytsen. He had read an article in which Pechersky's name was mentioned, and in this way he learned that Pechersky had not only survived the war but was still alive. He wrote a letter to the newspaper and asked about Pechersky. The newspaper replied that Pechersky was still alive and lived in Rostov-on-Don. Vaytsen then started corresponding with Pechersky, and finally, in 1963, they met. After celebrating the twentieth anniversary of the revolt in 1963, they met every five years.

Natasha said that her grandfather was rather busy as a veteran in the early 1960s with speaking in public as a war veteran—but not as the leader of the revolt of 1943:

> He visited different places, like Dagestan and the northern Caucasus, where he went to schools to meet children, and he was invited to different organizations too and he was asked to tell the story in his own words. But he was upset because he wasn't allowed to go to the trials (Nuremberg 1948; Jerusalem 1961; Hagen 1966, S.L.). At first he even didn't know that he had been invited to these trials, to these courts. In fact he didn't even receive the invitations. Somebody had answered in his place, saying for example that he was ill, or that he couldn't go to the trial. And when he found out, he was

176   *Return to Rostov*

very upset. He was also not really healthy, because in the seventies he had one kidney removed. And he had diabetes, so after the middle of the seventies he was not healthy.[36]

He corresponded with the world, assisted by Michael Lev. Of course he was not free in his written contacts since his letters were under strict surveillance by the KGB, and whatever Pechersky wrote at this period had to be coded in the language of that time. He complied, but his international contacts remained a threat to his life, which was already in danger. When she was interviewed after his death, Olga remarked that the authorities had seriously warned Pechersky to stop his correspondence. Contacts with foreigners were blocked; he was required more and more to stay in Rostov, and even travels on Russian territory were hindered. Contacts between East and West were difficult since the Cold War was raging, and the fight against imperialism was all over the place. The authorities knew he received invitations from the West, and therefore he was suspected by them being a spy. He had to fear for his own life. According to Olga, he survived only because his name was so well known in the West.[37]

He was invited to attend meetings such as the commemoration of Sobibor at the camp and the opening of the grounds as a memorial site in 1965. But like many Soviet citizens of the time, he could not leave the country, and his applications for a visa remained unanswered. That same year, trees were planted on the grounds of the former camp at Sobibor, and a sculpture of a grieving woman with her child was unveiled. The organizing committee had expected him to come, and a speech would even be given to honor him, but he did not show up since he was not allowed to go.

Survivor Thomas Blatt also began to correspond with Pechersky regularly in the 1970s and even visited him Rostov in 1980. Slowly knowledge about Pechersky's fate and isolation began to circulate. The survivors tried to reconstruct what had happened during the escape and who had been where; since everyone was on the run, they had not been able to keep an eye on one another during the revolt.[38] Later, during the decades after the revolt, they had scattered all over the world, and no one could tell a coherent story about the revolt nor about the camp. Fragments of fading memories had mingled with images of other camps, with anxiety and suppressed feelings of trauma, and with chaotic pictures. They felt the need to collect a shared story and to join a collective effort of reconstruction. While doing so they wanted to help each other, and they assumed that only those who had witnessed the revolt and who had been in the camp could understand each other. This is exactly what united many ex-inmates and survivors, as well as those who had been incarcerated in other camps.

Moshe Bahir tried to help by sending parcels from Israel, but there were taxes to be paid upon receipt, and there was not enough money to do so. An initiative to bring Pechersky to visit Israel failed. The others kept trying to support him and to show their gratitude, for he was their hero.

The author of *Escape from Sobibor*, Richard Räshke, met Pechersky, together with Thomas Blatt, later in 1980 in Moscow. In his book he described the somber

Intourist hotel where they met, one of those places where everything was perfectly organized and thoroughly monitored.[39] Thomas Blatt wanted very much to talk to Pechersky. Pechersky admitted he could still hear the children crying, and for him the wailing of these children had been the worst.[40] He had felt powerless to help them. The answers he gave to questions were politically correct, since everyone in the room knew that whatever was said could be heard by the KGB. Pechersky said he would like to go back to Sobibor to see the place and to verify his memories.

The organization of the Sobibor underground had given Pechersky hope at a time when one needed to believe in survival, he said. He felt that hope again when he was with his friends, the other survivors. He put an enormous amount of energy into finding all those who were still alive. And Thomas felt the friendship and solidarity. At that meeting with Richard Räshke, a small discussion started between Thomas and Pechersky about the way the Russian inmates had left the others after the escape. Pechersky defended himself by saying that he wanted to join the Red Army and to fight for Russia. Thomas has written about this conversation and tried not to blame Pechersky, but the accusation of having abandoned the others remained.[41] Indeed, it was something not to be proud of. But his heroism could not be stained, and understandably it was beyond imagination to accuse the great leader. As a result there were ambivalent feelings, even confusing feelings, as Thomas told me in 2010. As was the rule, Pechersky had been recognized for his service and for being wounded, and he showed his medal with pride. In Moscow there were two meetings at which not a word was uttered that could be used against him. Apparently Pechersky was quite emotional during the encounter, easily brought to tears. He had become a very emotional man. Räshke wrote: "There was gentleness about Sasha. He spoke with great humility, and as he talked about Sobibor, he showed more sadness than anger or hatred."[42]

On the fortieth anniversary of the victory, in the spring of 1985, Pechersky received the Order of the Great Patriotic War. This was an award given to all veterans. He was given another medal in 1951 for being a member of the partisans, but in fact he had received this award already in 1946. He did not know it until 1951, since the medal had been lost or hidden in the cupboards of the bureaucracy. According to his friends like Blatt and Lev, these honors were not enough, and in the following years new efforts were made for him to be nominated as a Hero of the Soviet Union, an order of the highest degree. No answer was ever received. In addition, Lazar Lubarsky had written to the President of the USSR, Nikolai Podgorny. Such *démarches* would be noted and kept in the files of the KGB. When Lazar Lubarsky was arrested and became a "prisoner of Zion," representing Jews who wanted to go to Israel, one of the first questions he was asked was why he had written such a letter.

Pechersky was no longer a member of the Communist Party. He felt his exclusion as a humiliation. After the Twentieth Congress of the Communist Party of the Soviet Union (February 14–25, 1956), which denounced the personality cult and dictatorship of Joseph Stalin, he was invited to reapply for party membership. However, the criminal case against Pechersky was still active. He replied he did

Figure 6.2 Aleksandr Pechersky at the Red Square in Moscow in 1980
Source: Photograph courtesy of Richard Räshke.

not want to do reapply, since he himself had never left the party. In a letter to author Valentin Tomin, he briefly described what had happened when he discussed his membership: "When I answered that I was a member of the Party and I had my Party membership card with me, the judge told the secretary: 'Write that he is expelled according to the decision of the city Party Committee.'"[43]

Most likely this means the following: At that time it was considered that a party member could not be held criminally responsible, so before a trial, a defendant would have been expelled from the party at a meeting of the primary party organization. In Pechersky's case, this procedure had evidently not been followed, so the city committee of the party expelled him ex post facto.[44] While all praised Pechersky as an excellent Communist worker—and in spite of his being nominated as a foreman—the directorship of the place where he worked did not support him. He landed in a vicious circle, while he kept striving for more recognition. In the same letter to Tomin in 1961, Pechersky announced that he would bring his case before the Central Committee. But at the regional level, he was told that he first needed rehabilitation, and this was rejected by a local court.[45]

Many Russian Jews chose to leave for Israel in the late 1960s and 1970s, but this was not an option for Pechersky. He was a citizen of the Soviet Union, and he wanted to stay. This was his home, here in Rostov-on-Don. He said so explicitly to Olga.[46]

The Post-War Trials and the Collective Punishment

As the Red Army reconquered terrain, the perpetrators were held liable for their crimes and sentenced to death. Lawsuits against these "criminals" started immediately after Soviet power recaptured the territory. Indeed, already during the war, Soviet persecution of "Nazis and other traitors" had started, with no mention of the murder of Jews.[47] The other traitors were those who had been collaborators as well as those suspected of collaboration because they had not evacuated when ordered or had tried to survive in occupied territory. Jews did not exist, and even the ghettoization of Jews by the Germans was presented as a forceful resettlement of Soviet citizens to the outskirts of the cities. The Soviet government conducted thousands of open and closed tribunals until the late 1980s, condemning tens of thousands of Germans and Soviet collaborators for crimes committed on Soviet territory. The 1943 Krasnodar trial was the first major open military tribunal to take place before the end of the war.

Ilya Bourtman has described how two institutions were assigned the task of investigating the crimes committed against Soviet citizens. One was the system of military commissions originally instituted by Leon Trotsky shortly after the Russian Revolution. As part of the Central Political Office of the Soviet armed forces, by 1940 the commissions had become a powerful element of every division in the Red Army. The other was the Extraordinary State Commission for the Ascertainment and Investigation of Crimes Committed by the German Fascist Invaders and their Accomplices.[48]

180 Return to Rostov

In Krasnodar in 1943 eleven Soviet citizens were accused and found guilty of treason and collaboration with the Nazis; eight of them were hanged in front of tens of thousands of cheering Soviet citizens. The trial served as a warning to all those who had collaborated with the Germans, and severe punishment was also threatened to family members and those in close contact with the defendants. Highly visible military tribunals served as the instrument for conveying this warning; at the same time, they prevented contact with "enemies."

In the following years "enemies" would include not only Germans but also many dissidents and people supposed to be non-Communist. Whatever its underlying rationale may have been, the military tribunal proved to be a flexible tool for the prosecution, and it was used to punish all opponents—foreign or domestic—of the Soviet state. It set in motion a series of public war crimes trials that continued through the 1940s and even into the 1960s, 1970s, and 1980s. The ultimate responsibility lay with the *individual* who had perpetrated the crime, but there was no discussion of collective guilt.

During the Nuremberg trials, the camps of Operation Reinhard were ignored. According to historian Donald Bloxham, this silence highly influenced the Western image of the Holocaust.[49] One explanation for this omission is that so few survived the camps of Operation Reinhard, and even more important, there was not the kind of proof favored by the Anglo-American judges. They wanted documents that would prove the killings beyond doubt. The court in Nuremberg considered eyewitness accounts unreliable, because the survivors were thought to "exaggerate."

The Soviets in turn were not keen to consider what had happened in eastern Poland as part of their history. The massacre at Katyn, where thousands of Poles had been killed by the Soviets in 1940, also happened in the "Bloodlands." The Soviets wanted to hide their murder of Polish officers and intellectuals and to highlight their own heroic struggle against fascism. Historians specialized in the field have argued that American-German collaboration during the Cold War also hindered the prosecution of the crimes of Sobibor. All attention fell on Auschwitz and camps to the west such as Belsen, for which famous film recordings of the Allied Forces entering the camp do exist.

Indeed, the elimination of the camps of Operation Reinhard was successful, even in an immaterial sense. The camps had vanished from memory. Sobibor mistakenly turned up in Nuremberg under the name "Wolzek," but no connection was made with Operation Reinhard and the murder of Polish Jews, who composed the majority of the victims of the three camps. The camps were understood as a looting exercise. In a vague sense, the massive murder was known, but the judges did not know where this had taken place. Belzec and Sobibor barely received any mention in the proceedings of the court, despite much anecdotal evidence about them. The ensuing distortion highlights the difference between legal and historical evidence, and this difference is crucial for understanding Pechersky's post-war despair. He was not allowed to testify as a witness in Nuremberg. Pechersky was convinced that only by testifying would he be able to spread the word about Sobibor.

The Emergence of the Voice of the Survivor and Oral History

The voices of the survivors remained silent during the early proceedings against the Nazi perpetrators, and not only in the case of Sobibor. Not until the Eichmann trial in 1961 in Jerusalem was attention given to the full narratives of survivors, including those who did not directly support the indictment. The statement of the Israeli prosecutor Gideon Hausner was broadcast worldwide:

> I am not standing alone. With me are six million accusers. But they cannot rise to their feet and point an accusing finger toward him who sits in the dock and cry: "I accuse." For their ashes are piled up on the hills of Auschwitz and the fields of Treblinka, and are strewn in the forests of Poland. Their graves are scattered throughout the length and breadth of Europe. Their blood cries out, but their voice is not heard. Therefore I will be their spokesman and in their name I will unfold the awesome indictment.[50]

During the Eichmann trial, witnesses Moshe Bahir and Ya'akov Biskowitz were major spokesmen for the survivors of Sobibor.[51] Again, the Soviet authorities did not allow Pechersky to give his testimony at the court in Jerusalem.

Before the Eichmann trial, the testimonies and accounts of survivors consisted mainly of answers to questions from the prosecution. These fragmentary narratives are truncated by the objectives of judicial procedure and fail to convey what the witnesses really wanted to say; they do not fully reflect what happened.

However, outside the legal framework, archivists and others began very soon after the war to collect testimonies about the lives of individual Jews and whole communities that had disappeared, along with stories of the camps. These were in most cases small projects conducted by researchers who were keen to investigate the fate of the Jewish survivors of the Shoah and their traumatization. In those years, however there was little demand among the general public for such information, and many people did not even want to listen. For example, the work of Primo Levi, who is now part of the Western canon, remained unrecognized until 1958, more than a decade later.

In the early years after the war, far from the world of literary and judicial eyewitnesses, the psychologist David Pablo Boder conducted interviews in displaced persons (DP) camps and created a series of magnificent audio documents in 1946.[52] Boder interviewed with two objectives: he wanted to preserve an authentic record of wartime suffering, and as a psychologist he was professionally interested in the impact of extreme suffering on personality. His magnificent interviews give us a glimpse of the German hell that slowly emerged from the historical blackout.

A great deal of oral history research into trauma during World War II arose in an unprecedented way in the 1970s when Jewish survivors wanted to tell about crimes that the perpetrators had chosen to hide. They also wanted to spread the word about ways of life that had been lost. Unlike the survivors of the Armenian genocide, the Jewish survivors had the means to tell their stories, and new

182 *Return to Rostov*

technologies and new ways to communicate facilitated this process. It became clear that telling about the past can be a tool for the reintegration of traumatic events, and for a long time it has been a useful discipline for the social regulation of traumatic war experiences.[53] Its model of the use of life-narratives has been taken over by other forms of trauma psychology.

The model of victims speaking up in court has also permeated Western jurisprudence. The spoken word became a source of "evidence" where written sources had been destroyed. From that moment, the Jewish tradition of *zakhor*—a concept that includes not only the commandment to remember through ritual and

Figure 6.3 Aleksandr Pechersky in his sixties
Source: Photograph courtesy of Selma Leydesdorff.

Return to Rostov 183

recital, but also an actualization of memory and a field of action—became part of the Jewish post-Holocaust mental world. It has become the ground for major oral history collections, such as the Fortunoff collection at Yale University and, on a much more massive scale, the Shoah Visual Foundation Collection in Los Angeles, where more than 52,000 audio-visual accounts are stored.

The genre of oral history of trauma is often interwoven with eyewitness accounts created as documents to bear witness to the "real truth" and to be used as evidence in court.[54] Elie Wiesel named our time "The Age of Testimony" because of the unprecedented way in which traumatic events are often no longer kept private but preferably shared with a wide audience.[55] Trauma must be acknowledged, and therefore those involved must speak up. But trauma stories are never straightforward accounts of "what happened"; like all memories, they are based on perceptions of the present. They are deeply moving accounts that shift back and forth between frozen memories of atrocities and the reconstruction and interpretation of the injuries suffered.[56] In turn, the stories give meaning to the present and constitute the survivors' longings and musings about their desired future world.

Often trauma has permeated not only the soul but also the body, which reacts and often hurts.[57] No story emerges spontaneously, since survivors prefer to repress the memory of their ordeals. Over the years there have been a plethora of debates about how to approach the narrator of a trauma story. How much empathy should be shown, and how much distance should be kept? And as trauma interviews are especially difficult to interpret, discussion arises regarding the various possibilities for interpreting what has been told.[58] The discussion on distance continues, with some arguing for traveling with the narrator through the obstacles of the unknown fields of memory, and others arguing for more objective distance.

All the above is true for the story of Pechersky. His memories changed and were influenced by the stories of other prisoners. He was not allowed to tell his story straightforwardly, but in his case he was also actively hindered from spreading the word about Sobibor, a camp kept secret by the Germans and kept in the dark by the authorities of the Soviet Union.

Notes

1 Jeffrey W. Jones, *Everyday Life and the "Reconstruction" of Soviet Russia During and After the Great Patriotic War, 1943–1948* (Bloomington: Slavica, 2008), 43.
2 Ibid., 80.
3 Exact data are not clear since the town was reconquered slowly. Some parts were invaded and liberated earlier than others.
4 Amir Weiner, *Making Sense of War: The Second World War and the Fate of the Bolshevik Revolution* (Princeton and London: Princeton University Press, 2001), 112.
5 Ibid., 43–82 (chapter "The Making of a Post War Elite").
6 Catherine Merridale, *Night of Stone: Death and Memory in Twentieth-Century Russia* (New York: Penguin Books, 2000), 16.
7 Ibid., 11.
8 Benyamin Lukin, "Rostov on Don," in *The YIVO Encyclopedia of Jews in Eastern Europe* (New York: YIVO Institute for Jewish Research, 2010).

184   *Return to Rostov*

9   Jones, *Everyday Life*, 762–764.
10 A typescript is held in the archives of NIOD (Netherlands Institute for War Documentation, Amsterdam), 804–19–00047. The interview was conducted in Russian and translated into Dutch. I have translated it from Dutch into English. See Ch. 1, note 13.
11 Ibid.
12 Lukasz Hirszowicz, "The Holocaust in the Soviet Mirror," in *The Holocaust in the Soviet Union: Studies and Sources on the Destruction of Jews in the Nazi-Occupied Territories, 1941–1945*, eds. Lucjan Dobroszycki and Jeffrey S. Gurock (Armonk, NY and London: M. E. Sharpe, 1993), 29–61, on p. 35.
13 Mikhael Krutikov, "Foreword to: Michael Lev, Sobibor and Soviet Yiddish Culture," in *Michael Lev, Sobibor, A Documentary Novel of the Sobibor Uprising* (Jerusalem: Gefen, 2007), xiii.
14 Yitzchak Arad, *In the Shadow of the Red Banner: Soviet Jews in the War Against Nazi Germany* (Jerusalem: Gefen, 2010). Arad estimates that 500,000 Jews joined the Soviet Army.
15 See, e.g., Marina Sorokina, "People and Procedures: Towards a History of the Investigation of Nazi Crimes in the USSR," *Kritika: Explorations in Russian and Eurasian History* 6:4 (2005): 797–831. Also: Kiril Feferman, "Soviet Investigation of Nazi War Crimes," *Journal of Genocide Research* 5:4 (December 2005): 587–602.
16 NIOD 804–19–00047.
17 Ibid.
18 Letter of a student in grade 8B, Tatiana Nekrasova, from the Pashinskaia School; archive of the family in Rostov, 1972.
19 NIOD 804–19–00047.
20 Gitelman, *A Century of Ambivalence*, 147–150.
21 Arno Lustiger, *Stalin and the Jews*, 195–247.
22 Amir Weiner, *Making Sense of War*, 89–95.
23 Simon Redlich, *War, Stalinism and the Holocaust: A Documentary History of the Jewish Anti-Fascist Committee* (New York: Routledge, 1995). See also Joshua Rubenstein and Vladimir P. Naumov, eds., *Stalin's Secret Pogrom: The Postwar Inquisition of the Jewish Anti-Fascist Committee* (New Haven, London: Yale University Press, 2001).
24 Redlich, *War*, 40–47.
25 Jonathan Brent and Vladimir P. Naumov, eds., *Stalin's Last Crime: The Plot Against the Jewish Doctors* (New York: Harper Perennial, 2004).
26 Gitelman, *A Century of Ambivalence*, 164–167.
27 Ibid., 171.
28 Christina Winkler, "2000 Jews Have So Far Been Detected," in *Холокост: 70 лет спустя*, eds. Ilya Altman et al. (Moscow: Научио-просветительиньый Цеитр "Холокост," 2015), 133–139.
29 Karel C. Berkhoff, "The Corpses in the Ravine Were Women, Men, and Children: Written Testimonies from 1941 on the Babi Yar Massacre," *Holocaust and Genocide Studies* 29:2 (2015): 251–274.
30 SVF, Los Angeles, code 5009, Iakov Krut; interviewed by Maria Lackman in Ashkelon, Israel, 10 October 1995. I thank Ina Gogina for her help with Russian slang.
31 NIOD 804–19–00047.
32 Lazar Lubarski, interviewed by author, Holon, 2012.
33 Ibid.
34 Ella Grinevich, interviewed by author, Rostov-on-Don, August 2013.
35 Ibid.
36 Natalya Ladychenko, interviewed by author, Rostov-on-Don, August 2013.
37 Vilensky et al., *Sobibor*, 130, from an interview with Olga by G. Belotserovski.
38 Much of what is written here I owe to the work of Lev Simkin.
39 Richard Raske, *Escape*, 465–478 (ch 43, "Sasha").

Return to Rostov   185

40 Ibid., 470.

41 See also chapter 3.

42 Raske, "Escape," 474.

43 Simkin, *Half an Hour of Retribution*, 184, letter of Pehersky to Valentin Tomin, Moscow, 25.1.1963.

44 Simkin, *Half an Hour of Retribution*.

45 Ibid., 189.

46 Vilensky et al., *Sobibor*, 130.

47 Alexander Victor Prusin, "'Fascist Criminals to the Gallows!': The Holocaust and Soviet War Crimes Trials, December 1945—February 1946," *Holocaust and Genocide Studies* 17:1 (2003): 1–30.

48 Ilya Bourtman, "Blood for Blood, Death for Death: The Soviet Military Tribunal in Krasnodar, 1943," *Holocaust and Genocide Studies* 22:2 (Fall 2008): 246–265.

49 Donald Bloxham, *Genocide on Trial, War Crimes and the Formation of Holocaust History and Memory* (Oxford: Oxford University Press, 2001), 109–129. See also Donald Bloxham, "Prosecuting the Past in the Postwar Decade: Political Strategy and National Mythmaking," in *Sixty Years after the Nuremberg Trials*, eds. David Bankier and Dan Michmann (Jerusalem: Yad Vashem, 2010), 539–554; and Donald Bloxham, "The Missing Camps of Aktion Reinhard," in *The Memory of Catastrophe*, eds. Peter Gray and Kendrick Oliver (Manchester: Manchester University Press, 2004), 118–131.

50 The Trial of Adolf Eichmann, session 6, 17 April 1961.

51 Proceedings Eichmann trial, Session No. 65, 21 Sivan 5721 (5 June 1961). Testimonies of Moshe Bahir, Ya'akov Biskowitz, and Moshe Bahir (concluded), Submission of documents relating to Sobibor, Testimonies of Michael Podchlewnik and Modechai Zurawski.

52 David Pablo Boder interviewed DPs (displaced persons); his work is a most impressive series of testimonies. Boder was a psychologist, not a historian. See *I Did Not Interview the Dead* (Urbana: University of Illinois Press), 1949. No longer available is *Topical Autobiographies of Displaced People Recorded Verbatim in the Displaced Persons Camps, with a Psychological and Anthropological Analysis*, 16 vols. (Chicago: D. P. Boder, 1950–57). For an extensive review of Boder's work, see Alan Rosen, *The Wonder of Their Voices: The 1946 Holocaust Interviews of David Boden* (New York: Oxford University Press), 2010.
Transcripts of his interviews are available online at http://voices.iit.edu/david_boder.

53 Erika Apfelbaum, "And Now What, After Such Tribulations? Memory and Dislocation in the Era of Uprooting," *American Psychologist* 55 (2000): 1008–1013; Dori Laub, "Truth and Testimony, The Process and the Struggle," in *Trauma: Explorations in Memory*, ed. Cathy Caruth (Baltimore: Johns Hopkins University Press, 1995), 61–76; Paul Gready, *Writing as Resistance: Life Stories of Imprisonment, Exile, and Homecoming from Apartheid South Africa* (Lanham, MD: Lexington Books, 2003).

54 See Nanci Adler and Selma Leydesdorff, eds., *Tapestry of Memory: Evidence and Testimony in Life-Story Narratives* (New Brunswick and London: Transaction Publishers, 2013).

55 For the history of Jewish eyewitness accounts, see Annette Wievorka, *The Era of the Witness* (Ithaca and London: Cornell University Press, 2006), translated from French. She describes how members of the Historical Commissions of the Central Committee of Polish Jews gathered 7,300 testimonies in 1944. See also Elie Wiesel, *Dimensions of the Holocaust* (Evanston: Northwestern University Press, 1977), 9.

56 Dori Laub and Nuri C. Auerhahn, "Knowing and Not Knowing Massive Psychic Trauma: Forms of Traumatic Memory," *The International Journal of Psychoanalysis* 74 (1993): 287–302.

57 See Albert Lichtblau, *To Engage and to Disengage: Keeping Distance in Oral History Interviews* (Oral History Productions Forum), www.oralhistory-productions.org/articles/keepingdistance.htm.

186 *Return to Rostov*

58 One name worth mentioning is that of the German historian Alexander von Plato, who developed a methodology during the International Forced Labour Project, which he directed. To create comparable interviews, he and his collaborator Christian Thonfeld developed guidelines. For an English translation, see www.oralhistoryforum. ca/index.php/ohf/article/viewFile/57/85. During this project, in which people from more than ten countries participated, he tried to get consensus about the interviewers' attitudes. Striking is his so-called fourth phase, during which interviews are criticized and scrutinized, preferably by a group in which scholars from other researches participate.

7 Traumatized and Alone in Front of "Justice"

The first Western judicial inquest into the "unknown" camp of Sobibor was held in Germany in 1959.[1] The senior prosecutor, Dietrich Zeug, had learned that there were survivors in the Netherlands; he had read excerpts from *The Black Book*, mentioned in earlier chapters, and in October 1960, an official investigation was launched, followed by the indictment of a dozen soldiers in 1964. The trial started in 1965 in Hagen.[2] Pechersky was probably testifying at that moment in Rostov-on-Don. Due to "imperfections in the accounts" of some witnesses, several defendants were acquitted. Five were convicted and sentenced, while a sixth would be re-tried later. Pecherksy was furious, as is clear from his epilogue to the 1972 edition of his book, written in a style typical of the political culture and jargon he lived in. He wrote,

> "The soil of Sobibor absorbed too much human blood and the perpetrators received such an insignificant punishment. Not only the perpetrators of Sobibor, but also of hundreds of other death camps founded by fascist Germany during the years of the Great Patriotic War, are still living in freedom. The imperialists are covering them in every way in the hope of setting them against the socialist countries and in the first place against the Soviet Union. But this is in vain: the people of the world will not let fascist rogues act freely. In 1962 I was present as a witness at the trial against eleven traitors [in Kiev, S.L.]. I could not watch them calmly. Cowardice and blankness were on their faces. Those "heroes" in front of defenseless women and children were trembling from fear for their paltry lives. Where had their aplomb and their "victorious" smile disappeared to? Twenty-two days in Sobibor flashed through my mind."[3]

He had spent twenty-two days in Sobibor, and he stood up against anyone who wanted to challenge his pride in being a Soviet citizen. The men tried in Kiev were Russians who had chosen the other side and had helped the Germans. He despised them. As he wrote expressing his feelings of disgust at what happened: "Every man has his Motherland where he spent the happiest days of his life, his childhood, his youth where he was raised and was living his life whether happily or not. It is always dear to him." However, the men who were on trial had no

188 *Traumatized and Alone*

such pride: "They had *cowardice*. In a cowardly way, they shifted the blame, trying somehow to soften and acquit not only their own high treason but also the mass killing of their brothers, sisters, and mothers. The Soviet court, the people's court passed its sentence on the traitors who had lost their human nature and had become helpmates to fascist cannibals." Many Russians were shocked when they learned about the crimes of the Germans. For them the punishment was never severe enough. The campguards and all those who had helped to kill were people without conscience. Pechersky continued:

> The Soviet experts on state security do not forget their duty in seeking out high traitors who have betrayed their people during the war. In 1965 there was a new trial of *vakhmans* [*Wachtmänner*, camp guards] in Krasnodar. As Lev Ginsburg, a special correspondent for *Literaturnaya Gazeta* (The Literary Gazette) wrote:
>
> The court will listen to the stories of six traitors and time-servers who betrayed their Motherland in order "to live," gorge themselves, appropriate the property of others, live in safety far from the front line, who without thinking and with no hard feelings changed one uniform for another and went over to the enemy's side as simply as a man crosses a street. In the condition of the fascist regime this time-serving led them to participate in mass killings, sadism, and turned them absolutely into brutes.

"And who were those people whom you were killing?" asked the prosecutors and the judges. "Did you not feel sorry, not even for the small children?"

"Matvienko (one of them) thought a bit and answered: "Of course, sincerely speaking, if I had been as smart then as I am now, it would have been better to shoot myself. Now I have a wife, children, have built a house. And of course if I had been intelligent as I am now, I . . .""

"One doesn't have to be clever to understand that killing people is a crime. Whom did you kill?"

"We killed children, old men, old women . . ."

"How did the doomed behave?"

"Of course they were crying, shouting, wailing—a terrible picture. Now it is impossible to imagine. . . . People were stripped naked, and *vakhmans* were pushing them and shooting them. A German *ober-vakhman* was standing behind me. What could I do? . . ."[4]

Pechersky continued with the story of the other survivor who was at the proceedings, his friend Aleksey Vaytsen. The arrogance and lack of compassion of the accused was a warning that left Pechersky amazed.

"I remember them all," concluded Pechersky, furious at a world that would not punish them enough. He was aghast that the perpetrators could live on without unbearable shame.

During the decades after the war, there existed a different pattern for the trials in the East and in the West. In the West, punishment was usually mild, certainly in Germany, where lawsuits became moments when memories, especially those of

Traumatized and Alone 189

surviving Jews, were scrutinized and questioned—and most cases in the West were heard before German judges. Many of these judges came from the élites who had collaborated with Nazism. They were hostile to the endless complaints of victims. The post-war literature of Germany contains a plethora of descriptions of how much people were hurt by the insensitivity of questions during court proceedings.

There were several trials in the Soviet Union in which Pechersky participated where the punishment was not mild at all. He agreed with this policy of condemnation, as we have seen, and did not realize that the trials served Soviet propaganda more than the struggle to come to terms with a painful past. The confusion was aggravated since only in court could surviving witnesses testify about the fate of the Jews.

In 1962, several guards (auxiliaries of the Germans) were sentenced in Kiev, and all were hanged. These trials were held pursuant to Soviet law, in which eyewitness testimonies and confessions were of crucial importance and often considered incontrovertible proof.[5] Such "confessions" were taken at face value, and the defendant's guilt was never doubted.

From the proceedings in Kiev it is clear the court's ideological framework was again the Soviet memory of the Great Patriotic War, and what happened in Sobibor was part of the "crimes against innocent 'Soviet Citizens.'" The trial took place in 1962, but for bureaucratic and unknown political reasons the date is remembered as 1963. Weeks of sessions went on behind closed doors. The proceedings were edited by the KGB, and a shorter, abridged version was stored both in Kiev and Washington (I have copies of both). We have the testimony of Pechersky, which is more extensive than others preserved from that trial. Since he was proud of the resistance, he wanted to talk about it. He also stressed that not *only* Jews were killed in Sobibor. When I read this, I wondered if he was yielding to the dominant discourse of that time, in which Jews were not singled out as particular victims of German atrocity. But in Moscow I learned that only by stressing that Russians were killed could he have hoped to attract the attention of judges who did not care much about Jews or were instructed not to care.

Pechersky was questioned and, as was normal in such proceedings in Russia at that time, no one doubted his words. The verdict was clear from the beginning. In response to questioning, Pechersky explained that there were very few Germans in Sobibor and many tasks were done by the auxiliary guards who were on trial. As everywhere in the USSR, these "helpers" were seen as traitors, and since there had hardly been any Germans, their criminality was worsened. In addition, he was given the opportunity to describe what happened in Sobibor. In gruesome detail he explained how the gas chambers worked and what had been the trajectory to the gas chamber. He wanted to explain how people were killed. He said,

> I cannot say what happened in the room where people were stripped naked. I know that people were invited to undress and go to "the bathhouse" and afterwards to work. People believed that they were going to wash and undressed voluntarily. I cannot say if there were cases of prisoners' resistance during undressing, since I had not been in the camp very long.

190   *Traumatized and Alone*

From the second zone people were directed to the third zone, where there were special chambers with water taps and even basins as if for washing. However, it was trickery. As soon as the people entered the chamber the doors were closed, the gas turned on, and people suffocated. There were special workers selected from the arriving troop trains to discharge the gas chambers. I was told that this team consisted of about thirty people. I did not know what exactly their function was because we were forbidden to move freely around the camp, but I heard from other Sobibor prisoners that they loaded the dead bodies of the suffocated people on trolleys, stacked them, and burned them.

He became graphic in his description, as was normal in such trials, and continued: "At that time our group was working in the fourth zone and we heard shooting and people shouting. One of the prisoners working with me suggested that we had to take advantage of the situation and escape from Sobibor, moreover since, during the extermination process, the Germans reduced the number of guards working in the camp."[6]

He then tried to convince the court that this had happened to Russians, and he abstained from mentioning Jews. Indeed, his whole strategy was aimed at explaining that fellow citizens of the judges (innocent Soviet citizens) were killed, interweaving the accusation with his own story: "*It should be noted that not only Jews arrived at Sobibor* [italics added]. Several Russians arrived at Sobibor with our car and they were also exterminated in the gas chambers. Such cases happened in other troop trains. Because in the work camp near Minsk we were kept together with Russian POWs."[7]

Shortly before the court proceedings began, Leonid Brezhnev (leader of the Soviet Union, 1964–82) enabled by special decree the verdict of the death penalty. Officially this penalty no longer existed, and the last time it had been imposed was more than fifteen years earlier. Lev Simkin has argued that the death sentences imposed in Kiev paved the way for subsequent death sentences for collaborators.[8] There have indeed been many cases since then. The need for a death penalty was never doubted, and sentences could not be severe enough. At several moments during his life, Pechersky looked back on his Kiev testimony and felt proud of what he had done. He had helped ensure that the auxiliaries of the Germans were condemned to death, and he had aided in bringing the perpetrators to judgment. He was the only survivor of Sobibor who spoke up in Kiev; reportedly, he also acted as a witness at the trial of Krasnodar in the 1950s, but I have not been able to locate the files containing his testimony.[9]

Documentation is available for two more cases in which Pechersky was asked to testify. In 1974 he went to Moscow for the case against Hubert Gomerski (1911–99), one of the major perpetrators at Sobibor as well as in other camps. At that time, Pechersky was not allowed to go to Hagen in Germany, where the proceedings took place.[10] He never received permission to leave the Soviet Union (except when he was too old and too weak), but he was allowed to speak to a delegation from the German court in Moscow. Since German law did not and does not allow collective responsibility for war crimes, the specific sadism, motives, and acts of each accused individual needed to be proven in every single case.[11]

During Pechersky's deposition, of course, the question of what the defendants had done—and not Pechersky's own story—was at the center of the proceedings. The representatives of the court were eager to know whether Gomerski had been such an awful perpetrator. Was he worse than the others? For the members of the court, any visible emotion made a witness statement unreliable, while all information needed to be given with extreme precision. German law focused on the individual perpetrators' separate acts of atrocity, which therefore received more attention than the complex crime of the destruction of Jews. The defendants went through a normal "criminal" procedure, typical for a legal system that was unable to admit that what happened at Sobibor was more than the sum of the crimes of certain sadistic individuals.

The questions from the German delegation centered on Gomerski, but Pechersky managed to insert some of the story of the revolt. He also recounted an extremely cruel episode during which Gomerski himself shot a Dutch prisoner after an atrocious beating. Pechersky had witnessed three more instances of the excessively cruel behavior of Gomerski. When asked, Pechersky doubted if he would be able to recognize Gomerski after so many years, and he struggled with his memory and his confusion. In order to have arguments in favor of the accused the defense asked if there were SS men who provided extra food to the prisoners, which of course was not the case.

Gomerski and other defendants had probably boasted of their "good" behavior and pretended it was true. During cross-examination, Pechersky had to admit time and again that he was confused about certain data, that there were contradictions in what he had said. He clearly suffered from the distrust he encountered from the official commission, which he perceived as hostility. The interrogation was very precise, and many questions involved details. He defended his lack of specific knowledge of names by saying that he had spent only twenty-two days in Sobibor, while, as we now know, he had at that time been very busy with planning and hiding.[12]

He was "accused" of having already testified against members of the guards of Sobibor in Kiev. There was the suggestion that one such performance was enough and that he was biased. He answered that when he had testified in Kiev, he did not know who the guards were or who was accused. He had been naïve and merely wanted to tell what had happened in the camp, which had indeed been the case.

One example of the stubborn questioning concerned whether Gomerski's whip was different from those used by other SS men. Clearly the prosecution wanted to know whether Gomerski had been more sadistic than the others and whether his instrument of torture had inflicted more severe wounds.[13] However, someone who is being beaten to death is unlikely to notice the exact shape of the weapon. Pechersky became so upset about the interrogation that he could no longer remember the names of other prisoners, not even the friends with whom he had escaped. While his words were being doubted, he testified: "I knew the

192   *Traumatized and Alone*

names of eight or nine inmates, but I have forgotten them now." He also did not know which of the men he had escaped with were still alive. He was asked if he ever had written about the crimes, and he answered that he avoided writing about the offenses because emotionally it was too hard for him. In his writings he had focused on the uprising and the battle of the people. He estimated that about six hundred people had participated in the revolt.

A similarly hostile attitude was felt at the trial in Hagen, a court he was not allowed to attend. Many questions put to the eyewitnesses were disrespectful and cast doubt on the veracity of their answers. The survivors were not believed, and the lawyers made an effort to support critics of the stories of the victims. Thomas Blatt remarked that it felt as if the accusation was against him instead of against the Nazi culprits.

Pechersky's reaction to the lenient punishment was violent. He was most shocked that apart from the three main perpetrators, the other accused were charged only with being accomplices and were judged not to have killed without orders.[14] "What hypocrisy! And what mockery of the hundreds of thousands of human beings who were murdered at Sobibor."

In 1984 Pechersky was interviewed again for the second German Sobibor trial a decade later.[15] The word about him had spread, and noticing these testimonies more and more, people became aware that he was alive, while his absence started the myths about him that still persist. One example is a tapestry on which Pechersky is portrayed as the centerpiece. Deep down in the image are the dark Germans. The whole scene looks like a Russian icon.

Pechersky was interrogated in Donetsk in Ukraine, which was then part of the Soviet Union. Here the questions put to him were of a different kind; this time, the case centered on the ways in which some defendants sought to exculpate themselves by accusing others. He was asked if he had noticed that the Germans who had to do the killing had also suffered, and he replied politely that it was a hard question for him to answer, for he had not seen any SS members suffering. When one reads the transcripts, there is again involuntary confusion; the interrogation was full of distrust of his words, and whenever mistakes were pointed out, they took the form of an accusation. In response to one question, Pechersky said he had not met any Germans who behaved better. One feels his embarrassment while reading the transcripts.

Alone, Isolated, and Bitter

Pechersky felt alone in these years, isolated from his most important friends and far from where he could pursue his mission. However, the Gomerski case was the beginning of lengthy correspondence with survivors and their organizations in the West, and especially with the Communist resistance fighter Hermann Langbein, who founded the International Auschwitz Committee and, after the Hungarian uprising of 1956, was removed from official positions by the Communist leadership of the Committee as a result of his criticism of Stalinism. In 1960 Langbein was also removed from his position on the International Auschwitz Committee.[16]

Traumatized and Alone 193

It had become difficult for Pechersky to remember, as he said later that year. The trauma occupied his brain, as he confessed to Breur and Schelvis while preparing for the already mentioned interview:

> When I tell a story, I'm not just recounting, but before my eyes I see those scenes unfold, you see, and I describe them. I'm talking in a really quick tempo with scenes passing before my eyes just as in a movie; I'm commenting like an anchorman on what was happening there. That's why I have stopped bearing witness completely for two or three years already. That's why it's hard for me to testify in court now, as it was in Donetsk. The judge would see the state I was in and would reassure me, he would allow me short recesses and let me talk about everything without stress. So people pay close attention to my mental state. What am I to do? I decided to dedicate my life to this case, but probably I won't be able to do so until the end of my life.[17]

Despite his exclusion (because he had spent "only" twenty-two days in Sobibor), the trial of 1984 was a crucial moment for the retrieval of knowledge about Sobibor, though during the court proceedings the views of the victims were neglected.[18] The victims were asked to testify only regarding data that supported the accusation, not about anything else they had seen. The main defendant was commander Karl Frenzel.

The trial in Hagen in 1984 was also attended by Jules Schelvis, himself a survivor of Sobibor. In 2010 I interviewed Schelvis, who had passed through Sobibor in transit to another camp, about the court proceedings in Hagen. His wife was murdered in Sobibor when she arrived, but until the Hagen trial he had not really been able to absorb mentally the nature of the Sobibor camp. Before the trial he had not been able to imagine what had happened and had blocked it from his brain—it was too awful. He had not been aware of the revolt because, in October 1943, he was already trying to survive in another camp elsewhere in Poland. Only in Hagen did he start to face what Sobibor really was, since he had not followed the court proceedings of the 1960s.

Schelvis found out about the second trial in Hagen by accident. He was visiting family in Australia when he heard that a survivor of Sobibor was living nearby. It was Chaskiel Menche, and during a visit he told Schelvis what had happened during the revolt. Chaskiel himself had killed a German, and he intended to go to the trial in Hagen. He felt obliged to testify against Karl Frenzel, but he was also scared that he would be accused of murder himself. As Schelvis said: "This man was very afraid. When I entered his hotel room, he would close the door to prevent someone from sneaking in to kill him." Jules Schelvis waited for him at the railway station. Menkel's fare from Australia and his stay in Germany were paid for by the German state.

But Dunya Breur and Jules Schelvis did not get such money. They had to stay in a caravan. They worked together on filming the testimonies, and for this purpose they traveled to Rostov to interview Pechersky. Dunya Breur, who spoke Russian, became a good friend of the family. The "Sobibor Interviews" they

194　*Traumatized and Alone*

started to make there would become major testimonies and played a major role in remembering.

The Trial and the Story

Pechersky wanted to tell the world about the revolt, and his hope was that during the sessions in court some attention would be paid to Sobibor. Although he had published a book in 1945 and had sent material to well-known Russian authors,[19] he did not manage to attract the attention he wanted. With our current knowledge about anti-Semitism under Stalin, we can now understand this, but Pechersky lived in the middle of it all. He must have felt everyday oppression, but the system behind the oppression would only be known much later. Maybe he still had hope.

During the trials the stories of the survivors were limited to "legal testimony" and thus marginalized. What he or she really wants to say is of no importance; the victims are actors in a script written by others. Especially in the trials of the Holocaust, victims wanted to be recognized in their extreme suffering and wanted to tell about their ordeals. They wanted the world to know and talk about what had happened in many traumatic ways, but the court is not the body that soothes the pain.

The victims also wanted the world not to forget the crimes that had been committed. In a letter written in 1978 to the other survivors, Pechersky wrote, "The nations of the world cursed Fascism and all its dark forces. . . . We cannot forget this. Each and every one must remember, so that nothing like it will ever be repeated. Because man was created for happiness and peace. And the joy of peace is worth fighting for."[20] By that time, thirty-five years had passed and "the earth once again is overgrown with grass. The wind completely sweeps away the ash of human bodies. Spring waters carry away with them the traces of spilled blood. But neither years nor centuries will efface the traces of the bloody crimes of fascism."[21]

The trials became a meeting place and an opportunity to spread the word. The three cases attracted wide attention and were marked by the impact of the political moment. The survivors came to testify because they expected to be heard and to be able to tell the world about the crimes. They wanted the criminals to be punished. But when I read the transcripts and listened to other survivors who were present, I also found the wish to express fury, trauma, sadness—and most of all pride—in how they had revolted and escaped. From my interviews with survivors who were present in one of the courts and had been invited to testify, I know that the trials enabled them to reconnect and to give interviews, and there was the beginning of a redemption that would later be frustrated. While listening to the proceedings, they began to create a total picture of the camp, which had been fragmented in their memories. Some of the panic was replaced by fury and an overview of the events. However, they were asked not to attend all at the same time, because the judges did not want them to hear each other's stories. The judges believed the eyewitnesses would use accusations made by others to strengthen their arguments.

One outcome of the trials, however, was unexpected. It enabled the survivors to testify and to meet, to be confronted with what had happened, which they had never been able to comprehend. It was an enormous help in recovering memories, and some of them became aware that there were more survivors than they had expected. They felt strong; they were reinforced in their wish to speak up and to break through the wall of silence that seemed unavoidable and incomprehensible. When I interviewed her in 2012 in Adelaide, Regina Zielinski told me how much the trial helped her to understand what she had experienced. Until then, Sobibor had been a black hole in her brain: a place of sadness, horror, and the struggle for survival. The picture in her mind was scattered, and she had found "standardized" narratives. With the help of these, she lectured about her experience, but she did not really know what had happened there. The killing had become an enigma hidden somewhere in her brain. The escape had become a chaotic memory, reshaped by stories she had heard from other survivors.

The same experience of emptiness and recovery was recounted to me by survivor Esther Raab in 2010 in New Jersey. We know it was also the case with Dutch survivor Jules Schelvis, who expressed how much meeting with other inmates and attending the trial enabled him to give Sobibor a place in his memory. After Hagen, he started his lifelong historical research. Indeed, the survivors started meeting and reminiscing, and he spoke up in favor of Pechersky, who so much wanted to join them.

When I asked her in Adelaide how she got in contact with the court in Hagen, Regina told me:

> That happened in 1983, but before that they called me to the German consulate in Sydney. Five men came over from Germany and one defendant was there for me, and they asked questions, a lot about Sobibor. And then I was telling them what I could, and about Gomerski, and what Wagner did to me. They wondered if I could recognize Gomerski? I said that if I saw him maybe I could. They brought out a very big album with pictures of SS men and normal soldiers. No longer in uniform, but in civil clothing, and I should recognize Gomerski. If I could recognize him, then they would know that I had been in Sobibor. I don't know how they found me, how they knew that I had lived.

One of the other survivors must have known she was alive, perhaps because she had put in a claim for restitution. Regina continued:

> I was called to Sydney, and then they wanted me to recognize Gomerski. I looked over that album, I looked as much as I could and I couldn't see him, and they gave up. But they took a break for lunch, and I didn't go with them for lunch, I stayed in the room and I asked a lady to leave that album with me. I wanted to go slowly over the images. And you wouldn't believe it: I found him. And, anyhow, they accepted it and after that I was called to

196 *Traumatized and Alone*

Germany in '83. I said I wanted an English interpreter, but you know what they did? They gave me a Polish interpreter, because I come from Poland.

In a frenzy she had rushed to Germany where everything was waiting for her. But she had counted on a positive attitude in the courtroom, which was not the case at all:

> When we got to Germany we got to Frankfurt, and from Frankfurt we boarded a train to Hagen; and when we arrived everything was really good.

She was indignant about the behavior of the lawyers: "And Frenzel's lawyer tried so very hard to discredit me. He tried very hard and I said to them you have everything black on white, or you have everything on tapes and I'm getting older, I'm not old yet, but I have to have everything in my head."

She had seen people walking naked to the gas chambers. She was asked to point out from where it was possible to see this and to show the place on a map.

> I went down to it and I looked at it and I looked at it, and I couldn't find it. And I said to the judge who joined me, "That is not the map of Sobibor." All the time that lawyer was smiling, he was so happy about it. So the judge Kramer came over to the map and he had a look at it and he said "Excuse me please, somebody turned it around, it's upside down." And he put it right on that stand where the map was, like a blackboard and I showed him there were the toilets and there's the brush fence. [She had watched from a window in the toilets.] And you should have heard the clapping in the courtroom. Because there were a lot of students, university students and other school people and ordinary people.

Regina was modest about how strong she had been. I imagined this small, rather ill woman defying judges and lawyers who wanted her to fail. I asked her who had tricked her, but she did not know. It could have been anybody, and maybe it was an accident, but probably not.

She had cornered them all; she just wanted Sobibor to be known. I asked her if she had contacts with other survivors, but apparently there were never two survivors in court at the same time, so they did not meet. But people in the court told her about the existence of the others. Afterward she started to write letters, and journalists would ask if they could interview her.

I use this example because the survivors of Sobibor were not recognized, and no one took account of their mental suffering. Especially in Germany, they felt hopeless, while in Russia the people they hated so much were punished. Pechersky was troubled and wrote, "I Still Hear the Cries of the Children, I hear it over and over again in my sleep and I wake up bathed in cold sweat."[22] He fulminated against showing any clemency, and pardon was out of the question. In that sense he was not different from the average Russian citizen, but I guess he must have known that not all of those condemned had helped the Nazis. He was never openly critical.

Pechersky had come back from the war expecting that the suffering would end and the criminals would be brought to trial. Probably he expected a warm welcome and recognition for his personal heroism. We can only imagine how great his disappointment must have been. He came back to a destroyed town, where his stature as a hero was not self-evident. Probably he was still loyal to his old ideals, ideals that had given him hope and the strength to organize the revolt. He had organized the revolt by using his creativity and fantastic imagination to serve his country. He could see how others who had done less to serve that country—but who knew better how to manipulate the post-war society—were making their careers and how they lived in better conditions. He could not manage this new world.

A Hostage of an Unwanted History

I am convinced that Pechersky believed that a new society had come with Communism, a society where people would be equal and where the minority status of Jews would no longer exist. But he returned to a world of authoritarian chaos. I suppose he had not reckoned with the tradition of anti-Semitism and the ways in which Stalinist politics would use this resentment and even make Jews the focus of renewed oppression. Though he was not a member of the Jewish Anti-Fascist Committee, he was in contact with people who belonged to that part of the Jewish intelligentsia.

Jewish intellectuals and leaders were suspect. Pechersky aspired to be a model worker, but at his workplace and in his social environment he would never be allowed to talk about his leadership and about how he had inspired resistance. Any mention of such personal courage was unwelcome in those Stalinist times. Moreover, the story he wanted to tell about the resistance of the Jews was also unwelcome. He could not be stopped from spreading the story of Sobibor, since telling it was like breathing. It was his incentive to live. The authorities were aware of this and kept him for long periods in Rostov-on-Don, although sometimes he was allowed to travel inside the Soviet Union. He became in effect a hostage of an unwanted history that was forbidden, yet needed at the same time to punish those who were on trial in the many local courts. The message he got was double. He was treated as a persona non grata and could not do what he wanted to do; he did not enjoy the respect he thought society owed him. He lived the life of a poor man who needed help from others, which was in sharp contrast with the tremendous admiration he got from the survivors of Sobibor. The KGB followed him, harassed him, and prevented him from leading a normal life. In 1965 he wrote in a letter: "They took away everything so that I could not be in correspondence."[23] Even though his letters were undoubtedly read and censored, he took the risk of writing this.

He tried to speak up, to tell his story, but slowly he exhausted his tremendous forces. This affected him both physically and psychologically. Disappointment alternated with hope of recognition. He complained of being excluded, and that except for his friends, the others from Sobibor, no one listened. The

198 *Traumatized and Alone*

other survivors from Sobibor had found him, and they remembered him and his leadership. The small group of survivors pieced together what had happened and started to write the history of the camp based on memory. Pechersky could not participate in commemorative meetings in Poland and waited for descriptions to reach him by letter in his isolation. Late in his life he was invited to attend the premiere of the film *Escape from Sobibor* in 1987, where he was to be honored, but Moscow made it impossible for him to obtain a visa for the United States. Everything was done to delay the official procedure for going abroad in spite of the coming of perestroika, glasnost, and telebridges between the United States and Russia. The decision was contested by the well-known journalist Vladimir Pozner, who was told that there was an instruction to the effect that an invitation to a capitalist country could only be from a direct relative.[24] In the end Pechersky was allowed to attend, but by then it was too late; he had lost his last bit of hope and began to withdraw into a bitter silence.

Always Alone: Bitterness, Depression, and Withdrawal from the World

On January 14, 1974 Pechersky wrote a letter to Naum Plotnitsky, a survivor of Sobibor, a former butcher, and (as mentioned in Chapter 5) his companion when the group of Russian soldiers finally reached the partisans. Naum had been sent with him to the Schors partisans. They had lost contact after the war, but had recently managed to reconnect and meet. They were both pitiably poor, and both could barely make ends meet. In a letter to Pechersky in Rostov-on-Don, Naum had expressed his discontent about the social and economic situation he had to endure and complained about the misery and the poverty. Pechersky's answer is bitter and full of irony. Pechersky compared the social position of Plotnitsky with his own. One of Naum's complaints was about the small amount of money they both received as a pension.

It was dangerous to write the way Naum had done, since grievances were usually considered a form of criticism of the authority that granted pensions—that is, the state. Did he realize he was writing to someone who was at risk and who was being monitored by the KGB? Maybe he was naïve. I found the letter in Rostov-on-Don, and I realized that this complaint had been written at a time when any criticism of the regime was extremely dangerous, even for someone who only received such illegitimate words. The ban on criticism had never been lifted, not even after Stalin's death, and the Soviet Union remained a totalitarian state. When Brezhnev came to power (1964), the intimidation and denunciations started again. The thaw was over, and this had dire consequences for Jews. The state no longer controlled the details of family life, as in the earlier period, but the world was grim and unfree, and daily life was permeated by pervasive corruption. For Jews in particular, the hard times were not over: the existence was difficult, monotonous and poor, travel was seldom allowed, and there was not enough food.

Plotnitsky had been sent a copy of a request to the authorities written by someone in Pinsk, the town in Belarus where he lived. This person (whose name we don't know) had tried to help increase his meager pension. Pechersky wrote back and made it clear that according to him Plotnitsky was in no position to receive more money. They just did not belong to the elite social network of those who received such rewards. In his reply, he advised Naum to take a look at the way the authorities had refused to grant extra money to Pechersky, who was of course absolutely more important than this supplicant from Pinsk. Pechersky's bitterness is clear in this letter. Years of exclusion and the damage done to him had probably compelled him to underline his strength and superiority to Plotnitsky and to bolster his ego. Pechersky wrote dismissively:

> I received the letter that has been written on your behalf. I don't know by whom—a relative or an acquaintance. One should really write such a letter oneself. What answers can I provide to the questions that are of importance to you? In order, it will all be clear, my approach will not be particularly diplomatic—it will only be the truth. Being in a Fascist death camp during World War II does not entitle one to receive a higher pension. According to Soviet law, the amount of the pension paid is related to the average wage. There is also the so-called personal pension, which is granted for special service to the state.
>
> I have been given a regional personal pension of 80 rubles for the wartime patriotic education of an urban population (over 400 lectures) and for the organization of the uprising in the camp. I was also a member of an executive committee.

The two men had met when Pechersky visited Plotnitsky. They discussed the many times Pechersky had made public appearances as a speaker and how he had talked to large audiences about Sobibor. Apparently Plotnitsky had not been a public speaker, and Pechersky wrote, "As I understand, Naum, you made no presentations, you did not conduct socially useful work—so you have no right to the personal pension. What kind of pension for work can you have? I am comparing you to me so that what I write will be clear to you."

Pechersky was not very kind in refusing to help, or maybe he was hiding his lack of power since he had no means to assist. However, he had made an earlier attempt, and he reminded Plotnitsky: "When I visited you, and you know this, I stopped in at the editorial office of your newspaper and told them about you. I left them ample material and they promised to publish it, but for some reason they didn't." He was surprised, since "Articles were published about all of the guys [in our Sobibor group] in the cities in which they live, after I visited their respective editorial offices. I don't understand why there were no articles published in Pinsk. Perhaps they inquired at the plant where you worked, and they were not given an entirely good characterization of what happened."

Sadly enough, Plotnitsky needed medical help, which required vouchers according to the system at the time. Pechersky advised him to get a voucher and continued his letter: "Aside from that, you should have an official certificate attesting to the fact that you were in a partisan unit, and when you go into the

200 *Traumatized and Alone*

office you should obtain a document in a clinic saying that you need treatment at a sanatorium and go to the city social security department and request assistance to obtain a voucher."[25] If I look carefully at the correspondence, I sincerely believe that Naum tried to do this. Such general advice (to obtain the correct documents) soothes the author, but it does not solve the problem. But maybe there were less conciliatory letters.

The correspondence between the two men started with the preparation of the twenty-fifth commemoration of the revolt in 1968.[26] Plotnitsky had not reacted immediately when he was invited to come to the meeting and dinner in Rostov-on-Don, and in a letter Pechersky reproached him for not sending a reply during the past two months: "A month and a half has passed since I visited you [at the beginning of May 1968] and I have not written you a word. The point is that I was ill and could not write, not only to you but to all our fellows about meeting you."[27] Maybe at that time the tone was set. It emanated bitterness as Pechersky wrote:

> After visiting you I took my wife and we went to Haivoron [a city in Ukraine]. We discussed how to arrange the celebration of the 25th anniversary of the Sobibor uprising. I've sent our plans to all our fellows, and since you are one of us I want to inform you about our plans. Please write me without delay whether you agree with our plan or not or if you would like to add something, etc.
>
> As I told you, all the prisoners with their wives are going to come. Some writers and other public figures are also invited. Altogether there will be 18–20 persons. We all will have our meals at home, not in a canteen. Then, on October 14, we'll organize a banquet at my home for 40–45 persons. We calculated roughly that the expenses for each of us will be approximately 150 rubles.

That was about an average monthly wage, and one gets the impression that Plotnitsky was really poor. It might have been a reason not to answer. While Pechersky's relationship with Plotnitsky was certainly more distant in comparison with the other survivors, Pechersky insisted on keeping Plotnitsky posted about what was happening, and even invited him to his birthday.[28] But Plotnitsky did not respond and did not reply.[29]

Both men were in the same economic situation. The economic and social position of veterans was precarious and was part of the post-war political turmoil. There were too many of them, and many had been uprooted. Millions of those who had been fighting returned afterward to join the masses of the unemployed and were a burden for the budgets of local authorities. Some veterans were celebrated as heroes without special merits, whereas others were scrutinized and suspected of collaboration. Officially, only those who had served as soldiers at the front were eligible for an extra pension, but those extras were dispensed arbitrarily. No one understood why some people got more money while others did not.[30] Pechersky was forced to live off the minimum, and he was not granted the extra food that some other veterans would get. He had been a POW who had been punished, and he was telling an unwanted story.

Getting Lost in a Hostile World; Unrecognized Trauma

In the early 1960s, none of the former inmates of the German camps were recognized as permanently traumatized. Pechersky wanted that particular story to be acknowledged, and he felt rejected again and again. His feelings were in accord with the reality he faced in daily life. Besides the psychological pain of the prohibition against speaking out, Pechersky faced physical impediments as he got older, and he became increasingly confined to the narrow space of his house. Years before, he had shown signs of psychological exhaustion. In 1963 Pechersky had written in a letter that he felt very tired. "I am depressed" he wrote. "Psykhovannyy," he called it, which can be interpreted as a vague feeling of being lost, which made him too lazy to write, as he phrased it.[31] He had just returned from court in Kiev, and what happened there had probably exhausted him. Also, we know now that traumatization can create an impediment in daily life.

Many survivors tried to reconnect with new social relations by embracing a new life and by moving on. They ignored their pain, suppressed their traumatic feelings, and never spoke about their emotional and psychological problems. There was no place to mourn, and it was impossible to acknowledge that they were hurting. All Pechersky could do was witness and say again and again that he still heard the cries of children who were being driven to the gas chamber. He complained that these cries kept him awake. His remedy was to talk about Sobibor in a prescribed vocabulary, but he was not granted respect for what he had to say, and the lack of freedom was possibly a major hindrance. When he was successful at speaking up or organizing a meeting, he would often be exhausted afterward. In the weeks at the end of 1968, he wrote from Sochi on the Black Sea that Olga and he were very tired.[32] Complaints about exhaustion are a major feature of his surviving letters. He replied to many of the letters he received, which kept him engaged but also involved a lot of work. In 1984 he told Schelvis and Breur, "And now for two or three years already, I do not perform, because I simply can't do it. I simply can't do it, I am getting spasms, I skip over those parts that are hard for me to talk about."

To Find the Others and to Remember

Pechersky's letters give us some indications of the urgency of his drive, which was at the same time his torment. When I survey his many letters in the archives of Moscow, at the U.S. Holocaust Memorial Museum, at Yad Vashem, at YIVO in New York, and those owned by the family in Rostov-on-Don, I get a glimpse of a desperate man who wanted to reach out to the world, but who was severely hindered by politics and secret services. The letters also reveal a lonely man who was fighting his depression. He wanted to get out of Rostov and meet the people who were most precious to him: his friends from the camp, especially the Soviet

202   Traumatized and Alone

soldiers among them. Without their loyalty and obedience, he could not have survived. He stood up against the Germans when it really counted, but he no longer had the energy and hope to resist his torturers in Russia, who did not beat him but isolated him and made him lonely. He needed his friends, and most of all he needed recognition.

However, as he was not allowed to leave, he had to wait and see whether his friends could manage to come see him. Like everyone living in Rostov-on-Don, Pechersky was far from the center of the world. Decisions made in Moscow would sometimes reach him, censored, several weeks later. In Rostov-on-Don, Pechersky had no opportunity to receive his friends the way he wanted to. His house was small, and there was no food. When he wanted to organize a meeting of survivors in 1963 to mark the twentieth anniversary of the revolt, he complained there was no money to do so since he had no work.[33] Poverty would be a permanent factor in his life, and as late as 1982 he still complained he could not properly receive people who wanted to meet and speak with him.[34]

As soon as politics seemed to permit, Pechersky began looking for ways to get the history of the camp written down and published for a large audience. His immense work started in 1959.[35] In 1961 he wrote to Valentin Romanovich Tomin to introduce himself. Tomin published *Return Is Undesirable*, together with Alexander Sinelnikov, in 1964, the same year in which Michael Lev published in *Kimat a Legende* in Yiddish.[36] As we have seen, Michael Lev would become a real friend to Pechersky.

These two are the first publications about the camp and the murder of Jews in Eastern Europe written for a Russian audience. It was a moment when in the West there was no more than fragmentary knowledge about Sobibor. The Polish government controlled the memorial site of the camp and was not eager to commemorate the slaughter of Jews. When I interviewed survivor Thomas (Toivi) Blatt in 2010, he was still upset about the way he found the camp when he visited the first time: it honored only the "Soviet Citizens, Victims of Fascism."

The search for survivors started in 1959, but Pechersky had already met Arkady Waiszpapir in 1953 in Lugansk.[37] At that time he started to look for documentation that would help Tomin to write about Sobibor.[38] Pechersky's name as the hero of Sobibor had already circulated, and in that same year he was invited to come to Warsaw to attend the commemoration of the Warsaw uprising in April 1960. The Polish Historical Institute had asked Pechersky for photographs and documents from the camp, but there was no such material.[39] In the revolt and ensuing escape, people had lost everything, and later there were hardly any images of Sobibor.

Pechersky would repeatedly write proudly that he had kept a photo of Ella, his daughter, hidden under his clothes and that the image had survived his miserable journey. To look at her face had helped him survive psychologically, since it gave him energy and hope. When he was invited to come to Warsaw, Pechersky replied that he would love to come and that he hoped to meet other survivors from the camp. He added he would also like to go to the places where the camp had been and to construct a more precise memory. Being there would be an aid to piece together his story, and he was keen to understand better. But he needed an invitation from the Polish government and perhaps permission to enter Poland. Under these conditions he would ask for a travel permit. He was filled with hope, but disappointment followed. He was also amazed that people kept asking for photographs, letters, and diaries. Why did they not understand that he did not have such things, so his answers always had to be negative?

As I argued before, the camps of Operation Reinhard were under-documented because the Germans deliberately wanted to keep the death industry a secret. Auschwitz-Birkenau, for example, was better known due to its satellite labor camps, as was for example Mauthausen. In Sobibor, however, the only work was in the death factory, and it was the intention of the Germans that no one, except the SS and the guards, would ever remember it. When the camp was destroyed in 1943, there were no poems and letters left; whoever had arrived there was dead or among the escapees. And the fleeing escapees did not carry bags with letters. Therefore the Polish invitation had a negative outcome, and they could have known there was no material. Without much reflection, they had reacted to a letter from September 4 in which Pechersky had introduced himself.[40] By writing them, Pechersky hoped he could find new information: "I, Aronovitch Aleksandr Pechersky [sic], a participant in the uprising in Sobibor, live in the city of Rostov-on-Don. I accidentally learned that you have at the Jewish Historical Institute an exposition dedicated to the uprising in Sobibor. Part of the exhibition is devoted to me as one of the active participants in the uprising." He asked for a photo of the exhibition. "I ask you, if it's not too difficult, to tell me everything you know about the fate of my fellow survivors and those living in Poland or other countries. I inform you that I live in Rostov-on-Don, and I work in a woodworking factory."[41]

In the following years, Pechersky would finally meet his friend Aleksey Vaytsen from Ryazan, who had been actively looking for him. Vaytsen joined Pechersky's search for the other inmates and started a correspondence with Tomin to inform him of his story of Sobibor and the German atrocities, while he also described his own role and trajectory after the war.

Simion Rosenfeld also joined in the search both for more detailed information and for the other survivors.[42] Pechersky was informed by letter in 1964 that Leon Feldhendler, the other leader of the revolt, had been killed after the war by Poles. Moshe Bahir, who had gone to Israel and who had testified at the Eichmann trial about Sobibor, reported this to him.[43] Bahir was happy he had finally found the man who would remain his venerated leader until his death in 1990. In the same letter he wrote that while everyone seems to have forgotten Pechersky's leadership, he never would, and he had praised his leader in his testimony about the revolt at the Eichmann trial.

During these years there was a busy exchange of letters and slowly a network was built. Pechersky himself participated, writing in Russian, and out of respect for him all of the Russian participants in the revolt joined in. They could not

204 *Traumatized and Alone*

have done otherwise when the initiative was taken by their beloved officer. They respected him and were happy to have found each other. During an interview in Ryazan in 2010, Aleksei Vaytsen told how happy he had been to find his hero and know that his hero was still alive.

Later, in 1968, Vaytsen wrote to Naum Plotnitsky:

> I found out you were alive from the security organs of the city of Dnetropetrovsk; they were given the information from Poland, but I didn't know your exact address. I just received a letter from Aleksandr Aronovich [Pechersky S.L.] with your address and I decided to write. Aleksandr Aronovich informed us that he went to visit you, etc. I am truly glad that you are alive and well and that soon, for the 25th anniversary of the uprising, we will see each other in Rostov-on-Don.

He continued: "My dear Naum! Tell me what your life is like, where you work. How did you end up in the army after the partisans? Where were you when the war ended? How did they find out about you in Poland? Tell me about your family."[44]

Together they tried to piece together what had happened and to break the silence, while they tried to correct each other's mistaken memories. Of course, they each had only a partial vision of the camp; there were many places they were not allowed to enter, places such as Camp III, where the killing took place. They had heard stories about events and cruelty so often that it felt as if they had been there. In the camp, they had been running around, as humiliated as slaves, and they had been silenced, which had numbed their senses.

Pechersky had scrutinized the camp in preparation for the revolt, but even he relied on information given by others. He had been in the camp for only twenty-two days, during which he attempted to hide and shield himself from death. But his strategic insight to stage the revolt was respected, which granted him the right to criticize the memory of another inmate, Livitnowsky, in a letter dated January 25, 1963. They had not been imprisoned in Smolensk, as Livitnowsky had suggested, but in Minsk, and several other mistakes were also corrected.[45] The criticism was accepted since they were all working on the same project of the history of the camp. Pechersky complained that Livitnowsky seemed to avoid him after the criticism.

Since the former inmates considered themselves to be friends, they wanted to meet, and some of them did so from 1968 on. The twenty-fifth commemoration was a moment together and consisted of a moment of silence, a dinner with speeches and toasts, and unavoidably the singing of partisan songs. In later years the group tried to gather on October 14, especially in 1973, when the thirty-year jubileum was important. For that commemoration, Pechersky had tried to get permission from Moscow for all Soviet former prisoners to meet with those from the West in Sobibor.[46] His request was turned down, and only the Soviet inmates met.

The effort to expand and meet internationally continued. Pechersky exchanged letters with those who started to describe the fate of the Jews and their resistance, including Herman Langbein, who represented the survivors of Auschwitz.

By sheer accident, I also found in YIVO Pechersky's letters[47] to Reuven Ainsztein, the chronicler of the resistance of Jews in Eastern Europe.[48] Pechersky sent Ainsztein the book written by Tomin and, in a later letter, tried to explain that he would be able to come to Poland for the inauguration of the monument in Sobibor. Ainsztein was uncertain about several pieces of information about Sobibor and had compared the work of Tomin with what he had found written by Michael Lev.[49] The information was confusing. Whom should he trust? Pechersky replied that one cannot compare historical data derived from literary publications, since that kind of work contains fictions.[50] Their correspondence continued for many years, and we might assume that every word was first checked by the KGB and worse: the KGB actively tried to hinder contacts with the West. "They" would turn up at odd moments and confiscated documents. In 1977 Pechersky wrote to Michael Lev that the police had been at his door. He could not leave Rostov-on-Don, even though he was keen to attend the trial in Hagen. He had managed to connect with former prisoners from Auschwitz, but that did not help him.[51]

There also seems to have been an exchange of letters with Paul Pesack Novich,[52] a journalist and left-wing political activist who had come to live in New York in 1920 and who published in Yiddish. He was the founder and longtime editor-in-chief of *The Morning Freiheit*, a left-wing Yiddish daily. The *Freiheit* had a daily circulation of over 14,000 at its peak.

Novich was an ardent member of the Communist Party until he became aware that many Jewish cultural leaders of the Soviet Union had been murdered. While still a member of the Communist Party, he pleaded for more support for Israel in its conflict with Arab states. He called his shift in political orientation a "new Jewish consciousness that was born in Auschwitz." His standpoint radicalized when he criticized the anti-Semitism of the Kremlin, and in 1973 he was expelled from the Communist Party.

Depression and No Freedom

These were clearly difficult years for Jews.[53] The anti-Semitic policies of the government were answered with massive requests to emigrate to Israel. But the exodus had an impact on all Jews, not only on those who "confirmed" they were loyal to Russia but were also committed to other roots. Pechersky wanted to stay in Rostov-on-Don. The psychological effect of being hindered from publishing freely was intertwined with his ailing health. In a letter to Michael Lev, his troubles in publicizing Sobibor were at the same level as his concerns that his diabetes was not going well. "I have one big weakness, I don't feel well."[54] Pechersky felt that work was the best remedy. Earlier that year his diabetes had worsened. "Olga is heroic," he wrote, "she had to work."[55] He praised her as the only one who could help him.[56]

The whole year of 1980 was busy, particularly when Thomas Blatt and Richard Räshke arrived in Moscow. Räshke described their meeting. Pechersky was weak, but strong since he had such an enormous personality. Pechersky expressed his pleasure with the way Langbein and Mirjam Novitch had started to explain that

206 Traumatized and Alone

the Jews had not been slaughtered like sheep but had resisted. He felt supported by Michael Lev, who visited often and who helped with his correspondence. Lev would also participate in celebrations, and there are many images of the two sitting and drinking together.

But Pechersky was too ill to write, and he frequently complained of pain in his heart. There were also better days when, although he was too weak to write, he doubted the urgency of his heart problem. He admitted the pain was not only physical. In a letter to Dunya Breur in 1982, he even denied the pain: "You asked if I suffer from pain? Seldom. Maybe twice a month my heart hurts." He had medications.[57] On normal days he took only his medicine against diabetes. And he wrote that everything was interwoven with his personal circumstances. All those visitors were expensive because they needed to be received. There was not enough food in Rostov-on-Don, and the prices at the food market were very high.

He never gave up, and even when he became ill he kept writing. Simion Rosenfeld also supported him, though he lived in Odessa, and they discussed daily life in their letters.[58] These letters are about Pechersky's ailing health and his lack of psychological drive; virtually all of his letters from that period include complaints about being ill and not feeling mentally well. Also, Rostov-on-Don can be very hot during the summer, but he had to remain there. I have the impression that Pechersky was more eager and asked more often to be allowed to leave the town than in previous decades. However, as he wrote, "being a retired person, I am not able to go anywhere."[59] Furthermore, writing all of these letters made him tired.[60] His body started to give up. He wrote that he felt bad and that everything was mixed up in his head.[61] His handwriting became almost unreadable. He scribbled to Lev: "I need help and I don't get the help I need. At certain moments my thoughts are gone, I don't control them any longer."[62] When I interviewed Michael Lev, he repeatedly told me how much he had appreciated the depth of the contact.

Pechersky withdrew from a world that had forsaken him. He no longer wanted to leave his house; he would hardly talk and could no longer express appreciation for the love of those who surrounded him. The various descriptions of this late period are certainly those of a man who had become old. He was clearly disappointed never to have been able to go back to Sobibor, and he could not know that, twenty-five years after his death, the world would want to know all about him. He had devoted his life to telling the story of Sobibor; he had even made a model of the camp, and he had tried to give a shape to his memories. He had tried to establish a map and show how there, in the interplay of light and shadow, shadow prevailed. He received support from the Sobibor survivors who sought to write their memoirs, and later Russian and Israeli activists would work together for his recognition.

In the minds of the other survivors, Pechersky was and would remain their leader. As Moshe Bahir said in January 1990, "I am at his bedside and see my commander close his eyes. Aleksandr Pechersky—my brother, my commander, the head of the uprising in the Sobibor camp. My general! To me, you have been and remain the most eminent general in the world."[63]

Figure 7.1 Aleksandr Pechersky with his family in Rostov-on-Don in the 1980s
Source: Photograph courtesy of Natalya Ladychenko.

Notes

1 For an account of these procedures, see Marek Bem, *Sobibor*, 303–321.
2 Michael S. Bryant, *Eyewitness to Genocide: The Operation Reinhard Death Camp Trials 1955–1966* (Knoxville: The University of Tennessee Press, 2014), 125–191.
3 Epilogue Pechersky 1972, 107.
4 Ibid.
5 Prusin, "Fascist Criminals," 17.
6 Testimony Kiev, 1962.
7 Ibid.
8 Lev Simkin, "Death Sentence Despite the Law: A Secret 1962 Crimes-against-Humanity Trial in Kiev," *Holocaust and Genocide Studies* 27:2 (2013): 299–312, 309.

208   *Traumatized and Alone*

9 For the various trials see Marek Bem, *Sobibor*, 303–337 (chapter 8, "Trials and War Criminals from Sobibor").

10 Protokoll einer Zeugenvernehmung Moskau den 17. Juli 1974, sta., Do. PROT.BAND III-Gomerski Verfahren.

11 Devin O. Pendas, *The Frankfurt Auschwitz Trial, 1963–1965: Genocide, History and the Limits of the Law* (New York: Cambridge University Press, 2006). "Genocide and the Limits of the Law," 288–307.

12 Protokoll, 1974, 25.

13 Ibid., 9.

14 Comment of Pechersky published in *Jewish Observer and Middle East Review* (22 July 1966): 13–14: "Revolt Leader's Impassioned Appeal."

15 *Protokoll über Zeugenvernehmung*, authorized translation, Donetsk, 15 March 1984.

16 Katharina Stengel, *Hermann Langbein: Ein Auschwitz-Überlebender in den erinnerungspolitischen Konflikten der Nachkriegszeit* (Frankfurt am Main: Campusverlag, 2012).

17 Interview, Schelvis and Breur, 1984. NIOD 804–19–00047.

18 Marek Bem, *Sobibor*, 309.

19 Ilya Ehrenburg, "Murderers of the Peoples," Newspaper *Izvestiya*, 1944);French translation of testimony given by Haim Powroznik, a survivor of Sobibor, to Ilya Ehrenburg on 10 January 1945, USHMM RG-41.010M, title "From Chelm to Sobibor."
   V. R. Tomin and A. G. Sinelnikov, *"Returning Is Undesirable"* (Moscow: Publishing House "Molodaya gvardia" [Young Guard], 1964).
   M. Lev, "Kimat a Legende," *Sovetish Heimland* (Moscow) no. 2 (1964), (in Yiddish).

20 Letter 119, collection Michael Lev, USHMM 68118.

21 Ibid.

22 A. Pecherski, "Für sie kan es keine Vergebung sein," translation from *Sovetish Heymland* 4 (1966): 21–24, 2; in NIOD 804 INV 19.

23 Pechersky to Reuven Ainsztein, 17 July 1965, YIVO, New York.

24 Simkin, 246.

25 Aleksandr Pechersky to Naum Plotnitsky, 14 January 1974, letter with the family in Rostov-on-Don.

26 Yad Vashem, Jerusalem O3.4123.3558242.

27 Letter of 28 June 1968, Rostov-on-Don.

28 Letter, 27 January 1969, Rostov-on Don.

29 Letter, 10 March 1969, Rostov-on-Don.

30 Mark Edele, "Collective Action in Soviet Society: The Case of War Veterans," in Golfo Alexopoulos, Julie Hessler, and Kiril Tomoff (eds.), *Writing the Stalin Era: Sheila Fitzpatrick and Soviet Historiography* (New York: Palgrave McMillan, 2011), 117–33.

31 USHMM, box 51, RG 68118, letter to Valentin Romanic, 29 June 1963.

32 Yad Vashem, undated letter.

33 USHMM RG68118, box 51, 23 March 1963, to Sara Jareimeievna.

34 USHMM RG 68118, to Michael Lev, 16 March 1982.

35 Letter to B. Mark, 4 September 1959, Moscow.

36 Michael Lev "Kimat a Legende," in *Sovetish Heymland* 2 (1964), Moscow.

37 Letter, 22 October 1959, Moscow.

38 Letter, 4 September 1959, Moscow.

39 Letter, 22 October 1959, archive Moscow.

40 Letter, 4 September 1959, to the Polish Historical Institute, Moscow.

41 Letter, 22 October 1959, Moscow.

42 Letter, Rosenfeld to Tomin and Sinelnikov, 30 April 1962, archive Moscow.

43 Letter, Moshe Bahir to Pechersky, 20 August 1964, archive Moscow.

44 Letter, Aleksey Vaytsen to Naum Plotnitsky, 1968, probably written before the commemoration in Rostov-on-Don.

45 Letter, Pechersky to Tomin, 25 January 1963, Moscow.

Traumatized and Alone 209

46 Letter to Naum Plotnitsky, 14 January 1974, Rostov-on-Don.
47 YIVO folder 144, RG 116, Poland II. Pechersky is written Pchorsky due to problems with transliteration of the Cyrillic alphabet.
48 Reuven Ainsztein, "Jewish Resistance,"ch 4.
49 Letter to Pechersky, end of 1964, YIVO.
50 Ibid., beginning 1965.
51 Letter, Pechersky to Michael Lev, 13 October 1977, USHMM 68118.
52 Pesach Paul Novick, Record Group 1247 of the YIVO Archives letter of 27 September 1965.
53 See Nora Levin, "Jews in the Soviet Union," II, 615–91.
54 Letter to Michael Lev, 10 November 1980, USHMM 68118.
55 Ibid., 28 February 1980, USHMM 68118.
56 Ibid., 17 February 1981, USHMM 68118.
57 Letter, 16 March 1982, USHMM 68118, which contains his answer to Dunya.
58 Letter to Michael Lev, 9 June 1983. He again says that they must remember, even though the revolt had been forty years ago, USHMM 68118.
59 Ibid., 17 August 1983, USHMM 68118.
60 Ibid., 22 August 1983, USHMM 68118.
61 Ibid., 26 January 1984, USHMM 68118.
62 Ibid., 7 November 1986, USHMM 68118.
63 Simkin, *Half an Hour of Retribution*, 244.

Conclusion

To Speak and to Be Silenced

In this book I have approached Pechersky's life as a window on the world of Russian Jews from tsarist times to the final decades of Soviet Communism. When Pechersky was five years old, World War I started, inaugurating thirty years of unprecedented violence, social upheaval, totalitarian revolutions, mass murder, genocide, misery, hunger, and despair. In 1945, Nazi Germany was defeated but Stalinism emerged victorious. In post-war Communist newspeak, World War II was referred to as the Great Patriotic War, in which countless "innocent Soviet citizens" were murdered by the "fascist hordes." That the Jews had been the victims of a genocidal extermination policy became literally unspeakable. All Russians who wrote or spoke in public had to frame their story in this official code. Those who openly defied the code risked degradation, the Gulag, or death.

Pechersky's self-assigned duty was to act as a witness of the Nazi extermination of the Jews, but also to recount the successful Jewish insurrection in Sobibor and thereby to question the stereotype of Jewish non-resistance. However, he had to tell his story in a language in which the word "Jew" was taboo. As we have seen in this book, his post-war life was a protracted struggle to tell his story and to gain recognition within the confines of the communist code. Psychologically, his predicament was complicated by his faith, or the remnants of his faith, in Communism. As a young man he joined the party and believed in the new world created by Communism. He had been elated to see how Communism created possibilities for Jews that had been unthinkable in tsarist times. But after 1945 the party would betray him and dictate how he should look at and speak about the Nazi hell he had survived. His story was completely different from the official version, but he could only tell it in the language of the communist collective memory. He could not say openly what he wanted to say, but in his many letters, and in his efforts to reconstruct the truth about Sobibor with the help of his friends, his view of the past is clear. He had experienced how the prisoners refused to surrender their dignity and he had seen resistance. His entire life after the war was focused on communicating the message of how people had resisted despite such horrendous conditions.

A first step in creating a history of Sobibor came in 1945, when a regional publishing house in Rostov-on-Don published "The Uprising in the Sobibor Camp,"[1] a report and an autobiographical narrative about how Pechersky remembered his

Figure 8.1 Aleksandr Pechersky in later life
Source: Photograph courtesy of Mirjam Huffener.

years during the war, with the revolt at the center of the story. As we have seen, Jews were not mentioned in the small booklet. After this publication, Pechersky stubbornly went on for all these years to make the history of the revolt known to the world. In a way, he acted like many camp survivors who urgently wanted to tell about their suffering.[2] There were individual and collective efforts to bear witness to what had happened in all of the countries that had been occupied by the Nazis. Documents stored in growing archives supported the various war trials and helped to inform the public.

In 1947, a year after the Nuremberg trials, delegates from a variety of commissions and documentation centers from thirteen nations met in Paris;[3] most of them were survivors. As Laura Jockush wrote in her book on the ways Jewish survivors tried to document the Shoah and to write the history of their ordeal: "The first Holocaust conference truly embodied the urgent and indefatigable efforts by

212 Conclusion

survivors across Europe to chronicle, witness and testify."[4] They acted out of fear that the Nazis had succeeded in destroying all the evidence and that the Jewish catastrophe would disappear into oblivion; they wished to document the deeds of the perpetrators. But there was no representative from the Soviet Union at the meeting. For the various trials in the Soviet Union, the authorities there had amassed their own documentation, which helped to condemn the mass crimes committed by the fascist invaders and their helpers. However, as we have seen, many of the confessions of those who were accused were ready-made for a verdict that existed even before the court proceedings began. The trials had started even before the war was finished.[5]

In Poland, the underground press documented what happened in Sobibor as early as 1943,[6] but in the Soviet Union the subject was silenced and taboo. In the beginning of this book, I described how Aleksey Vaytsen from Ryazan never spoke about Sobibor and how survivor Arkady Weiszpapir from Kiev only talked about the revolt in carefully composed heroic words that avoided mentioning Jewish suffering under Communism. In Weiszpapir's case, his story was very much about suffering under Communism. His father had been executed before the war, and he had to keep silent about him because his father had been targeted as an "enemy of the people" in the 1930s. This was the label attached to many, with or without a formal accusation, and it was always followed by punishment. When I interviewed Weiszpapir in 2010, he said: "I just didn't try to tell it to anyone." He did not refuse to speak to journalists about his time in Minsk and about Sobibor, but he never talked about his father's persecution. Journalists came to hear about the Holocaust, but as he said: "There were these correspondents, I would tell them everything, but the way I told you just now I never told to anyone. I'm saying to Olga [his wife]: before my death I will speak."[7]

To report about a camp no one knew about, a camp that had been razed to the ground and kept secret, seemed even more urgent to the survivors. If the camp and the killing were forgotten, then the Germans would have won, they thought. For Pechersky, there was yet another reason to write about the revolt. In his case, back home, he also had to distinguish himself from those accused of surrendering to the enemy, which was considered treason. As we have seen, Russian soldiers were expected to fight to the death and never taken prisoner. By publishing his book, Pechersky hoped to make his whereabouts and his resistance known to the authorities and to the KGB. The book, written in 1945, was the beginning of a canonized version of Pechersky's life, a standard narrative no longer questioned, and the story could be repeated to his family and friends. Even more important, he could not make a mistake as long as he followed the book. He knew how to stay within the language and terminology that was allowed under Stalinism and post-Stalinism. The book of 1945 and later testimonies were formalized and could hide his personal feelings, which were expressed in heroic and often bombastic language. He was watched by the KGB, he was under suspicion, and he could not allow himself any literary deviation. However, as we have seen, the KGB was not able to control the publication in other languages.

Conclusion   213

In this straight grand narrative of the Great Patriotic War, Pechersky repeatedly told the story of the revolt of Sobior. He talked to large audiences about Russian POWs, and he testified in courts. His wish to inform others came from a deep conviction that Jews had indeed fought back; they had not been led like sheep to the slaughter, as the dominant history claimed. He had witnessed another attitude, like the resistance in Borisov, escapes, acts of sabotage in Minsk; he had listened to many partisan stories, and all this culminated in his narrative of the revolt. I have not found any testimony from him about the time he spent with the partisans, except for official documents. Maybe he never spoke about these years. Over several decades, his allies would be political activists who professed the same attitude of resistance and who wanted this history to be written down and remembered. They helped Pechersky and his fellow survivors to tell the world and to keep the promise they had made after the revolt: Sobibor would not be forgotten.

Pechersky certainly had moments when his role was recognized, such as when the famous author Ilya Ehrenburg invited him to come live in Moscow and work with him on *The Black Book*. But Pechersky refused to leave Rostov-on-Don; his life was with his family, he replied. For Ehrenburg these were extremely tense times, and probably Pechersky knew how deeply Ehrenburg was in danger, and how much he might be obliged to compromise. Pechersky might have a very uncertain existence in Moscow's literary circles if he went there. There is also another explanation for his refusal: he did not want to leave Rostov for more personal reasons. Difficult times had started already, since from quite early on he seems to have been physically and emotionally unstable. This is understandable after such an ordeal, and we can surmise that he was wise enough to realize that he would be lost without the steady love of Olga, his friends, and his family. He needed emotional support. The biggest blow came when the Soviet authorities did not allow him to attend the premiere of the movie *Escape from Sobibor* in New York in 1987. By the time he had protested and finally been allowed to go, it was too late. His health was no longer good enough.

He had never wanted to leave Rostov-on-Don permanently, and he had doubts about friends who did leave for Israel and the United States. He just wanted to go and see, attend the premiere, and come back. He was exhausted and became depressed; what had happened felt like a total lack of recognition. As his granddaughter Natasha said in 2013 when I met her in Rostov-on-Don:

> They noticed this change very evidently, because before that, he was rather active. He could go to the kitchen and make something for himself, like cook his soup or something like that. But after this happened, he . . . kept sitting somewhere quietly, and even when they wanted him to move a little bit and they just said to him "let's go, you should walk, let's keep walking a little bit," he preferred to stay somewhere and sit quietly. So, the most difficult were the last two weeks. When he felt really bad, they called for an ambulance several times.

214   *Conclusion*

Aleksandr Pechersky saw himself as an envoy of the people killed in Sobibor. He stored all the letters and information he received; his wardrobe in Rostov-on-Don was packed with albums, books, audiotapes, and cards, all of which have been carefully preserved by his family.

We know now a victims' core desire is recognition. Political philosopher Nancy Fraser has described recognition as a reciprocal relation between subjects, in which each sees the other both as its equal and also as separate from it. This relation is constitutive for subjectivity: one becomes an individual subject only by virtue of recognizing, and being recognized by, another subject. Recognition from others is thus essential to the development of a sense of self. To be denied recognition—or to be "misrecognized"—is to suffer both a distortion of one's relation to one's self and an injury to one's identity because the ability of traumatized survivors to restore their identity depends on reconnecting to a society and a world that seem to have been lost.[8] Recognition could not happen as long as people did not even know that Sobibor had existed.

Still, it would take decades before Sobibor and the Camps of Operation Reinhard emerged from oblivion. There were not enough survivors to tell the story, and the memory of the massive killing of Jews was being manipulated and inserted in the post-war collective memories both in the East and in the West, though in markedly different ways.

Competing Victims and Historical Clarity

In the West, for a long time there was a great reluctance to remember the deportation of Jewish citizens. Remembering meant that people also had to acknowledge the massive participation of the non-Jewish population in the deportations and manhunts. Many people were uncomfortable speaking about it. In most countries of Western Europe the dominant ideology was that the Germans were the perpetrators (which they certainly were). Telling the story in this way had the effect of hiding and disculpating the non-German perpetrators. Condemning German atrocities does not preclude remembering the involvement of others who made it possible for the trains to run to unknown destinations. A special turn in this debate came when Michael R. Marrus and Robert O. Paxton's book *Vichy France and the Jews* was published, which highlighted the participation of the French population in the deportations.[9] In the epilogue to his book *Postwar*, historian Tony Judt remarked that, thanks to this recent publication, the question of collaboration could no longer be ignored.[10] There had been a moment of historiographical change. The same debate found its way into other countries, often despite emotional resistance against the theme.

Tony Judt also described how the cult of the victim had created a climate in which everyone claimed victimhood.[11] Jean-Michel Chaumont has shown how victims began to compete for acknowledgment of their claim to that role.[12] They may have had good reasons for such a claim, since if they could show that their suffering was worse than what others experienced, there might also be a claim for compensation. While victims are entitled to act and feel this way, there are

Conclusion   215

cases where victimization is an unjust term that is being used only to promote a particular interest.

At this moment and mainly in the east there are nationalist groups who see themselves as the ultimate victims because they lost their nations. In some places, such as the Baltic States, the victimization of Jews is contested by others who suffered under Communism. Jewish participation in the partisan struggle has recently been investigated by the courts, since Lithuanians were killed by partisans.[13] No one will deny the ordeal of those who have suffered, but such accusations are often used to cover up or excuse participation in the aggression against Jews. One particular form of it is the combination of nationalism, with the accusation that Jews are part of the Communist order ("Judeo-Communism"), or that Jews have been too involved with Communism. This is the form post-Communist nationalism takes: the Jews are forever the "other" and are always blamed. There are ample grotesque examples, and anyone who visits an international conference and wants to talk about Jewish victimhood might find opposition from those who consider their own victimization far more important.

I believe that the advocacy of these groups is rooted in what happened to historical consciousness in the former Communist orbit. So many histories have been silenced, and there have been so many lies and distortions. History needs to be (re)written and (re)framed, which can be done in widely different ways. Fortunately the revision of this historiography has started.[14] I feel that I am a part of this new historiography. Writing these words, I realize that my own research would have been impossible a few decades ago, and despite the changes and the new openness of certain places, I have been confronted with the fact that some archivists have no tradition of making documents available, so the archives are accessible only to insiders who speak the local language. The Moscow Holocaust Education and Research Center is an exception in this sense, since the archivist Leonid Teruschkin and I have shared all documents. But the opening of the archives is only a part of the story. There are major revisions in the historiography and new frames of interpretation.

Numerous new archival sources have become available and a new spate of oral history interviews is being produced. One example is the book by Anika Walke on memories of the Holocaust in Belarus. She has dared to address openly the problem of the relation between her interviewees and herself (she is of German origin), which would not have been possible in earlier times.[15] She writes about how the writing of history can only be the result of overcoming feelings of hatred, and she describes how her admission that she came from the country of the perpetrators (Germany) has helped her to overcome resentment and became one of the reasons she was so successful in her interviews.

Changing Perspectives

An impressive number of studies of memory have been undertaken that deal with the new political situation.[16] This research on memory is urgent, since memories are changing and produce new ones, on both a personal and a collective level.

216   Conclusion

What has been silenced suddenly becomes an open discourse and, in the case of the fall of Communism, new memories are competing for acceptance. As Tony Judt wrote:

> The Communist era did not forge new ways of identifying and describing local and national interests; it merely sought to expunge from public language all trace of the old ones. Putting nothing in their place, and bringing into terminal disrepute the socialist tradition of which it was the bastard product, it left a vacuum into which ethnic particularism, nationalism, nostalgia, xenophobia, and ancient quarrels could flow; not only were these older forms of political discourse legitimated again by virtue of communism's very denial of them, but they were the only real terms of political communication that anyone could recall, with roots in the history of the region.[17]

The memories of the camps of Operation Reinhard have been a major victim of the confusion in historical narration; they became invisible. The ban is now lifted, and many written memories have been published since the 1990s in Vlodava, a town near Sobibor. We are now able to read the stories of the escapees in all their variety, and we can begin to understand how what happened after the revolt has shaped memories of Sobibor. History is always changing, and it is currently being recast into new frames which reveal more of an ultra-nationalist counter-movement. In 2016 the Polish government introduced a new law whereby certain statements can be considered anti-Polish and can be punished severely. Criticism of the attitude of Poles and critical reflection are hindered, although awareness of the anti-Semitism of some Polish and Russian partisans is crucial for understanding why Pechersky and many others did not flee to the partisans in Poland. Only then can we understand why the Russian POWs fled eastward, and why Pechersky apparently never spoke in public about his time with the partisans. I am inclined to think being a partisan was a hazardous undertaking, and being a Jewish partisan was extremely risky. I guess many Jewish partisans were traumatized but never able to express their feelings.

Political barriers to open debate can become an obstacle and an impediment for a free discussion about the past. It is important to know and understand why these partisans were anti-Semitic, and I am not satisfied with any answer describing anti-Semitism as simply a part of Polish culture. It is true that many Poles helped with the extermination of Jews, but it is also true that more Jews were saved in Poland than in any other country. This can only be understood if we are able to study both sides.[18]

Any serious reconstruction of the past and remembrance requires a world with free speech and non-obstructed memories. In 2009, in an article in the *New York Review of Books* about the divergence of memories of the Holocaust in the East and West, historian Timothy Snyder wrote: "After World War II, West European Jewish survivors were free to write and publish as they liked, whereas East European Jewish survivors, if caught behind the iron curtain, could not. In the West, memoirs of the Holocaust could (although very slowly) enter into historical writing and public consciousness."[19] He added: "Auschwitz as a symbol of the Holocaust excludes those who were at the center of the historical event. The largest group of Holocaust victims—religiously Orthodox and Yiddish-speaking Jews of Poland, or, in the slightly contemptuous German term, *Ostjuden*—were culturally alien from West Europeans, including West European Jews."[20]

For decades in the Soviet Union and its satellites, the narrative of the "Great Patriotic War" was the only permitted form, and the special fate of the Jews disappeared from the historical consciousness represented by museums and school curricula. Paying special attention to a "minority" would have stained the purely Russian character of the fight against fascism.[21] Pechersky was expected not to deviate. World War II has been the prism through which Soviet citizens of all classes have come to look at their country and their society. Only since the fall of Communism have historians been able to question the official narrative of the heroic Great Patriotic War.

Unfortunately, many new mirror images have been created that are equally ahistoric. The museum commemorating the German occupation of Minsk shows us the pride of Belarus winning the battle against Hitler, which has become central to national self-definition.[22] According to this image, Belarus was liberated not by the Red Army, but by Belarusian strength and spirit. This is an example of the many new histories in that part of Europe, all of which express trauma and suffering, and many of which are introverted and centered on a national and xenophobic view of the past.[23] When Jews speak up about their suffering, they are too often regarded as hostile to the effort to stage the suffering of the nation.

The battles for memory are rooted in the interaction between two opposing totalitarian realities and ideologies that have dominated the lives of millions of people. Contradictory visions of history, and the violence and anger with which they are expressed, obscure mourning, loss, and most of all, individual agency. We still do not know very much about how the two interconnected systems of oppression have interacted when it comes to memory. Holocaust studies are published in a part of academia with their own journals and conferences different from where historians of Stalinism publish. There is a ban on comparative questions and since the so-called Historikerstreit people are afraid to research what the interaction has meant. It is politically more correct to keep the fields separated.[24]

Up to now, fruitful lessons have been learned by examining smaller samples and microhistories that leave the larger numbers for what they are but make use of local sources. Omer Bartov's study of Jewish-Christian relations in Buczasz in Romania has shown how easy it is to write and talk about religious hostilities in the town, while interethnic relations more generally are a far more complex subject and show a different pattern.[25] When I interviewed Esther Raab, a survivor of Sobibor, she was at pains to mention that she used to have many Christian friends. She had spent her childhood in Chełm (in eastern Poland), a town where relations between Jews and non-Jews were strained at the very least. Her account of good relations and the way neighbors tried to save her family should make us

218 *Conclusion*

curious about the later open hostilities that seemed to reach a climax after the liberation by the Red Army, when Jews were persecuted in Chełm and left.

Who Was Aleksandr Pechersky?

We should never forget that the sad story of Pechersky presented here is the story of a man who suffered the same fate as millions of people who lived in the "Bloodlands." They all survived the entanglements of being victimized by two oppressive systems, and many more died in the cataclysmic era inaugurated by World War I and the Russian Revolution, culminating in Stalinism, World War II, and the Holocaust, as well as the bleak decades of post-war Communism.

The year 1941 represented a major turning point in Pechersky's life, as it did for millions of Russians, Germans, Poles, and Ukrainians. Before World War II, Pechersky was an average Russian man from a lower-middle-class, partly secularized Jewish family that tried to rise with the Communist tide. Even so, they remained "aliens" in the eyes of most non-Jewish Russians and in the dominant mindset of Communist culture. In his youth, Sasha Pechersky profited from the new opportunities available to Jews to acquire knowledge and professional skills in post-revolutionary Soviet society. As a young man, he displayed—if we may credit the sources—above-average intelligence and stamina, and he impressed others with his courage and energy.

When the war came, Pechersky, like many millions of his countrymen, was swept along by the storm. The routines of his life in Rostov were disrupted overnight to make way for the cruel realities of war. Fighting the Germans, Pechersky may have felt more Russian than ever, but in German captivity his Jewish identity acquired a novel and sinister significance. Sobibor was meant to be a final destination for all the Jews sent there, but Pechersky managed to escape this fate. He was saved by Germany's need for manpower, but also by his strong self-image as a Red Army officer who remained loyal to his duty and his Communist homeland. After all, Pechersky, an assimilated Jew, had attained the rank of officer in the Russian Army, which would have been unthinkable in tsarist times. Regarding the Jews as inferior *Untermenschen* who could easily be intimidated, the Nazis who operated Sobibor were blind to the danger posed by a cohesive and disciplined group of Russian soldiers. Sheer luck also played a role, but it is probably not entirely coincidental that Pechersky and his group acted at a moment when the war had been turning against the Nazis for quite some time.

While Hitler was losing, Stalin was winning. Pechersky rejoined the Red Army very soon after his escape from Sobibor, only to face the consequences of having been a POW, and once again he was caught up in a massive current of repression that engulfed hundreds of thousands of his countrymen. Instead of thanking and honoring Pechersky for his uncommon courage, his country punished him. For the remainder of his life he was an unrecognized hero, admired and venerated only by a small minority of Russian and West European Jews, and relegated to oblivion by the state for which he had fought and risked his life. Disappointment, bitterness, and despair clouded his last forty years. He passed away in 1990, so he did not live to see the fall of Communism. What happened to Pechersky tells us about the bleak decades of Soviet society after Stalin. His mood and dying expectations resonate with the broader cultural and psychological currents of Russian life.

In 2016 he was posthumously awarded the Order of Courage, which was handed over by President Vladimir Putin to Natalya Ladychenko from Rostov-on-Don, Pechersky's granddaughter and the custodian of his heritage. A year earlier, Pechersky had been awarded a Polish order for his resistance in Sobibor. The Russian order is one of the highest in Russia and is awarded to those citizens of the Russian Federation who have shown dedication, courage, and bravery in protecting public order, fighting crime, and rescuing people during natural disasters, fires, accidents, and other emergencies, as well as for bold and decisive actions committed during the performance of military or civil duties under conditions involving risk to life. I consider this late recognition to be a hopeful sign.

In Sefat, in Israel, there is a street named after Pechersky. In Holon, near Tel Aviv, there is a small memorial site. And in front of his house in Rostov-on-Don, there is a stone in the pavement commemorating his life. Pechersky and Sobibor are slowly escaping from oblivion, with the help of so-called stumbling stones (*stolpersteinen*), little memorial plaques made of brass that stick out just above

Figure 8.2 The Lane of Memory in Sobibor
Source: Photograph courtesy of Mirjam Huffener.

220 Conclusion

sidewalk-level in ordinary streets throughout Europe. They are set into the pavement to mark the places where Jews lived and from where they were deported into the Holocaust. They remind present-day citizens that Jews once lived in many houses and streets of Europe.

Some of the questions I have dealt with in this book have not been and cannot be answered. In the end this volume represents what I was able to learn from fragments and letters. The person is there on film, in his own writings, and in the words of love from his family and friends. I have felt and witnessed the unlimited admiration and loyalty of those who owed him their liberation. One cannot doubt the strength and the leadership of this man, but we should also acknowledge his despair at never being allowed to express all he wanted to say, and his loneliness in his imposed silence. He was a persistent and obstinate person who lost his faith in Communism and in the future of the country that had given him so many chances.

His indisputable trust in the new world of Communism during his adolescence had come nearly automatically, his convictions inspired him to invent and stage the revolt, but it was also an act of incredible imagination that showed his ability to go beyond borders. I strongly believe that while the economic hardship and exclusion really existed and must have been hard to survive, Pechersky was most deeply hurt psychologically. The oppression of political control can asphyxiate a creative individual, and I would argue that Pechersky was not getting old, ill, and miserable only because he was not recognized. He was living in a world that remained dark.

Notes

1
2 Laura Jockush, *Collect and Record: Jewish Holocaust Documentation in Early Postwar Europe* (Oxford: Oxford University Press, 2012). Although the author collected a massive amount of material, Sobibor and much of the material mentioned in this book are, somewhat amazingly, ignored.
3 According to Jockush, the delegates came from Allied-occupied Germany, Austria, Sweden, France, Greece, Italy, Poland, Romania, Bulgaria, Great Britain, the United States, Palestine and Algeria. Jockus, *Collect and Record*, 3.
4 Ibid., 4.
5 *The People's Verdict: A Full Report of the Proceedings of the Krasnodar and Kharkov German Atrocity Trials* (Chinson & Co. 1943).
6 *Glos Warszawy* (Voice of Warschau), Organ of the Polish Workers Party, nr. 82/83, 16 November 1943.
7 Interviewed by author, Kiev, 2010.
8 Nancy Fraser, "Rethinking Recognition," *New Left Review* 3 (2000): 107–120. See also Nancy Fraser and Axel Honneth, *Redistribution or Recognition? A Political-Philosophical Exchange* (London: Verso, 2003).
9 Michael M. Marrus and Robert O. Paxton, *Vichy France and the Jews* (Stanford: Stanford University Press, 1981).
10 Tony Judt, *Postwar: A History of Europe Since 1945* (London: Penguin Books, 2005), Epilogue.
11 Arlene Stein, "Whose Memories? Whose Victimhood? Contests for the Holocaust Frame in Recent Social Movement Discourse," *Sociological Perspectives* 41:3 (1998): 519–540. Here one can find many examples.

Conclusion 221

12 Jean-Michel Chaumont, *La Concurrence des victimes* (Paris: La Decouverte, 2010).

13 Paulus Sužiedélis and Šarūnas Liekis, "Conflicting Memories, the Reception of the Holocaust in Lithuania," in *Bringing the Dark Past to Light: The Reception of the Holocaust in Postcommunist Europe*, eds. John-Paul Himka and Joanna Beata Michlic (Lincoln, London: The University of Nebraska Press, 2013), 338–339.

14 For instance: Yehuda Bauer, *The Death of the Shtetl*; Omer Bartov, *Erased*; Jan Tomasz Gross, *Golden Harvest*; Christopher Browning, *Remembering Survival*; Timothy Snyder, *Bloodlands*.

15 Anika Walke, *Pioneers and Partisans: An Oral History of Nazi Genocide in Belorussia* (New York: Oxford University Press, 2015).

16 Małgorzata Pakier and Joanna Wawrzyniak, "Memory and Change in Eastern Europe: How Special?," in *Memory and Change in Europe*, eds. Pakier and Wawrzyniak (New York: Berghahn Books, 2015), 1–20.

17 Tony Judt, "The Past Is Another Country: Myth and Memory in Postwar Europe," *Daedalus* 121:4, Immobile Democracy? (Fall, 1992): 83–118.

18 Joshua D. Zimmerman, ed., *Contested Memories: Poles and Jews During the Holocaust and Its Aftermath* (New Brunswick, NJ and London: Rutgers University Press, 2003).

19 Timothy Snyder, "Holocaust: The Ignored Reality," *New York Review of Books*, 16 July 2009.

20 Ibid.

21 Amir Weiner, *Making Sense of War: The Second World War and the Fate of the Bolshevik Revolution* (Princeton: Princeton University Press, 2002).

22 A good analysis of this mechanism can be found in this study by David Marples, which criticizes the official version of the Great Patriotic War in Belarus. *"Our Glorious Past": Lukashenka's Belarus and the Great Patriotic War* (Stuttgart: Ibidem Verlag, 2014).

23 John-Paul Himka and Joanna Beata Michlic, eds., *Bringing the Dark Past to Light: The Reception of the Holocaust in Post-Communist Europe* (Lincoln: University of Nebraska Press, 2013).

24 An exception is Norman M. Naimark, *Stalin's Genocides* (Princeton: Princeton University Press, 2011).

25 Omer Bartov, "Wartime Lies and Other Testimonies: Jewish-Christian Relations in Buczacz, 1939–1944," *East European Politics and Societies* 25:3 (August 2011): 486–487.

Bibliography

Adamushko V. I. et al., *Справочник о мастах принудительного содержания гражданского населения на оккупированной территории БССР 1941–1944 гг.* Минск, Государственный комитет по архивам и делопроизвоству Республики Беларусь, 2001. (Spravochnik o mestakh prinuditel'nogo soderzhaniya grazhdanskogo naseleniya na okkupirovannoy territorii BSSR 1941–1944 gg. Minsk, Gosudarstvennyy komitet po arkhivam i deloproizdvodstvu Respubliki Belarus', 2001). [Guide to Places of the Forced Detention of Civilians in the Occupied Territory of the BSSR in 1941–1944 (Minsk: State Committee on Archives and Records Management of the Republic of Belarus, 2001)].

Adler Nanci, *Keeping Faith with the Party: Communist Believers Return from the Gulag* (Bloomington: Indiana University Press, 2012).

Ainsztein Reuben, *Jewish Resistance in Nazi-occupied Eastern Europe* (London: Paul Elek, 1974); in German as *Jüdische Widerstand in deutsches Osteuropa während des Zweiten Weltkrieges* (Bibliothek und Informationssystem der Universität Oldenburg, 1993).

Altman, ed. *Жертвы ненависти. Холокост в СССР 1941–1945 гг.* Москва, Фонд "Ковчег", 2002. (Zhertvy nenavisti. Kholokost v SSSR 1941–1945 gg. Moskva, Fond "Kovcheg", 2002). [Victims of Hate: The Holocaust in the Soviet Union 1941–1945. (Moscow: Foundation "Kovcheg", 2002)].

Altshuler Mordechai, *Soviet Jewry on the Eve of the Holocaust, a Social and Demographic Profile* (Jerusalem: Ahva Press, 1998).

Apenszaik Jacob and Polakiewicz Moshe, *Armed Resistance of the Jews in Poland* (New York: American Federation for Polish Jews, 1944).

Arad Yitzhak, *Belzec, Sobibor, Treblinka: The Operation Reinhard Death Camps* (Bloomington: Indiana University Press, 1987).

Arad Yitzhak, *The Holocaust in the Soviet Union* (Jerusalem and Lincoln: University of Nebraska Press, 2009).

Arad Yitzhak, *In the Shadow of the Red Banner: Soviet Jews in the War Against Nazi Germany* (Jerusalem: Gefen Publishing House, Yad Vashem Publications), 2010).

Arendt Hannah, *Eichmann in Jerusalem: A Report on the Banality of Evil* (Revised and enlarged edition, New York: The Viking Press, 1965).

Arkad'eva Olga et al., *На перекрестках судеб: из воспоминаний бывших узников гетто и праведников народов мира.* Минск, изд-во "Четыре четверти", 2001. (Na perekrestkakh sudeb: iz vospominaniy byvshikh uznikov getto i pravednikov narodov mira. Minsk, izd-vo "Chetyre chetverti", 2001). [At the Crossroads of Fate: From the Memoirs of Former Ghetto Prisoners and the Righteous People of the World (Minsk: Publishing House "Chetyre chetverti", 2001)].

Bibliography   223

Asher Harvey, "The Soviet Union, the Holocaust and Auschwitz," in *The Holocaust in the East: Local Perpetrators and Soviet Responses*, eds. Michael David Fox, Peter Holquist and Alexander M. Martin (Pittsburgh: University of Pittsburgh Press, 2014), 29–51.

Babel Isaac and Nathalie Babel, "The Journey," in *Red Cavalry and Other Stories*, trans. Peter Constantine (London: Penguin, 1994), 80.

Barmatz Zeev, *Heroism in the Forest, the Jewish Partisans of Belarus* (Ramat Gan: Kotarim International Publishing, 2013).

Baron Nick and Gatrell Peter, "Population Displacement, State-Building and Social Identity in the Lands of the Former Russian Empire, 1917–1923," *Kritika: Explorations in Russian and Eurasian History*, Vol. 4, No. 1 (Winter 2003), pp. 51–100.

Bartov Omer, "The Conduct of War: Soldiers and the Barbarization of Warfare," *The Journal of Modern History (Supplement: Resistance Against the Third Reich)*, Vol. 64 (December 1992), pp. 32–45.

Bartov Omer, "Wartime Lies and Other Testimonies, Jewish Christian Relations in Buczaz, 1939–1944," *East European Politics and Societies*, Vol. 25, No. 3 (August 2011), pp. 486–487.

Bauer Yehuda, *They Chose Life: Jewish Resistance in the Holocaust* (New York: American Jewish Committee Institute of Human Relations, 1973).

Bauer Yehuda, *Rethinking the Holocaust* (New Haven: Yale University Press, 2002), 130.

Bauer Yehuda, *The Death of the Shtetl* (New Haven: Yale University Press, 2010).

Beevor Anthony, *Stalingrad: The Fateful Siege, 1942–1943* (New York: Viking, 1998).

Bem Marek, *Sobibor Extermination Camp 1942–1943*, trans. Tomasz Karpiński and Natalia Sarzyńska-Wójtowicz (Amsterdam: Stichting Sobibor, 2015).

Benz Wolfgang, ed., *Dimension der Völkermords: Die Zahl der jüdischen Opfer des Nationalsozialismus* (München: Oldenbourg Verlag, 1991).

Berger Sara, *Experten der Vernichting: Das T4-Reinhardt Netzwerk in den Lagern Belzec, Sobibor und Treblinka* (Hamburg: Hamburger Edition, 2013).

Berkhoff Karel Christian, "The Mass Murder of Soviet Prisoners of War and the Holocaust: How Are They Related?," *Kritika: Explorations in Russian and Eurasian History*, Vol. 6, No. 4 (2005), pp. 789–796.

Berkhoff Karel Christian, "The Corpses in the Ravine Were Women, Men, and Children: Written Testimonies from 1941 on the Babi Yar Massacre," *Holocaust and Genocide Studies*, Vol. 29, No. 2 (2015), pp. 251–274.

Bettelheim Bruno, *Surviving and Other Essays* (New York: Knopf, 1952).

Bialowitz Philip "Fiszel" and Bialowitz Joseph, *A Promise in Sobibor: A Jewish Boy's Story of Revolt and Survival in Nazi-Occupied Poland* (Madison: University of Wisconsin Press, 2008).

Black Peter, "Foot Soldiers of the Final Solution: The Trawniki Training Camp and Operation Reinhard," *Holocaust and Genocide Studies*, Vol. 25, No. 1 (2011), pp. 1–99.

Blatt Thomas (Toivi), *Sobibor, the Forgotten Revolt: A Survivor's Report* (Issaquah: H.E.P., 1996).

Blatt, Thomas (Toivi), *From the Ashes of Sobibor* (Włodawa, Poland: Muzeum Pojezierza Łęczyńsko-Włodawskiego, 2008).

Bloxham Donald, *Genocide on Trial, War Crimes and the Formation of Holocaust History and Memory* (Oxford: Oxford University Press, 2001).

Bloxham Donald, "The Missing Camps of Aktion Reinhard," in *The Memory of Catastrophe*, eds. Peter Gray and Kendrick Oliver (Manchester: Manchester University Press, 2004), 118–131.

Bloxham Donald, "Prosecuting the Past in the Postwar Decade: Political Strategy and National Mythmaking," in *Sixty Years After the Nuremberg Trials*, eds. David Bankier and Dan Michmann (Jerusalem: Yad Vashem, 2010).

224 Bibliography

Bluhm Hilde O., "How Did They Survive? Mechanisms of Defense in Nazi Concentration Camps," *American Journal of Psychotherapy*, Vol. 53, No. 1 (1999), pp. 96–122, here p. 98. The original study was made in 1948.

Boder David P., *I Did Not Interview the Dead* (Urbana: University of Illinois Press, 1949).

Boder David P., *Topical Autobiographies of Displaced People Recorded Verbatim in the Displaced Persons Camps, with a Psychological and Anthropological Analysis*, 16 vols. (Chicago: D. P. Boder, 1950–57).

Botvinnik Marat, *Памятники геноцида евреев Беларуси. Минск, изд-во "Беларуская Навука"*, 2000. (Pamyatniki genotsyda yevreev Belarusi. Minsk, izd-vo Belaruskaya Navuka, 2000). [Jewish Genocide Memorials in Belarus (Minsk: Publishing House "Belaruskaya Navuka", 2000)].

Bourtman Ilya, "Blood for Blood, Death for Death: The Soviet Military Tribunal in Krasnodar, 1943," *Holocaust and Genocide Studies*, Vol. 22, No. 2 (Fall 2008), pp. 246–265.

Brandon Ray and Lower Wendy, *The Shoah in the Ukraine: History, Testimony, Memorialization* (Bloomington: Indiana University Press, 2008).

Brent Jonathan and Naumov Vladimir P., eds., *Stalin's Last Crime: The Plot Against the Jewish Doctors* (New York: Harper Perennial), 2004.

Bruder Franziska, *Hunderte solcher Helden: Der Aufstand jüdischer Gefangener im NS-Vernichtungslager Sobibor* (Münster: Unrast, 2013).

Bryant Michael S., *Eyewitness to Genocide: The Operation Reinhard Death Camp Trials 1955–1966* (Knoxville: The University of Tennessee Press, 2014), 125–191.

Budnitskii Oleg, *Российские евреи между красными и белыми 1917–1920. Москва, изд-во РОССПЭН*, 2005. (*Rossiyskie yevrei mezhdu krasnymi i belymi 1917–1920. Moskva, isd-vo ROSSPEN, 2005*). [Russian Jews Between the Reds and the Whites. (Moscow: ROSSPEN, 2005)].

Butler Rupert, *Stalin's Secret War: The NKVD on the Eastern Front* (London: Pen & Sword Books, 2010).

Cantorovich Irena, "Jews and Non-Jews in the Partisan Movement in Belorussia 1941–1944," *Journal of the Study of the Holocaust and Antisemitism*, Vol. 11 (2014), pp. 98–144.

Chaumont Jean-Michel, *La concurrence des victimes* (Paris: La Decouverte, 2010).

Chernoglazova Raisa, *Масюковщина: Шталаг-352. 1941–1944. Документы и материалы. Минск, изд-во "Четыре четверти,"* 2005. (Masyukovshchina: Shtalag 352. 1941–1944. Dokumenty i materialy. Minsk, izd-vo "Chetyre chetverti," 2005). [Masyukovshchina: Stalag 352: 1941–1944: Documents and Materials (Minsk: Publishing House "Chetyre chetverti", 2005)].

Cholawskym Shalom, *The Jews of Bielorussia during World War II* (Amsterdam: Harwood Academic Publishers, 1998).

Clark Katerina, "Ehrenburg and Grossman: Two Cosmopolitan Jewish Writers Reflect on Nazi Germany at War," *Kritika: Explorations in Russian and Eurasian History*, Vol. 10, No. 3 (2009), pp. 607–628.

David Guy, *Innocence in Hell: The Life, Struggle and Death of the Minsk Ghetto* (New York: Guy David Publisher, 2004).

Davidson Shamai, "Human Reciprocity Among the Jewish Prisoners in the Nazi Concentration Camps," in *The Nazi Concentration Camps* (Jerusalem: Yad Vashem, 1984).

Davidson Shamai, *Holding on to Humanity* (New York and London: New York University Press, 1992).

Dekel-Chen Jonatah, Gaunt David et al., eds., *Anti-Jewish Violence: Rethinking the Pogrom in East European History* (Bloomington: Indiana University Press, 2011).

Desbois Patrick, *The Holocaust by Bullets: A Priest's Journey to Uncover the Truth Behind the Murder of 1.5 Million Jews* (New York: Palgrave Macmillan, 2008).

Des Pres Terence, *The Survivor: An Anatomy of Life in the Death Camps* (New York: Oxford University Press, 1976).

Duffy Peter, *The Bielski Brothers* (New York: Harper Collins, 2003).

Ehrenburg Ilya, "Накануне". Газета "Правда," 7 августа 1944 г ("Nakanune," gazeta *Pravda*, 7 avgusta 1944) ["On the Eve," Newspaper *Pravda*, 7 August 1944].

Ehrenburg Ilya and Grossman Vasily, *The Complete Black Book of Russian Jewry*, trans. and ed. David Patterson (New Brunswick and London: Transaction Publishers, 2002).

Ellman Michael and Maksudov Sergei, "Soviet Death in the Great Patriotic War: A Note," *Europe-Asia Studies*, Vol. 46, No. 4 (1994).

Epstein Barbara, *The Minsk Ghetto 1941–1943, Jewish Resistance and Soviet Internationalism* (Berkeley: University of California Press, 2008).

Ernst Federm, "The Terror as System: The Concentration Camp," *Psychiatric Quarterly Supplement*, Vol. 22 (1948), pp. 52–86.

Frankl Viktor E., *Man's Search for Meaning* (London: Random House, 2004).

Freiberg Dov, *To Survive Sobibor* (Jerusalem: Gefen Publishing House, 1988).

Friedländer Saul, *Nazi Germany and the Jews 1939–1945, the Years of Extermination* (New York: Harper Colins, 2007).

Gerasimova Inna, Selemenev Vyacheslav and Kagan Jack. *We Stood Shoulder to Shoulder: Jewish Partisans in Byelorussia 1941–1944* (Bury St. Edmonds, Suffolk: Arima Publishing, 2010), 272. There is also an edition in Belarus published in Minsk. (I found an article in Russian by Gerasimova I, Selemenov V. "To the question about the number of Jews in the Belarus partisan movement in 1941–1944—jewishfreedom.jimbo.com/к вопросу о численности евреев/).

Gerlach Christian, *Krieg, Ernahrung, Volkermord: Forschungen zur deutschen Vernichtungspolitik im Zweiten Weltkrieg* (Hamburg: Hamburger Edition, 1998), 10–84.

Gerlach Christian, "Die Ausweitung der deutschen Massenmorde in den besetzten sowjetischen Gebieten im Herbst 1941: Überlegungen zur Vernichtungspolitik gegen Juden und sowjetische Kriegsgefangene," in *Krieg, Ernahrung, Volkermord: Forschungen zur deutschen Vernichtungspolitik im Zweiten Weltkrieg*, ed. Christian Gerlach (Hamburg: Hamburger Edition, 1998).

Ginsberg Benjamin, *How the Jews Defeated Hitler: Exploding the Myth of Jewish Passivity in the Face of Nazism* (New York: Rowman & Littlefield Publishers, 2013).

Gitelman Zvi, *Bitter Legacy: Confronting the Holocaust in the USSR* (Bloomington: Indiana University Press, 1997).

Gitelman Zvi, *A Century of Ambivalence: The Jews of Russia and the Soviet Union, 1881 to the Present* (Bloomington: Indiana University Press, 1988, reprinted 2001).

Glantz David M., *And Their Mothers Wept* (Victoria, BC: Heritage House Press, 2007).

Glantz David M., and House Jonathan, *When Titans Clashed: How the Red Army Stopped Hitler* (Lawrence: University of Kansas Press, 1995).

Glass James M., *Jewish Resistance During the Holocaust: Moral Uses of Violence and Will* (Houndmills and New York: Palgrave Macmillan, 2004).

Gomberg Paul, "Can a Partisan Be a Moralist?" *American Philosophical Quarterly*, Vol. 27, No. 1 (1990), pp. 71–79.

Gross Jan Tomasz and Gross Irene Grudinska, *Golden Harvest: Events at the Periphery of the Holocaust* (New York: Oxford University Press, 2012).

Grossman Vasiliy, *With the Red Army in Poland and Byelorussia*, trans. Helen Altschuler (London and New York: Hutchinson and Co., 1945).

Hartmann Christian, *Operation Barbarossa: Nazi Germany's War in the East 1941–1945*, trans. Christian Hartmann (Oxford: Oxford University Press, 2011).

Heifetz Elias, *The Slaughter of the Jews in the Ukraine in 1919* (New York: Thomas Selzer, 1921).

226   *Bibliography*

Hellbeck Jochen, "The Diaries of Fritzes and the Letters of Gretchens: Personal Writings from the German-Soviet War and their Readers," *Kritika: Explorations in Russian and Eurasian History*, Vol. 10, No. 3 (2009).

Hilberg Raul, *The Destruction of the European Jews* (New Haven: Yale University Press, 1961).

Himka John-Paul and Michlic Joanna Beata, *Bringing the Dark Past to Light, the Reception of the Holocaust in Postcommunist Europe* (Lincoln, London: The University of Nebraska Press, 2013).

Hirszowicz Lukasz, "The Holocaust in the Soviet Mirror," in *The Holocaust in the Soviet Union: Studies and Sources on the Destruction of Jews in the Nazi-Occupied Territories, 1941–1945*, eds. Lucjan Dobroszycki and Jeffrey S. Gurock (Armonk, London: M. E. Sharpe, 1993).

Hughes Paul, *Retreat from Rostov* (London: Random House, 1943; reprinted Columbia: University of South Carolina Press, 2011).

Jockush Laura, *Collect and Record, Jewish Holocaust Documentation in Early Postwar Europe* (Oxford: Oxford University Press, 2012).

Jones Jeffrey W., *Everyday Life and the "Reconstruction" of Soviet Russia During and After the Great Patriotic War, 1943–1948* (Bloomington: Slavica, 2008).

Judt Tony, "The Past Is Another Country: Myth and Memory in Postwar Europe," *Daedalus*, Vol. 121, No. 4, Immobile Democracy? (Fall, 1992), pp. 83–118.

Judt Tony, *Postwar: A History of Europe Since 1945* (London: Penguin Books, 2005).

Kagan Jack and Cohen Dov, *Surviving the Holocaust with the Russian Jewish Partisans* (Edgware and Portland: Vallentine Mitchell, 1998).

Kay Alex J., "German Economic Plans for the Occupied Soviet Union and Their Implementation, 1941–1944," in *Stalin and Europe: Imitation and Domination, 1928–1954*, eds. Timothy Snyder and Ray Brandon (New York: Oxford University Press, 2014).

Kohl Paul, *Ich wundere mich, daß ich noch lebe: Sowjetische Augenzeugen berichten* (Gütersloh: Gütersloher Verlagshaus Gerd Mohn, 1990).

Komitee für Archive und Archivangelegenheiten beim Ministerrat der Republik Belarus, Lager Sowjetischer Kriegsgefangenen in Belarus, 1941–1944 (Minsk: 2004), 6–8.

Kowalski Isaac, *Anthology of Armed Jewish Resistance 1939–1945* (New York: Jewish Combatant Publishing House, 1985).

Krakowski Shmuel, *The War of the Doomed, Jewish Armed Resistance in Poland, 1942–1944* (New York, London: Holmes and Meier Publishing, 1984).

Krutikov Mijhal, "Introduction to: Michael Lev, 'Sobibor', and Soviet Yiddish Culture," in *Michael Lev, Sobibor* (Jerusalem: Gefen Publishing House, 2007), I-IX.

Kuromya Hiroaki, *Freedom and Terror in the Donbass, a Ukrainian-Russian Borderland 1870s—1990s* (New York and Cambridge: Cambridge University Press, 1998).

Langer Lawrence L., *Versions of Survival: The Holocaust and the Human Spirit* (Albany: State University of New York Press, 1982).

Leder Mary M., *My Life in Stalinist Russia: An American Woman Looks Back* (Bloomington: Indiana University Press, 2001).

L'Einwohner Rachel, "Leadership, authority and Collective Action," *American Behavioural Scientist*, Vol. 50, No. 10 (June 2007).

Leoni Eliezer, ed., *Wolozin, the Book of the City and of the Etz Hayyim Yeshiva* (Tel Aviv: Yizkor Book Project, 1970).

Lev Michael, "Kimat a Legende" [Almost A Legend], *Sovetish Geimland*, Vol. No. 2 (1964), Moscow.

Lev Michael, *Sobibor* (Jerusalem: Gefen Publishing House, 2007).

Levine Allan, *Fugitives of the Forest: The Heroic Struggle of Jewish Resistance and Survival During the Second World War* (Guilford, CT: The Lyons Press, 1998).

Levin Nora, *Paradox of Survival, The Jews in the Soviet Union Since 1917* (New York: New York University Press, 1988).

Leydesdorff Selma, "The State Within the State: An Artisan Remembers His Identity in Mauthausen," *Studies on the Audio-Visual Testimony of Victims of the Nazi Crimes and Genocides*, Vol. 10 (2004), pp. 103–117.

Liempt Ad van, *Selma, de vrouw die Sobibor overleefde* (Laren: Verbum, 2010).

Lohr Eric, *Nationalizing the Russian Empire: The Campaign Against Enemy Aliens During World War I* (Cambridge: Harvard University Press, 2003).

Lopukhovsky Lev, *The Viaz'ma Catastrophe: The Red Army's Disastrous Stand Against Operation Typhoon* (Solihull, UK: Helion and Company, 2013).

Lukin Benyamin, "Rostov on Don," in *The YIVO Encyclopedia of Jews in Eastern Europe* (New York: YIVO Institute for Jewish Research, 2010).

Lustiger Arno, *Stalin and the Jews: The Tragedy of the Soviet Jews and the Jewish Anti-Fascist Committee* (New York: Enigma Books, 2003).

Maher Thomas V., "Threat, Resistance and Collective Action: The Cases of Sobibor, Treblinka and Auschwitz," *American Sociological Review*, Vol. 75, No. 2 (April 2010), pp. 252–272.

Markham Walsh Ann and Wijnberg Engel Saartje (Selma), *Dancing Through Darkness: The Inspiring Story of Nazi Death Camp Survivors, Chaim and Selma Engel* (Portland, ME: Dunham Books, 2012).

Marples David R., *"Our Glorious Past": Lukashenko's Belarus and the Great Patriotic War* (Stuttgart: Ibidem Verlag, 2014).

Marrus Michael R., "Jewish Resistance to the Holocaust," *Journal of Contemporary History*, Vol. 30, No. 1 (1995), pp. 83–110.

Marrus Michael R., and Paxton Robert O., *Vichy France and the Jews* (Stanford: Stanford University Press, 1981).

Meltser David and Levin Vladimir, *The Black Book with Red Papers* (Cochesville, MD: 2005).

Merridale Catherine, *Night of Stone, Death and Memory in Twentieth-Century Russia*, edited by Albert Todd and Yakov Polyakov (London: Granta Books, 2000).

Merridale Catherine, *Ivan's War: The Red Army, 1939–1945* (London: Faber and Faber Ltd., 2005).

Michman Dan, "Bloodlands and the Holocaust: Some Reflections on Terminology, Conceptualization and their Consequences," *Journal of Modern European History*, Vol. 10, No. 4 (2012), pp. 440–446.

Milyakova Lidiya, ed., *Книга погромов. Погромы на Украине, в Белоруссии и европейской части России в период Гражданской войны 1918–1922 гг.Москва,, РОССПЭН, 2007.* (Kniga pogromov: pogromy na Ukraine, v Belorussii i Yevropeyskoy chasti Rossii [v period grazhdanskoy voyny 1918–1922). [The Book of Pogroms: The Pogroms in the Ukraine, Belorussia, and the European Part of Russia During the Civil War in 1918–1922 (Moscow: ROSSPEN, 2007)].

Molokiv-Zhurskiy Pavlo, *Кременчук (короткий довідник),Кременчук, 1929 Kremenchuk: (A Short Handbook)* (Kremenchuk: Kremenchuk Association of Local History, 1929).

Movshovich Evgeniĭ Veniaminovich, *Очерки истории евреев на Дону.Ростов-на-Дону, Донской издательский Дом, 2006.* (Ocherki istorii yevreev na Donu. Rostov-na-Donu, Donskoy izdatel'skiy dom, 2006) [Essays on the History of the Jews in the Don Region. (Rostov-on-Don: Don Publishing House, 2006)].

228 Bibliography

Movshovich Evgeniy Veniaminovich, "Глава 18: Александр Печерский. Руководитель восстания в лагере смерти Собибор," *Очерки истории евреев на Дону. Ростов-на-Дону: ЗАО "Книга"*, (2011), *стр.* 320–324 ("Glava 18: Aleksandr Pecherskiy. Rukovoditel' vosstaniya v lagere smerti Sobibor," *Ocherki istorii yevreev na Donu. Rostov-na-Donu: ZAO "Kniga"*, (2011), str. 320–324) ["Chapter 18: Aleksandr Pechersky, Leader of the Uprising in the Sobibor Death Camp," *Essays on the History of Jews in the Don Region*, Rostov-on-Don: ZAO "Book", (2011), pp. 320–324].

Murphy Brian, *Rostov in the Russian Civil War 1917–1920: The Key to Victory* (London and New York: Routledge, 2005).

Musial Bogdan, *Sowjetische Partisanen: Mythos und Wirklichkeit* (München: Paderborn, 2009).

Nirestein Albert, ed., *A Tower from the Enemy: Contributions to a History of Jewish Resistance in Poland* (New York: The Orion Press, 1959).

Novitch Miriam, *Sobibor, Martyrdom and Revolt* (New York: Holocaust Library, 1980).

Overy Richard, *Russia's War: A History of the Soviet Effort: 1941–1945* (New York: Penguin Books Ltd., 1998).

Pakier Małgorzata and Wawrzyniak Joanna, eds., *Memory and Change in Europe* (New York: Berghahn Books, 2015).

Pendas Devin O., *The Frankfurt Auschwitz Trial, 1963–1965: Genocide, History and the Limits of the Law* (New York: Cambridge University Press, 2006).

Pipes Richard, "Catherine II and the Jews: The Origins of the Pale of Settlement," *East European Jewish Affairs*, Vol. 52 (1975), pp. 14–17.

Pohl Dieter, "Nationalsozialistische Judenverfolgung in Ostgalizien, 1941–1944," in *Reihe: Studien zur Zeitgeschichte* (Munich: Oldenbourg, 1996), 50.

Polian Pavel, "First Victims of the Holocaust: Soviet-Jewish Prisoners of War in Captivity," *Kritika: Explorations in Russian and Eurasian History*, Vol. 6, No. 4 (2005), pp. 763–787.

Porter Thomas Earl, "Hitler's Forgotten Genocides: The Fate of Soviet POWs," *Elon Law Review*, Vol. 5 (September 2013), pp. 359–387.

Power Rhoda, *Under Cossack and Bolshevik* (London: Methuen, 1919).

Prusin Alexander Victor, "Fascist Criminals to the Gallows! The Holocaust and Soviet War Crimes Trials, December 1945—February 1946," *Holocaust and Genocide Studies*, Vol. 17, No. 1 (2003), pp. 1–30.

Redlich Simon, *War, Stalinism and the Holocaust: A Documentary History of the Jewish Anti-Fascist Committee* (New York: Routledge, 1995).

Reinhard Otto, *Wehrmacht, Gestapo und sowjetische Kriegsgefangenen im deutschen Reichsgebiet 1941/42* (Munchen: R. Oldenburg, 1998).

Rentrop Petra, *Tatorte der Endlösung: Das Minsk Ghetto und die Vernichtungsstätte Maly Trostinez* (Berlin: Metropol, 2011), 157.

Reuss Anja and Schneider Kristin, eds., *Berlin Minsk, Vergessene Lebensgeschichten: Ein Gedenkbuch für die nach Minsk deportierte Berliner Jüdinnen und Juden* (Berlin: Metropol, 2013).

Rosen Alan, *The Wonder of Their Voices, the 1946 Holocaust Interviews of David Boden* (New York: Oxford University Press, 2010).

Roskies David G., *Against the Apocalypse: Responses to Catastrophe in Modern Jewish Culture* (Cambridge: Harvard University Press, 1984).

Rubenstein Joshua and Naumov Vladimir P., eds., *Stalin's Secret Pogrom: The Postwar Inquisition of the Jewish Anti-Fascist Committee* (New Haven, London: Yale University Press, 2001).

Rubinstein Joshua and Altman Ilya, eds., *The Unknown Black Book, the Holocaust in the German-Occupied Soviet Territories* (Bloomington: Indiana University Press, 2010).

Rutman A., and Krasil'shchik S., "Фабрика смерти в Собибуре", газета "Комсомольская правда", 2 сентября 1944. ("Fabrika Smerti v Sobibure": Gazeta "Komsomol'skaya Pravda", 2 sentyabrya, 1944). ["The Death Factory," in *Sobibor*, ed. Ehrenburg Ilya].

Schechtman Joseph, *Погромы Добровольческой армии на Украине (Pogromy Dobrovol'cheskoy armii na Ukraine)*. [The Pogroms of the Volunteer Army in Ukraine] (Berlin: Ostjüdisches Historisches Archiv, 1932).

Schelvis Jules, *Sobibor: A History of a Nazi Death Camp* (Oxford and New York: Berg Publishers, 2010).

Schelvis Jules, *Ooggetuigen van Sobibor* (Amsterdam: Ambo/Anthos, 2010).

Sereny Gita, *Into That Darkness: From Mercy Killing to Mass Murder* (London: Pimlico, 1974).

Shenker Noah, *Reframing Holocaust Testimony* (Bloomington: Indiana University Press, 2015).

Shneer David, *Through Soviet Jewish Eyes: Photography, War and the Holocaust* (New Brunswick: Rutgers University Press, 2012).

Shtif Nokhem, *Погромы на Украине: Период Добровольческой Армии (Pogromy na Ukraine: Period Dobrovol'cheskoy armii)*. [The Pogroms in Ukraine: The Volunteer Army Period] (Berlin: Vosto, 1922).

Simkin Lev, "Александр Печерский свидетельствует: неизвестные страницы истории концлагеря Собибор." ("Aleksandr Pecherskiy svidetel'stvuet: neizvestnye stranitsy istorii kontslagerya Sobibor"). [Aleksandr Pechersky Testifies: Unknown Pages of the Concentration Camp Sobibor History], Russian electronic historical magazine *Bylye Gody*, Vol. 27, No. 1 (2013).

Simkin Lev, "Death Sentence Despite the Law: A Secret 1962 Crimes-Against-Humanity Trial in Kiev," *Holocaust and Genocide Studies*, Vol. 27 (2013), pp. 299–312.

Simkin Lev, *Полтора часа возмездия*. (Poltora chasa vozmezdiya). [Hour and a Half of Retribution] (Moscow: Zebra, 2013).

Slepyan Kenneth, *Stalin's Guerillas: Soviet Partisans in World War II* (Lawrence, KS: University Press of Kansas, 2006).

Sloan Stephen M., and Cave Marc, eds., *Listening on the Edge: Oral History in the Aftermath of Crisis* (New York: Oxford University Press, 2014).

Smilovitsky Leonid, "Ilya Ehrenburg on the Holocaust in Belarus: Unknown Testimony," *East European Jewish Affairs*, Vol. 29, No. 1–2 (1999), pp. 61–74.

Smilovitsky Leonid, *Holocaust in Bieolorussia, 1941–1944*, trans. Irene Newhouse (Tel Aviv: Biblioteka Motveya Chernogo, 2000).

Smoliar Hersh, *Fun Minsker geto* [Resistance in Minsk] (Oakland, CA: Judah L. Magnes Memorial Museum, 1966).

Smolar Hersh, *The Minsk Ghetto: Soviet-Jewish Partizans Against the Nazis* (New York: Holocaust Library, 1989).

Snyder Timothy, "Holocaust: The Ignored Reality," *New York Review of Books*, Vol. 56, No. 12 (2009).

Snyder Timothy, *Bloodlands: Europe Between Hitler and Stalin* (New York: Basic Books, 2010).

Snyder Timothy, *Black Earth: The Holocaust as History and Warning* (London: The Bodley Head, 2015), 201.

Sorokina Marina, "People and Procedures: Towards a History of the Investigation of Nazi Crimes in the USSR," *Kritika: Explorations in Russian and Eurasian History*, Vol. VI, No. 4 (2005), pp. 797–831. Also: Kiril-Feferman, "Soviet Investigation of Nazi War Crimes," *Journal of Genocide Research*, Vol. V, No. 4 (December 2005), pp. 587–602.

Speeches That Changed the World (London: Quercus, 2014).

Stahel David, *Operation Barbarossa and Germany's Defeat in the East* (Cambridge: Cambridge University Press, 2009).

230 Bibliography

Stein Arlene, "Whose Memories? Whose Victimhood? Contests for the Holocaust Frame in Recent Social Movement Discourse," *Sociological Perspectives*, Vol. 41, No. 3 (1998), pp. 519–540.

Stola Darius, "A Spatial Turn in Explaining Mass Murder," *Journal of Modern European History*, Vol. 11, No. 3 (2012), pp. 299–305.

Suhl Yuri, *They Fought Back: The Story of the Jewish Resistance in Nazi Europe* (New York: Shocken Books, 1967).

Tcherikower Elias, *История погромного движения на Украине 1917–1921 гг. Антисемитизм и погромы на Украине 1917–1918 гг. (Istoriya pogromnogo dvizheniya na Ukraine 1917–1921 gg. Anisemitizm i pogromy na Ukraine 1917–1918)*. [The History of the Pogrom Movement in Ukraine in 1917–1921: Anti-Semitism and Pogroms in Ukraine in 1917–1918 (Berlin: Ostjüdisches Historisches Archiv, 1923)].

Tec Nechama, *Defiance* (New York: Oxford University Press, 2009).

Thruston Robert W., and Jonowetch Bernd, *The People's War: Responses to World War II in the Soviet Union* (Champaign: University of Illinois Press, 2000).

Ticho Kurt, *My Legacy, Holocaust, History and the Unfinished Task of Pope John Paul II* (Włodawa: Muzeum Pojezierza Łęczyńsko-Włodawskiego, 2008).

Tomin Valentin and Sinelnikov Aleksandr, *Возвращение нежелательно. (Vozvrashchenie nezhelatel'no).* [Return is Undesirable (Moscow: Molodaya Gvardiya, 1964)].

Treister Michael, *Gleamps of Memory* (Minsk: History Workshop, 2011).

Vasilyev Ilya, *Александр Печерский, прорыв в бессмертие (Alexander Pecherskiy, proryv v bessmertie).* [Aleksandr Pechersky, Breakthrough to Immortality (Moscow: Vremya 2013)].

Vilenskiy Semen Samuilovich; Gorbovitskiy G. B., Terushkin Leonid A., and *Собибор. Восстание в лагере смерти. (Sobibor: Vosstaniye v lagere smerti).* [Sobibor: Uprising in the Death Camp. (Moscow: Vozvrashcheniye, 2008)].

Vyrskiy Dimitrii, "Єврейський погром у 1905 року у Кременчуці" [The Jewish Pogrom in 1905 in Kremenchuk], *Historical Journal*, Vol. 2 (2006), pp. 110–117.

Wachsmann Nicolaus, *A History of the Nazi Concentration Camps* (London: Little Brown, 2015).

Waitman Beorn Wade, *Marching into Darkness: The Wehrmacht and the Holocaust in Belarus* (Cambridge: Harvard University Press, 2014).

Wewryk Kalmen, *To Sobibor and Back* (Włodawa, Poland: Muzeum Pojezierza Łęczyńsko-Włodawskiego, 2008).

Wiechert Ernst, *Forest of Death* (New York: Greenberg, 1947).

Winkler Christina, "2000 Jews Have So Far Been Detected," in *Холокост: 70 лет спустя*, ed. Ilya Altman et al. (Moscow: Научио-просветительный Цеитр "Холокост," 2015), 133–139.

Witte Peter and Tyas Stephen, "A New Document on the Deportation and Murder of Jews During 'Einsatz Reinhardt' 1942," *Holocaust and Genocide Studies*, Vol. 15, No. 3 (Winter 2001), pp. 468–486.

Yatskevich Natalia, "Das Lager in der Schirokaja-Straße in Minsk," in *Existiert das Ghetto noch?*, ed. A. Klein (Berlin: Hanser Literatur Verlage, 2003), 220–221.

The Yivo Encyclopedia of Jews in Eastern Europe, *Rostov on Don* www.yivoencyclopedia.org/article.aspx/Rostov-on-Don.

Zavadivker Polly, "Blood and Ink: Russian and Soviet Jewish Chroniclers of Catastrophe from World War I to World War II" (Ph.D. dissertation, University of California at Santa Cruz, 2013).

Zavadivker Polly, "Minsk-Shirokaia Street," in *The United States Holocaust Memorial Museum Encyclopedia of Camps and Ghettos 1933–1945*, vol. V, vol. ed. Martin Dean, *Extermination, Transit, and Forced Labor Camps for Jews* (Bloomington: Indiana

University Press in association with the United States Holocaust Memorial Museum, forthcoming).

Zeits Dan, "Was Minsk Really Different?" (Professor Barbara Epstein and Soviet Internationalism) unpublished manuscript.

Zielinski Andrew, *Conversiations with Regina* (Włodawa, Poland: Muzeum Pojezierza Łęczyńsko-Włodawskiego, 2008).

Zimmerman Joshua D., ed., *Contested Memories: Poles and Jews During the Holocaust and Its Aftermath* (New Brunswick, NJ and London: Rutgers University Press, 2003).

Index

Ainsztein, Reuven (Reuben) 17–18, 50, 74, 113, 119, 120, 121, 205
AK army (Armia Krajowa) 114, 139
Aleichem, Sholom: *The Big Lottery* 172
Altman, Ilya 17
Amigoe di Curacao 82
anti-Semitism 6, 16, 22–3, 28, 29–30, 33, 35–6, 38, 67, 81, 85, 114, 138, 165, 167–9, 170, 171, 172–5, 194, 197, 205, 216
Antokolsky, Pavel Grigoryevich 81, 160
Arad, Yitzhak 25, 90, 123
Arendt, Hannah 117
Armia Krajowa (AK army) 114, 139
Atashinsky, Abram 72–3
Auschwitz camp 6, 11, 77n69, 148, 180, 181, 203, 204, 205, 217

Bahir, Moshe 6, 120, 176, 181, 185n51, 203, 206
Bakalczuk, Meilech 152, 155, 162n5
Barbarossa, Operation 42, 54
Barin 35
Bartov, Omer 18, 217
Battle of Moscow 52–3
Battle of Stalingrad 4, 59, 60, 72, 93, 109, 111, 123, 154, 155
Bauer, Erich 96
Bauer, Yehuda 117
Belarusian State Museum of the Great Patriotic War History 74, 154
Belzec camp 6, 24, 26, 67, 90, 97, 98, 111, 113, 180
Bem, Marek 3, 97, 101, 120, 121, 122, 130–1, 140, 141, 162n6, 207n1, 208n9
Bemporad, Elissa 39
Benz, Wolfgang 20n11, 90
Beorn, Waitman Wade 53–4
Bettelheim, Bruno 102, 102

Bialowicz, Philip 3, 129, 131
Bialowicz, Simcha 95, 122
Białystok ghetto revolt 113
Biskowitz, Ya'akov 181
Blatt, Thomas (Toivi) 3, 90, 95, 98–9, 129, 131, 133, 134, 147, 176–7, 192, 202, 205
Bloodlands 24, 58, 180, 218
Bloxham, Donald 180
Bluhm, Hilde O. 102–3
Boder, David Pablo 181, 185n52
Bogdanova, Svetlana 11
Boiko, Tanya 65
Bolshaya Bronaya synagogue 11
Bolshevism 22, 33, 42
Breur, Dunya 7, 116, 166, 168, 173, 193, 201, 206
Brezhnev, Ehen 198
Brezhnev, Leonid 190
Brodyanskaya, Rebecca 41
Bruder, Franziska 13, 74
Brzecki, Kapo 126, 127
Budnitski, Oleg 29, 38
Butler, Rupert 158–9

Camp I 84, 91, 96, 97, 126, 127
Camp II 89, 91, 96, 124, 127, 128
Camp III 89, 91, 92, 93–4, 95, 96, 116, 120, 122, 128, 204
Camp IV 84, 122, 127
Charny, Israel W. 103
Chaumont, Jean-Michel 214
Cibulsky 132
Communism 2, 3, 8–9, 11, 13, 14, 18–19, 36–7, 38–9, 40, 41, 44, 52, 61, 68, 98, 142, 154, 155, 156, 157, 161, 164, 165, 167, 168, 170, 171, 173, 177, 179, 192, 197, 205, 210, 212, 215–17, 218–19, 220; Byelorussia

Index 233

152–3; language 50; propaganda 51; revolution of 1917 22–4
Conference of Jewish Material Claims against Germany 20n22
cosmopolitanism 169
Cossacks 28, 33, 34, 36, 74, 166

Dachau camp 11, 148
Davidson, Shamai 103–4
Demjanjuk, John 1, 2, 3, 19n1, 134
Denikin, Anton 33
deportation 14, 29, 48, 53, 60, 67, 69, 70, 81, 85, 90, 99, 112–13, 138, 214
Deryugin, I. K. 62
Desbois, Patrick: *The Holocaust by Bullets* 25
Des Pres, Terrence: *The Survivor* 101–2
displaced persons 146, 181, 185n52
Distel, Barbara 90
Dombrovsky, Yuri 43–44
Duniec, Josef 95

Eastern Front 105, 109, 157
Educational Holocaust Center 9, 17
Ehrenburg, Ilya: *The Complete Black Book of Russian Jewry* 56, 61, 62, 68, 81, 82, 83, 125, 160, 187, 213
Eichmann, Adolf 6, 13, 117, 181, 203
Engel, Chaim 82, 144
Engel-Wijnberg, Selma 82, 144
Epstein, Barbara: *The Minsk Ghetto 1941–1943* 67–8, 69, 70, 135n7
Escape from Sobibor (movie) 7, 17, 198, 213
Extraordinary State Commission 159, 160, 163n69, 179

fascism 12, 16, 23, 24, 51–2, 84, 104, 152, 154, 168, 169, 170, 180, 194, 217
Feldhendler, Leon 82, 85, 95, 100, 104, 115–16, 123, 124, 125, 126, 127, 128, 203
Five Year Plan 39, 164
Frankl, Viktor E. 102–3
Fraser, Nancy 214
Freiberg, Ber (Dov) Moiseevich 82, 87, 91–2, 115, 131, 142
Frenzel, Karl 96, 97, 104, 117–18, 120, 127, 128, 131, 140, 142, 193, 196

gas chamber 66, 80, 82, 86, 87, 88, 91, 92, 93, 94, 95, 97, 98, 99, 101, 109, 119, 120, 122, 123, 126, 134, 139, 152, 189–90, 196, 201
Gatrell, Peter 35

Gebelev, Mikhail 65
Geneva Convention 60, 111
genocide: Armenian 181; Russian 17; Wehrmacht 54
ghetto fighters 11, 109
Ginsburg, Lev 188
Gitelman, Zvi 169, 171; *A Century of Ambivalence* 39
Glass, James 118
Globocnik, Odilo 97–8
Golba, Josif 42, 61
Gomerski, Hubert 81, 85, 106n7, 190, 191, 192, 195
Grafeneck Castle 97
Great Patriotic War 3, 42, 51, 74, 98, 154, 168, 177, 187, 189, 210, 213, 217, 221n22
Great Purges 40
Great Terror 41, 51, 153
Grinevich, Ella (Pechersky's daughter) 7, 16, 17, 30, 36, 86, 160–1, 173, 174, 202
Grossman, Vasily 56, 113–14; *The Complete Black Book of Russian Jewry* 56, 61, 62, 68, 81, 82, 83, 125, 160, 187, 213
GRU 153
Gulag 6, 7, 23, 54, 68, 158, 165, 210
Guy, David: *Innocence in Hell* 73
Gypsies 99, 112

Hadamar Euthanasia Center 97
Hague Convention 54
Harvest Festival, Operation 141
hyadamaks 33
Hess, Franz: *The Trial of the Nazi Invaders Who Committed Acts of Horror in Belarus* 25
Heydrich, Reinhard 110
Hilberg, Raoul 117
Himmler, Heinrich 25, 80, 141
Hirszowicz, Lukasz 167
History Workshop of Minsk 67
Hitler, Adolf 8, 24, 49, 52, 53, 54, 83, 94, 99, 170, 217, 218
Hitlerites 98, 126, 170
Holocaust Memorial Board of the Russian Jewish Congress 43
Hughes, Paul: *Retreat from Rostov* 44

International Auschwitz Committee 192
Itzhak Katzenelson Holocaust and Jewish Resistance Heritage Museum, Documentation, and Study Center 12

JAC *see* Jewish Anti-Fascist Committee
Janowska Street camp 114

234 Index

Jewish Anti-Fascist Committee (JAC) 170, 171, 197
Jewish prisoners of war 61–4, 65
Jews in post-revolutionary world 22–44; crossing borders, looking at the region 24; dangerous trek through chaotic territory 34–6; Kremenchuk: family background and memory of persecution 27–34; Operation Reinhard 24–7 (*see also* Operation Reinhard); Rostov-on-Don 36–42; war comes to Rostov-on-Don 42–4
Jewish resistance 2–3, 13, 19, 32, 60, 116–21, 161, 173
Jockush, Laura 211–2, 220n3
Jones, Jeffrey W. 164

Kaverin, Veniamin Alexandrovich 81, 160
KGB 8, 9, 81, 154, 167, 176, 177, 189, 197, 198, 205, 212
Khrushchev, Nikita 7, 171
Kibbutz Lohamei HaGeta'ot 11, 12, 174
Koldczewo camp 114
Komsomolskaya Pravda 161
Kotova, Olga 160
Krasnaya Zvezda (Red Star) 113, 161
Krut, Iakov 41, 172
Kube, Wilhelm 70, 110, 111
Kurlandskaya, Sofia 65, 70, 74

Ladychenko, Natalya (granddaughter of Pechersky) 17, 167, 175, 213, 239
Laitman, Shlomo 74, 86, 97, 116, 123, 127, 128, 132
Langbein, Hermann 192, 204, 205
Lanzmann, Claude: *Sobibór* 85
Leder, Mary M.: *My Life in Stalinist Russia* 40
Lehrer, Yehuda 85
Lerer, Samuel 99
Lev, Michael 12, 13–14, 96, 132, 159, 160, 173, 176, 177, 205, 206; *Kimat a Legende* 202; *Sobibor* 19n2, 30–2
Lev, Polina 20n19
Levi, Primo 15, 181
Levin, Nora 22
Levin, Sara 65
Levine, Allan: *Fugitives of the Forest* 114
Leydesdorff, Selma: "The Long Shadow of Sobibor" 82
Liulyeva, Tesya 41
Lokshin, M. 72
Lubarsky, Lazar 7, 8, 11, 173, 177

Maher, Thomas 118, 119
Majdanek camp 77n69, 114, 141, 160

Makhortykh, Mykola 45n18
Maly Trostinets death camp 68, 69, 70, 74, 77n69
Marrus, Michael 116, 117, 118; *Vichy France and the Jews* 214
Marutyan, Aleksander 7, 20n14, 160, 173
Mathematical Calculation of Freedom 7
Mauthausen camp 148, 203
Meir, Golda 170–1
Menche, Chaskiel 193
Merridale, Catherine 165; *Ivan's War* 50, 51, 52, 54
Metz, Zelda 101, 115, 120
Meyerson (Meir), Golda 170–1
Michel, Hermann 79
Mikhoels, Solomon (Shloyme) 170
Minsk ghetto 65, 67–9, 70, 76n49, 122, 135n7
mistrust, culture of 155–6
Moiseevich, Lev 72
Molotov, Vyacheslav 50–1, 60
Molotov-Ribbentrop Pact 42, 52
The Morning Freiheit 205
mythology 2, 4, 12, 17, 36, 38, 49, 96, 98–9, 129–34, 151, 156, 192

Nebenklager 2
Netherlands Institute for War Documentation (NIOD) 20n13, 106n8, 167, 184n10
New Economic Policy 38
Nieman 127
NIOD *see* Netherlands Institute for War Documentation
NKVD 51, 153, 154, 158, 159
Novitch, Miriam 11, 81, 83, 86, 87, 89, 95, 101, 104, 120, 205–6
Nuremberg trials 13, 160, 161, 163n69, 180, 211

Operation Barbarossa 42, 54
Operation Harvest Festival 141
Operation Reinhard 1, 7, 24–7, 90, 109, 113, 141, 148, 180, 203, 214, 216
Order 227 156, 158
Order 270 54–5
Order of Courage 219
Order of the Great Patriotic War 177
Order of the Red Banner 150
Otherstein, Tanha 41

partisans 6, 8, 59, 65, 66–7, 68, 69–70, 72, 74, 85, 97, 99, 118, 119, 122, 123–4, 131, 132, 138–61, 177, 198, 199–200, 213, 215, 216; life as 154–5; Minsk 14,

16, 112; Poland and Byelorussia 10, 111–15; under the control of Moscow 153–4

Paxton, Robert O.: *Vichy France and the Jews* 214

Pechersky, Aleksandr ("Sasha"; Aleksandr Aronowitch Pechersky): after the escape 138–61; alone, isolated, and bitter 192–4, 198–201; arrival in Sobibor 65, 70, 73, 81, 105; born 12, 27; captured at the Battle of Moscow near Smolensk 49, 52–3, 55, 56; Communist 129; conscription into army 48, 52; death 6, 13, 18, 23, 203, 206, 218–19; deportation to Sobibor 15–16, 48, 53, 83–5; depositions 9–11, 16, 48, 61, 64, 65, 73, 81, 83, 87, 123, 191; early years in Kremenchuk 14, 27–34, 35, 44; false accusation of corruption 6; hospital 160; imprisonment: Vyazma, Borisov, Minsk, Stalag 352 55–8; Kremenchuk: family background and memory of persecution 27–34; marriage to Lyudmila Vasilyevna 23, 36; marriage to Olga Kotova 160; Medal of Courage 19; memoir 13; memories of survival after the escape 142–7; military service 23, 45n4, 48–74, 157; October 14, 1943 1, 127, 131, 140–1; partisans 6, 8, 10, 138–61; post-revolt 17–18; psychological survival 99–102; rejoining of Red Army in 1944 6, 218; Rostov-on-Don 14, 16–18, 34–7, 36–42, 164–83; Schors Battalion 149, 150, 156–57; September 18, 1943 65, 70, 73, 81, 105; Stalag 352 57; travel from Kremanchuk to Rostov-on-Don 34–7; *see also* Shirokaya (Broad) Street Prison; Sobibor camp: revolt

Petliura, Symon 33

Plato, Alexander von 186n58

Plotnitsky, Naum 124–5, 149, 150, 198–200, 204

Podgorny, Nikolai 177

pogroms: 1905 28–9, 45n22; 1918–20 32, 33–4; Kremenchuk 28–9, 32, 33–4, 45n22; Ukraine 32

"Politics of Reconstruction" 164

Poppert-Schonborn, Gertrude 104

POWs *see* prisoners of war

prisoners of war (POWs) 55, 56, 70, 73; Russian 1, 9, 15, 48–9, 54, 58, 61–2, 67, 71, 72, 84, 85, 95, 99, 103, 104, 111, 115, 116, 119, 122, 133, 139, 148, 153, 158, 161, 166, 167, 190, 213, 216;

Russian Jewish 65; Soviet 7, 52, 54, 64, 69, 95, 126, 127, 128; Ukrainian 74, 98

project details 1–6; February 2013 13–14; how started 2–6; May 2013 14–15; Michael Lev and other friends of Pechersky in Israel 11–13; Minsk research 14–15; Moscow research 9–11; October 2012 9–11; political and academic silence 8–9; reshaping narratives, changing memories 18–19; unknown camps in eastern Poland 6–8; Washington, D.C. research 13–14

Putin, Vladimir 19, 219

Raab, Esther 6, 79, 100–1, 105, 115, 134, 147, 195, 217

Rabbi Israel Miler Fund 20

Räshke, Richard: *Escape from Sobibor* 96, 176–7, 205

Red Army 2, 6, 8, 17, 23, 27, 33, 38, 41, 42, 48, 51, 52, 60, 70, 79, 80, 99, 100, 109, 111, 113, 114, 122, 123, 132, 133, 138–52, 153.54, 155, 156, 157, 177, 179, 217, 218; joining 158–60

Red Star (*Krasnaya Zvezda*) 113, 161

Reinhard, Operation (Aktion) 1, 7, 24–7, 90, 109, 113, 141, 148, 180, 203, 214, 216

revolts 118; *see also* Białystok ghetto revolt; Sobibor camp: revolt; Treblinka camp: revolt; Warsaw ghetto revolt; Włodawa revolt 119

Revolution of 1917 22, 29–30

Rosenfeld, Simion 11, 66, 69, 74, 84, 94–5, 203, 206

Russian Civil War 27, 29, 30, 32, 34, 38, 150

Russian prisoners of war 1, 9, 15, 48–9, 54, 58, 61–2, 67, 71, 72, 84, 85, 95, 99, 103, 104, 111, 115, 116, 119, 122, 133, 139, 148, 153, 158, 161, 166, 167, 190, 213, 216

Russian Jewish prisoners of war 61–5

Russian Research and Educational Holocaust Center 9, 17

Russian Revolution 24, 27, 29, 35, 179

Schelvis, Jules, 3, 7, 90, 92, 106n8, 116, 122, 127, 129–30, 162n5, 166, 167, 173, 193, 195, 201

Schors Battalion 156–7; partisans 16, 198

Sereny, Gitta: *Into that Darkness* 110

Shalek, Moshe 6; *see also* Bahir 6

shame and guilt 27, 128, 134, 188

Sheinman 56, 61

236   Index

Shenker, Noah 4
Shirokaya (Broad) Street Prison 61–2, 64,
   65, 66, 67, 69–74, 83, 94, 138, 139
Shoah 2, 9, 24, 40, 42, 117, 181, 211
Shoah Visual Foundation 40, 172, 183
Shoah Visual History Archive 42, 92, 115
shtrafniki 158
Shubaev, Aleksandr 74, 132, 150
Simkin, Lev 96, 190
Sinelnikov, Alexander 32, 106n29;
   Returning Is Undesirable 202
slave labor 59–61, 90, 146
Slepyan, Kenneth 150, 155
SMERSH 153, 154
Smilovitsky, Leonid 55; "Ilya Ehrenburg
   on the Holocaust in Byelorussia" 77n69
Smolar, Hirsh 59, 70, 73
Snyder, Timothy 24, 58, 80, 216
Sobibor camp 2, 48, 60, 83, 91–3, 141,
   151, 193, 206; accounts of a death
   factory 87–9; after the escape 138–61;
   anniversaries of revolt 149–50, 177,
   200, 202, 204; August 1943 69; Camp
   I 84, 91, 96, 97, 126, 127; Camp II 89,
   91, 96, 124, 127, 128; Camp III 89, 91,
   92, 93–4, 95, 96, 116, 120, 122, 128,
   204; Camp IV 84, 122, 127; Dutch 122;
   eighty Russian soldiers 84–6; escapes
   120, 121–5; experienced perpetrators
   96–8; first person and other narratives
   89–91; fortieth anniversary of revolt
   177; gas chamber 86–7; human
   bonding and hope for a better world
   102–5; memories of survival after the
   escape 142–7; narratives 80–4; non-
   Jews and Jews 98–9; October 14, 1943
   1, 127, 131, 140–1; psychological
   survival and Russian soldiers 99–102;
   revolt 1, 2, 7, 8, 15, 18, 23, 50, 65, 74,
   79–81, 82, 83, 96, 99, 100, 104–5,
   111, 114, 115, 116, 118–19, 120,
   121–34, 138–9, 140, 141–2, 143, 144,
   147, 149–50, 151, 159, 160, 167, 168,
   175, 176, 191–2, 193, 194–5, 197,
   200, 202–4, 210–1, 212–13, 216,
   220; revolt: myth and reality 129–34;
   Russians 99–102, 115–16 sixty-
   fifth anniversary of revolt 149–50;
   survivors' narratives 79–105; twentieth
   anniversary of revolt 175, 202; twenty-
   fifth anniversary of revolt 200, 204;
   violence and death 91–4
Sobibor Foundation 2, 3, 11, 82

"Sobibor Interviews" 167, 193–4
Sovetish Heymland 12, 89, 172
Soviet POWs 7, 52, 54, 64, 69, 95, 126,
   127, 128
spies 29, 155, 166
Stalag 352 14, 57, 62, 63, 67
Stalin, Joseph 8, 50, 129–30, 153, 154,
   168, 218; anti-Semitism 174, 194, 197;
   death 23, 171, 174, 198; denouncement
   1956 177; "Not a step back!" 54–5;
   Order 227 156, 158; Order 270 54–5;
   persecution 6, 24, 40; post- 19, 56, 212,
   219; repression 23
Stalin Brigade 150
Stalingrad, Battle of 4, 59, 60, 72, 93, 109,
   111, 123, 154, 155
Stalin's Guerillas 150
Stalinism 41, 44, 40, 155, 170, 192, 210,
   212, 217, 218
Stangl, Franz 110
starvation 49, 52, 53, 59, 60, 73, 105,
   118, 175
Stepan, Trutnev 63
Stola, Darius 24
Subaiev 127
Suhl, Yuri 125
suicide 49, 102, 120
Szmajzner, Stanislaw 26, 127

Taborinski, Boris 84
Tarnow ghetto revolt 113
Terushkin, Leonid 9, 14, 163n75
Ticho, Kurt 93, 94
Tolstoy, Alexei Nikolayevich 30, 159
Tomin, Valentin 32, 45n4, 179, 203, 205;
   Returning Is Undesirable 202
traumatization 3, 42, 44, 48, 85, 102, 134,
   144, 146, 147–8, 161, 165, 166, 168, 176,
   181, 182, 183, 187–206, 214, 216, 217
Treblinka camp 6, 11, 20n11, 25,
   26, 77n69, 90, 109, 110, 111, 181;
   destruction 118–19, 131, 141; revolt
   113–14, 121
Treister, Michael 64, 70–1, 72
Trostinets death camp 68, 69, 70, 74,
   77n69
Trotsky, Leon 179
Tsibulsky, Boris 16, 63, 74, 95, 104, 123,
   126, 127, 128, 149

Ukrainian prisoners of war 74, 98
unknown camps in eastern Poland 6–8; see
   also Sobibor camp

"The Uprising in the Sobibor Camp" 210–1
U.S. Holocaust Memorial Museum 13, 20n11, 25, 100, 159, 201

Vasilyevna, Ilya 19
Vasilyevna, Lyudmila 36
Vaytsen, Aleksey 8, 134, 156, 175, 188, 203, 204, 212
The Voice of Warsaw 81
Von dem Bach-Zelewski, Erich 25
Voroshilov Brigade 149, 153, 156

Wachsmann, Nikolaus 49
Wagner, Gustav Franz 88, 97, 127, 195
Waldlager 64
Walke, Anika 215
Warsaw ghetto revolt 60, 121
Wehrmacht 53, 54, 158–9
Weiner, Amir 165, 169
Weiszpapir, Arkady 60, 128, 212

Wewryk, Kalmen 88–9, 99, 115–16, 129, 130, 143
White Guards 32, 33, 38, 66
White Movement 33
Wiesel, Elie 15, 183
Włodawa revolt 119
Wulfowna, Frida 67

Yad Vashem 55, 62, 105n6, 173, 201
YIVO 17, 201, 205

Zamynetzky, Vasily 36
Zavadivker, Polly 64, 65, 69, 78n75
Zeits, Dan 20n27, 68, 76n39, 151, 162n27, 162n29
Zelikman, Arkadi 73
Zielinski, Regina 4, 90–1, 195
Zionism 40, 169
Znamya 160
Zukerman, Hershel 87

Printed in the United States
By Bookmasters